Augustine

by Antonello da Messina, 1430c-1479

National Gallery of Sicily, Palermo

THE IRISH AUGUSTINIANS IN ROME, 1656-1994

AND

IRISH AUGUSTINIAN MISSIONS THROUGHOUT THE WORLD

edited by

F. X. MARTIN, O.S.A.

and

CLARE O'REILLY

St Patrick's College, Rome, 1994.

ISBN No. 0 952488 2 0 5

Published by
Augustinian House of Studies,
Ballyboden,
Dublin 16.

and

The Augustinian Fathers,
St. Patrick's College,
Via Piemonte 60,
Rome.

Production by OMAH Printing Ltd., Cork, Ireland.
Cover Design: Ron Rigby, Epic Design, Cork, Ireland.

TABLE OF CONTENTS

BLESSING OF ST AUGUSTINE

May the Lord Jesus Christ give you

A heart to love Him,

A will to choose Him,

An understanding to know Him,

A spirit which may always be

united to Him

And may the God of Love and

Mercy love you for ever.

Amen.

PREFACE

We preface this volume with a note of explanation and a word of apology.

The explanation concerns the scope of the book. In 1992 the Irish Augustinians celebrated the centenary of the foundation of St Patrick's College, Rome. To mark the occasion it was decided to publish a comprehensive account of the development of the Irish Augustinians' base in the Eternal City, from its first foundation at San Matteo in Merulana in 1656, through the vicissitudes of five displacements, before its final establishment at St Patrick's, on the site of the Villa Ludovisi on what is now the present Via Piemonte.

From their base at Rome the Irish Augustinians reached out to all the world and this volume, in celebrating the centenary of St Patrick's College, would seek to recognize also the valuable work of Irish Augustinians in every one of the five continents. A survey of this valiant missionary activity over the years is captured in a series of varied outline histories sketched by the contributors to this book.

The Augustinian friars first came to Ireland about 1280 and have continued to operate there without a break up to the present day, in 1994. It is high time to put on record their service to Ireland and to the Catholic Church.

In the thirteenth century the Irish Augustinian unit was in fact, and still is in 1994, a small part within the international framework of the Augustinian Order. It has nevertheless made a world-wide contribution quite positively disproportionate to its size and to the number of its members within the Order and within the Catholic Church.

In medieval times the thirteen Irish Augustinian houses were concentrated in the traditional civil provinces of Leinster, Munster and Connacht. It was not until the turbulent seventeenth century that the Augustinian friars established houses in Ulster - until then largely unapproachable territory for anyone except "the mere Irish". This the Augustinian friars did surprisingly in the 1630s, at Derry and elsewhere, amid the bloody anti-Catholic welter of the Cromwellian onslaught in England and Ireland.

As the dust settled on the religious battle-fields of the 30 Years' War (1618-48) the limited Augustinian base in Ireland expanded to Newfoundland in 1756, to the United States of North America in 1794, then to British India in 1834, next to Australia in 1838, then to England in 1864.

By any standards it was a remarkable story. During those years the Irish Augustinians produced extraordinary individuals, notably the Gaelic scholar, Fergal Dubh Ó Gara, who doggedly continued his recording of traditional bardic poetry even when he was a heart-broken exile at Lille in the Low Countries (1656) during the persecution of the Irish Catholics by the Lord Protector Oliver Cromwell. Dr William Gahan (1732-1804) was the foremost Irish religious writer in the 18th century. Towering over them all was the figure of the immortal Bishop James Warren Doyle (1786-1834), who first captured much public attention by issuing a brilliant series of pamphlets under the anonymous, and apparently baffling, initials "J.K.L.", but which signified 'James, bishop of Kildare and Leighlin'.

Doyle went to London as the leading Irish spokesman on the explosive question of Catholic Emancipation. He was interviewed by a Select Committee of the Houses of Parliament, but he quickly turned the tables on his interviewers by his self-confidence and his incisive replies, combined with fluency of language. The result was clearly signalled by one member of the Committee, who chanced to leave the room and encountered a friend who asked how the interview was proceeding. 'We', he replied wryly, 'are not interviewing Doyle. He is interviewing us'.

Doyle was a strong character who was given full scope by Augustinian superiors to utilise his talents, largely at his own discretion. This free rein for individual activity became a characteristic of Irish Augustinians, and has remained so to the present day.

In those decades of the late 18th century when Doyle was growing up in Wexford as a resolute Roman Catholic, but the son of a mixed Catholic-Protestant marriage, another famous Irish Augustinian, a cheerful rapscallion, Tomás Ó Caiside, - *An Caisideach Bán* - was embarked on his colourful career which encompassed Ireland, England, France, Prussia, and Germany. Throughout those turbulent years Ó Caiside attempted, not altogether successfully, to reconcile his loyalty to the priesthood with fraternity for the Augustinians, as well as with his loving attachment to the renowned Máire from Ballyhaunis and to at least one other female competitor for his affections, Brigid Ní Bheirn.

Ó Caiside joined the famous invincible six-foot-plus Prussian Guards, deserted from them and from two other armies, in France and England, then returned to Ireland in an attempt to rejoin his Augustinian brethren, and carrying with him a chalice - the symbol of his priesthood, which he never could forget.

Outstanding - and more orthodox, if less flamboyant - individuals continued to mark the history of the Irish Augustinians in the 19th and the 20th century.

The chapters in this volume show clearly how much the influence of the Irish Augustinians, their contribution to the life of the Catholic Church on a world-wide missionary stage, and their success in often very difficult conditions, depended on the strength and confidence of individuals of ability and flair - exemplified in recent decades in many spheres, from men like Malachy Cullen, labouring in the mission fields of Nigeria, to Martin Nolan who became the first Irishman to be elected Prior General of the Order. The characteristic of individual decision has remained a mark of Irish Augustinians to the present day. Long may it last!

The apology, referred to at the beginning of the Preface, must be made to the contributors to this volume whose patience has been sorely tried. They had to bear with initial demands from the editors that certain deadlines should be met in 1992, and then they found that the promptness of their response could not be reciprocated. Problems which arose - some simply of a technical nature, even in this advanced computer age ! - entailed postponement of the publication date for what must have appeared an inordinate length of time.

No one was more concerned than the editors at the postponement and the long delay. No one is more relieved than the editors that the difficulties - which at times seemed endless - have finally been resolved, and that now this volume may relate the world-wide labours of the Irish Augustinians down the years, just as their present base at Rome, St Patrick's College, begins its second century of life.

F.X. Martin.
Clare O'Reilly.

Dublin, 26 April 1994.
Feast of Our Lady of Good Counsel.

THE IRISH AUGUSTINIANS IN ROME, 1656-1994

F.X. Martin, O.S.A.

THE IRISH AUGUSTINIANS IN ROME, 1656-1994
F.X. Martin, O.S.A.

The Irish Augustinians were granted a house in Rome during the year 1656, at a time of the gravest crisis. The Order in Ireland was struggling for its very existence.

An exiled friar, William Meagher, O.S.A., had written despairingly to the prior general, Lucchini, from La Rochelle in France on 28 October 1650:[1]

'Very Reverend Father,

I have thought it well to let you know of the destruction of Ireland, where it would appear that not merely our Order but the Faith itself is on the point of being exterminated. Many religious of our Order have been put to death in the persecution by the Reformed heretics; among their number is Father Peter Taaff. I beg your Paternity to write down this martyrdom in the registers of the Order, so that this mention of them may serve as their funeral oration. I have made up my mind to go to Canada, to the New World, that I may be of better service to God and to my Order. In conclusion I desire to kiss your Paternity's hand with deep affection,

Your Paternity's very devoted and humble servant,

Father William Meagher, La Rochelle, 28 October 1650.'

In 1649 Cromwell's mailed fist struck the country. The Lord Oliver himself tells that at the siege of Drogheda he captured the Augustinian, 'Father Peter Taaff (brother to the Lord Taaff) whom the soldiers took, the next day, and made an end of'[2]. During the following ten years the roll-call of Irish Augustinian martyrs steadily increased - the ascetical William Tirry, publicly executed at Clonmel on 22 April 1654[3]; Fulgentius Jordan, 'the golden-mouthed preacher' of the West; the faithful lay brother, Thomas Deir, struck down in 1652; Denis O'Driscoll, provincial and man of integrity; Donogh O'Screnan, 'the Irish Juvenal'. And these are but a few of the names that spring to mind. James MacCarthy O.S.A., Irish Augustinian procurator in Rome, wrote a report on the persecution for the Holy See on 14 August 1657[4]. In it he gave the names and some details of eleven Augustinians who had suffered martyrdom. He added that for the sake of brevity he was omitting the names of forty other Augustinians who were in prison, in exile, or in hiding in Ireland.

JAMES MacCARTHY: THE FIRST VICAR PRIOR

It was this same James MacCarthy who was mainly responsible for establishing an Irish

---

1. In López Bardón, *Monastici Augustiniani R.P. Nicolai Crusenii continuatio,* II, Valladolid 1903, pp 535-36.
2. Cromwell to William Lenthal, Speaker of the House of Commons, Dublin 17 Sept. 1649, in *Letters and Speeches of Oliver Cromwell,* ed. T. Carlyle, re-ed. S.C. Lomas, i, London 1904, p. 471.
3. William Tirry was one of 17 Irish Martyrs beatified by Pope John Paul II in St. Peter's Square, Rome, 27 Sept. 1992. For Tirry, see John O'Connor, O.S.A., *A Priest on the Run. William Tirry, O.S.A., 1608-1654,* Veritas, Dublin 1992.
4. *A.P.F.,* 'Miscellanea Diverse', vol. 20, 'Relatio di Varie Missioni', ff 413-416. In 1655, the year before the Irish friars took possession of San Matteo in Rome, James O'Mahony, O.S.A., the provincial in exile, published a pamphlet at Brussels, *Sanguinea Eremus Martyrum Hiberniae Ord. Eremit. S.P. Augustini,* ed. F.X. Martin, O.S.A., in *Archivium Hibernicum,* XV (1950) 74-91, giving a moving account of the sufferings of the Irish Augustinians. This supplies details further to MacCarthy's account. For new information on the Irish O.S.A. martyrs, particularly on Tirry, see M.B. Hackett and F.X. Martin in *Archiv. Hib.,* XX (1957) 69-122.

Augustinian college in Rome[5]. We have few details of his life, but sufficient to indicate that he was a remarkable and zealous individual. He appears to have been a Corkman[6], and one whose abilities secured his appointment at Rome as representative of the Irish Augustinians during the Cromwellian period. When the restoration of the Polish province was undertaken during the 1660s James MacCarthy was the man chosen by the prior general to direct the work. Here in the unfamiliar scene, among a foreign people and difficult circumstances he and his fellow-friars laboured with such success that within the space of ten years nineteen Augustinian houses were founded[7].

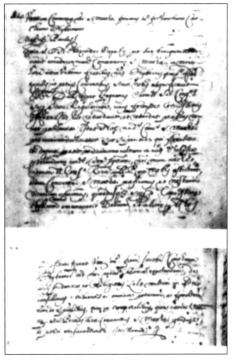

Entry in the Generals' Registers recording the appointment of James MacCarthy to the vicar-priorship of San Matteo in July 1656.

MacCarthy's missionary zeal led him to a more dangerous scene, but nearer home. During the year 1669 a papal agent, Claudio Agretti, went on a secret mission to England, to investigate the condition of Catholicism. In his revealing report, dated 14 December 1669, he stated that James MacCarthy was residing in London as provincial of the Augustinians in England, and that he was accustomed to say Mass in the house of the Venetian ambassador[8].

The most enduring of all MacCarthy's works was the part he played in securing the establishment of the Irish Augustinians at Rome. At present we have no details of the negotiations which he conducted to secure this foundation in the Eternal City, but we may safely assume that he had to overcome a host of difficulties in order to attain his objective[9].

UNSUCCESSFUL ATTEMPTS, 1620-56

For thirty-six years the Irish Augustinians had been seeking to establish a college on the continent where they might train their students before sending them back to the dangers of Catholic life in Ireland. On 23 June 1620 the Irish Augustinian provincial, Dermot MacGrath, received the prior general's permission to accept a house from the French Augustinians as a training centre for students[10]. Nothing further came of that permission though in 1630 the prior general ordered that the provinces of France, Toulouse and Belgium were to accept and train Irish novices[11]. However, the Irish brethren considered that the kindness of foreign provinces was too uncertain a factor on which to build the future of the Order in Ireland. During the year 1638 Maurice O'Connell, O.S.A., a member of that noble Kerry family which has distinguished itself on several occasions in Irish history, was in Spain negotiating for a college at Madrid or at one of the university towns[12]. These negotiations bore no fruit.

5. Declaration by James MacCarthy to the Congregation of Lecceto, 2 March 1661 (Biblioteca Comunale, Siena, C.X.5, f. 184r). I am indebted to my Dutch *confrère,* the late Benignus van Luijk, O.S.A., († 1974), for my knowledge of the Irish Augustinian documents at Siena.

6. At the Irish provincial chapter of 1649 he was appointed 'praedicator major' in the Cork house, cf. acts of chapter in A.G.A., Ff 2, f. 1418.

7. G. Uth, *Szkic historyczno-biograficzny Zakonu n Augustjanskiego w Polsce,* Cracow 1930, pp 115, 132-5, 201, 289; F. Gössmann, in *Analecta Augustiniana,* xiv (1931-32) 379.

8. Cited in W.M. Brady, *Episcopal succession in England, Scotland and Ireland, 1400-1875,* iii, Rome 1877, p. 115.

9. For the "Irish seminary movement" on the European continent in the sixteenth and seventeenth centuries see John J. Silke, 'The Irish abroad, 1534-1691', in *N.H.I.,* Vol. III, pp 587-633.

10. A.G.A. (Archivium Generale Augustinianorum, Romae), Dd 62, f.30v.

11. Ibid., Dd 69, f.35r.

12. Applications of Maurice O'Connell to Propaganda, undated, but discussed at meetings of the Congregation on 16 March 1638, 9 Aug. 1638 (Archiv. Propaganda Fide, Scritt. rif. cong. gen., 399, ff 104r, 133r).

A further attempt was made in the year 1640 when the Irish provincial chapter assembled at Ballyhaunis, County Mayo, petitioned the prior general for permission to establish a college in the Low Countries[13]. Though the permission was readily granted, and the prior general exhorted the Belgian Augustinians to assist the Irish friars in every way, the college was never established. This was probably due in great measure to the outbreak of the rebellion of 1641. With a large part of Ireland under the control of the Irish Confederates it may have seemed unnecessary to establish a college abroad when this could be done with greater facility at home.

THE COLLEGE AT DUNMORE, 1641

It would appear that even before the outbreak of the rebellion the Augustinians had established a college for students at Dunmore, in east Galway. A Protestant remonstrance of the year 1641 complained, 'The friars swarm *hic et illic,* and are often to be met with on the highways in their habits. In Dunmore is a house consisting of a prior and thirty friars, which have their oratory, dormitory, refectory, etc., and observe the rites of their Order as fully as when they were in Spain'[14].

This happy state of affairs did not last for long. The strength of the Confederates was weakened by internal dissensions, then shattered by the arrival of Cromwell. We have already noted that the Augustinians were made to pay in blood and suffering for their religion and patriotism. Their houses were sacked or confiscated. Dunmore friary was emptied by the Parliamentarians in 1654[15].

THE CRISIS OF SURVIVAL

The Irish Augustinians were now face to face with the crisis of survival. Their houses in Ireland were destroyed or confiscated. Some of the friars had been martyred, others were in prison, the remainder were in hiding at home or in exile abroad. A report of the year 1655 spoke of the exiled Irish Augustinians scattered throughout the provinces of France, the Low Countries, Germany and Spain[16]. If there were to be any real security for the future it was necessary that a college should be established on the continent. There the Irish youths who wished to become Augustinians might be trained and educated. It is to the lasting credit of James MacCarthy that he was instrumental in solving the critical problem. Where the previous Irish Augustinian attempts had failed in Spain, France, and the Low Countries, he succeeded in Rome. His efforts might well have been in vain had he not found a kindly patron in the reigning pontiff, Alexander VII.

By coincidence a notable Irish Augustinian Gaelic scholar, Fergal Dubh Ó Gara, was living as an exile in the Low Countries, during that same year, 1656, when an Irish Augustinian house was founded in Rome. In a valuable collection of bardic poetry, now in the Royal Irish Academy, MS 23.F.16, Ó Gara has left a touching marginal note, explaining that on that day, 12 February 1656, he was 'deep in gloom and sorrow at Lille in the Low Countries', wishing he was back in Ireland. Happily he and the MS did return to Ireland.

THE FIRST FOUNDER, POPE ALEXANDER VII

Paolo Lucchini, the Augustinian prior general, appointed James MacCarthy vicar prior of the house of San Matteo in Merulana by a decree of 2 July 1656[17]. The general remarked that MacCarthy was appointed as Superior because of the esteem in which he was held for his prudence and his zeal for the Order. Lucchini stated that it was Pope Alexander VII who had ordered that the

13. A.G.A., Dd 76, f.42v.
14. Cited in O.J. Burke, *History of the Catholic archbishops of Tuam,* Dublin 1882, p. 125.
15. E.A. D'Alton, *Hist. archdiocese Tuam,* II, Dublin 1928, p.268.
16. Visconti Register, April 1655 - A.G.A., Dd 89, ff 337v-338r (recte 338-339), ed. M.B. Hackett in *Archiv. Hib.,* XX (1957) 98-122, at pp 104-115. Visconti adds that he will try to get them a house in Rome.
17. A.G.A., Dd 91, f. 42r-v.

Irish Augustinians were to be given a house in Rome, and this because they were exiles for the sake of religion[18].

It was fortunate that when the Irish Augustinians looked for a friend in this year of crisis they found a pope who had both a keen interest in the Irish struggle and a warm attachment to the Augustinians[19]. Fabio Chigi, before his election as Alexander VII (1655-67), served as nuncio and

 envoy extraordinary in Germany (1639-51). Here he gained a first hand knowledge of the intensity and complications of the struggle between Catholics and Protestants. It fell to his lot as papal secretary of state (1651-5) to hear little else from Ireland but a story of division, disaster and persecution. Added to his sympathy for a Catholic people in agony there was the traditional patronage of the Augustinians by his family. The city of Siena, the home of Fabio Chigi, looked upon the nearby Augustinian monastery of Lecceto as a nursery of saints. The Chigi in Rome, bankers like their cousins in Siena, were traditional patrons of the Augustinian church of Santa Maria del Popolo. When Fabio Chigi came to Rome as secretary of state he showed himself a munificent patron of the friars at del Popolo. We can thus see how James MacCarthy's efforts for a house in Rome were favoured by the circumstances of the time.

Fabio Chigi, from Siena, who as Pope Alexander VII (1655-1667) founded the first Irish Augustinian house at Rome.

FOUNDATION IN ROME, 2 JULY 1656

The Augustinian prior general made known in a decree of 2 July 1656 that the Irish Augustinians had been donated the church and priory of San Matteo by Pope Alexander VII. It was not to be expected that they would be given a well-endowed friary. But San Matteo was rich in religious associations[20]. Some would trace the history of the church back to the fifth century, when christianity was still a novelty in Ireland. However, the first certain reference to San Matteo is from 28 November 1216. Towards the end of the thirteenth century the church came into the care of the religious known as the *Cruciferi* or Crutched Friars. This Order later fell into decline, and the church and friary were given into the possession of the Roman province of the Augustinian friars in the year 1477. Under their care the church was renovated, and a spirit of activity manifested itself. One of the most important events in the history of San Matteo occurred in the year 1499, while Stefano da Genazzano was prior. On 27 March 1499 the picture of Our Lady of Perpetual Succour was enthroned above the high altar of the church. The history of the painting need not detain us here[21]. It came originally from Crete, where it was venerated as miraculous. It was stolen by a Cretan merchant who came to Rome. There he fell greviously ill, and before dying committed the picture to the care of a friend in Rome, by whose

18. 'Quia S.D.N. Alexander Papa VII pro sua benignitate decrevit concedere unum conventum S. Matthaei in Merulana intra Urbem fratribus nostris Hybernis propter fidem exulis a patriis conventibus', ibid., f. 42r. The papal brief of 2 March 1739, restoring San Matteo to the Irish Augustinians, mentioned that the priory was first given in 1656 'fratribus eiusdem Ordinis Eremitarum ex provincia Hiberniae inter alios sub Cromwellis Tirannide ad hanc Almam Urbem semper tutum omnium Orthodoxae Fidei cultorum portum confugientibus', cit. in W.J. Battersby, *History . . . of the Hermits of St. Augustine in Ireland,* Dublin 1856, p.99.

19. For Pope Alexander VII, cf. L. Pastor, *History of the popes,* XXXI, London 1940, pp 1-313.

20. For the history of San Matteo cf. C. Henze, C.SS.R., 'San Matteo in Merulana', in *Miscellanea Francesco Ehrle,,* ii, Rome 1924, 404-14.

21. The classic work on the subject is C. Henze, C.SS.R., *Mater de Perpetuo Succursu,* Bonn 1926. For a further authoritative discussion on the picture and the devotion cf. D. Buckley, C.SS.R., *The miraculous picture of the Mother of Perpetual Succour,* Cork 1948.

wife it was presented to the church of San Matteo in Merulana.

The picture was unlikely to create a sensation in a city which already possessed so many pictures and images of the Madonna credited with miraculous intercessory powers. It did, however, become one of the popular Marian shrines in the city. San Matteo was raised to the dignity of a cardinalate church in 1517. Perhaps its most famous cardinal patron was its first, the Augustinian reformer and humanist, Giles of Viterbo[22].

THE CHURCH AND FRIARY IN THE 17th CENTURY

From an apostolic visitation made in October 1629 we gain some idea of the church of San Matteo as it must have been when the Irish friars acquired it twenty-seven years later[23]. The church was well-equipped, with altars dedicated to SS Matthew, Paul, Joachim and Anne, and Nicholas of Tolentine. The centre of devotion was the high altar with the picture of Our Lady of Perpetual Succour, surrounded by its many votive offerings. From other descriptions of the late sixteenth century we know that the church was between 100 and 108 palms long, and between 44 to 55 palms wide[24]. Not many years before the Irish friars came into possession of San Matteo the church was beautified with a series of paintings from the brush of the Roman artist, Giovanni Antonio Lelli († 1640)[25].

Our Lady of Perpetual Succour.

The priory attached was not small - the visitation of the year 1629 stated that there was a dormitory and cells for six friars - but it was apparently poor. The income was sufficient to support only four friars. All such small religious houses in Italy were suppressed by a decree of Innocent X, *Instaurandae* of 15 October 1652[26]. The house became derelict for four years, and it was in these circumstances that it was offered to the Irish Augustinians. Beggars cannot afford to be choosers, and the exiles were glad to take what was offered to them.

The grant of 1656 was confirmed by a papal decree of 18 September 1658[27]. Alexander VII stated that, moved by the sight of the Augustinians driven from Ireland because of their religion, he was donating them the church and priory of San Matteo, with all their possessions. He added that no less than five priests were to live there. To ensure that they would have adequate means of support he ordered that the Augustinian house of Sant'Agostino was to donate them an annual sum of fifty Roman *scudi,* on the feast of All Saints.

DISPUTED POSSESSION OF SAN MATTEO

The Irish friars had a short tenure of San Matteo. The church and priory were handed over

---

22. Cf. G. Signorelli, *Il Cardinale Egidio da Viterbo,* Florence 1929, p.271, for a copy of the inscription in San Matteo, recording the work of restoration due to Giles. For Giles of Viterbo there is an abundant literature, for which see, F.X. Martin, O.S.A., *Friar, Reformer, and Renaissance Scholar. Life and Work of Giles of Viterbo, 1469-1532,* ed. John E. Rotelle, O.S.A., Villanova, U.S.A., 1992, and a fundamental work by the American Jesuit scholar, John W. O'Malley, *Giles of Viterbo on Church and Reform,* Leiden, 1968. See also bibliography, complete up to 1982, by F.X. Martin in *Biblioteca e Società,* [Viterbo], iv, no 1-2 (June 1982) pp 5-9, i11.
23. Archiv. Segret. Vat., Acta S. Visit. Apostol. sub Urbano VIII, Pars II; Henze, in *Miscell. Ehrle,* cit. ii, 410.
24. Henze, 412.
25. Ibid.
26. *Bullarium Romanum,* XV, Turin 1868, pp 696-700.
27. Bibl. Comm., Siena, C.X.5, f.183r. There is a contemporary copy of the brief in the Posterula *Liber Instrumentorum* now in the archives of St. Patrick's College, Rome.

to the Italian Augustinian Congregation of Perugia by a papal brief of 26 March 1661[28].

Why did the house pass so quickly out of Irish hands? A papal brief of the year 1739 mentioned that the Irish ceded San Matteo to the Perugians because there was insufficient income to support a community of five[29]. Undoubtedly this was a governing factor. Even with the extra fifty Roman *scudi* provided for by the papal decree of 18 September 1658 the Irish at San Matteo could not make ends meet. But the determination of the Perugian friars to outmanoeuvre the Irish, and to incorporate San Matteo into their own Congregation, was one of the main causes for the change. Indeed, it is probable that this was the deciding factor.

James MacCarthy did not yield without a struggle. When the intention of the Perugian Congregation came to his ears he wrote directly, as prior of San Matteo, to Alexander VII asking that the grant of 18 September 1658 be confirmed[30]. His purposeful mood is evident in the criticisms he launches against the Perugian friars. He reminded the pope that San Matteo was given to the Irish in recognition of the fourteen martyrs of the Irish Augustinian province who had testified to their faith by their blood. The Perugians, he commented with a note of bitterness, had neither shed a drop of blood for their religion nor had they ever to endure the hardships of exile. He admitted that the Irish were involved in financial difficulties, but these, he added hastily, he hoped to overcome with assistance from the king of Spain. He admitted to fears because the Perugians had powerful friends in the papal curia who were endeavouring to turn the pope against the Irish community.

It was another petition sent in the name of the Irish Augustinian province which really revealed the tense state of affairs[31]. The Perugians were accused of actively hindering and even opposing the Irish community. They had not hesitated, we are told, to stoop to bribery and influence. They maltreated one friar who was questing for bread on behalf of San Matteo; they prevented Irish friars from joining the community; they were interfering with the payment of the small annual rents which supported San Matteo. The petition anticipated a likely objection from the Perugian Congregation by remarking that a full and regular life was followed at San Matteo, and that even more was to be hoped for if His Holiness, the Pope, would deign to extend a helping hand.

MacCarthy was sufficiently well versed in curial affairs to know how poor were the chances of the Irish community unless it had some powerful backing with higher papal circles. He showed a gift for strategy by trying to rally another Italian Augustinian Congregation to his side. In a document, dated 3 March 1661, he suggested that San Matteo and its Irish community should be affiliated with the Congregation of Lecceto in Tuscany[32]. The community at San Matteo was to remain Irish, but the prior might alternately be of the Lecceto Congregation. The friars at San Matteo, while remaining members of the Irish province were also to have the rights and privileges of being sons of the Congregation of Lecceto. It was assumed that the Congregation would help to support the community at San Matteo.

MacCarthy was somewhat optimistic in his proposals. He was doubtless aware that the

---

28. Mentioned in the papal brief of 2 March 1739, cf. in Battersby, *Hist. Aug. Ire.,* p. 100. My account of the events governing the change at San Matteo in 1661 was revised in the light of suggestions from M.B. Hackett, O.S.A., and the documents from the Vatican Archives which he generously placed at my disposal.

29. The brief of 2 March 1739 stated that the Irish brethren were forced to leave San Matteo in 1661 because of the lack of economic support, quoted in Battersby, *Hist. Aug. Ire.,* pp 99-100.

30. Vatican Archives, Miscellanea, Arm. VII, 64, no. 6, f.282r. This is a holograph letter of James MacCarthy. It is undated but by internal and external evidence has been dated by M.B. Hackett, O.S.A., as written between 18 September 1658 and 3 March 1661.

31. Ibid., f.283r. It is obviously written about the same time as the document on f.282r. It is difficult to know how much truth there was in the accusations against the Perugian friars.

32. Bibl. Comm., Siena, C.X.5, f.184r-v. The document is in James MacCarthy's hand and name. It is not formally addressed to any particular body, but was obviously a petition to the Congregation of Lecceto. It is to be found with the other papers of the Congregation in the Biblioteca Comunale at Siena.

Congregation of Lecceto were as anxious as were the Perugians to have a foothold in Rome. Also, he probably believed that any canonical difficulties to such a union would be smoothed out by the interest of the reigning pope, Alexander VII, who as a Sienese was aware of the high reputation of the friars at Lecceto. Nevertheless, MacCarthy's proposals could hardly be regarded as attractive. The Lecceto friars, while making no secret of their desire for a house in Rome, wanted San Matteo on their own conditions. These were stated by Ambrogio Landucci, then papal sacristan and the leading light of the Congregation of Lecceto[33]. San Matteo was to have a community of six, of which one or two might be Irishmen, but the remainder were to be members of the Congregation. The Lecceto friars were to manage the public church services and business affairs. The Irish would be supported by the Congregation, would have the opportunity to study and learn Italian[34] - this was a smart dig at the Irish friars - as well as the advantage of being entitled to stay at any of the houses of the Congregation in Tuscany. Crumbs for the beggars from the table of the master!

Though both sides were anxious for agreement, nothing practical came of the negotiations. The Perugian Congregation was put in charge of San Matteo by a papal brief of 26 March 1661[35]. At present we do not know sufficient about the legal arguments of the case or of the interplay of ecclesiastical forces to grasp why the Perugian Congregation succeeded in their objective. It is difficult to understand why the Congregation of Lecceto, strengthened by the influence of Ambrogio Landucci in the papal court, could not have proved an adequate counterweight to the Perugians. The Irish must have had a poor case to defend, particularly because of their economic instability[36]. The fact that they were in canonical possession of San Matteo, and apparently had the sympathy of the Lecceto friars, did not outweigh the reasons and influence marshalled by the Perugian Congregation. The Perugians were given San Matteo in recompense for their friary of Santa Maria Novella at Perugia, which had been transferred by papal authority to the Benedictine nuns[37].

MacCarthy was hampered in his negotiations because he was not free to make the important decisions. The Irish Augustinian provincial, James O'Mahony, was living in exile at Brussels[38], and nothing could be concluded without his consent[39]. The practical difficulty of exchanging news and views between Rome and Brussels prevented immediate decisions. The Irish Augustinian interest was probably also influenced by hope of religious toleration in Ireland which the restoration of Charles II to the throne of England brought among Irish Catholics. A continental refuge for the Irish Augustinians did not then appear to be the pressing necessity it had been during the Parliamentarian and Cromwellian days.

MacCarthy, the one man who might have set about the restoration of an Irish Augustinian house in Rome, and probably the only member of the Irish province at this time capable of treading successfully through the maze of Roman curial subtleties, was appointed vicar general of the Polish province in 1662. His departure marks off one phase of Irish Augustinian history in Rome.

33. Ibid., f.185r. For Landucci, who was appointed papal sacristan and bishop of Porphry in 1655, and died on 16 Feb. 1669, cf. D. Perini, *Bibliographia Augustiniana,* ii, Florence 1931, pp 143-5. Since Landucci moved in the inner papal circles one may see a particular reason why MacCarthy conducted the negotiations with the Congregation of Lecceto.

34. A document from the Lecceto friars, written about 1660, stated that the Irish at San Matteo were seriously hampered 'per non haver la lingua italiana et per non haver conoscenza', in Bibl. Comm., Siena, C.X.5, f. 186r.

35. M.B. Hackett, O.S.A., informed me that a copy of the brief of 26 March 1661 is in A.G.A., Bullarium 4 (1644-1721), from the original in Archiv. Vat., Reg. Brevium, 1230, f.567.

36. The statement by the Lecceto Congregation mentioned that there were only two Irish and two Italian friars at San Matteo, and that the house 'sta spogliato di ogni utensile', Bibl. Comm., Siena, C.X.5, f. 186r.

37. Mentioned in the papal brief of 2 March 1739, cit. in Battersby, *Hist. Aug. Ire.,* p.100.

38. Cf. biographical note on O'Mahony by F.X. Martin, O.S.A., in *Archiv. Hib.,* XV (1950) 74-75.

39. MacCarthy added a note to his proposals of 3 March 1661, stating that from the Irish side all depended on the final consent of James O'Mahony and the Irish provincial diffinitory, cf. Bibl. Comm., Siena, C.X.5, f. 184v. He mentioned the difficulty of treating with a provincial so far away. The same point was made about this time by the Lecceto Congregation, cf. ibid, f. 187r. The Irish at San Matteo were also weakened by dissension within the community. The 'Libellus supplex', written about this time states that one friar, Thady Colgan, was a trouble maker, and requests the Augustinian prior general to remove him, cf. A.G.A., Ff 33, ff 1421r-2.

BROTHER DONOGH IN ROME, 1661-1700

The Irish association with San Matteo did not end in 1661. One Irish lay brother, Donogh, remained at the friary. It is he who has immortalised Irish devotion to Our Lady of Perpetual Succour. Fr J.B. Coyle, C.SS.R., with full justice, dedicated his work, *Our Lady of Perpetual Succour and Ireland*[40], to 'the memory of *Donogh,* the exiled Irish friar who for forty years loved and guarded the shrine and sacred picture of Our Lady of Perpetual Succour at old St Matthew's, and was buried under its shadow'.

Brother Donogh was an ex-soldier of the days of Eoghan Ruadh O Neill, a man of remarkable simplicity and striking sanctity[41]. Lay folk, clergy, prelates and cardinals at Rome revered him for his holiness of life. Even during his lifetime miracles were supposed to have been worked through his intercession.

Though circumstances beyond their control forced the Irish Augustinians to leave San Matteo in 1661 their connection with Rome was by no means severed. This is evident from the careers of Patrick of St Augustine, Christopher Marcellus [Marshal?], Francis Bermingham, Fulgentius Butler, Marcus Kirwan, Nicholas Blake, Thomas Berrill, Hilary Flood and Luke Geoghegan - to mention but a few of those who studied and worked in Rome between 1661 and 1739[42].

Before Brother Donogh died in 1700 the Irish Augustinians were once more looking for a house of their own in Rome. When James II fell in 1688 the hopes of Irish Catholics crumbled to the ground. The Battle of the Boyne (1690), the Treaty of Limerick (1691), and the first of the Penal Laws (1695) removed what little hope may have remained. The iron grip tightened in 1697 with the introduction of 'An act for suppressing all fryerys, monasterys, nunneryes, etc.'. All religious were to be quit of Ireland by 1 May 1698. The Irish Augustinians were once more driven into exile. A report from Paris in January 1699 stated that at that city alone financial assistance had been given to twenty-six refugee Irish Augustinians[43].

The Irish provincial, Francis Bermingham, went to Rome in 1698, principally to act as a representative to the pope from the Irish clergy, but also to find a home for exiled Augustinians[44]. While in Rome he must have visited the holy Irish lay brother at San Matteo. Yet it was not San Matteo in Merulana but Santa Prisca on the Aventino that he tried to secure as a refuge for the Irish brethren. Neither Brother Donogh nor Francis Bermingham lived to see the return of the Irish Augustinians to San Matteo.

PERSECUTION IN IRELAND: VOCATIONS MULTIPLY

Despite the rigour of the Penal Laws there was no lack of vocations for the Augustinians in Ireland. The friars improvised as best they could to ensure that a regular supply of young men would continue to be received into the Order. The house at Dunmore was re-established secretly as a novitiate. The prior, Patrick Brehon, posed as a landowner who employed a number of young men as "farm hands" or "apprentices"[45]. Though the essential training for novices could be given at Dunmore there was little hope that the studies in theology and philosophy could be made satisfactorily in Ireland. The students were, therefore, sent to the houses of the Order in the Low Countries, France, Germany, Italy, Spain and Portugal. But the charity of the continental brethren grew strained as the number of Irish students continued to increase over the years. The provincial,

40. 2nd ed., Dublin 1912.
41. Cf. account in J. Lanteri, *Postrema Saecula Sex Religionis Augustinianae,* iii, Rome 1860, pp 40-3.
42. Cf. A.G.A., Ff 22, ff 1425, 1427; Dd 125, ff 211-2; *Analecta Augustiniana,* XI, 208, 276, 281 (bis), 379; Vienna State Library MS 7239, fasc. 20; Burke, *Irish priests in the penal times,* pp 256-7; De Burgo, *Hibernia Dominicana,* p. 751.
43. A return of charitable grants made to the Irish exiles by order of the Holy See, Paris, 17 Jan. 1699, signed by the archbishop of Armagh and bishop of Ossory. In *Spicilegium Ossoriense,* ed. P.F. Moran, ii, Dublin 1878, pp 347-8.
44. Cf. W.P. Burke, *The Irish priests in the penal times, 1660-1760,* Waterford 1914, p.133.
45. Burke, cit., pp 255-6.

Edmund Byrne, wrote to the prior of Dunmore on 18 October 1722, 'If you have sent any of the young men to the province of Andalusia they will not be taken by reason of the great number of ours that is there already. All Spain complains of us for receiving so many in this kingdom, and so do all other countries'[46].

The next provincial, Peter Mulligan, wrote to the prior of Dunmore on 3 September 1725 that sixteen youths had offered themselves to the Order, but that all had to be refused for the time being since there was no place in which to house them[47]. Even the training of novices in Ireland was seriously jeopardized when the Dunmore friary was raided by government officials in 1732, all documents seized, and the Augustinians driven from their house[48].

AGAIN, THE QUESTION OF SURVIVAL

The crisis over student training, indeed of survival, once more faced the Irish Augustinians as in the days of Cromwell. If the Order were to survive and progress in Ireland a college devoted exclusively to the training and education of young Irish Augustinians was needed on the continent. In their perplexity the friars looked instinctively to Rome. A powerful patron was needed to sponsor their cause, and the Augustinians turned to James III. It was because the Irish Catholics had supported the Stuart cause that they were suffering the degradation of the Penal Laws. It was, therefore, a consolation that it was the Stuarts who were directly responsible for re-establishing the Augustinians in San Matteo.

JAMES III, THE SECOND FOUNDER

James III has as much claim to be styled the second founder of the Irish Augustinian house in Rome as Pope Alexander VII has to be called the first founder. It is not surprising that one notable Irish Augustinian who studied at San Matteo during the 1740s, the Gaelic poet Liam Inglis, should have sung in defiance to George II[49]

'Yes, George! and a brilliant career lies before us
The God we have served will uplift and restore us
Again shall our Mass hymns be chanted in chorus
And our prince, without name, our beloved, shall reign o'er us'

*Liam Inglis, O.S.A.,
the Gaelic poet.*

James has little of the romantic appeal of his son, Bonnie Prince Charlie. James, however, did make an attempt during 1715 to raise the standard of rebellion in Scotland. The story of the rescue of his intended wife, the Polish princess, Clementina Sobieski, by Charles Wogan and some other Irish nobles from the imperial guards at Innsbruck, is one of the stirring chapters of Stuart history. In proposing the re-establishment of the Irish Augustinians at San Matteo James was undertaking something of more lasting importance than the majority of his ineffectual political schemes.

James III, founder of the second Irish Augustinian house at Rome. From miniature in oils in possession of Miss Maria Widdrington, Berkeley Square, London. The miniature set in a case of diamonds, as part of a necklace, is supposed to have been the property of Clementina Sobieski, wife of James III (Reproduced with permission).

---

46. Ibid., p. 258.

47. Ibid., p. 256. For information on Peter Mulligan, for many years a zealous missionary in Scotland, see chapter by M.B. Hackett in this volume. Mulligan later became bishop of Ardagh, province of Armagh, 1730-1739.

48. Ibid., p. 254.

49. R. Ó Foghludha, *Cois na Bríde* [The Life and poems of Liam Inglis, O.S.A.], Dublin 1937, pp xvii, 36. See Conor Cruise O'Brien, *The Great Melody*, (London, 1992), p. 22 n.1.

THE AUGUSTINIANS AND THE STUARTS

The Irish Augustinians were not without some influence at the Stuart court. When Francis Bermingham came to Italy in 1698 seeking financial support for the Irish clergy he was fortified with a letter to the duke of Tuscany from Queen Mary of Modena, wife of James II[50]. His successor as provincial, Bernard O'Kennedy, when dying at Madrid signed a statement on 29 February 1704 in which he mentioned that he was agent for James II and Mary of Modena at the court of Spain[51]. O'Kennedy nominated another Augustinian, John Kelly, to act in his place as agent for the Stuarts.

There was another distinguished Augustinian friar, John Dowdall, who may have had some part in securing the support of James III[52]. Dowdall had been court preacher to James II during his brief unfortunate spell in Ireland, 1689-90. After a lengthy exile in London and on the continent Dowdall returned to Dublin about 1727, was elected provincial for the years 1730-3, and died on 14 November 1739. The negotiations at Rome could not have been concluded without the consent of George Vaughan, who was Irish provincial in March 1739, and was then, with John Dowdall, a member of the Dublin community. Dowdell's advice as an ex-provincial, and his influence as a former court official of James II, were likely to have been availed of.

Nevertheless, who in fact were then the Irish Augustinian influences in the court circles of James III is at present unknown. We are as much in the dark about the forces behind the transfer of San Matteo from the Perugians to the Irish in 1739 as we are about the legal arguments and inner influences which wrested San Matteo from the Irish in 1661. The only certain information of an Irish Augustinian effort is that three of the friars, Thomas Berrill, Luke Geoghegan, and Hilary Flood, petitioned Clement XII that San Matteo be granted to the Irish province[53]. Presumably this strengthened James III's request to the pope, but it can hardly have been a decisive factor.

SAN MATTEO IN THE 18th CENTURY

The brief of Clement XII, granting San Matteo to the Irish Augustinians contains some enlightening information. It stated that San Matteo was being established as a house of studies, and that its very secluded position on the Via Merulana made it suitable for such a purpose[54]. The papal brief of 1739 also mentioned the proximity of the Irish Dominican house of San Clemente as an advantageous factor for San Matteo[55].

The church and priory were situated on the Via Merulana, which runs between the basilicas of St John Lateran and St Mary Major. It is difficult at the present day, as one looks at this busy thoroughfare with its constant stream of traffic, to realize that in the year 1739 the Via Merulana was an unspoiled suburb of the city. By a stroke of good luck an engraving of San Matteo, for long overlooked, has come to light[56]. Since it dates from the year 1731 we may feel with

---

50. Burke, *Irish priests in Penal Times*, cit., p. 133.

51. Cited in Battersby, *Hist. Aug. Ire.*, pp 67-9.

52. For Dowdall, cf. W. Harris in J. Ware, *History of the writers of Ireland*, Dublin 1764, p. 94. The dates of the offices he held in Ireland, given by Harris, are to be corrected from the acts of the Irish provincial chapters as found in Liber A 2, Irish Augustinian Provincial Archives, Dublin. I am indebted to the late Stanislaus Roche, O.S.A. (†1973) Archivist, for these corrections and for several other points of information throughout this article. Harris, who was a contemporary of Dowdall, and displays an almost personal knowledge of his life, states that he was provincial in 1739. This is incorrect, but Harris's statement probably mirrors the influential position Dowdall held among Irish Augustinians in the eyes of outside observers.

53. T. de Burgo, *Hibernia Dominicana*, Cologne [Kilkenny] 1762, p. 751.

54. 'in eam sententiam devenimus, ut iisdem fratribus [Hibernicis] aliquem conventum, seu domum hujus Almae Urbis, ad effectum ut aliquot iuxta inferius statuenda juniores fratres ejusdem provinciae Hiberniae sub vigilanti et immediato prioris generalis Ordinis praedicti regimine, ac inspectione sedulam doctrinarum studiis operam navarent, opportunam destinaremus, nec aliam ob causam, quam ut iisdem omnino doctrinarum studiis instructi, in eadem morum consuetudine formati, ab iisdem superioribus viventes, atque ad animas fratrum suorum in patria positorum lucrandas seinvicem adhortantes, et collaborantes, quem in similibus collegiis instituti religionis viri uberem nationibus suis

confidence that we are seeing San Matteo as it was when the Irish Augustinians returned to take possession in 1739. The neatly walled property, the carefully spaced trees, the pretty façade of the church, the adjoining priory, compact and solid, tell that the friars of the Perugian Congregation had lavished more than average care upon San Matteo during the years between 1661 and 1739.

We have already noted that in the year 1629 San Matteo was a poor house capable of supporting only four friars. Though the Irish Augustinians who acquired San Matteo in 1656 were granted an annual supplementary income of fifty Roman *scudi* from Sant'Agostino, by the papal decree of 18 September 1658, they found it impossible to maintain a community of five there. After the Perugian Congregation acquired San Matteo in 1661 it was decided that the advantage of having a church and priory in Rome justified a special effort to develop the foundation. The

San Matteo in Merulana: The first home of the Irish Augustinians in Rome, from A. Hoeggmayr, O.S.A.,
Monasteria Fr. Ord. Erem. S. Augustini, *Munich 1731, f. [10r].*

golden opportunity came when Francesco Nerli (†1705) was declared cardinal of San Matteo in 1673[57]. Here was a prince of the Church with far-reaching influence - he was cardinal secretary of state, acknowledged as a man of exemplary life, and known to be zealous for the glory of the house of God.

Nerli's generous patronage allowed the church to be renovated and the priory to be rebuilt. Under this new regime of comparative prosperity the Perugian Congregation was able to maintain a community of twelve at San Matteo[58]. Popular devotion to the picture of Our Lady of Perpetual Succour continued to increase, as we know from a sermon preached in Rome by the Jesuit Father

afferre pergunt fructum, ipsi quoque deinceps uberiorem in Hibernia producere possint . . . : eo dumtaxat fine, ut studiorum sive philosophiae sive theologiae curriculum in eodem conventu S. Matthaei inire possint, et non aliter quocumque praetextu remoto . . .' in Battersby, *Hist. Aug. Ire.*, cit., pp 100-1, 103. The actual brief is in AGA, Hh 7, 70.
55. Ibid., p. 101.
56. Cf. [A. Hoeggmayr, O.S.A.] *Monasteria Fr Ord. Erem. S. Augustini,* Munich 1731, f. [10r].
57. For Nerli, cf. Pastor, *Hist. popes,* XXXI, London 1940, p.477.
58. Henze in *Miscell. Ehrle,* cit., ii, p.411.

Carocci on 31 August 1715[59]. The reputation of the Italian friars at San Matteo may be concluded from the fact that the ascetical Dominican pope, Benedict XIII (1724-30), dined there with the community on several occasions when he was in residence at the nearby Lateran Palace[60]. It was thus the good luck of the Irish Augustinians that they re-acquired San Matteo when the condition of the church and priory had so much improved since the year 1656. One wonders what were the sentiments of the Perugian friars on receiving orders to transfer San Matteo to the Irish brethren!

We have the names of some of those who were connected with the new start in 1739. The papal brief mentioned that an Irishman, Augustine Higgins, was immediately to be placed in possession of the priory on behalf of the Irish province, but that the acting prior was to be Xavier Valletti, an Italian friar, who was to remain as Superior until the arrival of a prior sent by the Irish provincial and confirmed by the prior general[61]. The Irish Augustinians allowed no grass to grow under their feet. On 1 April 1739 Thomas Berrill was inducted as prior of San Matteo. Thomas de Burgo, the Irish Dominican historian, and later bishop of Ossory, was present on this occasion. He mentions that Berrill was one of those who petitioned the pope to transfer San Matteo to the Irish brethren[62].

It is odd, very odd, that a veil of mystery, or at least a surprising silence, surrounds the inner story about the return of San Matteo to the Irish friars in 1739. Normally in such Roman ecclesiastical manoeuvres, and consequent bitter wrangles, there is a spate of documents available giving the arguments for and against, from persons of authority. Nevertheless, so far nothing of the kind has come to light about San Matteo, but it is almost inevitable that such documents do exist and will come to light. Blessed is the researcher who will discover them!

PURPOSE OF SAN MATTEO

The brunt of the papal document, *Aspera Temporum Conditio* (2 March 1739) was that San Matteo was now established specifically as a house of studies[63]. It mentioned that the staff of the college was to consist of a prior or rector, a sub-prior, a procurator and two lectors - one for philosophy and one for theology. It was conceded, however, that the prior, sub-prior and procurator might act as lectors. The prior general was instructed to create two lectors for the college, and the lecturing was to be regarded as part of the qualification for the much-coveted magisterium in theology. The brief stated that the community was also to include some lay brothers and at least four students[64].

One might have expected that due to the need for priests in the British Isles a shortened course of studies would have been allowed. Instead it was ordered that the course was to occupy eight years - two years for philosophy, three for the usual branches of theology, and three for the study of the scriptures and of controversial issues[65]. It was added that these latter three years of study were not to be frittered away on side-issues and irrelevant matter, but were to be devoted to questions of practical import. The object was to produce priests for pastoral work in the Irish province. The students on entrance to the college were to take an oath that after their eight years of study they would return without delay to this work. Nobody but the pope was entitled to grant exemption from the oath. It was described as having the same binding force as all other such oaths

59. Henze, *Mater de Perpetuo Succursu,* Bonn 1926, p. 56.

60. Henze in *Miscell. Ehrle,* cit., ii, p.411.

61. Cf. Battersby, cit., pp 102-4.

62. De Burgo, *Hibernia Dominicana,* cit., p.751.

63. Cf. supra n.54.

64. Evidence that the formalities about qualification for the magisterium (i.e., the doctorate in theology) were observed is seen in a printed broadsheet of theses defended by Nicholas MacCann at San Matteo in the mid 18th century. There is a copy of the broadsheet in the Angelica Library, Rome, and in the O.S.A. Provincial Library, Ballyboden, Dublin 16.

65. 'Studiorum curriculum in Collegio S. Matthaei explendum, octo annorum spatio terminetur; nimirum per duos quidem philosophiae tres vero theologiae scolasticae, tres denique in quibus etiam S. Scripturae lectio per horam quotidie habeatur, controversiis in patria praesertim vigentibus annos incumbant', in Battersby, cit., p. 107.

in pontifical missionary colleges[66].

We know of one notable Augustinian, Nicholas Molloy, who was lector of philosophy and theology at San Matteo in the early 1790s[67]. Molloy was gifted intellectually, but his later fame was to rest on his ability as a preacher. While a deacon at Rome he preached in Italian. After his return to Ireland in 1796 he was acknowledged, even by the *Hibernian Magazine* and the *Dublin Mirror*, as the leading Catholic pulpit orator of his day. He died in 1810. His change from a professor's chair in Rome to the active ministry in Ireland was in accordance with the purpose for which San Matteo was re-founded as an Irish Augustinian college in 1739.

The appointment of the prior of San Matteo was not left directly to the Irish Augustinians. According to the brief of 1739 the Irish provincial was to forward three names to the prior general who had the right to select any one of the three[68]. The matter was taken entirely out of Irish Augustinian hands by a brief of Benedict XIV, dated 17 March 1746, which left the appointment at the discretion of the prior general[69].

From the time of its second foundation in 1739 until the end of the century the Irish Augustinian college appears to have followed a placid existence. The uneventful daily life is well caught in a letter, dated Rome 31 August 1763, from John Corban, the prior of San Matteo, to the provincial in Dublin[70]. Corban mentioned business of the province which he had conducted with the general curia, he told of an Irish friar who had come from France to live at Sant'Agostino, and he assured the provincial that all were well at San Matteo. He gave a homely touch with his comment that 'our vineyard promises nothing extraordinary this year, on account of the continual rains and foggs of this season'. He mentioned in passing, what is of special interest, that San Matteo was also a novitiate[71].

The main source of information about life at San Matteo has been lost since the disappearance of the greater part of the archives during the destruction of San Matteo by French troops in 1798[72]. However, from scattered sources we can piece together some information about one prior of San Matteo who has a special place in the history of the Irish province.

PHILIP CRANE, 1791-8: FOUNDATION IN AMERICA

Fr Philip Crane, an outstanding member of a remarkable County Wexford family, was agent in Rome for the wardenship of Galway during the years 1792-6, in the dispute between the bishop and the citizens[73]. The wardenship had been established in the city with quasi-episcopal rights, because of local racial conditions during the late medieval period. The dispute at the end of the eighteenth century was one of several attempts by the bishops of Galway to limit these rights.

Philip Crane was also agent for something of far greater importance - the foundation of the Augustinian Order in the new republic of the United States. The story of the development of the Augustinians in North America is told by Rev. Joseph Schnaubelt, O.S.A., in another contribution to this volume. One may here recall that the foundation letters for the new province were granted on 27 August 1796 at the request of Philip Crane, then prior of San Matteo[74].

66. Ibid.
67. For Molloy, cf. Battersby, cit., pp 133-6; J. Walsh, O.S.A., ed., *Molloy's practical sermons,* Dublin 1859, v-vii.
68. Battersby, cit., p.105.
69. Letter of prior general, F.X. Vazquez, to the Irish diffinitory, Rome 12 September 1758, reminds the Irish fathers of the Brief of Benedict XIV, in Liber 100, Irish Aug. Prov. Archiv., 64.
70. In Battersby, cit., pp. 118-19.
71. The house at Rome was again used as a novitiate during the 1880s. Cf. the house diary, "Records of the Irish Augustinians in Rome, 1875-1936", St. Patrick's College Archives, pp 5-13.
72. For the little archival material which has survived cf. F.X. Martin, O.S.A., 'Archives of the Irish Augustinians, Rome', in *Archiv. Hib.,* XVIII (1955), 157-63.
73. Cf. E. MacLysaght, 'Report on documents relating to the wardenship of Galway', in *Analecta Hibernica,* xiv (1944) 70-1.
74. Cf. documents quoted in *Anal. Aug.,* iii, p. 396. The close relationship between the American and the Irish Augustinians was still in evidence in the year 1881 when three students from the United States came to follow their theological course with the Irish Augustinians in Rome, cf. house diary of Posterula, pp 9, 14.

Fr John Rosseter, who had been parish priest of Enniscorthy, County Wexford, before he became an Augustinian novice, was one of the two founders of the Order in the United States. After his novitiate at Dublin he went to Rome, and was a member of the community at San Matteo during the years 1788-90[75]. George Staunton was the third Augustinian to serve in the United States[76]. He was rector of San Matteo during 1787-91, also served in Spain and Portugal, and was appointed vicar of the Catholic troops at Gibraltar by the commander-in-chief, Henry Fox, on 13 March 1805.

Today, when one considers the progress of the Order in the United States, the parishes, schools and university colleges under American Augustinian care, the splendid expansion they had made in Cuba, before the arrival of Fidel Castro, with their then Catholic University and other thriving houses, their foreign Mission in Japan, with six centres at different cities, and the American Augustinian Mission in Peru, South America, one can only marvel at the growth which has come from the humble beginnings made with the assistance of the friars at San Matteo.

DESTRUCTION OF SAN MATTEO, 1798

That glorious chapter of Augustinian history in the United States lay in the future, unknown to Philip Crane. He lived in a Europe where the Catholic Church was on the defensive. It fell to his sad lot to be prior of San Matteo when the French marched into Rome on 9 February 1798 under General Berthier[77]. A week later the "Free Republic of Rome" was declared, and the ailing Pius VI was haled away as a prisoner, with his chaplain, the Augustinian Bartholomew Menochio, whose cause for beatification is now well advanced in Rome. Berthier was succeeded by Massena, and under his regime the work of destruction began. It was first believed that San Matteo would suffer only suppression and sale, as occurred with the other Irish, English and Scottish colleges in the city. So much we may gather from a letter of the Irish Dominican, Connolly, written from Rome in March 1798 to Dr Plunkett, bishop of Meath. 'The French have seized on and sold everything belonging to the English and Scotch Colleges here; the former was worth three thousand pounds a year . . . I suppose they will do the same at the Irish Convents of St Matthew's, S. Isidore's and S. Clement's, notwithstanding the efforts of the incumbents of these houses to prevent it'[78].

But the fate of San Matteo was to be even more melancholy than Connolly had foreseen. It was not merely sold, but was one of more than thirty churches in Rome declared to be 'superfluous'. This meant it was to be razed to the ground. The levelling began in June 1798. A further letter from Connolly, 18 January 1800, supplies the sad information that 'the purchaser of the Irish Augustinian convent here demolished the church and the greatest part of the convent, and the same was to happen the Irish Franciscan Convent, had the purchaser a little more time'[79].

So thoroughly did the demolition squads do their work that a papal bull of 23 December 1801 declared that it was difficult at that time to find even a trace of the former buildings of San Matteo[80].

Meantime, what of the Irish community? Philip Crane, driven from Rome, made his way towards Ireland. A revealing story is told of his stay in Paris[81].

---

75. Cf. F.X. Martin, O.S.A., 'John Baptist Rosseter, O.S.A., family background and pre-American years', in *The Past,* vi (1950) 26-38.

76. For Staunton cf. Battersby, cit., pp 137-8.

77. Henze in *Miscell. Ehrle,* cit., ii, 413.

78. L. Nolan, O.P., *The Irish Dominicans in Rome,* Rome 1913, p. 55.

79. Ibid., p. 56.

80. Henze in *Miscell. Ehrle,* cit., ii, 413, quoting the bull *Christiani gregis pastor* (23 Dec. 1801).

81. See Thomas C. Butler, O.S.A., *Near Restful Waters: The Augustinians in New Ross and Clonmines,* Good Counsel Press, Ballyboden, Dublin 1975, pp 99-101. See also J.B. Cullen, 'The Augustinians in New Ross', in *Irish Ecclesiastical Record,* ser.5, XV (1920) 308-9.

It is a dramatic story, sharply reminiscent of the incident related by Charles Dickens in *A Tale of Two Cities*.   There Dickens gives the heart-rending fictitious account of the noble-minded Englishman, Sydney Carton, who allowed himself to take the place of an innocent Englishman, and so go to the guillotine, accompanying a totally innocent French girl, whose sole crime was to have been a seamstress for an aristocratic lady.   The seamstress went with confidence in the company of Sydney Carton, while the Parisian harridans sitting around the scaffold cheered as the heads were lopped off and the spurting blood encrimsoned the knitting of those blood-thirsty creatures. Dickens's is a memorable - indeed immortal - story, with Carton declaring, 'It is a far, far better thing that I do, than I have ever done'.

A similar situation posed a real problem for the Irish Augustinian, Philip Crane, when he arrived at Paris from Rome on his way to Ireland.   He was travelling externally as an Irishman, and therefore in favour with the French revolutionaries who knew of the radical Irish revolt against their British overlords.   When he arrived at Paris he stayed with a clerical friend, whom he had known at Rome, but who was not suspect at Paris as an enemy of the French Revolution.   This friend quietly let Crane know that a fellow-Irishman, Charles Tottenham, from New Ross, was in prison, awaiting public execution on a trumped-up charge of being an English spy.

Crane's initial reaction was understandable in the circumstances of the degrading anti-Catholic legal system enforced in 18th century Ireland.   He knew the local circumstances at New Ross where the Tottenham family were all-powerful as British agents.   Instinctively he bitterly commented, 'He is no friend of ours', but then his christian conscience asserted itself - probably also a special sympathy for a fellow Wexfordman in dire trouble.

Crane decided on a very risky venture.   He went to the prison, disguised as a miller, delivering the daily supply of bread.   He took the place of Tottenham in the condemned cell, so allowing Tottenham to get away.   Later Crane managed to secure his own release from the gaol, by pretending that he was a chaplain who had defected to the stupid doctrine and altar of the Goddess of Liberty, recently crowned at the cathedral of Notre Dame.   Obviously - his critics could comment - he was a product of the Jesuit system of casuist theology!

So both Tottenham and Crane made good their escapes from the prison and from France. Crane returned to Ireland and became prior of the Augustinian community who were living in dingy quarters at New Ross.   Tottenham was now mayor of New Ross, with much wealth and almost unlimited local power.   When Crane looked around for a site for a new church Tottenham decided to repay the extraordinary debt he owed to the resourceful Augustinian.   He offered Fr Crane, for the nominal annual rent of 10/-, the former Catholic parish chapel site which had a commanding position on the hill, overlooking the town[82].   Needless to say the offer was accepted and this explains why the Augustinians are now on such a prime site.

Since there was now no college in Rome for the students Crane established one at New Ross in the year 1809.   Here as his assistant he had James Warren Doyle, O.S.A., later famous as the "J.K.L." of Emancipation fame[83]. Meantime, the Irish Augustinian connection with Rome was not completely broken.

When Philip Crane left Rome in 1798 some of the community appear to have remained on. They were given possession of the church and priory of Sant'Eusebio which had belonged to the Celestines, a branch of the Benedictines[84].   Little was saved from nearby San Matteo.   The

82. Battersby, cit., pp 213-14.
83. Ibid., p.214.
84. Cf. F.X. Martin, cit., in *Archiv. Hib.,* xviii (1955) 158-61. An Irish Augustinian student community returned to Rome, to Sant' Eusebio, early in the first decade of the 19th century. Then in May 1809 Napoleon annexed the papal states, including the city of Rome. British subjects were arrested, but the Irish clerics were allowed free. At Paris we find, from Rome, two Irish Dominicans, six Irish Franciscans, and ten Irish Augustinians (including their prior, ? Fr Keating). Cf. document in Maynooth Library, Index Room, in French Colleges MS section, catalogued in 1950 by Fr Joseph Kelly. Copy sent to F.X. Martin by Fr T.J. Walshe, P.P., Durrus, Co. Cork, 15 July 1968.

archives and library were dispersed; eight marble statues from the church found their way to the Lateran basilica[85]. But the friars brought with them one object of special value, the picture of Our Lady of Perpetual Succour.

William Keating, O.S.A., who had been regent of studies at San Matteo, and who had been driven from Rome at the same time as Philip Crane, was sent back to Rome during the Napoleonic wars to salvage whatever he could of the Irish Augustinian rights and properties. He acted as prior in Rome during the years 1807-15. We are told, with an annoying lack of detail, that 'he fulfilled his trust with great risk, but with good effect'[86].

JOHN RICE, 1819-40

A new era dawned for the Irish Augustinian position in Rome with the election of Philip Crane as provincial in 1819. However much the college at New Ross for Irish Augustinian students may have tided over a difficult period it would not be an adequate substitute for training in Rome. The new beginning was due to the interest of Philip Crane, and to the exertions of John Rice, the man who was sent as prior to Sant'Eusebio in 1819.

John Rice is described as having been 'amiable in his manners, dignified in his person and possessed of considerable abilities'[87]. He is perhaps best known not for his own considerable talents but for the fact that he was brother of Edmund Ignatius Rice (1762-1844), founder of the Irish Christian Brothers, whose Cause for Beatification is now (1994) well advanced at Rome. During the difficult years when the early Christian Brothers were trying to obtain recognition of their Institute from the authorities in Rome John Rice proved to be of invaluable help[88].

Edmund Ignatius depended greatly on his Augustinian brother, John, for the recognition and defence of the Irish Christian Brothers, when under heavy attack from Robert Walsh, bishop of Waterford, 1817-1821. Walsh savagely assailed not only the moral behaviour of Edmund Ignatius, who he asserted had a bastard child in every parish in Waterford diocese, but wrote with even greater vehemence against his brother John. These charges from an apparently reputable authority, a bishop, had to be taken seriously in Rome. As a result of Walsh's charges John was called to Rome - he had not yet been appointed to Sant' Eusebio - and had to stand trial on the charge by the bishop of Waterford of being a practising homosexual. It was a humiliating experience even for a completely innocent man.

What emerged, much later, was the startling recognition that Bishop Walsh was totally untrustworthy, his charges were diversionary, and he was protecting a friend of his, the parish priest of Dungarvan, who was conducting a heated love affair with the female organist of the parish church, even in the organ loft during interludes in religious ceremonies.

Fortunately, at the time of the charges, John Rice had staunch friends in Rome who knew his character and behaviour over many years. He had in particular the confidence of Dom Mauro Cappellari, the Camaldolese abbot of San Gregorio in Celio, who was later elected pope as Gregory XVI (1831-46)[89]. The pontificate of Gregory XVI were crucial years for the development of the early Christian Brothers. They were also crucial for the history of the Irish Augustinians in Rome.

It was at Pope Gregory's express wish in 1835 that John Rice was appointed Assistant General for Germany and all other provinces outside Italy, except those of Spain[90]. It was this

---

85. Statues of SS John the Baptist, Peter, Paul, Matthew, Mark, Luke, Laurence, and Simplicianus. Cf Henze, cit., in *Miscell. Ehrle,* ii, 413.
86. Battersby, cit., p. 191.
87. Battersby, cit., p. 204.
88. Cf. Rev. J.D. Fitzpatrick, *Edmund Rice,* Dublin 1945, p. 55.
89. Apart from Battersby, cit., pp 204-5, there was an unpublished account of John Rice by the late E.A. Foran, O.S.A., in the *Good Counsel Quarterly* files, Augustinian priory, Dublin, in 1956. This is now missing. The latest information on John Rice's death at Valletta in Malta 12 December 1840 and his burial in the crypt of the Augustinian church at Rabat (Gozo), is to be found in, Fr Julius Bonnici, O.S.A., *Grajjiet Agostinjani F'Malta,* Valletta, Malta, 1990, based on documents in the Maltese Provincial Archives at Valletta.
90. Battersby, cit., p. 205.

personal friendship too, between Dom Mauro Cappellari and John Rice. which had, much earlier, helped largely to obtain a new home for the Irish Augustinians, a notable victory. During 1819, when John Rice was prior at Sant' Eusebio, the Augustinians were granted the church and priory of Santa Maria in Posterula, situated not far from the Vatican, on the left bank of the Tiber between the Via Zanardelli and what is now the Ponte Umberto[91].

SANTA MARIA IN POSTERULA, 1819

Posterula was the third building occupied by the Irish Augustinians in Rome, and represented the fourth occasion on which they had to find themselves a home in the city. It remained in their hands until 1888.

The little church of Santa Maria already existed in the ninth century[92]. Santa Maria, like Sant'Eusebio, had been in the care of the Benedictine Celestines, who built a college beside the church in 1626. It was the only church in Rome dedicated to the Blessed Virgin under the title of

Our Lady of Grace which is now venerated in Saint Patrick's Church is a fourteenth century fresco which the Irish Augustinians brought with them from their former church of Santa Maria in Posterula.

the Presentation, and the feast was always held there with full solemnity on the twenty-first of November. Santa Maria in Posterula enjoyed a certain fame in Rome because it contained a picture of Our Lady of Grace, reputed to be miraculous. It was crowned by the Chapter of St Peter's in 1573 in recognition of the favours granted at the shrine[93].

The title "in Posterula" came from a nearby postern gate which gave access across the Tiber to the Vatican and the Castel Sant' Angelo.

THE REVOLUTION OF 1848-49

The Irish Augustinians in Rome seemed destined to suffer from the scourges of revolution and war. When the flag of revolt was raised over Rome in November 1848 Santa Maria was too near the Vatican to escape the attention of the revolutionaries. James B. Hayes, a student at Posterula, has left a description of the frightening scene as a band of armed men, headed by a well-known bearded leader, Callimaco Zambianchi, burst into the college[94]. A retired Italian Augustinian bishop, playing chess with an Irish friar in one of the rooms, was thrown roughly aside and the table overturned as the revolutionaries rushed through the building, unaware of what or whom they were seeking. What might well have been the fate of the Irish Augustinians may be judged from the murder of the Dominicans and other priests by Zambianchi and his terrorists at the convent of San Calisto. However, the revolution passed, and life went on as before at Posterula.

When the Irish friars came to Posterula from Sant'Eusebio they brought with them the picture of Our Lady of Perpetual Succour which they had salvaged from the destruction at San Matteo. Since there was

91. Cf. letter of John Rice to Philip Crane, Saint Augustine's, Rome, 23 Dec. 1819, telling of his negotiations about the properties of Sant 'Eusebio and San Matteo. I am indebted to the late S. Roche, O.S.A., for a transcript of this letter from Irish Aug. Prov. Archiv., C 44 I.

92. For a brief account of Santa Maria in Posterula, cf. M. Armellini, *Le chiese di Roma,* 2nd ed., Rome 1891, pp 347-8.

93. See illustration.

94. A typescript copy of this letter was in the *Good Counsel Quarterly* files, Augustinian priory, Dublin. It is now missing.

already a strong devotion at Posterula to the Blessed Virgin, under the title of Our Lady of Grace, the picture of Our Lady of Perpetual Succour was placed in the private oratory of the college. The fascinating story of how it was "discovered", and of how it was transferred at the express order of Pope Pius IX on 19 January 1866 from Santa Maria to the church of Sant'Alfonso (newly built on the site of the former church of San Matteo in Merulana), is told elsewhere in full detail[95]. Here we need only bear in mind that it was the Irish Augustinians who saved the picture from destruction 1n 1798, and that it was, in particular, one faithful lay brother, Agostino Orsetti, an Italian member of the San Matteo community who lived on into the middle of the nineteenth century, who kept alive the knowledge of where the picture of Our Lady of Perpetual Succour was preserved. It is opportune, also, to pay tribute to the zeal of the Redemptorist Fathers, who during more than 100 years have spread devotion to Our Lady of Perpetual Succour to the four corners of the earth[96].

MISSIONARIES TO AUSTRALIA, 1838

We have noted that the Irish Augustinians in Rome were intimately associated with the despatch of missionaries to North America at the end of the nineteenth century. Perhaps even more important was the contribution made by Posterula to the infant Church in Australia. As the history of the Augustinians in Australia is dealt with in a lively contribution in this volume by Fr Thomas A. Hunt, who was first provincial of the Australian Province, we need recall but a few facts for the general picture.

James Alypius Goold, O.S.A., (1812-86), first bishop, then archbishop of Melbourne, was one of the founders of the church in Australia[97]. His biography has yet to be written in detail, but it is already evident how much Catholicism in Australia owes to his practical zeal and shrewd foresight. Goold's future took a new direction because of a chance meeting in Rome while he was a member of the community at Posterula.

During Easter 1837, when coming out of the Augustinian church of Santa Maria del Popolo, after a visit to the Blessed Sacrament, he casually met Dr Ullathorne, then vicar general of New Holland [i.e. Australia], who was on the alert for volunteers to his mission. Goold, in his characteristic manner, offered himself for the work, was accepted, and received the necessary permission from the Irish provincial on 22 September 1837. Throughout the remainder of his life, Goold retained his links with Posterula which remained ever close to his heart[98].

Fr T.A. Hunt, O.S.A., who in 1952 became the first Provincial of the Augustinians in Australia, seen here in 1982 with Pope John Paul II, with whom he had concelebrated Mass in the Holy Father's private chapel, on the occasion of the Golden Jubilee of Fr Hunt's ordination.

Goold alone among the Catholic bishops in Australia fought with courage and persistence for

95. Cf. for e.g., Buckley, *Mother of Perpetual Succour,* cit., pp 69-76, and elsewhere.

96. Ibid., pp 88-110 for the spread of the devotion up to 1948.

97. No full biography of Goold has yet been published, but much useful material is to be found in P.F. Moran, *History of the Catholic Church in Australia,* Sydney-Melbourne 1895, pp 723-831. This includes lengthy extracts from his diaries which were missing, but have recently come to light, due to Very Rev. Dr Francis Little, Archbishop of Melbourne. Mention must also be made of a fine partial study made by Frances O'Kane, *A Path is Set,* Melbourne University Press 1976.

98. See T.A. Hunt, O.S.A., 'Australia remembers Rome and Ireland', in *The Irish Augustinians in Rome,* ed. J.F. Madden, O.S.A., Rome 1956, 89-94, at p. 94.

the right to have government financial support for Catholic schools. Virulent anti-Catholic opposition did not deter him.

When he died in 1886 his cathedral at Melbourne - he had incredibly scrapped the first two versions of the building as the city and its Catholic people quadrupled - remained in a primitive state of development. He was a Corkman with vision who had seen the hidden chapels in Ireland replaced with magnificent cathedrals throughout the country, and the official government poor-houses replaced with efficient large-scale Catholic hospitals independent of the English government.

St. Patrick's Cathedral, Melbourne, Australia. The cathedral was first planned and partially built by Dr Alypius Goold, O.S.A., the first bishop, then archbishop, of Melbourne.

It was appropriate that Goold's two dreams - first a Catholic cathedral at Melbourne on an elevated position he had carefully selected, secondly a system of government support for Catholic schools - were attained only some 70 years later by another indomitable Corkman, Daniel Mannix, a legend in his own lifetime. Goold and Mannix are still undoubtedly the two most important figures in the history of the Catholic Church in Australasia.

Who else but Mannix could have defeated the attempt by the prime minister of Victoria, William Hughes, to introduce army conscription to Australia in 1917? Who else in 1920 could have mustered a demonstration of 10,000 ex-servicemen and women, on Saturday 13 March 1920, through the main streets of Melbourne, led by 14 ex-servicemen - not all were Catholics - on white horses, who had won V.C.s in World War I?

It was Mannix too, who when travelling from the U.S.A. to Ireland across the Atlantic on a passenger-steamer, *The Baltic*, during 1920 to participate in anti-British political demonstrations in his native country, had his journey shadowed by, incredibly, a succession of ten British destroyers. As his ship neared Ireland *The Baltic* was ordered to halt, and on the high seas Mannix was removed to one of the British destroyers, *Wyvern*. He submitted peacefully, but as he was escorted aboard *Wyvern* he quipped, with almost malicious satisfaction, to his embarrassed host, the British naval commander, that this was the greatest British victory at sea since the Battle of Jutland (on 31 May - 1 June 1916) off the Baltic coast. Both he and the British commander knew that Jutland was a drawn affair with each side contending to its own advantage, even to the present day, that it was a decisive victory. Arresting Mannix's journey was unintentionally another victory for the cause of Irish Independence, which came shortly afterwards with the Anglo-Irish Peace of 6 December 1921.

Martin Crane, O.S.A., first bishop of Sandhurst (1874-1901), was a contemporary of Goold, and also a distinctive figure in the early history of the church in Australia[99]. Crane was appointed

---

99. For Martin Crane, cf. Moran, cit. n.97, pp 845-8; S. Roche, O.S.A., *Good Counsel*, ii, no. 8 (Jan.-Mar. 1940) 977. See also, Stan Arneil, *Out Where the Dead Men Lie,* Augustinian Historical Commission, Brookvale, N.S.W., Australia 1992, pp 287-290. Arneil's book is a comprehensive history of the Augustinians in Australia.

prior of Posterula in 1850[100]. He was grand-nephew of Philip Crane, whom we have seen as prior of San Matteo in 1798. Martin Crane was one of the leading figures in the history of the Irish Augustinian province in the nineteenth century. It was he who undertook the building of the present Augustinian "John's Lane" church in Dublin, "the poem in stone", as Ruskin called it. Crane also re-introduced the Augustinians to England by establishing them at Hoxton, London, in 1864[101]. His life's work was crowned by his years as bishop in Australia, and in particular by the ambitious Sacred Heart cathedral which he began to build at Bendigo, in Victoria.

Two other Augustinian missionary bishops were alumni of Posterula. Dominic Murray, vicar apostolic of Cooktown in Northern Queensland (1898-1914)[102], and Alphonsus J. Heavey, vicar apostolic of Cooktown (1914-41), and first bishop of Cairns (1941-8)[103]. We have no space here to mention the many other past students of Posterula and of St Patrick's College who have given service to the Church in Australia. The first Australian vocation to the Order, Laurence Moran of Melbourne, followed his studies at Posterula[104].

Architect's etching of the "John's Lane" church, Dublin.

POSTERULA IS AGAIN THREATENED

Confiscation threatened Posterula during the 1870s. When the Piedmontese troops seized Rome in 1870 the suppression of the religious houses was announced. Most of Sant'Agostino, the magnificent head-house of the Order, was confiscated in 1871 - one small part of it has by now (1994) been restored to the Italian Augustinians - as were the other Italian Augustinian friaries in Rome. The prior general and his curia, driven from Sant'Agostino, came for refuge to the Irish Augustinian house in April 1871[105]. This was a noteworthy event.

Posterula itself was next threatened. The Augustinians, in common with the Irish Franciscans at Sant'Isidoro, and the Irish Dominicans at San Clemente, claimed exemption as colleges under protection of the British government[106]. Probably this alone saved them from confiscation. It was something of a paradox that all three colleges, founded in the seventeenth century because of the religious persecution by the English in Ireland, should have been saved by English intervention in the nineteenth century.

100. This does not appear in the acts of the provincial chapter. Fr S. Roche, O.S.A., located the reference for me in the diary of the provincial, John Walsh, in Liber A 10, Irish Aug. Prov. Archiv., 7, 22, 194, 200, 201, 203.

101. Cf. the chapter in this volume by Rev. M.B. Hackett, O.S.A.

102. Contemporary references to Murray's student days in Rome are in the Posterula house diary, cit., 1-2. Cf. biographical notice of Murray in *Anal. Aug.*, v, 333. See also Arneil, cit.n.99, pp 296-298.

103. Cf. contemporary references to Alphonsus Heavey in the Posterula house diary, cit. 26-36. Heavey was a student both at Posterula and at San Carlo al Corso. He was also present at the inauguration of the temporary chapel in St Patrick's, 17 March 1891. Cf. obituary notice of Dr Heavey in *Good Counsel*, v, no. 7 (Oct.-Dec. 1948) 14. See also Arneil, cit. n.99, pp 290-292.

104. Cf. references to Moran in Posterula house diary, cit. 4-12. See article, 'The first Australian Augustinian', by F.X. Martin, in Irish Augustinian P.N.L. *(Provincial News Letter)*, July 1975, pp 33-37.

105. Cf. documents from the general archives published in *Anal. Aug.*, xiv, 26.

106. Cf. documents of the years 1873-5, St. Patrick's College Archives, listed by F.X. Martin, cit. in *Archiv. Hib.*, XVIII (1955), 162, n.42.

PATRICK GLYNN: THE VILLA AT SAN PIO, 1880

Patrick Glynn was appointed prior of Posterula at the Irish provincial chapter of 1879. It would be difficult to exaggerate the debt which the Irish province owes to this Limerick-born friar. His first service was to secure a summer villa for the students of Posterula. Rome, even at present, during the summer months is not considered suitable for the health of foreign students. One may imagine how doubly serious was the state of affairs in the nineteenth century when the Pontine Marshes around Rome were still for the most part undrained. The problem was particularly grave for the Irish Augustinians. Their college was situated on the banks of the Tiber, in an unhealthy part of the city[107]. Whenever the Tiber overflowed its banks the Posterula house was invaded by the waters at ground level[108].

Glynn saw a solution for the problem when he heard that the former Conventual Franciscan house and property at San Pio, in the hills of Lazio, were due to come under the auctioneer's hammer[109]. The estimated cost of the property and of the renovation of the buildings was £3,000, a considerable sum of money in those days, though the property was reckoned to be worth three times that amount. Glynn had no capital at his disposal, but he appealed to the Irish people. Within less than two months the £3,000 was paid by public subscription[110].

The Villa, San Pio.

San Pio has a special attraction for the Augustinians. It is situated about half a mile above the town of Genazzano, where rests the reputedly miraculous picture of Our Lady of Good Counsel[111]. The proximity of San Pio to Genazzano explains in part why the Irish Augustinians of the past seventy-five years have shown such a devotion to Our Lady under this title. Archbishop Goold of Melbourne included the image of the Mother of Good Counsel in his coat of arms; Bishop Martin Crane dedicated the diocese of Sandhurst, Victoria, Australia, to the Blessed Virgin, under her title of Good Counsel. Pope John Paul II, during his official visit to Albania in 1992, reminded his audience of the Mother of Good Counsel shrine at Genazzano. The present day devotion to Our Mother of Good Counsel propagated by the Irish Augustinians is perhaps best exemplified by the popularity of the shrine in the "John's Lane" church, Dublin.

---

107. The worst period of ill-health occurred during the building of the Ponte Umberto I, when the house diary records, 'May 1888 . . . At this time, owing to the works on the new bridge, Ponte Umberto I, Posterula became very unhealthy, so much so that three fourths of the community were at one time ill in bed'.

108. The house diary under 14 Nov. 1878 mentions, 'The Tiber overflowed its banks and inundated a good portion of the city, the water raised to the height of seven feet in our yard, and about 4 feet in the church, and continued on for four days. Provisions were supplied by boats during this time'. Another inundation is recorded under 10-11 April 1885.

109. For a history of San Pio, cf. Rev. J.A. Meagher, O.S.A., 'San Pio and Genazzano', in *The Irish Augustinians in Rome*, ed. J.F. Madden, O.S.A., Rome 1956, 109-115.

110. G.F. Dillon, *The Virgin Mother of Good Counsel: a history of the ancient sanctuary in Genazzano, with an appendix on San Pio*, Dublin 1884, pp 540-59, gives a brief account of San Pio and mentions the price paid by Glynn as £3,000. The house diary, under 17 March 1880, gives the price in international exchange as 9,100 francs.

111. Cf. Dillon, *Virgin Mother of Good Counsel,* cit., which remains the standard work on the subject in English.

THE END OF POSTERULA, 1888: A BLESSING IN DISGUISE

Prior Glynn's ability to solve a practical problem was put to the test in 1886. By 1883 he already knew from the Roman municipality that Santa Maria in Posterula was due to be demolished in order to allow for the construction of the outworks of a new bridge, the Ponte Umberto I. It was said in 1886, and later, that this decision was due to Freemasonry and to anti-clericalism[112]. There appears to be no real foundation for the charge. The occasion may have suited the anti-clerics, but that had little to do with the main issue. A new bridge was badly needed across the Tiber, and the Augustinian church and college happened to stand at the point most suitable for the construction. The demolition of Posterula, however much of a disaster it may have first appeared to the Irish Augustinians, proved to be a blessing in disguise. Glynn made the most of the opportunity. He conducted a stiff dispute with the Roman municipality over the compensation to be awarded. He was granted £16,000, a reasonable and, at that time, an even generous sum. He realized he was then in a position which had not come the way of the other Irish communities in Rome. Instead of having to accept some existing church and priory, as the Irish Augustinians had already done four times during their history in Rome, he would be able to select a site and build a college according to modern specifications, and with an eye to the future needs of Catholic Ireland and of the Irish Augustinian province. He chose a plot of ground in the Villa Ludovisi, in an elevated unbuilt area overlooking the city. It was a secluded unspoilt spot, and yet within easy walking distance of the centre of the city, and of educational establishments such as the Jesuit Collegio Romano, and of the Propaganda Fide and other university colleges.

THE IRISH NATIONAL CHURCH OF ST PATRICK, ROME

Prior Glynn's ambitions soared still higher. In a private audience with Pope Leo XIII during the year 1886 he told of the fate which was to befall Posterula, mentioned that a plot of land had been secured as a site for a new college in the Villa Ludovisi, and added that he proposed to build a church in honour of St Patrick beside the college. This was a project which had been already discussed three years previously between Archbishop Croke of Cashel and Prior Glynn[113]. The pope, a warm friend of the Augustinians and a lover of Ireland, gave his immediate approval to the project[114]. A letter signifying his support was issued by the Congregation of Propaganda Fide, on 21 July 1886[115]. Pope Leo gave practical evidence of his approval by heading the subscription list with the generous sum of £2,000[116]. The pope's enthusiasm proved infectious. The Irish hierarchy, at a meeting in Maynooth College on 8 September 1886, were told of the proposed church in Rome, and of the pope's full approval of the project. Archbishop Croke of Cashel proposed a motion, seconded by Archbishop McEvilly of Tuam and adopted by the hierarchy as a body, that 'we express our united thanks to His Holiness for the special interest he has been pleased

---

112. For example, the *Catholic Telegraph* of Cincinnati, Ohio, 9 Dec. 1886 stated, 'In the course of its piratical policy of sequestration of ecclesiastical property to which it takes a fancy, the unprincipled government of Italy has laid its hands on Santa Maria in Posterula, the home of the Irish Augustinians'.

The house diary of Posterula, under July 1886, simply records without emotion, 'At this time, on account of the construction of a bridge [Ponte Umberto I] close to Posterula, the site on which our convent stood was needed to form the entrance to the bridge. Compensation was sought for by the prior [V. Rev. P.J. Glynn], and after great exertion on his part the sum of £16,000 was obtained'. It will be noted that, according to this reference, the exact location of the buildings was at what is now one entrance of the bridge.

113. Croke to Glynn, Thurles, 1 Sept. 1886, 'I believe, indeed, I was the first of your numerous friends to promise a subscription towards it, when about three years ago, you intimated to me your desire and determination to set such a project on foot with a view to its ultimate realization', in *Annals of the Irish National Church of St Patrick, Rome,* Dublin 1889, p. 8.

114. Cf *Annals National Church,* cit., pp 3, 25.

115. The Latin text and English translation are given in ibid., pp 42-3.

116. The Posterula house diary states under 'July 31, 1886. The pope, Leo XIII, gave a subscription of 4,000 francs to the National Church of St Patrick, which is to be erected at Irish expense on the grounds of the once Villa Ludovisi (Orti Sallustiani) and is to be attached to our convent about to be erected there, and will perennially be served by members of the Irish province of our Order'.

28

to manifest in this most desirable work, and we promise to favour and support the undertaking as far as possible'[117].

A central committee for the "Irish National Church of St Patrick, Rome" was formed, with Archbishop William Walsh of Dublin as chairman, and Dr Robert Browne, president of Maynooth College, as one of the secretaries[118]. Archbishop T. Kirby, rector of the Irish College, Rome, gave his warm support to the project[119].

It will be noticed that the letter of approval issued in Leo XIII's name by the Congregation of Propaganda Fide did not formally title the proposed church as "The Irish National Church". This was perfectly understandable in the political circumstances of the time, when nationalism on the continent particularly in Italy and in France was so often closely associated with anti-clericalism, and sometimes with anti-religion. The Irish hierarchy, however, who were best qualified to judge the relation of Irish nationalism to Catholicism did not hesitate to give their support for the project of a "national church". Their attitude was clearly expressed by Bishop Nulty of Meath in a letter of 16 October 1866 to Prior Glynn[120], 'I feel great pleasure, indeed, in concurring in the cordial and emphatic approval

Executive Committee St Patrick's National Church, Rome.
Most Revd P.J. Ryan, Archbishop of Philadelphia; Most Revd W.J. Walsh, Archbishop of Dublin; Very Revd P.J. Glynn O.S.A. Prior, Rome; Most Revd R. Browne, President Maynooth College; Comm. Hickey, New York; Dr Kenny, Melbourne; Revd D. Pettit, Dublin; Revd P.F. O'Hare, Brooklyn, N.Y.

given by all the bishops of Ireland to the project of erecting at Rome a National Church which would symbolise the faith and religion of our race abroad as well as at home, and be dedicated to God under the invocation and name of St Patrick, our National Apostle'. It was probably this assurance from the Irish bishops which induced *Osservatore Romano,* the semi-official organ of the Vatican, to refer in glowing terms to St Patrick's, in an article of 2 February 1888, not merely as the future Irish church in Rome but to style it "national" in the same sense that St Louis' was for the French, St Anthony's for the Portuguese, Santa Maria dell'Anima for the Germans, and St Gregory's for the English[121].

---

117. *Annals National Church,* cit., p. 6.
118. Cf. their appeal to the Irish people, ibid., pp 11-12.
119. Cf. his letter to Glynn, Irish College, Rome, 20 July, 1886, ibid., p.9.
120. Ibid., pp 11-12.
121. 'Come ad ognuno è già noto, la Cattolica Irlanda era, si può dire, la sola nazione la quale non possedesse nella Città Eterna una chiesa veramente nazionale. Eravi, sì, e vi è tuttora, la chiesa di S. Isidoro la quale ha grati ricordi e preziosi tesori per l'Irlanda. E vi è pure, sul Gianicolo, quella storica chiesa francescana, dove dormono il sonno del giusto gli esiliati Principi del Nord. Ma queste due chiese non rappresentano che un asilo offerto dalla Roma Cattolica a figli sventurati. Ivi il cuore irlandese può battere di gratitudine per chi l'ospita, ma non può ripetersi quella parola così dolce ad ogni straniero pellegrino: "Qui sto come sul suolo patrio: Sto in casa mia". Il francese invece va giustamente altero per la magnifica chiesa di S. Luigi; il portoghese per la ricchissima di S. Antonio; lo spagnuolo per quella maestosa di Nostra Signora di Monserrato; l'inglese per quelle di S. Gregorio et di S. Tommaso di Canterbury; l'Austro-Ungherese per quella devotissima di S. Maria dell' Anima'.

THE IRISH PEOPLE RESPOND

Subscriptions began to flow in from the Irish and their descendants all over the globe, from Ireland, England, Scotland and Wales, from Gibraltar, Italy, the United States of America, Canada,

Copy of postcard issued by Father Glynn on the occasion of the appeal for funds to build an Irish National Church in Rome.

British Guiana, the West Indies, South Africa, Australia and New Zealand[122]. The political and cultural resurgence then taking place in Ireland gave an added impetus to Irish generosity. Michael Davitt, that admirable Irish patriot, sent his subscription with a long letter expressing his satisfaction that Ireland would at last be represented properly in Rome, and would have a recognized centre from which to counteract English intrigues at the Vatican[123]. On the other hand Cardinal Manning sent his subscription with sentiments of warm approval for an Irish church in Rome[124]. The duke of Norfolk, though bearing the reputation of being anti-Irish, was present at the laying of the foundation stone of St Patrick's in Rome, and gave a subscription of £50[125].

The solid expression of Irish piety was represented by subscriptions from groups in Dublin such as the Breadvan Drivers' Society, the Coopers' Society, the Operative Horseshoers' Society[126]. It was noticeable how many subscriptions came from individual members or groups of the Royal Irish Constabulary[127]. There was the touching letter and the subscription of 10s-6p from the poor Irish patients in St Elizabeth's Hospital, London[128]. And one can see the faith and the fighting spirit in the letter sent with a subscription by William Dwyer from a mining camp in the wilds of the Rocky Mountains, in the U.S.A.[129]

In March 1899 Matt Talbot and his brother, Charles, joined the St Patrick's Roman Legion, an Association headed by an Augustinian priest, to raise funds for St Patrick's National Church in Rome[130].

The foundation stone of St Patrick's Church was laid on the feast of St Brigid, 1 February 1888, with much solemnity. A large space had been excavated in the shape of a Greek cross, around which were erected tribunes, draped in scarlet and gold, for the more distinguished guests from different parts of the world. By permission of Pope Leo XIII Archbishop Walsh was allowed to perform the ceremony, and was granted the use of the papal vestments for the occasion. As a symbol of the bonds between Rome and Ireland, the foundation stone was set in earth brought from St Patrick's grave at Downpatrick. Archbishop Ryan of Philadelphia, "The American Chrysostom", delivered a moving sermon. The official record on parchment, which was buried with the foundation stone, stated that the new church was to rise beside the Augustinian college. Did any of those at the ceremony, flushed with the satisfaction of initial success, foresee the broken hopes and unhappy years which were to pass before the project was completed?

122. Listed in *Annals National Church,* cit., pp 58-68.
123. In *Annals National Church,* cit., pp 18-20. A similar comment was made in John Boyle O'Reilly's newspaper, the *Boston Pilot,* 18 Dec. 1886, with reference to 'the intrigues of a political Catholic, like Mr Errington'.
124. In *Annals National Church,* cit., p.7.
125. Cf. ibid., p.48.
126. Listed, ibid., p.66.
127. Listed, ibid., pp 65-8.
128. Ibid., p.24.
129. Ibid., pp 23-4.
130. Mary Purcell, *Matt Talbot and his time,* Dublin: Gill, 1955, pp 103-4.

Trowel used at laying of the first stone of the Irish National Church of St Patrick, Rome 1888. (Illustration taken from a tracing of the trowel made by Diarmuid Kerrisk, O.S.A.

SAN CARLO AL CORSO, 1888-92

The notice from the Roman municipality in the summer of 1886 gave the friars a year of grace in which to find themselves a new home. Even though they managed to have this extended for a further year they found themselves in a predicament by early summer 1888, with Posterula due to be demolished that same year while the new college of St Patrick was yet unbuilt. Leo XIII generously gave them temporary possession of the spacious church and adjoining presbytery of San Carlo al Corso until such time as the new college would be built. During June and July the movable property of Posterula was changed to San Carlo. The last Irish Augustinian link with Posterula was sundered when Fr Glynn left on 1 August 1888 for holidays in Ireland[131].

LIFE BEGINS AT ST PATRICK'S COLLEGE, 1892

The building of St Patrick's College went steadily ahead, and a substantial part was completed by Spring 1891. Archbishop Walsh of Dublin, the faithful friend of the Augustinians, was in Rome on St Patrick's Day 1891 to celebrate the first Mass in a temporary chapel in the college. A year later St Patrick's was ready for occupation. On 5 March 1892, a little before the "Ave Maria", as the house diary notes, the community of twelve changed from San Carlo to their new home on the Via Piemonte. This was the sixth occasion on which the Irish Augustinians in Rome had to transplant their roots. St Patrick's is the fifth building to serve as their home.

The first solemn profession to take place in the new college was not without significance for the future. Joseph Hennessy from County Limerick was solemnly professed on 13 November 1892. Thirty-eight years later, when provincial, he was instrumental in restoring St Patrick's to the Augustinians. This brings us to a sad chapter in the history of the college.

ST PATRICK'S COLLEGE: AN AMBITIOUS ACHIEVEMENT

A temporary chapel in the college was blessed by the Irish Cardinal Logue of Armagh on 20 February 1893, in the presence of a large number of pilgrims from Ireland. The chapel was designed to serve as the sacristy for the National Church. It was hoped that the church would be granted the status of

St Patrick's College, Rome.

a minor basilica. A beautiful ciborium to act as a canopy over the high altar was bought by Fr Glynn, and was much admired by Cardinal Parrochi, the cardinal vicar of Rome. Nevertheless, despite these gestures, the building of the church had made no progress since the laying of the

---

131. The house diary comments, '1 Aug. 1888. The prior, Very Rev. P.J. Glynn, left Posterula for Ireland, being thus the last Irish Augustinian to leave the house with which are connected so many traditions of the Irish Augustinian Province. Let Posterula be remembered for the glorious Irish names inseparably connected with it'. Unless otherwise stated the remaining facts in this article are taken for the most part from the house diaries. The first house diary was commenced in Sept. 1875.

foundation stone in 1888. By the year 1893 no more than the foundations for the walls were visible. At the time this did not occasion any disquiet or alarm. It was understood that it would be best to complete the college before commencing in earnest on the National Church[132].

Prior Glynn planned a college which would be an object of admiration for the Irish colony and for visitors to Rome. As a model there was taken the Palazzo Strozzi in Florence[133]. This palace, projected in 1489 and completed in 1539, is typical as an expression of Renaissance cultural life. It follows the style set by Michelozzo with the Palazzo Cosimo de' Medici at Florence. The

construction displays an embossed uniformity, enriched with Albertinian decoration and suggestion. Throughout there is economy of detail, organic unity, energetic projection of mass. The most striking single feature is the beautiful and vigorous cornice, executed, as was the *cortile,* by Simone del Pollaiolo, called *Il Cronaca.* Classicism, with the notes of harmony and symmetry, is all-pervading. The building expresses something of the serene and grave dignity of the ancient Roman buildings, yet with a definite imprint of the medieval Italian castellated mansion, as seen in the biforated windows and the general stonelike defensive appearance.

Florence: The Strozzi Palace.

The building on the Piemonte was intended not merely as a college for the Irish Augustinian students but also as a centre at which the Irish and Irish-descended prelates visiting Rome from various parts of the world might stay. The workmanship was executed with a generous hand. Mosaics with the shamrock design as the dominant motif were laid out on the first and second storey floors. A mosaic harp design in the centre of the refectory was surrounded with the

St Patrick's College: Ground floor corridor

St Patrick's College: Students' corridor, first floor.

132. This was presupposed in the historical record which was engrossed on parchment, and enclosed in a leaden case, and placed with the foundation stone - 'the new Church, dedicated to St Patrick, the Apostle of Ireland, which will rise close to the new Augustinian College' - in *Annals National Church,* cit., p.47.
133. For photographs showing the similarity between the Palazzo Strozzi and St Patrick's College, cf. pp. 31, 32. For a discussion on the architecture of the Palazzo Strozzi, cf. V. Costantini, *Storia dell 'Arte Italiana: Il Rinascimento,* Milan, 1948, p.19.

renowned dictum of St Patrick, *Ut Christiani ita et Romani sitis.* The solidity of the structure, the restrained decoration, the two *cortili,* the spacious corridors and the high-ceilinged rooms proclaimed that Ireland could be represented by a building which would compete with any of those belonging to the other nationalities in Rome. It was only then, on completion of the college, that the grim realities of the financial situation became apparent.

BUILDING OF THE NATIONAL CHURCH CEASES

The project for an Irish National Church in Rome began with the disadvantages of unanimous approval and too rosy hopes. The attitude was clearly reflected in the letter of Archbishop Croke to Prior Glynn, 1 September 1886, 'Funds for it, I feel assured, will not be found wanting. The whole Irish race will subscribe. Were it necessary I should gladly go a-begging for it myself. But, happily, there will be no need of doing so. Simply make known your project and requirements to your countrymen in and out of Ireland, and money will come pouring in on you from all quarters in golden showers'[134]. St Patrick's College was built, and the National Church was planned, on the supposition that Archbishop Croke's statement would come true - 'Simply make known your project and requirements to your countrymen in and out of Ireland, and money will come pouring in on you from all quarters in golden showers'. The readiness with which £3,000 had been subscribed for the summer villa at San Pio after Fr Glynn's appeal in 1880 created an optimistically false impression.

Fr Glynn began with the sum of £16,000, the compensation money granted by the Roman municipal authorities for the site and buildings at Posterula. With this he was able to buy a site in the then country area on the outskirts of Rome, the part of the Villa Ludovisi, for college and church, and have at hand an initial sum for the building of the college. The appeal for the Irish National Church in Rome was launched in July 1886. By 1889 the sum of £18,561-9-6 had been subscribed[135]. Under the impulse of these first generous offerings Fr Glynn began to build on an ambitious scale. By the year 1893 he found himself with the college built, but with little money forthcoming for the National Church which was now due to take shape. The 'golden showers' were no longer in evidence!

In these circumstances it is not surprising that recriminations and accusations flew fast. Even during these bitter years nobody seriously questioned Fr Glynn's intentions and good faith. But his practical abilities as an administrator and financier deservedly received scant sympathy. One may well understand the chagrin of those, particularly the subscribers, who had expected an Irish National Church to be completed within a few years. As almost inevitably happens in such a crisis one man, in this case Prior Glynn, was picked upon as the scapegoat. Though he was the one mainly at fault, a fair measure of the blame should also be meted out to the other members of the Central Committee for the Irish National Church of St Patrick. They were aware of how much money was at Fr Glynn's disposal, and knew, or ought to have made it their business to know, how it was being used. The Committee left the expenditure to Fr Glynn. He continued with the original plan in his big-hearted impractical way, confident that the money would continue to come.

Fr James Anderson, O.S.A., patriot priest, who undertook a fund-raising visit to Australia on behalf of St Patrick's National Church, Rome.

The fundamental fault throughout this affair was lack of business acumen. The crisis

134. In *Annals National Church,* cit., p.8. The same sentiments were expressed by the editor [Fr. Glynn?] of *Annals National Church,* p.31. 'We may expect Irishmen the wide world over to answer to the call, speeding to the Eternal City the golden stream which will soon raise beneath the sky of Italy in the City of the Soul, a pile becoming alike the hearts, the genius, and the resources of St Patrick's sons'.

135. Listed, ibid., pp 58-68.

developed because there was no active body with regular meetings to ensure continuous publicity and a steady flow of subscriptions. Glynn did make special efforts to raise money. In April 1887 he and Bernard O'Hanlon, O.S.A., went on a visit to the United States to collect funds. James Anderson, O.S.A., a well-known patriot priest, the friend of the Fenians, of Arthur Griffith, of D.P. Moran (founder and editor of *The Leader*), of Maude Gonne MacBride and of Padraig Pearse, set out from Rome for Australia in October 1891 for the same purpose. Neither of these schemes yielded much money. The world-wide economic recession was against them.

ST PATRICK'S COLLEGE CHANGES HANDS, 1899

The Irish Augustinian province found it had to bear the responsibility of the crisis. In April 1896 the Irish provincial, John Furlong, and his secretary, Dr Thomas Kenna, came to Rome. They spent a month in their investigations. The student community was transferred to Ireland. Fr Glynn came to Rome in the autumn of 1896, and said his last Mass in St Patrick's on 27 July 1897. He returned to Ireland a broken man, and resigned his priorship a short time afterwards. He died at Limerick on 1 January 1909, a victim of circumstances and his own enthusiasm[136].

At this time the Irish province had no "Central Fund" which could have been used to supply sufficient money to keep the building scheme at least partly in operation. The head house of the province at Dublin was struggling under a grave debt incurred by the building of the striking "John's Lane" gothic church in Thomas Street. The generous Irish Catholics in the vicariate of Cooktown in Northern Queensland might well have seemed to be the answer to the financial problem. This territory was given into the care of the Irish Augustinians in 1883, and developed a sudden "boom" due to the discovery of mineral wealth, particularly at Cooktown itself. Plans were made for a cathedral at Cooktown and for ecclesiastical expansion throughout the vicariate. These hopes faded when some of the mines failed and others were flooded. Cooktown became a "ghost city". The bishop, Dr Dominic Murray, was forced to go on a begging tour to the United States in order to try and raise money for the needs of his diocese. Apparently there remained no source from which the committee for the National Church in Rome could get a substantial loan.

St Patrick's College: Main staircase. The statue is now (1994) installed in the vestibule of the new St Patrick's College.

The Augustinians wished to make an honourable settlement, agreeable to all. They formally offered St Patrick's College to the Irish hierarchy, but this too generous offer was magnanimously refused. Dr Kenna, O.S.A., returned to Rome in September 1898 to negotiate the sale of the college. Before the end of the year he had arranged for the transfer of the property to a community of English Benedictine nuns, for the sum of 600,000 francs, to be paid at the end of six years. In the meantime an annual amount of 1,400 lire was to be paid. Fr Joseph Hennessy, the sub-prior, left for Ireland on 26 November, and Dr Kenna betook himself to the Augustinian head house of Sant'Agostino. Thus by Christmas 1898 St Patrick's had passed from the hands of the Irish Augustinians.

Meantime Fr Glynn was at Limerick, eating his heart out at the thought of the magnificent college of St Patrick being relinquished. More painful still was the reflection that the Irish Augustinian house in Rome, a proud heritage from the times of persecution in 1656, was being abandoned due to his unwitting mistakes. Yet before he died, on 1 January 1909, he had the consolation of knowing that the Irish Augustinans had resumed their place in Rome, and that the building of an Irish National Church in Rome had been energetically undertaken.

---

136. Cf. the brief uninspiring obituary notice of Fr Glynn in *Anal. Aug.* III (1909-10) p.24. He never sought power in the Augustinian Order or personal wealth.

The Benedictine nuns who entered into possession of St Patrick's in January 1899 depended for the purchase money on one richly-endowed junior member of the community. She, however, left after a short time. The nuns were thus unable to pay more than the rent for the first quarter. They were forced to leave in August 1901, but the finely carved throne of the lady abbess was left in the possession of the Irish Augustinians. The Irish Augustinians had continued to appoint a prior to Rome in the vague hope that some suitable solution would eventually be found to the problems. Fr Robert O'Keeffe, appointed prior in 1899 and re-appointed in 1903, leased St Patrick's to the "Convitto Nazionale" for four years, at 33,000 lire per annum. Before the lease expired he tried to sell St Patrick's, negotiating with the Jesuits and with the Holy See. The negotiations with the Jesuits were on the way to completion[137] when some unexpected factor caused the scheme to be dropped. It would have been a considerable bonus for the Society of Jesus to have acquired such a site, on such a central Roman position, with great potential for the future.

DR A.M. McGRATH, 1907-11

The great change came in 1907. When Dr Alphonsus Maurice McGrath was elected diffinitor to the provincial council of the Irish Augustinians he found that the then provincial, Dr Bowen, had made up his mind to sell St Patrick's. McGrath alone resisted strongly. One great difficulty at the time was that no-one was willing to go to St Patrick's as prior. It was a sea of troubles, both to Ireland and Italy[138]. As a solution, Dr McGrath, himself, was appointed prior in 1907 - to a "mission impossible"!

McGrath had been one of the Irish students in their temporary base at San Carlo and at St Patrick's. His heart was set on re-establishing an Irish Augustinian college in Rome. As a former subject of Fr Glynn he also wished to fulfil the dream of building an Irish National Church in the Eternal City. Early in 1908 he got into communication with the Ministry of Posts and Telegraphs about the renting of St Patrick's for a lengthy period. Negotiations eventually concluded with the agreement that St Patrick's was rented for nine years, as from June 1908, at 33,000 lire per annum.

Very Rev. Dr M. McGrath who built Saint Patrick's Church. Marble bust presented to the community by Dr Thomas Kiernan, Irish Minister to the Holy See.

With a certain financial stability thus secured, and St Patrick's still an Irish property, Dr McGrath explored the possibilities of building a National Church. The only money at his disposal was the rent from St Patrick's. He still held fast to the apparently impractical ideal of re-establishing the Irish Augustinian students in Rome though the plot of ground beside St Patrick's College was left vacant on the assumption that a church, and not more, would be built there. The broad foundations for the National Church were still visible in the excavated ground, like a monument to a fallen ideal.

Aristide Leonori, architect of St Patrick's Church, Rome.

THE IRISH NATIONAL CHURCH IS BUILT, 1911

An ingenious plan was evolved with the aid of a shrewd architect, Leonori[139]. A combined church and college would be built on the Via Boncompagni, on the plot intended for the church of St Patrick. The church would be cast in fourteenth century Lombardo-Gothic style, with the façade conforming to

---

137. The story was told by Fr Patrizio Manfolini, a contemporary, that negotiations had got to such a final stage with the Jesuits that a Jesuit laybrother and a dog were in occupation. Told by Patrizio Manfolini to G.T. Broder who told F.X. Martin in 1958.

138. I am indebted to Fr T.D. Tuomey for this information, which was given to him by Dr McGrath in the 1940s.

139. It is deserving of note that Leonori (1856-1928) was a man of exceptional holiness of life. The cause for his beatification has been introduced at Rome.

an orthodox architectural design yet masking the college apartments whose windows would form part of the facade itself.

Through the good offices of Monsignore Piffieri, O.S.A., the papal sacristan, Dr McGrath managed to get a loan of the money necessary for the building scheme. The loan was at 3% interest, and was to be paid back at 5,000 lire per annum. Since there was now an annual rent of 33,000 lire paid by the Ministry of Posts and Telegraphs for St Patrick's College Dr McGrath was receiving sufficient to pay off the annual debt and to have an income to support a body of students in Rome.

Work began in the autumn of 1908, and the church was opened amid great jubilation on the feast of St Patrick, 1911. The blessing was performed by Sebastiano Cardinal Martinelli, O.S.A., who had been professor at Posterula for sixteen years, 1872-88, and master of professed students

St Patrick's Irish National Church, Rome.

both at Posterula and at San Carlo. Some further work had yet to be done to the college, but it was finally completed by September 1912. The entire cost of the project was 367,261 lire. It was not without significance that Dr McGrath was elected provincial of the Irish Augustinians in July 1911. He had saved the reputation of the Irish Augustinians.

The Irish Augustinian college resumed its life in Rome when five students arrived from Ireland on 16 October 1913. Since that time its life has continued uninterrupted, even by two world wars. The college built-in with the church on the Via Boncompagni became officially known as "St Patrick's", but the adjoining *palazzo* (the original St Patrick's on the Via Piemonte) towered overhead, a reminder of Prior Glynn's dream. In 1917 the lease of the *palazzo* to the Ministry of Posts and Telegraphs was renewed, but when it expired in 1929 the then provincial, Joseph Hennessy, decided that the acceptable hour had come. Though at this time the junior students followed their course of philosophy in Ireland, at Orlagh College, Co. Dublin, the number of theological students in Rome had so increased that the college on the Boncompagni was no longer adequate to house them. Some were sent for their theological studies to Valladolid in Spain, but this could be no more than a temporary solution. Already there was talk of undertaking a foreign mission. Expansion was planned for the Augustinian secondary schools at Dungarvan and New Ross, and an increasing number of vocations to the Order was foreseen.

Despite the *festina lente* advice of older heads, Fr Hennessy took his courage in his hands.

The postal officials evacuated the *palazzo*, and the keys were handed to the Augustinians on 11 January 1930. The then considerable sum of £3,000 was spent during the following twelve months in adapting the building as a students' residence. Finally, on 15 February 1931 the building on the Via Piemonte was re-occupied by the Irish Augustinian community. Fr Bernard T. White was prior. The adjoining students' house which had been built on the Via Boncompagni became known as "St Brigid's". The number of students so increased during the 1930s and again after the second world war, that St Brigid's had to be used conjointly with St Patrick's.

St Patrick's Church, Rome, in the 1950s.

It was a happy coincidence that when the silver jubilee of the opening of the National Church occurred in 1936 the prior of St Patrick's was Dr A.M. McGrath, the man who was mainly responsible for building the National Church and for re-establishing an Irish Augustinian college in Rome. It may here be mentioned that three of the Augustinians associated with the early history of the National Church and of St Patrick's College played their part in the Irish national movement. James A. Anderson, O.S.A., (†1903), spared no effort to collect funds in Ireland for St Patrick's church, and even went to Australia for that purpose. He was the beloved friend of Fenians, Gaelic Leaguers, Home Rulers and all who moved on the road towards separation from England[140]. Joseph Hennessy, O.S.A., (†1941), was no less resolute in his patriotic purpose. He marched as chaplain with the city battalion of the Limerick Volunteers when they mobilized for the rebellion at Killonan on Easter Sunday 1916[141]. Alphonsus M. McGrath, O.S.A., (†1944), is remembered with affection by nationalists for his open sympathies and active interest on their behalf in Ireland during the political turmoil of the years 1917-22[142]. It should be noted in particular that Dr

140. For Padraig Pearse's comments on Fr Anderson, cf. *An Claidheamh Soluis,* 1 Aug. 1903, p.4; 27 Oct. 1906, p.7. Cf. also Maud Gonne MacBride, *Servant of the Queen,* Dublin 1950, pp 279-80.
141. Cf. D. Ryan, *The Rising,* Dublin 1949, pp 234-5.
142. Cf. F. O'Donoghue, *No other law,* Dublin 1954, p.288.

McGrath was friend and admirer of Cathal Brugha and kept on a wall of his room at St Patrick's a photo of Brugha, and underneath it the signature of Brugha from one of his letters to Dr McGrath.

The church which Dr McGrath was instrumental in completing by 1911 was at first only a shell. Even the altars were temporary, and remained so for many years. Gradually over the years most, but not all, of the desired fittings and decorations were added. On several scores, the most valuable object brought from Posterula was the picture of Our Lady of Grace. By Christmas 1916

Saint Patrick's Church:
The Madonna Altar

this was set in a marble shrine. The beautiful marble floor of the sanctuary was laid during 1924-5, and the marble altar rails were added during Spring 1925. A permanent high altar of carved marble was added in 1930. Early in the same year the most striking feature in the church was completed - the mosaic apse depicting St Patrick on the Hill of Tara, explaining the mystery of the Trinity to King Laoghaire and his court. This is a work which because of its scale, its blended colours, its sense of movement combined with unity, excites the admiration of the experts.

DR CANICE O'GORMAN, 1923-30

Dr Canice O'Gorman (†1941), who was responsible for many of these improvements, deserves more than a passing reference. He was elected assistant general of the Augustinian Order in September 1913, was chosen as prior of St Patrick's in 1915, was appointed a consultor of the Holy Office in June 1916, was selected as procurator general of the Order in January 1917, and became commissary general (or acting prior general) in January 1919. He was appointed prior of St Patrick's for two terms of office, 1923-7, 1927-30[143].

St Patrick's Church, Rome. High Altar and Apse (before changes to the sanctuary after Vatican Council II).

He and Fr Crotty, O.P., were the two priests selected by the Holy See in November 1916 to visit the Irish prisoners of war at Limburg in Germany, where Sir Roger Casement had been trying to form an Irish Brigade to fight on the side of Germany. Though Dr O'Gorman differed from Casement in his political outlook he always expressed a deep respect for Casement's character. Doubtless because of his known sympathy for the Allied forces in their struggle against Germany, he got permission from the British authorities to visit Casement in the Tower of London in 1916, when Casement was awaiting execution by hanging[144]. Fr O'Gorman always expressed admiration for Casement as a dedicated idealist.

DR McGRATH RESUMES HIS WORK

When Dr McGrath was reappointed to St Patrick's in 1936 he set about a systematic completion of the work he had begun a quarter of a century earlier. Unfortunately the outbreak of the second world war curtailed his plans. Nevertheless, he accomplished much. He first attended

---

143. See the tribute to Dr O'Gorman by Sir Alex Randal, the British representative in Rome, in *Vatican Assignment,* London 1957 ed., pp 89-90.
144. Professor Denis Gwynn of University College Cork discusses Dr O'Gorman's visit to Casement in *Studies*, Vol. 54 (1965), pp 64-65

to the students' needs. He installed extra bathrooms in the college, and replaced the inadequate pieces of furniture with a plain but comfortable set for each student's room. By March 1937 he had the inner *cortile* roofed over and transformed into a spacious "Tara Hall".

St Patrick's College : Tara Hall

At San Pio, the summer villa, he accomplished what had been declared impossible. By July 1939 he succeeded in having running water piped across country, from the main line serving the nearby village of Cave, and uphill to the villa. A further large wing, containing many bedrooms, kitchens, and refectory was added to San Pio between April 1938 and July 1939.

But it was the National Church in Rome which claimed his special care. The mosaic lunette of St Patrick over the main door of the church was inset by March 1937. Flood-lighting was added throughout the church by March 1938. A soft golden light was diffused throughout the upper part of the church by rich cathedral glass in celtic design.

This was completed by March 1939. Between June 1938 and January 1939 the pillars of the church were encased in marble and alabaster. Above the marble altar to the left of the high altar a simple and beautiful painting of the Sacred Heart was set in harmony against a background of

St Patrick's Church: St Oliver Plunkett's Shrine.

St Patrick's Church: St Brigid's Shrine.

mottled marble, and the whole was crowned with a striking mosaic by Galimberti in the apse overhead.

Two shrines were constructed at the end of the church. One, in honour of St Brigid, was completed by December 1938, the other, dedicated to the then Blessed Oliver Plunkett, had been ready for the feast of St Patrick 1938. It is claimed that the shrine to Blessed Oliver was the first dedicated to his honour in any church. The well-known Italian painter, Rosa, invested St Brigid, in a full length portrait, with an ethereal quality. The same painter presented Oliver Plunkett in an attitude of that strong dignity which he is said to have carried with him to the brutal ceremony of the scaffold at Tyburn. The beauty of the apse was completed by June 1939 after the high altar had been shorn of its more ornate decorations and set against a background wall of green marble, which hung like a curtain from the mosaic high up in the apse. Unfortunately the striking and beautiful effect of this green backdrop was largely lost when changes were made to the sanctuary in the late 1970s, to accommodate changes in liturgy after Vatican Council II.

St Patrick's Church: Some of the Stations of the Cross. The Stations, sculpted in marble by Alceo Dossena, were presented to St Patrick's by Mr Wm Macauley, Irish Minister to the Holy See.

Dr McGrath was instrumental, also, in procuring the Stations of the Cross which so quicken the interest of the artistic-minded who visit the church. The work is by Alceo Dossena, and each Station is carved from a single piece of Carrara marble. They were originally commissioned by the papal duchess, Genevieve Brady, who later married William Macauley, Irish minister to the Holy See. After her death in November 1938 her husband presented them to the Irish National Church in her memory. Previously, when set in her villa at Rome, they were admired, and frequently followed, by Eugenio Cardinal Pacelli, later Pope Pius XII (1939-1958).

There is an intriguing twist to the story of Alceo Dossena's career and work. Dossena said of himself, 'I was born in our time, but with the soul, taste, and perception of other ages', and in the 1920s the simple stone mason was happy to receive small amounts of money from local dealers for pieces which he thought were being sold as modern imitations. The dealers, however, knew a good thing when they saw it. They sold on, as originals, with false authentification and for large sums, many of Dossena's "Etruscan" terra-cottas, his "Greek" gods, and his "Gothic" statues. Some of these made their way even into holdings in museums. When Dossena learned what had been happening he was appalled and angry at the misrepresentation and swore that he would not produce any more antique sculpture in his work. Karl E. Mayer in his book, *The Plundered Past*[145], states that the naïve artisan was 'the greatest modern Italian master of the fake antique. . . [but] was by all accounts not a party to deceit. Dossena had a passion for every kind of ancient art and could uncannily imitate the style of any period, producing works that were never literal copies but, instead, brilliant originals'. Dossena died in 1937. It is believed that some of his production is still exhibited in museums as ancient art.

---

145. See Karl E. Mayer, *The Plundered Past*, London 1974, pp 108-110.

THE SECOND WORLD WAR, 1939-45

The outbreak of the World War II on 1 September 1939 arrested the development of St Patrick's College at an important stage of growth in the life of the Irish province. The college had a community of forty-seven for the scholastic year 1938-9, the largest number up to that date in its history. No further students were able to come until September 1946. During the war years the young priests managed to return gradually to Ireland by devious and difficult routes, travelling from Spain and Portugal by air or sea. The death of Dr McGrath on 1 January 1944 was a severe blow in strained conditions, but life continued under a capable vicar prior, Thomas D. Tuomey.

During these difficult war years St Patrick's received much support and encouragement from the Irish minister to the Holy See, Dr T.J. Kiernan, and from his wife, Delia [Murphy], later well known as the popular singer of Irish songs. The bust of Dr McGrath in St Patrick's College, presented to the College by Dr Kiernan, is a memorial to the deep friendship that existed between the community of St Patrick's College and the Kiernan family. Dr Kiernan's son, Colm, was later to be the Professor of Australian History at University College Dublin, 1980-85.

Fr Michael Damian Curley, O.S.A., receives Eamon de Valera at St Patrick's College during Mr de Valera's visit to Rome, March 1939, for the coronation of Eugenio Pacelli as Pope Pius XII.

When the German army occupied Rome in August 1943 St Patrick's College was selected as a billet for officers of the Wehrmacht. The attempt was thwarted when the Irish flag was flown overhead, and a declaration by Dr Kiernan of the immunity of St Patrick's as Irish property was hung inside the main door. The German army representative who came to the College for a reply accepted the information in silence, clicked his heels, saluted, and left. St Patrick's remained untouched.

Several Allied soldiers, escaped prisoners of war, recall with gratitude the refuge given to them at St Patrick's. One of the community, Canice Madden, O.S.A.. was later awarded the O.B.E. for his part in this work, which included supplying religious habits, food, and false passports to the escaped prisoners of war.

MISSION IN NIGERIA, 1940

The outbreak of the war in 1939 retarded the early growth of the Mission of Yola, in the province of Adamawa, Northern Nigeria. This territory was accepted by the Irish Augustinians on 14 March 1938 as a foreign mission. In January 1940 the three pioneers, Frs A. Dalton, B. Power and G. Broder, who had been in training elsewhere in Nigeria and Rhodesia, began their work in the Mission. The three priests were alumni of St Patrick's College, Rome. Fr Broder is now the sole survivor of those pioneers.

During the war some of the newly ordained priests at St Patrick's, who foresaw the difficulties of returning to Ireland, volunteered to travel directly to the Mission in Nigeria. The suggestion while laudable was considered neither practicable nor advisable.

Despite the ruthless warfare at sea priests were sent from Ireland to Nigeria. Two of the missionaries, Frs J.K. Anderson and J.C. Fitzsimons, who had already experienced the difficulties of a journey from Rome to Ireland during the war years, had the still more unpleasant experience of being aboard a ship which was bombed and sunk off the African coast. Fortunately, the two Augustinians made their escape in a lifeboat. During the war the supply of priests to the Mission

41

Missionary survivors from the S.S. California, *July 1943. The troopship on which the missionaries from various religious orders, bound for West Africa, were travelling, was bombed when some days out from Glasgow and 120 lives were lost. The ship was abandoned, survivors took to lifeboats and, after a couple of hours, were picked up by other ships. Brought to Casablanca, the missionaries were kitted out in borrowed clothing - American G.I. uniforms! Back row (standing): at extreme right is J.C. Fitzsimons, O.S.A.; third from right is J.K. Anderson, O.S.A.*

was maintained.

This is not the place to discuss the numerous difficulties of the Mission to a mixed population of pagans and Mohammedans. Elsewhere in this volume Fr Raymond Hickey tells the story of the Irish Augustinians in Nigeria. Suffice to say that despite many obstacles the Augustinians forged ahead with the missionary work in Nigeria. The missionary spirit, so much a part of the history of St Patrick's College, is a central tradition which has always been intimately associated with an Irish Augustinian College in Rome.

THE STUDENTS RETURN, SEPTEMBER 1946

By the time of Germany's capitulation in May 1945 there was no more than a skeleton community in charge of St Patrick's. Fr A.L. Doyle was appointed prior in July 1945. Normal life was once more resumed in September 1946 when the first group of eight students arrived from Ireland. By October 1950, when Fr T.J. Coffey was prior, the community counted fifty-two members. Of these the student body numbered forty-six. It was a heartening contrast with the ten students at Posterula in 1880.

BUILDING FOR THE FUTURE, 1955

During 1954 the Irish provincial diffinitory decided that a college should be built at Dublin for the students of philosophy and for those attending University College, Dublin. Even with these students subtracted from the community in Rome it was foreseen that within a few years, due to the increasing number of vocations to the Order in Ireland, St Patrick's in Rome would not be large enough to house even the students of theology.

Due to the initiative of the then provincial, Fr Nicholas P. Duffner, and under the direction of the then prior, Fr J. Finbarr Madden, decisive steps were taken. During the summer and autumn months of 1955 a further floor was made serviceable in St Patrick's, by converting a series of storerooms which had been constructed above the upper storey during the time when the *palazzo* was occupied as a general post office. After other extensive renovations and changes had been made for showers, sanitary arrangements, and such like, there was accommodation in the college for a community of sixty-two apart from servants' quarters. There were also 16 bedrooms and various living rooms in the adjoining building, named as St Brigid's. Altogether rooms for 78 Augustinians. It was the high point for St Patrick's.

At this time too the setting up of a library was begun in the College, utilizing some of the high corridors on the first floor. Hitherto the students had to depend on the copies of their text books and on the notes taken during the lectures. The establishment of a library, which was a new venture, undertaken for the most part by Fr Edmund Colledge, made a significant difference to the quality of the students' intellectual life.

A reminder of how much St Patrick's owed to the courage of individual men was made in 1950 when the gifted Irish sculptress, Breeda O'Donoghue Lucci from Cork, was commissioned to carve a marble bust of Joseph Hennessy, O.S.A. This delicate work, which conveys so well the impression of that strength of character which marked Fr Hennessy out among men, is now on view in St Patrick's.

A further work of art was added to St Patrick's in the same year when Bernard McDonagh was commissioned to paint The Last Supper in the refectory. The scene was skilfully designed to fill a large lunette at the end of the refectory, and earned the praise of art critics in Rome. It was intended that the remaining lunettes would be similarly decorated in due time when funds and sponsors would be available.

Very Rev. Joseph Hennessy. Marble bust by Mrs Breeda O'Donoghue Lucci.

By the late 1950s St Patrick's College had reached the final stage in its physical expansion. While on-going improvements in facilities would continue and minor details be completed, the College provided adequate space for its considerable community of priests and students. The 1950s were years of flourishing student activity and full occupancy of the building.

St Patrick's College: 'The Last Supper' painted by Bernard McDonagh in the college refectory in 1954.

SPIRITUAL IDEALS

So far in this account of the Irish Augustinians in Rome little has been directly mentioned about two of the most important aspects of the students' training - their spiritual ideals, their intellectual programme.

A religious Order such as the Augustinians is designed to produce men of prayer and of apostolic activity. The history of the Irish Augustinians explains why so little appeared in print about the men who fulfilled these ideals. It was only at a mature stage of organization that the Irish province could pause to consider, understand, and record its past. One may sense, however, what ideals were continually held up before the students by recalling three figures in the history of the Irish Augustinians in Rome - Brother Donogh, Philip Crane, Tommaso Martinelli.

Brother Donogh, the ex-soldier and exile from the Cromwellian persecution, was one of the first Irish occupants of San Matteo in Merulana. His life of mortification and his burning devotion to the Blessed Virgin set an ideal which was never to be effaced from the history of the Irish Augustinians in Rome.

Philip Crane was prior of San Matteo, 1791-8. He, as provincial in 1819, was partly responsible for establishing the Irish friars at Santa Maria in Posterula. When he returned to New Ross, in Ireland, people came to him for confession from places such as Dungarvan, forty miles distant, and this in the days of difficult transport. He died at New Ross on 28 July 1823. Forty years after his death people were still taking earth from his grave as from that of a saint[146].

Tommaso Martinelli, though an Italian from Lucca by birth, was, like his brother Sebastiano, an Irish Augustinian by adoption. He lived at Posterula as spiritual director for the students. Even when created a cardinal he continued his simple life at Posterula. He was styled "jewel of the college of cardinals" by Pope Leo XIII. He died on Good Friday, 30 April 1888, acknowledged by his contemporaries as possessing the qualities of a saint[147].

Cardinal Tommaso Martinelli, O.S.A. who lived with the Irish Augustinian community at Santa Maria in Posterula and was spiritual director of the students there.

INTELLECTUAL PROGRAMME

In dealing with the re-establishment of the Irish friars at San Matteo in 1739 mention was made of the precise regulations laid down by the Holy See for a thorough course of studies, with special attention to scriptural and polemical questions. When the Irish Augustinians entered into possession of Posterula in 1819 the former system of having resident professors and lectures in the college was continued. Usually the professors were Irish, but a fortunate exception was made for the two Martinelli brothers, Tommaso (†1888) and Sebastiano (†1918), men of sanctity and profound theological learning, both of whom became cardinals.

When the Irish Augustinian students returned to Rome in 1913 they attended the theological lectures at the International Augustinian College of St Monica. This continued for two years. On 5 November 1915 they began to attend the lectures at the Propaganda College in the Piazza di Spagna. A gracious tribute to the impression made by the Irish Augustinians is to be found in the recollections of one who was then a student in the North American College[148]. Writing of the members of the different seminaries and religious institutes who attended lectures at the Propaganda College he comments : 'Another group of monks, the Irish branch of the Augustinian Order, used to set me musing frequently on the history of monasticism. The habit was black and plain, an excellent example of simple neatness. Without exception these young monks were all, handsome, bright-eyed, intelligent. They had dignity without ostentation, light-heartedness without frivolity or boisterousness, courtesy without condescension or servility. They seemed to have gathered all virtues unto themselves, and to have combined them in a most appealing pattern'.

At the distribution of prizes in the Propaganda College on 28 November 1918 an Irish Augustinian, Augustine Doyle, was awarded the medal for first place in dogmatic theology. During the years that followed several of the Irish Augustinian students gained prizes or merited distinction.

Numbers from the different seminaries and religious institutes attending the Propaganda College had so increased by October 1926 that at least one professor was lecturing from a rostrum situated at an L-corner. The "hall" was composed of the two converging arms of the corridor.

146. Cf. J.B. Cullen, 'The Augustinians in New Ross', *I.E.R.,* ser.5, xv (1920) 309, n.2; W.J. Fitzpatrick, *Life, times and correspondence of Rt Rev. Dr Doyle,* i, Dublin 1880, p.13.
147. Cf. biographical notices in D. Perini, *Bibliographia Augustiniana,* ii, Florence 1931, pp 186-7; C. De Romanis, *L'Ordine Agostiniano,* Florence 1936, pp 225-6; Posterula house diary, under 30 April 1888.
148. Martin W. Doherty, *The House on Humility Street,* New York 1942, p.96.

Plans were made for a new Propaganda College on the Gianicolo, and since this was considered too far a distance from St Patrick's the Irish Augustinian students began to attend the Gregorian University on 3 November 1928. The practice also began of sending the Augustinian students to Rome for philosophy. The names of the first *baccalaureati* in philosophy, Aloysius Dooley, Vincent Conway and Joseph Curtis, appeared on the lists on 7 November 1931. The first doctorates in philosophy were gained by Joseph Curtis and Finbarr Madden, in 1931 and 1932 respectively.

Returning from class at the Gregorian University. Note the Augustinian religious habits and the mandatory "soup-plate" hats of the 1950s.

The first Irish Augustinian of the younger generation to gain the licentiate in theology at the Gregorian was Laurence Cotter, in July 1935. Thomas D. Tuomey was awarded the doctorate in theology in December 1941, the first graduate from St Patrick's to gain the degree at the Gregorian. Since that time an increasing number of students from the Irish Augustinian College have been presented for higher degrees in the various branches of the sacred sciences at the Gregorian and at other university colleges in Rome.

DEVELOPING THE WHOLE MAN

There is no space here to dwell at length on the lighter aspects of the students' life at St Patrick's over the years, those other activities which developed the whole man. Various house committees provided relief and developed the latent talents of the young professed - The Cumann Gaedhealach, the English Debating Society, the Musical Society, the Sports Committee, the Entertainments Committee, the annual house magazine - *An Mac Leighinn.* Friendship with the other colleges was stimulated by the annual gaelic football match with the Irish College, the soccer and rugby matches with various other colleges, the Christmas play at St Patrick's which drew the English-speaking students and their visitors together for some happy hours.

The opportunities for cultural development were not missed by those assiduous *camerate* (distinguishable always by their cameras and well-thumbed guide-books) which made systematic visits to the churches, museums, historic monuments, archaelogical sites and artistic attractions in Rome. Then came those glorious summer months when the *camerate* set off in carefree style from San Pio, on long hikes across the sunny hills and dusty roads of Lazio.

Cardinal Sebastiano Martinelli, O.S.A.

MASTER OF PROFESSED STUDENTS

Any account of the religious formation of the students in Rome would be incomplete if tribute were not paid to those who have acted as masters of professed students. It has been their duty to mould the students in religious discipline and the Augustinian spirit. It would appear that the offices of prior and master of professed were often held by the one person. When the number of students in Rome was small, and there was a shortage of priests in the Irish province, it was difficult to spare a special priest as master of professed. Furthermore, in several instances the admirable qualities of the man appointed as prior rendered him particularly suitable as master of professed. Among the masters of professed special mention should be made of Sebastiano Martinelli, master of professed for sixteen years at Posterula and San Carlo. He was elected prior general of the Order in 1889, was appointed apostolic delegate to the United States in 1896, and was created a cardinal in 1901.

ST PATRICK'S COLLEGE IN CHANGING TIMES-1970-1994

After Vatican Council II (1962-1965), in the turbulent and challenging years for the Catholic Church, and with the change in general life style in an ever-increasing materialistic age, the Augustinians, in common with other religious orders and the secular clergy, began to see a falling-off in religious vocations. Fewer students were, consequently, being sent to study at Rome. By the mid 1970s, what had now become a sharp decrease in numbers meant that space in St Patrick's College, conceived on a grand scale to meet the need of an earlier day, became superfluous to requirements, and in time threatened to become a liability.

There was, and had been for some 10 years, a certain income due to rents received from the Roman carabinieri to whom space for offices had been leased in what had become surplus space in St Brigid's, the part of the building above St Patrick's Church. In the early 1960s, too, an area adjoining the College, on the corner of the Via Boncompagni and the Via Piemonte, had also been

1984. The Prior General, Most Rev. Martin Nolan, O.S.A., with Pope John Paul II and His Eminence Paul Poupard, President of the Pontifical Council for Culture, on the occasion of the celebration of the first Centenary of the death of Gregor Mendel, O.S.A.

leased and was in use as an office and showroom by the automobile firm, Alfa Romeo. However, in the 1970s the upkeep of the massive building of St Patrick's, only part of which was by then actually in full use, became ever more difficult. Successive priors were faced with the necessity to provide an answer to this growing problem. Various solutions were attempted but inevitably, given the circumstances, these met with less than complete success.

In 1980 the top floor of St Patrick's was leased to the Irish Spiritans - C.S.Sp - (Holy Ghost Congregation) to provide a base for their members stationed at Rome. Shortly after that St Patrick's also accepted some priests from Irish diocesan colleges who were studying in Rome. However the numbers were still insufficient to make the maintenance of the huge building

viable and, as the years passed, it became apparent that a real crisis was looming for the College.

But all was not gloom. While struggling with the difficulties of an uncertain future, St Patrick's College received a heartening boost in spirits. In 1983 its then prior, Fr Martin Nolan, became the first Irish Augustinian in the history of the Order to be elected to the post of Augustinian Prior General. Shortly afterwards Brother Cyril Counihan became the first Brother ever appointed as Secretary of the Order. In 1985, Fr Brian O'Sullivan became prior and an ambitious - and what proved to be an inspired - survival plan for St Patrick's was set in train.

Concerted attempts were made to find a way to lease a major part of the building but these attempts ran into various technical difficulties, despite the evident potential value of the site. Then a welcome light appeared on the horizon. The section of the semi-state body I.R.I. (Istituto per Riconstruzione Industriale) with responsibility for management training, renewal and up-dating, showed interest in establishing its headquarters on the site, but it was clear that extensive

Cyril Counihan, O.S.A., first Augustinian Brother to become Secretary of the Order.

46

modifications would be needed in the internal lay-out of the building. After much deliberation and consultation a leasing contract was signed on 23 December 1987 and formally ratified on 29 January 1988. A vital radical step had been taken which was to save St Patrick's College and put it once again on a firm footing.

I.R.I. had leased a great part of the vast internal space in the College and, as part of its plan for the adaptation of this space to meet its needs, it included appropriate reconstruction of the area to be retained by the Augustinian community. This self-contained area was to include and be on all floors of the building, would provide ample accommodation for the community with all modern facilities, and make adequate allowance for eventual future increase in student numbers.

Work commenced in summer 1988. Already in autumn 1986, at a time when the future of St Patrick's was under review, the students had been transferred, with their master, Fr Kieran O'Mahony, to the international college at St Monica's, the Augustinian General House near St Peter's Basilica. The top floor of St Patrick's, which had been leased to the Spiritans, had been vacated even earlier and so it was that, in May 1988, the two remaining members of the community, Fr Brian O'Sullivan, the prior, and Fr T.A. Hunt, the Rector of St Patrick's Church, left to take up temporary residence in an apartment at the nearby Piazza Fiume. From there they could conveniently deal with the affairs of St Patrick's while the work on the College was in progress.

Services at St Patrick's Church continued as usual, while a monitoring eye had to be kept on reconstruction work in the part of the College being arranged for the Augustinian community. On this practical reconstruction side the Augustinians were fortunate in that Fr O'Sullivan was able to avail of the helpful advice, and expertize, of his brother Jerry, who is well experienced in the construction scene in Ireland. At St Patrick's Church, which was not affected by the reconstruction work, the normal Masses were said, the needs of the regular congregation catered for, and numerous wedding ceremonies performed. These marriages, of couples coming from Ireland to St Patrick's for their weddings, have increased quite considerably over recent years and the Rector of the Church is not only concerned with the actual ceremony but is committed to administrative work of ensuring that necessary documentation between the couple's parishes in Ireland and Rome is

14 March 1990. Formal inauguration of the new St Patrick's College.
Seated (from left):-Frs. G. MacDonagh; T.A. Hunt (Rector, St Patrick's Church); J. Byrne (Irish Provincial);
Miguel Angel Orcasitas (Prior General); B. O'Sullivan (Prior, St Patrick's); T. Cooney; T.J. Coffey; D.B. Ormonde.
Standing (from left):-Jerry O'Sullivan; Frs M. Leahy; K. O'Mahony; K. McManus; T. Tevington; J.A. Meagher;
T.D. Tuomey; M.B. Hackett; P. Tinney.

47

complete and in order.

By the end of 1989 the alterations to St Patrick's were finished. Fr O'Sullivan and Fr Hunt could quit their apartment at the Piazza Fiume and take up residence again at the College in time for Christmas 1989. On 14 March 1990, the new St Patrick's College was formally inaugurated by the Father General, Miguel Angel Orcasitas, accompanied by the Irish Provincial, Fr John Byrne, and many of the former priors and masters of students.

CHARACTERISTICS OF IRISH AUGUSTINIAN HISTORY IN ROME

In a general account such as this, covering more than three hundred years, there has been time only for mention of the main external events.

Even from the outline account in this article it will be seen that the chequered history of the Irish Augustinian house in Rome has manifested three clear characteristics - i) patronage by the popes and by the Stuart kings; ii) Marian devotion; and iii) missionary zeal and activity.

Gold Chalice presented to Saint Patrick's Church by Pope Saint Pius X; it bears the inscription: PIUS PAPA X ECCLESIAE S. PATRITII DE URBE DONAVIT XII KAL MAII MCMXI.

(i) Patronage by the Popes and the Kings of England

It was Pope Alexander VII who brought the Irish Augustinians to Rome and to the house at San Matteo in Merulana in 1656. They were restored to San Matteo in 1739 by a brief of Clement XII, granted at the intercession of the exiled Stuart King James III of England. After the destruction of San Matteo by the French invaders in 1798 Pius VII donated the church and priory of Sant'Eusebio to the homeless friars. Finding that this arrangement did not prove satisfactory he transferred them to Santa Maria in Posterula in the year 1819. When the Augustinians were forced to leave Posterula in 1888 they were given temporary occupation of San Carlo al Corso by Leo XIII. It was he also who gave his blessing and substantial financial support to the project for the Irish National Church in Rome. The chalice presented by St Pius X on the occasion of the opening of the church in 1911 was another token of papal interest. This is now considered as one of the treasures of the church.

(ii) Marian devotion

When the Irish Augustinians were granted the church of San Matteo in 1656 they became custodians of its great treasure, the reputedly miraculous picture of Our Lady of Perpetual Succour. Ireland's devotion to the Blessed Virgin under this title began with Donogh, the saintly lay brother, who served the shrine for over forty years. When the friars were driven from San Matteo in 1798 the picture of Our Lady of Perpetual Succour was practically the only object of artistic value they managed to save. It was transferred to Posterula in 1819, and remained there in safe keeping until handed over to the Redemptorists in 1866.

In acquiring the church of Santa Maria in Posterula the Irish Augustinians added another chapter to the history of their Marian devotion. Posterula had a local fame as the shrine of the reputedly miraculous picture of Our Lady of Grace. During the nineteenth century the Irish Augustinians spread devotion to Our Lady of Grace both among the Romans and among the English-speaking visitors to the church in Posterula. The picture was touched up by painters on several occasions in order to preserve the colours from fading. Finally in 1955, at considerable expense, the picture was restored to its original appearance and beauty by experts from the Vatican art restoration workshops.

Another chapter in the history of Irish Augustinian devotion to the Blessed Virgin was begun in 1880 when the friars at Posterula bought a derelict Franciscan house at San Pio, as a summer villa for their students.   San Pio lies near to Genazzano where the reputedly miraculous picture of our Mother of Good Counsel is venerated in the church of Santa Maria, served by the Augustinians of the Roman province.   The opportunities for frequent visits to the shrine at Genazzano from San Pio undoubtedly help to explain why devotion to the Mother of Good Counsel is to-day the most popular Marian devotion among the Irish Augustinians.   That devotion is evident in the readiness with which the Mission of Yola, in Northern Nigeria, was placed under the patronage of the Mother of Good Counsel.

La Madonna in Campo, by Antoninasso Romano, 15th century.
Nardo Matteo Arcangeli, in his will of 23 Dec. 1483, ordered that the picture be painted and left ten ducats for the execution of the work.

It is also worthy of note that when the Irish Augustinians took charge of the church at San Pio they became possessors of a picture of our Lady entitled *La Madonna in Campo*.   This enjoyed a local veneration, and is of considerable artistic value.   It is now preserved at St Patrick's College.

(iii) Missionary zeal and activity

The missionary spirit was evident in James MacCarthy the first Irish vicar prior of San Matteo in Merulana. He acted as procurator for the Irish Augustinians during the years of persecution, encouraged the friars who remained in Ireland, and protected those who were driven into exile.   He was not content to remain a spectator of the missionary activity.   During the 1660s he acted as vicar general of the Augustinians in England.   The history of his later life in Poland has yet to be investigated.

We know that individual Augustinians were at work in England and Scotland even before San Matteo was restored to the Irish province in 1739[149].   After that year the security of having a college in Rome allowed for more ambitious missionary projects.   Thus we find that the first Irish Augustinian arrived in Newfoundland in the year 1756[150].   His name has so far escaped identification.   He was the first Irish priest of that period to work in the country, and was the first of a succession of Augustinians who for fifty years gave service to the people of Newfoundland.

Mention has already been made of the intimate part which San Matteo played in the foundation of the Augustinian Order in the United States of America, in the year 1796.   The letters of foundation for the new province were negotiated by Philip Crane, prior of San Matteo.   Two of the three pioneer missionaries, Frs John Rosseter and George Staunton, had been members of the community at San Matteo in Merulana.

After the destruction of San Matteo in 1798, and the period of transition at Sant'Eusebio, the Irish Augustinians were given the church and priory of Santa Maria in Posterula.   Once again the opportunities of having an adequate college meant a fillip to missionary effort.   In the year 1834 an Irish Augustinian, Daniel O'Connor, was appointed bishop of Madras, the first British-born subject to be appointed a Catholic bishop in India[151].   He, with some Augustinians and secular priests, laboured with signal success in India from 1835 to 1841, and earned the warm commendation of Pope Gregory XVI.   Dr O'Connor was forced to leave India at the end of 1840, due to ill-health, and resigned from his diocese, but continued manifold spiritual and cultural activities until his death in Ireland in 1867.

---

149. Cf. the chapter in this book by M.B. Hackett on the Augustinians in England and Scotland.
150. Cf. E.H. Burton, *Life and Times-of Bishop Challoner, 1691-1781,* London 1909, ii, p.126.
151. Battersby, *Hist. Aug. Ire.,* cit., 152. For an account of Bishop O'Connor's Mission to Madras, 1834-41, see the chapter in this book by Fr Peter Clancy, P.P., of the Dublin archdiocese. Fr Clancy is the first to undertake detailed research on Bishop O'Connor from a wide variety of published and manuscript sources in Ireland, England, Rome and India. He intends to publish a separate study on Bishop O'Connor.

Even before the Irish Augustinians relinquished the work at Madras their missionary zeal had already found a new outlet in Australia. This was associated particularly with the college in Rome. James Alypius Goold was a member of the Posterula community when he volunteered for service in Australia. He landed there in 1838, was later appointed first bishop, then archbishop, of Melbourne, and died in 1886, leaving a rich heritage of example and good works to his flock.

Dr Martin Crane, first bishop of Sandhurst (1874-1901), had been vicar prior of Posterula in 1850. Two other bishops in Australia were alumni of the college in Rome - Dr Dominic Murray, vicar apostolic of Cooktown (1898-1914), and Alphonsus J. Heavey, vicar apostolic of Cooktown (1914-41) and first bishop of Cairns (1941-8). From the year 1883 until 1948 the Irish Augustinians alone had charge of the Catholics scattered throughout the 137,000 square miles of the Cooktown vicariate. Many of these missionaries were products of the college in Rome, as are still some of the Augustinians who are at present ministering in Australia.

The missionary spirit has intensified rather than slackened with the years. The Yola Mission in Northern Nigeria, accepted in 1938, was staffed to a great degree by priests trained in St Patrick's College, Rome. The interest of the students at Rome in the progress of the Mission has been stimulated by the frequent visits of the missionaries who stayed at St Patrick's when passing by air from Nigeria, via Rome, to Ireland.

The Irish Augustinian contribution to the foreign missions at various Times-and in different continents has been possible only as long as the college at Rome has remained in a sound condition. This is not surprising. The college in Rome, be it San Matteo in Merulana, Sant'Eusebio, Santa Maria in Posterula, San Carlo al Corso, or St Patrick's, has been the main training centre for the young Irish Augustinians during the past three hundred and more years. While it is undoubtedly true that circumstances in Ireland affected the condition of the college it is equally true that any setback to, or progress of, the house in Rome has had a corresponding effect on the Irish Augustinian province as a whole, and in particular on its work in the foreign missions. It is for this reason that the college has been of such importance in the history of the Irish Augustinians.

The original purpose of an Irish Augustinian house on the continent in 1656 was to train students so that they might return as priests to Ireland in order to sustain the faith of a people who were undergoing the harrow of Cromwellian persecution. There was an obvious advantage when this training was followed in Rome, near to the common father of Christendom. The young men were (and are) moulded in an atmosphere which inevitably leaves that distinctive mark of the *romanità* upon them. When the weight of religious persecution was lifted from Ireland in the eighteenth century the zeal of the young Augustinians was diverted to missionary work in Newfoundland and North America. During the nineteenth century the missionary spirit found its outlet in India and Australia, and this present generation

St Patrick's Church: Vestibule.

produces rich fruits in Nigeria, Ecuador and Kenya. The purpose for which the college was founded in Rome partly explains why the character of the Irish province - as contrasted, for example, with that of the Italian Augustinian provinces, devoted to studies and publications - has been formed with its main concentration on pastoral activity.

IRISH HEARTS AND ROMAN FAITH

After the Allied occupation of Rome in June 1944 the ubiquity of the Irish race was strikingly demonstrated. St Patrick's church welcomed soldiers in American, Canadian, English, South African, Australian and New Zealand uniforms, men who were Irish by birth or by descent. After the war St Patrick's resumed its normal functions for the pilgrims of Ireland. The Irish colony in Rome long remembered with a thrill of joy the sight of the Irish National Pilgrimage as it filled St Patrick's church during the Holy Year, 1950, and listened to the inspiring sermon by His Eminence John Cardinal D'Alton. A year later, May 1951, the Irish colony assembled in a

Holy Year, 1950. The Irish National Pilgrimage assembled in St Patrick's Church to hear Cardinal d'Alton preach.

different mood in St Patrick's to assist at the official requiem Mass for His Excellency Archbishop Ettore Felici, who had died in Dublin while acting as papal nuncio to Ireland. And each year on St Patrick's Day the ceremonies brought special exhilaration to the Irish hearts as the voices in the National Church rose in powerful unison to the strains of "Faith of our Fathers". An experience not easily forgotten!

Over the past 40 years the improvement in financial standards of people in Ireland and the ease of travel by rail, sea and air, have seen an ever-growing stream of Irish visitors come to Rome - pilgrims to the Holy City who have found a warm welcome at the Irish National Church. And since 1976 the facilities at San Pio - the summer house at Genazzano, now no longer needed for the Augustinian students who for the summer used to stay at San Pio but who now return to Ireland for the holidays or who go to other European countries for study and experience - have been used to good advantage. Groups of Irish students from the Augustinian secondary schools at St Augustine's College, Dungarvan, and Good

In St Patrick's Church the Irish honour the National Apostle on St Patrick's Day. In the foreground is Mr Joseph Walsh, then, in the 1950s, the first Ambassador to the Holy See.

Counsel College, New Ross, have had the opportunity to spend summers at San Pio, and to learn and to appreciate, with those who really know and love the Eternal City, the richness and the wonder that is Rome.

In 1991, on 8 December, the feast of the Immaculate Conception, St Patrick's Church resounded to joyous Irish celebration when the newly consecrated Cardinal, Cahal Daly, Primate of All Ireland, arrived to take over formally St Patrick's as his titular church. In autumn of the following year, 1992, Irish pilgrims once again arrived in force to celebrate a very special day - the Beatification by Pope John Paul II, in St Peter's Square on 27 September, of 17 Irish Martyrs. Among those Irish

Senator Mary Robinson, now President of Ireland, visited St Patrick's College with her husband, Nick, in April 1985. Seen here with Pope John Paul II, her father, Dr Aubrey Bourke, and Fr F.X. Martin, O.S.A.

martyrs honoured was William Tirry, an Irish Augustinian friar, executed publicly in dramatic circumstances at Clonmel on 12 May 1654. During ceremonies in St Patrick's Church to mark the occasion, the Irish Augustinian community were joined in their rejoicing by fellow friars from far and near, by many prelates of the Irish church, and by proud and loyal friends from every part of Ireland.

So the rich life of St Patrick's College and the Irish National Church at Rome goes on, the union of Irish hearts and Roman faith. *'Ut Christiani ita et Romani sitis'* - 'As you are Christians, so you are Romans'. That is the significant declaration glowing in the mosaic circle over the high altar at St Patrick's National Church in Rome.

The Pietà *in the vestibule of St Patrick's Church, Rome.*

52

SUPERIORS OF THE IRISH AUGUSTINIAN HOUSE IN ROME 1656-1994[152]

1656   James MacCarthy, vicar prior

. . . .

1739   Xaverio Valletti

1741   Thomas Berrill

1744   Augustine Waldron, vicar prior

1745   James MacKenna

1747   Patrick Casey, vicar prior

1751   Sylvester Fleming

1754   "   "

1759   John Martin

1762   John Corban, vicar prior

1766   "   "

1770   "   "

1774   "   "

1778   "   "

1782   "   "

1787   Augustine Staunton

1788   Philip Crane, vicar prior

1791   "   "

1795   "   "

1799   "   "

. . . .

1803   Michael Wall

1807   William Keating

1811   "   "

---

152. The list of priors up to 1954, was compiled by the late Rev. Stanislaus Roche, O.S.A., and Rev. M.B. Hackett, O.S.A., from the Irish Augustinian Provincial Archives, Dublin, and the International Augustinian Archives, Rome.

1815 George Staunton

. . . .

1819 John Rice

1823 John Shea

1827 " "

1831 James Spratt

1835 " "

1839 Matthew Downing

1843 Philip Lynch

1847 Patrick Kelly

1850 Martin Crane, vicar prior

1851 James Spratt

1855 Patrick Lyons

1859 Dermod O'Brien

1863 " "

1867 Robert O'Keeffe

1871 " "

1875 John Kehoe

1879 Patrick J. Glynn

1883 " " "

1887 " " "

1891 " " "

1895 " " "

1899 Robert O'Keeffe

1903 " "

1907 Alphonsus M. McGrath

1911 Patrick Raleigh

1915 Canice O'Gorman

1919 Michael Connolly

1923 Canice O'Gorman

1927   "   "

1930 Bernard T. White

1933   "   "   "

1936 Alphonsus M. McGrath

1939   "   "   "

1942   "   "   "

1944 Thomas D. Tuomey, vicar prior

1945 Ambrose L. Doyle

1948 Thomas J. Coffey

1951 Finbarr J. Madden

1954   "   "   "

1957 J.A. Hooper

1960 N.P. Duffner

1963 N.P. Duffner (resigned in August 1964)

1964 A.J. Meagher

1966 J.B. O'Flynn

1969 Thomas D. Tuomey

1973 Gabriel MacDonagh

1977 D.B. Ormonde

1981 Martin Nolan (elected as prior general in Sept. 1983)

1983 Kevin McManus

1985 Brian K. O'Sullivan

1989   "   "   "

1993 Patrick Ryan

THE IRISH AUGUSTINIANS IN ENGLAND AND SCOTLAND, 1539-1992

The Irish Province - Restorer of its Anglo-Scottish Mother Province

Michael Benedict Hackett, O.S.A.

THE IRISH AUGUSTINIANS IN ENGLAND AND SCOTLAND, 1539-1992

The Irish Province - Restorer of its Anglo-Scottish Mother Province
Michael Benedict Hackett, O.S.A.

I

It must be unique or nearly so in the history of the order, or of any order, that a daughter province was providentially destined to become the restorer of its mother province. This in a nutshell was the destiny, by no means the only destiny, of the Irish province with regard to the English province which was restored in 1977 under the title of the Anglo-Scottish province[1].

In 1539 the English province, in what was virtually the third centenary of its beginnings, ceased to exist *de facto* when the last of its thirty-five houses, the friary at Hull, was surrendered to the crown on March 10 by its prior, Alexander Ingram[2]. He did so at the behest of the royal agent, an ex-Dominican apostate, Richard Ingworth, the same man whom St John Stone had resisted to his face in no uncertain terms at Canterbury three months earlier (14 December 1538) when he came to suppress the friary in the name of the king as supreme head of the Church. John Stone paid with his life as a martyr for his refusal to give to Caesar the things which are God's - the Augustinian friary and church at Canterbury.

It was prognostic of the future that when the first native superior of the friars in Ireland, Maurice O'Flynn, was appointed on 6 August 1556, the prior general, Cristoforo da Padova, expressed the hope that from the few surviving Irish houses the seed might be sown for the recovery of all the lost English houses. The general reiterated this hope in a second letter written on the same day to O'Flynn in which he mentioned the idea of sending some exemplary Irish friars to England 'so that our order would recover again its pristine status through new planters' of the seed, namely the Irish friars[3].

In the event, more than seventy years were to pass before the Irish province, juridically constituted in 1620, could do anything to realise the hope expressed by the prior general in 1556 of refounding the order in England. It would take the nascent Irish Province all it could do to put its own house in order to restore regular life.   Indeed there was real danger of its losing provincial status[4].

At all events it was totally unrealistic - pure wishful thinking - on the part of the prior general to speak of the restoration of the English houses; in other words the restoration of the province, even after Mary Tudor became queen of England in 1553.   Incidentally, Cristoforo da Padova never informed O'Flynn that he had appointed on 13 November 1555 a Portuguese friar, Sebastião Toscano, as his vicar in England, with the express object of recovering the former monasteries of the order.   It may be that before writing to O'Flynn the general learned from Toscano that he had had to give up the mission entrusted to him.   The general still hoped that he would succeed, but it was evident that Toscano was not up to the job.

He was replaced in 1558 by a Spaniard, Fray Bernardo de Atienza, but it was now too late. Mary Tudor had died on 17 November 1558, just a few weeks before Bernardo received his

1. It is a sign of the vitality of the Irish province that also in 1977 it gave birth to the vice-province of Nigeria.
2. F. Roth, *The English Austin Friars 1249-1538,* ii (New York, 1961), no. 1154.
3. F.X. Martin and A. de Meijer, 'Irish material in the Augustinian archives, Rome, 1354-1624', *Archivium Hibernicum,* xix (1956), no.151a; cf n.151.
4. Ibid., no. 185.

commission as vicar of the general for England. With the death of the Catholic queen, all hope of a restoration of the Augustinian order in England at that juncture died with her[5].

There could no longer be any serious hope of restoring the order in England either by Irish friars or any from the continent during the reign of Elizabeth I (1558-1603). The situation as regards the Catholic religion hardly improved under her successor, James I, but in any case the most that could be achieved was a presence maintained by an individual or two. The few English and Scottish Augustinians whose names have survived for the reign of James joined the order abroad. Of the English there was Christopher Dixon, reputed to have been martyred in London in November 1620, Benedict Baxter who was professed at Antwerp on 21 May 1612, but later became a Carthusian, and a lay brother Thomas Sanders, who was at Seville by 16 February 1625 when the prior general gave him permission to return to England, where, so the general stated, there was then not a single Augustinian[6]. Another Englishman had joined the order in Lisbon in 1605. He was Mathias de Spirito Santo, son of Robert Roquevodi (Rochford?) and Dorothy Drury. He did not return to England. Instead he went to India as a missionary of the Portuguese province[7].

As with these English members of the order, there were Scottish contemporaries of theirs who likewise joined the order outside their country. The best known of these is William Paterson, author of *The Protestants Theologie* (1620), Just (?) Nicolson, who like Baxter, made his profession (5 October 1612) at Antwerp, and Thomas of the Mother of God, son of John Andrew Burd (Burt?) and Mary Lindsay of Cupar, Fife. He joined the Recollect Augustinians at their foundation house, Talavera in Spain on 14 October 1598. After ordination he returned to Scotland where he exercised a marvellous apostolate despite the danger to his life. He also laboured in England. Called back to Spain by his provincial who feared for his life, Thomas died on the way, at Nantes, on 30 October 1617[8].

There was indeed an Augustinian presence of a sort in London by 1605 when Fray Juan de San Agustin was confessor to the Spanish ambassador, Don Pedro de Zuniga, who became the first Marquis de Flores. Fray Juan was accompanied by another Augustinian of the Castile province of which Juan became provincial in 1618, but there is no evidence that he made any attempt to rekindle Augustinian life in London. The attempt in any case would be virtually hopeless, or at any rate inopportune, if indeed the thought of restoring the order ever crossed his mind[9]. As Fray Juan would have been aware, there were infinitely weightier considerations than the revival of the Augustinian order. The preservation of the faith and the need of persons, priests or lay people alike, to witness to it, even if it meant dying for it, far outweighed a revival of that kind.

One such witness during the reign of James I was an Irish Augustinian who is said to have been martyred in England, probably in the 1620s. He was Thomas Furlong alias Thomas of the Holy Cross, son of Richard Furlong and Johanna Sinnot of Wexford. It was at Salamanca as a student of the Irish College that he discovered his vocation to the Augustinian order rather than to

5. For the story of the efforts to restore the order in England in 1555-8 see the splendid study by Alberic de Meijer, 'The attempts to re-establish the English Augustinian province under Queen Mary Tudor', *Analecta Augustiniana,* xxiv (1961) 5-29. The immediate predecessor of Cristoforo da Padova as general, Cardinal Girolamo Seripando, after relinquishing office was also interested in the matter. He hoped, perhaps, through his friendship with Cardinal Pole, that an accommodation might be reached with the crown. Cf. C. de Frere, *La restaurazione cattolica in Inghilterra sotto Maria Tudor nel carteggio di Girolamo Seripando* (Naples, 1971).
6. For Dixon see G. Maigret, *Surculi sacri pulluantes e palma primorum, ord. erem. S. Augustini martyrum* (Liège, 1620), sig. 02r-3v. Baxter's parents may have been Scottish in view of his surname, but the deed of his profession states that he was born in England. Cf 'Liber professionum' (Augustinian Archives, Ghent) under the date 21 May 1612. For Sanders see AGA, Dd 65, f.109r.
7. For his profession on 16 March 1606 cf. C. Alonso, 'Las professiones religiosas en la provincia de Portugal durante el periodo 1513-1631', *Anal. Aug.,* xlviii (1985) 363. On his missionary activity in Persia, following his coming to Goa, and in Iraq at Basra cf. A. da Silva Rego, *Documentação para a historia das missões do Padroado Portugues do Oriente, India,* xi (Lisbon, 1955) 216, 268; T. Aparicio Lopez, *La orden de San Agustin en la India (1572-1622)* (Valladolid, 1977), pp 214-5, 221-2, 230.
8. For Paterson and Nicolson see Roth, *The English Austin Friars,* i (New York, 1966) 132-3. For Thomas see Andres de S. Nicolas, *Historia general de los religiosos descalzos del orden de los ermitanos,* i (Madrid, 1664) 512-6. There is a reference to both friars in D. Conway, 'Guide to documents of Irish and British interest in Fondo Borghese, series I', *Archiv. Hib.,* xxiii (1960) 126.
9. C. Maria Abad, *Una misionera española en la Inglaterra del siglo XVII - Doña Luisa de Carvajal y Mendoza (1566-1614),* Comillas [Santander], 1966. pp 194-5, 216, 220; T. Herrera, *Historia del convento de san Augustin de Salamanca* (Madrid, 1652), p.39.

the Dominicans or the Jesuits who were keen that he should join them. He was received into the order at St Augustine's, Salamanca, and was professed on 5 April 1615. He would have finished his studies and been ordained priest in or about 1622. It may be taken for granted that he returned to Ireland as soon as possible after ordination. We do not know what were his movements after arriving home, but according to Thomas Herrera, the soundest and most perceptive Augustinian historian of the time, the Wexford friar suffered martyrdom in England for the faith[10].

Another Irish Augustinian, a contemporary of Furlong, was also martyred in England. There is a problem, not a serious one, about the identity of this second Irish witness to the faith in England, Cornelius Egan *alias* Augustine of Holy Mary[11]. His parents were Eugene and Leonora Egan. Unlike other Irish contemporaries of his who entered the order in Salamanca, he was received as a novice at the historic monastery of San Felipe el Real at Madrid on 13 December 1618[12]. He took as his religious name that of Augustine of Holy Mary. It may be safely assumed that he was professed on 14 December 1619. He was noted for his spirit of humility and obedience, his love of prayer, but also his sense of humour. After profession he studied arts and theology at Burgos, and then proceeded to Salamanca to complete his preparation for ordination to the priesthood.

He returned home in 1625, but was betrayed by some informers, and arrested for being a priest and religious. When charged with this double offence under the law, he defended his calling with spirit. He was not condemned to death, however. Instead he was sent to London where he was imprisoned in the New Prison and tried under his baptismal name, Cornelius Egan, by March 1626[13]. At the request of the Venetian ambassador, who guaranteed to transport him (and his fellow priests) out of the kingdom, neither he nor they were condemned to death. Instead they were released into the custody of the ambassador who had them transported to Flanders. Cornelius lay low for two months and then made his way back to England where he operated as a priest, in disguise of course, but was spied upon and arrested. This time there was no delay in having him executed. Though there is no record extant of his death, there is evidence that he suffered the supreme penalty for the faith in 1626[14].

Although an Irish Augustinian mission to Ireland, England and Scotland was proposed to Propaganda Fide in 1627[15], it was rejected 'lest there should be disputes with missionaries of different orders as happened in Japan, Aleppo, etc.[16]' One may ask, however, whether the province within a few years of its establishment was really in a position to send a mission to England? Seemingly it was numerically strong enough, since a report of 1625 or 1626 states that there were many Augustinians in Ireland, and what is more, some were worthy of praise as theologians[17].

10. Herrera, cit., p.430; cf. p.415. See also his *Alphabetum Augustinianum* (Madrid, 1644), ii.447. Cf. also M. Vidal, *Agustinos de Salamanca. Historia de observantissimo convento de S. Agustin*, ii (Salamanca, 1758) 51. D.J. O'Doherty in *Irish Theological Quarterly*, xi (1915) 18, cited the title of Vidal's work incorrectly, and on p.17 confuses Augustinians with Recollects.

11. There is no verifiable proof that Augustine and Cornelius were one and the same person, but I believe that I have demonstrated their identity in a lecture which I gave at Villanova University, Pennsylvania, in 1990. The lecture is due to be published by the Augustinian Historical Institute of the said university.

12. Archivo Historico Nacional, Madrid: 'Clero 6842', f.97^v.

13. *Calendar of State Papers, Domestic, 1625, 1626*, p.297. Three more priests were fellow prisoners with him. All seem to have been Irish: Augustine Goul (Gould?), Robert Wading *(sic)* and Malachias Mechor. Egan's name is printed as 'Egen'.

14. This fact is vouched for by a contemporary Spanish Augustinian chronicler, fray Juan Quixano. Cf. 'Memorias para la historia de la provincia de Castilla N.P. San Agustin escritas por el P. Fr. Juan Quixano [Quijano], hijo de la misma provincia', ed. I. Aramburu, *Archivo Agustiniano*, lvii (1963) 31-4, which describes the career of Augustine of Holy Mary, the religious name, I believe, of Cornelius Egan. Patrick K. O'Brien, O.S.A., kindly provided me with a translation of the text.

15. Propaganda Archives, SOCG, vol. 387, f.299^r. Cf. also B. Jennings, 'Acta Congregationis de Propaganda Fide', *Archiv. Hib.*, xxii (1959) 45.

16. Jennings, cit., 46.

17. P.J. Corish, 'Two reports on the Catholic church in Ireland in the early seventeenth century', ibid. 146.

Even though the political situation was not helpful, provincial chapters were held on a regular, or nearly regular, basis from 1630 to 1649. Actually the first detailed acts of a provincial chapter derive from that fateful year of 1649. They prove conclusively that the province had reached a high degree of organization by June 15, even though nothing is said about studies. Still more to the point is the fact that no reference is made to England[18].

Whatever hope that may have existed in the mind of the new provincial, James of St William *alias* James O'Mahony, and his definitory, of reviving the order in England was doomed to be nullified exactly to the day, two months later, of Oliver Cromwell's arrival in Dublin on August 15. The invasion and persecution which followed - it is no exaggeration to say - went within an ace of destroying the church in Ireland[19]. The organization of the Augustinian province that reached a peak in 1649 was rudely swept away. O'Mahony, the provincial was forced, or perhaps thought it better, to take refuge on the European Continent, at Brussels in fact. The friars were scattered both at home and abroad. Some idea of the disruption may be gained from the fact that out of an estimated 90-100 Augustinians in Ireland by 1643, only forty priests and six lay brothers could be accounted for by 1657[20].

Yet before the darkest night gave way to a fitful dawn, the depleted numbers were already in the process of being made up, thanks to the drive of a friar who stood head and shoulders above his Irish confrères at this time. He was James MacCarthy master of theology. As procurator or agent of the province in Rome, not only was he the decisive figure in organizing a mission to Ireland in 1657, but he recommended at the same time to Propaganda that another mission should be sent to the Orkney Islands. His knowledge of geography was not too good, for he thought that these islands lay between Ireland and Scotland. He was thinking no doubt of the western isles. But he also urged, and this is exceedingly relevant to our theme, that Augustinian missionaries be sent to England and Scotland, 'because onetime the English province was one of the leading provinces of our order'[21].

Nothing could be done in pursuit of this objective until the Cromwellian regime was overthrown in England. Obviously the restoration of the Stuart king, Charles II, to the throne in 1660 brought some badly needed relief to the church in Ireland and England, but as far as the government was concerned it was most certainly not freedom for Catholics to worship openly. It is an indication of the unsatisfactory situation even within the Catholic church itself in England that it lacked a head, that is a vicar apostolic, from 1655 to 1685[22].

The pressure, however, of the anti-Catholic policy of the state definitely eased. Within a year of the restoration of Charles, the friars in Ireland were able to assemble (in 1652 this had been deemed impossible) for a provincial chapter at Dunmore on 6 May 1661. It was the first chapter of the province to be held in twelve years[23]. Meanwhile an English Augustinian suddenly makes his appearance out of the blue, the first in a quarter of a century. He was John of St Augustine, son of Rupert and Esther Shaw, citizens of London. Friar John made his profession as a member of the Castile province on 23 December 1660 at the monastery of S. Felipe el Real, Madrid[24]. Cornelius Egan as we have seen, was received into the order at the same monastery in 1618. How or where John of St Augustine found his vocation to the order we do not know. He certainly did not find it in London. As we shall shortly see he became vicar general of the order in England by 1688, but

18. AGA, Ff 22/2, pp 1417-21.
19. R.D. Edwards, 'Irish catholics and the puritan revolution', *Father Luke Wadding: a commemorative volume* (Dublin, 1957), p. 100.
20. J. Hagan, 'Miscellanea Vaticano-Hibernica', *Archiv. Hib.*, vi (1917) 123; Prop. Arch., 'Miscellanee Diverse', 20, ff 413r-416v.
21. Prop. Arch., cit., f. 416v.
22. W.M. Brady, *Episcopal succession in England, Scotland and Ireland, A.D. 1400-1875,* iii (Rome, 1877) 104-39.
23. AGA, Ff 22/2, ff 1425r-1428v.
24. Arch. Hist. Nac., Madrid, MS 251-B, f.115r. John's parents' surname is written 'Shau' ibid. He is mistakenly called Irish in AGA, Dd 128, f.189v, that is unless there was an Irish John of St Augustine contemporaneously with him.

for the moment the spotlight must be on James MacCarthy.

He followed up his petition of 1657 to the Holy See for missionaries - Augustinians - to be sent to England and Scotland with yet another petition, this time apparently to the general of the order. Actually the document containing the request is neither signed nor dated, but there can be little or no doubt but that it emanated from MacCarthy. For one thing it calls on the general to appoint an Irish friar as his vicar in England[25]. Nothing came of the request. Instead the general found a more realistic, but hardly less difficult mission, for MacCarthy himself, a mission to Poland where the order was experiencing grave problems. The crucial question, as the general saw it, was the revival of religious observance. It would take a friar of exceptional skill and drive to bring this about.

The one best suited to do it, in the general's eyes, was James MacCarthy. He accordingly appointed him visitor general and commissary general for the Polish province on 13 March 1661. His commission was an unenviable one. We are not concerned here with this assignment except to say that he was well received by and made an excellent impression on the king of Poland. All went smoothly for a year or two, and there is no doubt that the general's envoy did really good work, but he fell foul of some of the friars - there were faults on both sides evidently. The upshot was that MacCarthy was recalled to Rome towards the end of 1664[26].

James MacCarthy was not, one imagines, unduly upset by his Polish experience. Another mission beckoned to him, one next door to Ireland this time and close to his heart - a mission to revive the order in England's green and pleasant land. Did he not himself propose in effect this very object seven years earlier in 1657?

The project mooted in 1555 by the then prior general never got off the ground, as we have seen. A second attempt was now about to be made. The omens were good. So in June 1667 the general, Girolamo Valvasori, appointed MacCarthy provincial in England. This would seem to be an odd appointment. There was no province of England since the Reformation. Yes, but the order still continued to speak of a province of England. The general chapter of 1685, for example, issued a decree for the *provinces* of England and Ireland[27]. In other words it refused to accept the forced suppression under Henry VIII as legal. It was of course a case of *fictio iuris*. The anomaly continued until 1773 when the phrase 'Province of England' was marked for expunction from the constitutions of the order. At all events, in June 1667 the general wrote to Charles II's queen, Catherine of Braganza, on behalf of MacCarthy, recommending him to her good graces[28]. By 14 December 1669 he was resident in London and was saying Mass at the home of the Venetian ambassador, Piero Mocenigo, with whom he was evidently on excellent terms. The embassy was just off Piccadilly in Suffolk Street.

Catholics were free to hear Mass and receive the sacraments there, as at all the other five embassies of the Catholic powers accredited to the court of St James. Ambassadors like Mocenigo have been rightly praised for employing chaplains such as MacCarthy to provide Mass and the other sacraments for the persecuted Catholics in London. In addition to MacCarthy there were three more Augustinians in London, possibly but not necessarily living with him so as to avoid

25. AGA, cit., f.1421ᵛ. In 1660 Tadhg Coghlan, O.S.A., from Leinster, asked Propaganda for missionary faculties for his going to Ireland and Scotland. It appears that his request was not granted. Cf. B. Millett, O.F.M., 'Calendar of volume 15 of the *Fondo di Vienna* in Propaganda Archives', *Collectanea Hibernica,* 33 (1991) 60. Coghlan was a student at Perugia by 30 Jan. 1655 (AGA, Cc 82, p.463).
26. G. Uth, *Szkic historyczno biograficzny Zakonu Augustjanskiego w Polsce* (Cracow, 1930), pp 132-5; F. Gossmann, 'De rebus ordinis nostri in Polonia gestis', *Anal. Aug.,* xiv (1931-2) 379.
27. *Anal. Aug.,* xii (1927-8) 57.
28. A. de Meijer, 'James Willemart OSA at the court of James II. The fourth attempt to re-establish the English Augustinian province', ibid., xli (1978) 118, n. 14. In that same year 1667 Denis Kennedy, Irish Augustinian, asked Propaganda for faculties for himself and a companion to go on the Scottish mission (Arch.Prop. Acta, 1667, under the date 28 Nov. 1667). I owe this reference to F.X. Martin, O.S.A.

suspicion. They were Walter Wall, Gerard Baly or Rawley and Christopher French[29].

It may be asked what was the so-called provincial and his confrères doing in London, apart from saying Mass? What efforts, if any, were made to attract English aspirants to the order? We simply do not know. But whatever MacCarthy did or did not do, his mission certainly did not lead to the restoration, or even the beginnings of the restoration, of the order in England. After 1660 not a single English aspirant to the order appeared until about 1680 or a little earlier. He was William Morris. Nothing is known of his history except that he was promoted bachelor of theology by the prior general on 24 May 1686, possibly with a view to his returning to England as part of the team being got ready to work there for the restoration of the order[30].

Was he one of the first fruits of the apostolate of perhaps the most remarkable Irish Augustinian of the second half of the seventeenth century - John Skerrett, or Esquerret as he was known on the Continent and in the New World, and which he signed himself in 1673 as fourth definitor of the Irish province[31]. Skerrett had been a long time, so the record states, in England before 1685. There is a problem of chronology here, but for the moment, we may leave this pass because it is more important to emphasise that Skerrett was not the prime mover in the greatest yet attempt to restore the order in England[32].

Charles II died on 6 February 1685 and was succeeded as king by his brother James, Duke of York, a convert to Catholicism. This heralded the dawn of a new age for English Catholics, and indirectly for the revival of the Augustinian order in England. It has to be said *proh dolor* that the order in the person of a new general, Fulgenzio Travalloni, was unduly slow in grasping the golden opportunity of resuscitating the onetime great province of England. In the event, it was not the centre of the order that spearheaded the endeavour, nor was it an Irish friar, but a Dutch Augustinian, James Willemart. How this came about is interesting.

The new king, James II, and his brother before him, the late Charles II, had been entertained during their exile by the Augustinians at Bruges. Willemart was closer to Charles than to James. This did not matter: what did matter was that the new king and Willemart knew each other[33]. It explains why the prior general, Fulgenzio Travalloni, himself newly elected as general, made this Dutch friar the bearer of a letter dated 22 September 1685 to the king congratulating him on his accession to the throne of England and Scotland, while also recommending to him the renewal of the order in the kingdom. But the king could hardly have been impressed that the general had delayed for seven months before congratulating him on succeeding to the throne[34]. At all events, Willemart delivered the general's letter in person to James II, who together with his wife, Mary da Modena, received him most kindly. His majesty promised to remember the Augustinian friars whom he held in high regard - so he assured Willemart. The queen for her part also informed him that she too would do anything she could to further the restoration of the order to England.

Willemart duly reported to the general the good news of his visit to the court of St James. Now that for the first time since 1558 the political situation was right, the greatest yet effort to re-establish the order in England was about to be made. Yet Willemart, despite being the friar who had made direct contact with the king and his queen, was not chosen by the general to direct the

---

29. Brady, cit., iii.115. He cites a report made to Propaganda by Abbate Claudius Agretti, 14 December 1669, in which he mentions the enmity in England between the English and Irish clergy. He singled out Christopher French as one of the chief trouble-makers, not only in London, but also in Ireland. No word is said about the secret mission which brought the celebrated Augustinian missionary of Bengal, Friar Sebastião Manrique, to London that very same year. The story of his life as a missionary and how he met his death in London is the subject of Maurice Collis's enthralling book, *The land of the great image - being experiences of Friar Manrique in Arakan* (London, 1943).

30. AGA 125, f.213[v].

31. Ibid., Ff 22/2, f.1432[r].

32. For Skerrett see F.X. Martin, '"Obstinate Skerrett", missionary in Virginia, the West Indies and England, c.1674-c.1688', *Journal of the Galway Archaeological and Historical Society,* 35 (1976 [1977]) 12-51. For his first term as a missionary in England cf. p.28.

33. A. de Meijer, cit. (n.28), 122-3.

34. Ibid., 127.

effort. The man chosen was the Irish friar, John Skerrett. It does not take too much imagination to detect his prompting behind the enactment by the general chapter of 1685 of the decree which stated that 'men of our order, esteemed for doctrine, virtues and zeal, be sent [to England] . . . so that the ancient splendour of our order be restored there'[35].

In order to entice men to volunteer, a reward - not a spiritual one! - was promised. The coveted, privileged degree of master of theology would be awarded to those who spent three years in England, teaching and preaching[36]. The general, Travalloni, who does not appear to have had as a priority the restoration of the order in England, had to act in accordance with the directive of the general chapter. His problem was to find the right men to go to England and work there. There were no takers for the reward offered by the general chapter. In the end he had to fall back upon Ireland. Advised doubtless by Skerrett, he invited seven Irish friars on 16 March 1686 to go to England. As a group they were, perhaps, the pick of the Irish province. The leader was Peter Wynn, prior of Dublin. The others were Bernard Kennedy, master of theology and future provincial (1699), Martin French, prior of Cork, Dominic Martin, prior of Galway, William Gibbon, prior of Murrisk, John de Burgo and Peter (?) Rushe[37].

None of them apparently accepted the general's invitation, but other friars came forward. It was all to the good that four of these were English born: William Coulson, doctor of theology, Gregory Smith - he had been a missionary in Yorkshire about 1680, John of St Augustine whom we met before, and Laurence Tool, all of whom were active in London, most probably between 1686 and 1689. Indeed Coulson was organizing the Cincture confraternity in 1687[38]. In addition there were three Irishmen: Augustine O'Shea, doctor of theology, John Madden, and John Skerrett himself whom the general named head of the mission as vicar and commissary general on 2 November 1686[39].

Time was not on Skerrett's side. By 1688 he was dead. John of St Augustine was appointed to succeed him as vicar general, and John Madden, who returned to Ireland, was replaced by the distinguished John Dowdall. But the effort to restore the order in England was doomed from the day, 11 December 1688, when the Catholic king James II fled the country. With the advent of the so-called Glorious Revolution that led to the accession of William III, prince of Orange, to the vacant throne on 13 February 1689, the writing was on the wall. The vicar general, John of St Augustine, got leave from the general, one month later (March 25), to leave the country, so did Laurence Tool on August 9[40].

Travalloni's successor, Antonio Pacini, appointed Dowdall on 17 June 1693 as the new vicar general. He was joined within a short time by three more Irish Augustinians, William Carroll, Francis Kelly and Edmund Byrne who was later to become provincial in Ireland in 1717[41]. It is not known how these three newcomers fared as missionaries in England.

---

35. *Anal.Aug.*, xii (1927-8) 57.
36. Ibid.
37. A. de Meijer, cit., 131-2. Rushe's name is written as 'Pr. Rustea' in the general's register. Prof. F.X. Martin holds that the friar was in fact William O'Shea. Cf. ibid., 122, n.81.
38. For these friars see ibid., 132-4.
39. Ibid., 132-3. A copy of the form used by the prior general in commissioning a vicar and commissary general for England is in AGA, Cc (not numbered), pp 87-9. It may well have been devised in the first place for the commissioning of Skerrett. The commission was for all Great Britain, thus including Scotland. The appointee had to have spent many years in England, as Skerrett was said to have done. The vicar and commissary general was granted most ample faculties, but was explicitly forbidden to receive any Irish aspirants to the order. Evidently the intention was the creating, or restoration, of a purely English province embracing Scotland.
40. A. de Meijer, cit., 134-5. The general accepted the resignation of John of St Augustine on 22 Oct. 1693, and described him as a member of the province of Castile and 'lector jubilatus' of theology (AGA, Dd 133, p.256). Travalloni had already granted James Wale (Wall?), master of theology, permission on 26 May 1692 to go as a missionary to England 'ubi divina gratia appulserit'. (Ibid., Dd 132, f. 49r).
41. A. de Meijer, cit., 135-6. We have no information as to how these intrepid missionaries fared in England. For Byrne as provincial see T.C. Butler, *John's Lane - history of the Augustinian friars in Dublin 1280-1983* (Dublin, 1983), p.91, n.9. In Dublin he adopted the guise of a soldier in order to escape detection as a priest friar, and was known as 'Colonel Byrne'. Did he do the same when he was in England?

A Connacht friar, Eugene O'Connor, is erroneously stated to have been appointed vicar general for England by February 1695[42].

He may have been there, however, when he did a singularly curious thing. He actually praised the Protestant monarch, William of Orange, in writing! Given the vicious round of the penal laws introduced at this time, O'Connor's action, however well-intentioned, could not but appear incomprehensible, even scandalous in the eyes of Catholics. His unfortunate lauding of the king apart, in all other respects, the Irish friar was regarded as a splendid religious[43].

Despite the disappointment that must surely have attended the failure of the fourth attempt to restore the order in England during the last quarter of the seventeenth century, the commitment of the Irish Augustinians continued none the less. If it appeared to peter out by the end of the eighteenth century this may in part at least be connected with a possible shift of interest elsewhere occasioned by the foundation of the order in north America by the two Irish pioneers, John Baptist Rosseter and Thomas Matthew Carr. They arrived respectively in Philadelphia in 1794 and 1795.

Shortly after the dawn of the eighteenth century there were four Irish Augustinians doing pastoral work in London under the leadership of John Dowdall the vicar general. They were William Carroll, Nicholas Fallon, John Henegan and Fulgentius Butler[44]. We do not know where the small Irish Augustinian mission in London resided, or what precise sector of the population it ministered to. The friars were in contact with the centre of the order in Rome more than once in 1705[45]. That they had to live in separate lodgings and go about their work, offering the Mass and administering the sacraments, surreptitiously goes without saying. Indeed if proof were needed, the fate of Fulgentius Butler provides it. He had the misfortune to be discovered as a priest in London and was imprisoned for nineteen months, during five of which he was extremely ill[46].

On 24 April 1706 the general appointed Nicholas Fallon to succeed John Dowdall as commissary and vicar general in the kingdom of England. He in turn was succeeded in 1714 by none other than his immediate predecessor Dowdall who was joined by two other Irish friars, Francis Comyn and Andrew Peppard[47].

Meanwhile a new and striking pastoral initiative was made north of the English border by Peter Mulligan, the most distinguished Irish Augustinian of the eighteenth century. He was most probably a native of Galway. After entering the order he studied in Rome where he was ordained by 1697[48]. He was still in Rome when he was accosted by a Scottish prelate, James Gordon, from Banffshire who had just been appointed coadjutor vicar apostolic of Scotland. He invited Mulligan to come back with him to Scotland as a missionary and help to save the Catholic faith in the Highlands. Mulligan agreed.

Gordon, as yet only bishop-elect, decided to have his consecration at Montefiascone, north of

---

42. Butler, pp 87, 164, would have avoided his error if he had cited F.X. Martin, 'Provincial rivalries in eighteenth century Ireland (an Irish Augustinian document of 1722)', *Archiv. Hib.,* xxx (1972) 131, n.27. The prior general, Pacini, appointed O'Connor on 11 Feb. 1695 as his vicar and commissary general 'in toto Hiberniae Regno' (AGA, Dd 134, pp 322-3). In the register, O'Connor's name is written as 'Eugenius de O Konor, Hibernus ex Provincia nostra Bethicae' [Andalusia]. Cf. ibid., p.323.

The reason why the general appointed O'Connor as his vicar and commissary general is doubly interesting. The general thought that there were no Augustinians left in Ireland who would be able to restore there the Catholic faith which has almost collapsed. He orders O'Connor to restore the order in Ireland 'vbi olim tam splendide floruit' (Ibid.). But when O'Connor arrived back in Ireland, he found that the order was anything but moribund. In fact it was very much alive and operating fairly normally with eighty members, despite the persecution. It is clear, however, that religious observance obtained only in the houses in Connacht and in the Dublin friary. Cf. AGA, Dd 135, pp 364-5.

43. Cf. Martin (n.42), 131. An Irish friar, James Daly, had received permission from the general on 6 September 1695 to go to England (AGA, Dd 135, p.187). There appears to be no evidence that he actually went there.

44. AGA, Dd 145, p.373.

45. Martin (n.42), 118-9.

46. Ibid., 119, 133.

47. Butler, loc.cit. Comyn was arrested on arriving back in Ireland at Wexford in 1722. Bail was refused despite a plea from the Spanish ambassador in London. Comyn was transferred to Newgate gaol in Dublin and orders were issued on 28 June 1723 for his immediate transportation to Spain. If he was in fact transported, he managed none the less to return to Ireland where he was appointed prior of Galway that very same year and in 1727 provincial. Cf. Martin (n.42) 130, n.26.

48. AGA, Dd 136, p.354.

Rome, in order to avoid publicity. The danger of being reported to the British government by an informer was very real. Montefiascone, celebrated for its wine, was still more popular for devotion to St Margaret whose body is enshrined there in the Augustinian church. Incidentally, at least two English Augustinians in pre-Reformation days visited the shrine: John Waldeby, possibly the most outstanding preacher in the England of the fourteenth century, and Osbern Bokenham of Clare Priory, one of the most popular religous writers of the fifteenth century.

Peter Mulligan attended the consecration of his Scottish friend, James Gordon, on 11 April of that same year 1706. After the ceremony the two set off together for Scotland. They travelled via Paris where they rested until June 25 when they left for Holland to sail from there to Scotland. A month later, on July 27, they landed at Aberdeen[49]. The greatest need for priests was in the Highlands, and it was there at Glengarry, west of Invergarry between Fort Augustus and Fort William, that Peter Mulligan lived and worked as a missionary under the most trying conditions. He stayed there for sixteen years, that is until 1722[50]. He is last mentioned in the annual list of missioners under the year 1721 as 'Father Mulagan *al.* M'Donald, Augustinian'[51]. Evidently he adopted the alias McDonald in order to pass himself off as a Scotsman and thus less likely to incur suspicion as a priest. When he was recalled to Ireland in 1722 by his provincial, Edmund Byrne, who himself had come as a missionary to England in 1698, as we have seen, Bishop Gordon reported to Rome that, 'Mr Mulligan has left us after sixteen years in the Highlands. He wishes to serve his own countrymen, and during the many years he has been on the Mission he has reaped most abundant fruit of his labours, having reconciled over 700 persons to the Church[52]'.

Back in Ireland this valiant, self-sacrificing missionary was elected provincial in 1724[53]. He served as prior of Galway from 1727 to 1732 when he was made bishop of Ardagh. He ruled the diocese until he died on 23 July 1739. During his years as prior of Galway he catalogued its splendid library, which was built up and preserved in Times-that were anything but conducive to collecting, purchasing and preserving spiritual and theological works in particular. Even when Mulligan was arranging and cataloguing the books the community had to shut the church four times in November-December 1731 because of persecution[54].

The pendulum now reverts to its accustomed place - England. Once again the materials for a fairly continuous and revealing narrative are unavailable. It is a classical case of our having to make do with nothing more than *membra disiecta,* if one may so describe the friars who served in London in the eighteenth century. They being Irish were not wanted by the English clergy because they were regarded as troublemakers, but the prejudice may have been generated at bottom by the friars receiving financial aid, which meant that less was available for the secular clergy. Actually, the animus may simply have been an offshoot of the much bigger problem, the independence of the regulars *vis-à-vis* the bishops.

A victim of the anti-Irish feeling was friar Thomas Hagherin. In 1729 the agent of the English bishops in Rome, Laurence Mayes, protested to Propaganda that he should not be sent to England because such a policy with regard to Irish priests was resented by the English priests and

49. W.F. Leith, *Memoirs of Scottish Catholics during the XVII and XVIII centuries* (London, 1909), p.225.
50. O. Blundell, *The Catholic highlands of Scotland: the western highlands and islands* (Edinburgh & London, 1917), pp 173-4. Cf. J.F.S. Gordon, *The Catholic church in Scotland* (Aberdeen, 1874), pp 630-2. I cannot express too deeply my gratitude to Dr Christine Johnson, keeper of Scottish Catholic Archives, Edinburgh, for bringing to my notice William Forbes Leith's studies and that of Odo Blundell. Dr Johnson also very kindly provided me with photocopies of the references in these works to Mulligan.
51. Gordon p.632.
52. Blundell, p.174. I have agreed at the request of the editor of the *Innes Review* to submit for publication therein a fuller study of Mulligan's career with particular reference to his missionary work in the Highlands.
53. W.P. Burke, *The Irish priests in the penal Times-(1660-1770)* (Waterford, 1914), pp 255-9, 261-5, 337. Mr Diarmuid Ó Catháin, one-time pupil of Good Counsel College, New Ross, and now a practising solicitor in Cork, is making a study of Peter Mulligan as a member of an Irish literary society in Dublin during his time as provincial.
54. The catalogue has been edited by Hugh Fenning, 'The library of the Augustinians of Galway in 1731', *Collectanea Hibernica,* 31 and 32 (1989-90) 162-95. I am indebted to Fr F.X. Martin for a photocopy of this publication.

hence could only lead to trouble[55]. They may have also resented friars securing cushy appointments as chaplains to foreign embassies or English lords, but they could only envy such friars their good fortune. One such friar was Michael MacNarheny. He got permission on 18 October 1732 from the general to become chaplain to the Venetian embassy at the request of the ambassador, Giovanni Domenico Imberti[56].

Another friar, Peter Kilkehy (Killykelly), was in tow later on with an English noble. On 31 July 1758 Bishop Richard Challoner, vicar apostolic of the London district, informed Propaganda that the 13th earl of Stafford, John Paul Stafford-Howard, wanted Kilkehy, an Irish Augustinian, as his chaplain[57]. It would be interesting to know how this came about. Assuming, as one may, that the earl got his wish, we may presume that Kilkehy took up residence at Stafford House, the earl's London home which overlooked St James's Square, the oldest in London. Incidentally, John Paul Stafford-Howard succeeded to the earldom only because the rightful heir, Matthias Stafford-Howard, died without issue. His wife, and this is the interesting thing, was Henrietta Cantillon, a Parisien whose family originated in Ballyheigue, Co. Kerry, and became bankers in Paris[58].

To return to our main theme: Patrick Canton, a Leinster man, was appointed by the prior general, Felice Leoni, as vicar and commissary general for England on 11 June 1739[59]. He in turn was succeeded some years later by Luke Geoghegan on 29 September 1744[60]. He was doubtless one of the two Irish Augustinians who were working in the London district in 1746. As superior he was placed in a difficult position by the intransigence of the other religious orders who refused to accept the decrees of Propaganda concerning the need to receive faculties from the bishops and do pastoral work in accordance with their instructions. Geoghegan was singled out in 1748 by Bishop Challoner as the one and only religious who submitted without hesitation to the decrees. For this he fell foul of the two other orders of friars, the Franciscans and the Discalced Carmelites. It may be that he then lodged a complaint with the Nuncio in Brussels, for Challoner stated that he saw a letter from the Nuncio to the superior of the Augustinians praising the friar and wishing that the others would do as he had done[61].

For the remainder of the century, while it cannot be doubted that Irish Augustinians continued to do pastoral work in England with London as the centre, all that we know for certain is that the Irish provincial, Richard Talbot, was appointed commissary general for Great Britain by 5 March 1762[62], and that an unnamed friar was working in London in 1773[63]. The last Irish Augustinian known to have served in the city in the eighteenth century was Michael Clement Ryan who died there on 30 December 1798[64].

In or about this same year, a friar from Rathangan, county Kildare, Nicholas Molloy, whose title to fame rests on his reputation as one of the outstanding preachers of his time, travelled more than once from John's Lane, Dublin, to the Isle of Man to say Mass for the handful of Catholics living in Douglas. In doing so he was taking a risk in going to the island, for he had to say Mass for the tiny congregation behind closed doors in a parlour in the rear of a tavern. Nicholas Molloy was probably the first priest since the Reformation to bring the sacraments to the island's

55. H. Fenning, *The undoing of the friars of Ireland: a study of the novitiate question in the eighteenth century* (Louvain, 1972), pp 22-3.
56. Idem, 'Irish friars in the Augustinian schools of Italy: 1698-1808', *Anal. Aug.*, xliv (1981) 341.
57. Prop.Arch., Missioni Miscellanee, ii, f.65ʳ. 'Peter Kilkehy' is most probably a misspelling of the name of a Galway friar, Patrick Killykelly, who was a novice by 7 August 1737 and was ordained priest in May-June 1745. Cf. Fenning, pp 85-6.
58. *Complete Peerage*, xii, part 1 (London, 1953), 195.
59. AGA, Dd 181, f.32ᵛ.
60. Fenning, p.340.
61. E.H. Burton, *The life and Times-of Bishop Challoner (1691-1781)* (London, 1909), i.260-1. Cf. ii.171n for the reference to the two friars who were serving in London in 1746-8. It is not absolutely certain that Geoghegan was the superior in 1748, but there is no evidence that he was replaced by another.
62. IAPA, vol. 71, p.61.
63. Burton, ii.171n.
64. Fenning, p.347.

Catholics[65].

The nineteenth century, in so far as it concerns the revival of the order in England by the Irish province, presents a very different picture from the foregoing. For the first time since the suppression of the English province the foundations for its restoration were at length solidly laid. It must have seemed like the beginning of a second spring when a young English aspirant applied to join the order. He was William Morley. We know little or nothing about him, unfortunately, except that on 19 October 1803 the prior general sent him to do his novitiate at Perugia with two Irish aspirants, Thomas Power and James Kirwan[66]. A problem arose about his affiliation. The last that we hear of William Hart Morley is in a letter of November 16 in which the commissary general of the order, Nicola Salerno, who was also the assistant general for Italy, wrote, so it seems, to the Irish provincial, James Fleming, about the problem, suggesting that Morley be affiliated to the Dublin convent[67]. Evidently the young man did not persevere.

An attempt to revive the order in England by two Irish friars was projected in 1847, not on behalf of the Irish province but on behalf of the then American commissariate of the order. The attempt was focused on Bristol. Here it would be out of place, and in any case it would demand undue space, to recount the bizarre story, but as the Bristol foundation, or rather its demise, needs to be correctly understood, the facts are as follows.

The idea was the brainchild of one of the most charismatic, entrepreneurish and tempestuous characters in Irish Augustinian history. He was Patrick Eugene Moriarty, a Dubliner whose father was a lawyer and relative of Daniel O'Connell. Born in 1805, he joined the order in 1822, studied and was ordained in Rome in 1828. The first indication of his unusual temperament is that on the way home from Rome he tried to be taken on as chaplain to a Brazilian fleet then anchored at Genoa. Not succeeding in this, he continued on his way and managed to get a parish near Bordeaux!

He did not stay long there. In 1829 he was appointed to John's Lane, Dublin, and in 1835 volunteered for the Madras mission on which he accompanied Bishop Daniel O'Connor. He came to Rome in 1838 at the request of the bishop to report to Propaganda Fide on the success of the mission. In no time he was off to Philadelphia, where he was appointed superior of the Augustinians in America, and became co-founder in 1841 of a school which he christened Villanova. It was destined to develop into the present magnificent university. Moriarty returned to Europe to collect money for the rebuilding of St Augustine's, Philadelphia. It was then that his mind turned to the question of restoring the English province.

The idea may have been suggested to him by Charles Talbot, 19th earl of Shrewsbury, whose wife was a Wexford lady, Maria Theresa Talbot. He took on Moriarty as his chaplain at his manor house, Alton Towers, Staffordshire, on a temporary basis. Moriarty also stayed with the Benedictines in Liverpool, doubtless when he was collecting for St Augustine's in Philadelphia. Matters now moved rapidly as regard a foundation in Bristol. At the Augustinian general chapter of 1847 Moriarty was elected assistant general. He was told by John Lynch, prior of S. Maria in Posterula, that Bishop William Bernard Ullathorne, O.S.B., was willing to give the order a parish in his vicariate, the western district of England. Moriarty contacted the bishop and it was agreed in November that the order would open a parish in Bristol. Moriarty proposed that his confrère and intimate friend, Nicholas O'Donnell from near Cahir, Tipperary, who had been pastor of St Paul's, Brooklyn, be appointed prior and parish priest of the new foundation. Moriarty refused to have it affiliated to the Irish province. It was to be juridically an American Augustinian foundation. Moriarty persuaded an English convert to Catholicism, Timothy Crowther, and an Irishman, Joseph

65. IAPA, P(Philip). A. D(Doyle), 'Irish Augustinians deceased, in memoriam, documenta', p.17.
66. Fenning, p.358, citing AGA, Dd 243, reg. III, f.33. William Morley's full name was William Hart Morley.
67. IAPA, vol.71, p.25.

MacDonnell, to join the English offshoot of the foundation[68].

O'Donnell took up residence at Stapleton Road, Bristol, in March 1848, and erected a small chapel which was dedicated to his patron saint, Nicholas of Tolentine on 24 June. He received a rude shock, however, four months later when Moriarty decided that the mission could not survive financially and therefore should be given up. He informed the prior general, and wrote to the bishop, Joseph William Hendren, O.F.M., that in virtue of his authority as assistant general he there and then resigned the parish into the hands of the bishop. O'Donnell was appalled and protested in no uncertain terms. The bishop offered him another church, but when he declined the offer the bishop did not persist. In fact he continued to recognize O'Donnell as the parish priest of St Nicholas's, and in September 1849 he blessed and laid the cornerstone for the new church.

After Bishop Hendren was translated to Nottingham, his successor, a former Benedictine, Thomas Burgess, sought to reclaim the parish for the diocese, while O'Donnell was absent. Fr Crowther, his assistant, who had been ordained in 1850 and assigned to the parish in 1852, sided with the bishop and left the parish for a position in the bishop's household. Subsequently he had a chequered career, wandering all over the place. He died apparently in 1898, having become a secular priest in or about 1860[69].

When O'Donnell returned to Bristol he was up in arms and made his feelings known to both the bishop and the prior general, Giuseppe Palermo. He appealed to Propaganda Fide, so did the bishop. On 27 March 1854 Propaganda decided that justice was on the side of O'Donnell and that the parish was to be restored to the Augustinian order. The bishop refused to give way, but died in November before he could make a personal visit to the Congregation.

Archbishop George Errington was then appointed administrator of the diocese, which had been erected in 1850 as the diocese of Clifton. To resolve the impasse he proposed that the Augustinian order could keep the parish, provided it assigned three priests to care for it and pay the diocese £1,970 (it is not clear why this large sum of money, very large at the time, was stipulated). But if the order would relinquish the parish, then it would be compensated, but by not more than £200 for the cost incurred by Fr O'Donnell in building the church. The Augustinian order in 1856 acquiesced in this latter proposal, and that was the end of the Bristol foundation and with it the fifth abortive attempt hitherto to revive the English province[70]. It is pleasant to record that the church and presbytery of St Nicholas of Tolentine in Bristol still retain their Augustinian character, complete with a statue of the saint. It is a happy coincidence that the present parish priest, Canon Jeremiah O'Brien, is a brother of Fr Nicholas Bernard O'Brien, O.S.A., in Nigeria.

II

The first permanent Augustinian foundation in England since the Reformation was made at Hoxton Square, London, in 1864[71]. The credit belongs to the great Wexford Augustinian, Martin Crane, a man of vision and drive, who was elected provincial for a first term in 1863. He was the moving spirit behind the resurgence of the province after the Great Famine had run its hideous course. It is significant that the president of the chapter in 1863 was a Maltese prior general, Paolo Micallef. He is said to have urged Crane to set about making a foundation in England as a first

68. Crowther's first name varied from time to time as Timothy, Thomas, Alphonsus. He had a chequered career. Cf. Pejza (n.69), loc. cit. Eventually, he got permission to go to Australia and serve under Goold of Melbourne (AGA, Dd 259, p.III). So too did MacDonnell. Neither of them appears to have availed of the permission. Crowther left the order with the consent of the general. MacDonnell returned to Ireland but became rather a problem.

69. I am most grateful to Canon Maurice Abbott, parish priest of Meols in the Wirral, for information about Crowther. See also J.P. Pejza, 'Nicholas O'Donnell, O.S.A.', *The Tagastan*, 22 (1960) 35, n.43.

70. The story of the Bristol affair is set forth and documented by Pejza (cit.) in two excellent articles, (i) 'Second founder: Patrick E. Moriarty, O.S.A.', ibid., 21 (1959) 9-25, especially 18-20; (ii) 'Nicholas O'Donnell', cit., 22-35, in particular 27-31. The author also published a study of O'Donnell's career down to the year 1838 (ibid. 9-20). The order officially relinquished the Bristol mission in June 1856.

71. With the foundation of Hoxton we enter the early modern period. Hence it is not necessary to annotate in this necessarily short survey the subsequent history of the actual restoration of the order in England and Scotland by the Irish province, except where this would appear to be required.

With the establishment of a house at Hoxton, East London, in 1864, the Augustinians returned once more to England.

step towards the restoration of the mother province of the Irish province.

The history of the Hoxton foundation, as indeed of all the subsequent foundations, is amply documented. Fr Crane lost no time in seeking an interview in May of the following year (1864) with the archbishop of Westminster, Nicholas Cardinal Wiseman, who welcomed him, literally, with open arms. He is on record as saying during a visit to Carlow College in September 1858 that the Catholics of the United Kingdom owed a very great debt to one Irish Augustinian, James Doyle alias J.K.L., to whom said Wiseman he himself was particularly indebted[72]. From the pastoral point of view the cardinal's principal concern was the area of Hoxton which had a Catholic population of some 4000, mostly Irish or of Irish descent. It was the most deprived and poorest area of the archdiocese.

Unlike Patrick Moriarty and Bristol in 1848, Martin Crane was not put off by the poverty of the people and the prospect that the mission, as things were then, would need to be subsidised at least for some time to come by the Irish province. In August 1864 he accepted the mission on behalf of the province, and appointed the first community which consisted of three priests, John Maxwell, rector, with William O'Sullivan and Michael Kelly as his assistants. Maxwell soon retired, and O'Sullivan, who was slightly older than Kelly, was appointed prior and rector of the parish. One year later, he made way for Kelly to become rector and then prior. Kelly had scarcely been ordained more than a year in 1863, but he enjoyed the fullest confidence of Crane who told him he was 'the fittest man for the work'[73]. The Hoxton mission would test his mettle to the full.

Michael Kelly stood the test magnificently and became the embodiment of the Hoxton mission for the next fifty years without a break until the day he died, 26 January 1914. But it was Crane himself who did all the preparatory work. He bought the site and acquired temporary lodgings in which he himself lived for a time until the foundations were well and truly laid. He collected funds to pay for the undertaking, and finalizing the canonical arrangements with the curia in Rome and the diocese. The only problem in this respect was that the rescript granted for the foundation by Propaganda Fide at Rome went missing. It was still missing from the Westminster archives when Henry, later Cardinal, Manning succeeded Wiseman in 1865. The loss was made

---

72. N. Wiseman, *Sermons, lectures and speeches delivered during his tour of Ireland, August-September 1858* (Dublin, 1859) pp 309-10.
73. Cited in Hoxton centenary booklet, p. [18].

Fr Michael Kelly, O.S.A. - the "Saint of Hoxton", whose entire priestly life, 1864-1914, was spent among the poor of East London.

good by the issue of a new rescript dated 3 September 1865, which technically remains the date of the foundation.

It was on the basis of this new rescript that Crane presented Michael Kelly from Inistioge, Co. Kilkenny, on 8 November 1865 to the cardinal for institution as the first parish priest of Hoxton. The parish and church were dedicated to St Monica when the foundation stone of the new church was laid on 20 September 1864. The church was erected on the north side of Hoxton Square on the site of no.18, one of the three houses whose freehold Crane had purchased. The church was opened, appropriately, on 4 May, feast of the patron, St Monica, 1866.

The history of the parish is described in outline in the commemorative booklet published to mark the first centenary of St Monica's in 1964. There is need and room still for a full length history of the parish for which there is no shortage of materials. Here, however, it may be of interest to record a matter that did not fit into the plan or object of the booklet, but is entirely relevant within the context of this chapter. In passing a word deserves to be said about a forgotten community of nuns who were invited and came to Hoxton in 1867.

They were Franciscan sisters from Rosentaal in Holland. They were asked to come and take charge of a vital, if not the most vital, part of the mission - a school for the children of the parish. Education of the poor was one of the greatest neglects of the Catholic church in England in the nineteenth century, even after the restoration of the hierarchy in 1850. The friars at Hoxton heard about these sisters in Holland, probably through the Dutch Augustinians. They arrived in Hoxton and were accommodated at no.3 Hoxton Square in the summer of 1865. The house has long since been demolished. The sisters did splendid work in managing the school and teaching. They also held evening classes for girls. As the house was too confined they moved their residence to Victoria Park Road towards the end of 1866. Things looked ever so much more promising when the then new schools were built in 1870, but the sisters were forced to give up as they did not have the qualifications needed for government aid. And so, to the very great regret of priests, people and children, they had to leave.

Hoxton was Michael Kelly's first, greatest and last concern, but he was above all a great Augustinian. He was involved in the foundation at Hythe in 1891, for it was he who dealt with Rome through the prior general, Sebastiano (later Cardinal) Martinelli, and with the bishop of

Nestling peacefully in the Dublin mountains is Orlagh novitiate.

Southwark. He was even more directly involved in the foundation of Hammersmith in 1903. He wrote to various bishops inquiring about the possibility of foundations in their dioceses. In 1899 he sought a foundation in South Croydon, but without success. He was a man of other Augustinian interests, those of his own Irish province naturally, and was delighted by its acquisition of Orlagh, county Dublin, for a novitiate.

In addition he had very much at heart the progress of the order in Australia. After all, his great friend Martin Crane was bishop of Sandhurst (now Bendigo) in Victoria. Moreover, two of the friars who served under him in Hoxton became the one after the other bishops of the vicariate of Cooktown, as it then was, in north Queensland. They were John Hutchinson, a fellow Kilkenny man, who was appointed vicar apostolic of Cooktown in 1883, and James Dominic Murray, from county Westmeath, his immediate successor in 1897. But, apart from, or rather connected with, Hoxton, was the hope which Kelly cherished for the restoration of the centuries-long defunct English province.

In 1881 the then commissary general of the order, Pacifico Neno, had discussions in Hoxton with Michael Kelly about securing candidates specifically for the order in England, preferably English youths, or failing that, boys from Ireland. A product of this move was Edward Dominic Reid, who was born in Hoxton parish in 1868. When he left St Monica's school he had to work to support his widowed mother, but in 1886 he was able to follow his vocation, which was to be an Augustinian. He did his novitiate in Orlagh, was professed in 1887 and ordained in 1895. His first appointment was naturally to Hoxton. There we must leave him for the moment.

The prior general, Neno, followed up his talk with Kelly in 1881 with a letter the next year in which he urged him to get vocations for England and said that postulants could be sent to Italy for novitiate. He was to treat the matter as confidential. Kelly did so. When he encouraged and helped Edward Reid to join the order it was not to Italy but to Ireland that he sent him for novitiate.

Nothing more was heard of restoring the order in England after Pacifico Neno's letter to Kelly until 1898 when suddenly out of the blue the question was put directly to the Irish provincial, John Furlong, by Thomas Rodriquez, the general. On July 4 he wrote him a letter in which he asked him for his opinion and that of his definitory with regard to the erection of an English province. The provincial and definitory replied on July 12 that they were not opposed to the idea, but that it was impractical, because there were only two houses in England, Hoxton and Hythe. Moreover, since a gentleman, Mr Robert Banks Lavery, had promised to finance the erection of a third house, this should be done before any further steps were taken towards restoring the English province. The provincial later spoke to the priors of Hoxton and Hythe and to Mr Lavery. All agreed that the dismemberment of the Irish province should be deferred. Subsequently the provincial, accompanied by Fr Kelly, approached the archbishop of Westminster for the grant of a second foundation. When this was refused, the provincial, accompanied by the prior of Hythe, Richard A. O'Gorman, waited on the bishop of Southwark with a similar request. The answer again was in the negative.

In the meantime, the general dropped a bombshell by separating Hoxton and Hythe from the Irish province and appointing Kelly as commissary general, thus restoring at one fell swoop the old English province. The Irish provincial and his definitory, to say the least, were stunned. The villain of the piece in their eyes was the assistant general, Maurice M. Ryan, whom they castigated in no uncertain terms in a letter of 1 September 1898 to the general, who took umbrage at the contents and tone of the letter[74]. The upshot was that on 27 April 1899 the general suspended the provincial and his definitory. They appealed against the decree but in vain. Eventually peace was restored. Kelly was relieved of the office of commissary general and the re-erection of the English province was voided. In retrospect, it is obvious that whatever the rights and wrongs of the matter, the creation, for this is what it amounted to, of an English province in 1898 was both unrealistic and

---

74. Maurice Ryan was from Glynn, county Wexford. He was elected assistant general for the fourth assistancy in 1895, but lived at St Patrick's not at S. Monica. After relinquishing office he was appointed to John's Lane, Dublin, in 1903.

premature[75].

The foundation of Austin Friars, Hythe, has been mentioned in passing. If one takes as the date of foundation the rescript granted by the Holy See, through the Congregation of Propaganda Fide, the priory was founded on 30 October 1891. Rather appropriately the first prior and rector of the parish, was himself an English friar, Edward A. Selley, but it was his immediate successor, Richard A. O'Gorman of New Ross, county Wexford, who secured the present site and saw to the building of the church which was solemnly opened by the bishop of Southwark, John Butt, on 6 August 1894. The first centenary of the foundation was fittingly celebrated last year (1991)[76].

A gap of twenty-seven years yawned between the foundation of Hoxton and that of Hythe. It was a little less than half of that when the third post-Reformation foundation was made. This was at Hammersmith, in west London - one of the oldest and most historic Catholic districts of the city. It was because of the deep regard in which the then archbishop, Francis Cardinal Bourne, held Michael Kelly of Hoxton, that permission for the foundation was granted. The parish assigned to the care of the order was originally centred on west Kensington, and was taken possession of at Easter 1903 by Patrick Raleigh and John A. Condon. They lived at 71 Comeragh Road in a house that also served as a chapel. The boundary of the new parish was subsequently readjusted, and the parish itself was centred on Fulham Palace Road. A site was secured by Raleigh in September 1905, and a temporary church was built and opened exactly twelve months later. When Raleigh was appointed prior of St Patrick's, Rome, in 1911, the first English-born prior of an English Augustinian foundation since the Reformation, Edward Dominic Reid, succeeded him. He was, as we have seen, a product of Fr Kelly's mission at Hoxton.

By then the community which now consisted of Reid, William O'Sullivan (first prior of Hoxton) and Bartholomew Bowen, was living at 9 Palliser Road, Barons Court, while a new priory, the present one, was being built. It was ready for occupation by 26 August 1914. The foundation stone of the present church was laid on 25 March 1915 by Cardinal Bourne. Reid did not live to see the completion of his undertaking. He died prematurely of cancer on 6 June 1916. His successor was Edward A. Foran[77]. A man who combined in himself literary and artistic gifts with a deep interest in the history of the order, especially the English province, he saw to the completion and beautifying of the new church of St Augustine. It was to have been ready for the official dedication on August 28, but it was not until October 14 that it was solemnly blessed and dedicated by the cardinal archbishop of Westminster.

A totally new initiative by Augustinian standards was launched under the auspices of the Irish province at St Augustine's, Hammersmith, in 1967. It was directed to helping Irish people with social needs and problems in the Hammersmith area, but this was not and could not be divorced from pastoral considerations. The work had extremely humble beginnings in a basement room actually of the priory on Fulham Palace Road. But from those early, tentative beginnings, the work has expanded and the rewards in terms of christian social welfare have exceeded all expectations. The extent of the spiritual achievement must remain of its nature beyond analytical assessment.

It is good to recall that the founder of what was originally called the Irish Welfare Bureau, Brian Lawlor, at the end of his nineteen years as director, spoke in his final report of the

---

75. There is a printed copy of the unfortunate contretemps between the Irish province in the person of the provincial with his definitory and the prior general of the order in IAPA. For the inside story of the project to restore the English province, including a transcript of the dramatic letter, otherwise unknown to exist, of the prior general, dated 24 June 1898, to Mr. Lavery, see the contemporary account by R.A. O'Gorman, the instigator of the project, in his 'Records of the Mission of the Virgin Mother of Good Counsel, Hythe, Kent' (Archives of the English Province), pp 32-53 *bis*.

76. It is unnecessary to trace even in broad outline the history of the foundation, thanks to Michael A. Roche whose *The Austin Friars in Hythe 1891-1991* was published by SBS Publishing, Hythe, 1991.

77. Like his fellow Wexfordian, Richard A. O'Gorman, under whom he had served in Hythe, Fr Foran acquired his parochial pastoral experience at Hoxton as assistant to Michael Kelly. There is a well deserved tribute to Foran in T.C. Butler, *Near restful waters - the Augustinians in Co. Wexford* (Dublin, n.d.), pp 134-5.

'tremendous debt of gratitude . . . due to my Augustinian brethren for their tolerance and support over the years'. On 3 January 1986 he was succeeded by his confrère, Jim Kiely, as director, and he has more than maintained since then the excellent tradition inherited by him; indeed he has reached new heights, no longer as director of the Hammersmith apostolate, but by choice of the Irish hierarchy that of head of the Irish chaplaincy in London.

What may be called the turning point that led eventually to the formal erection of the Anglo-Scottish province in 1977 was the year 1950, sandwiched as it was between two highly significant events, the one in 1948, the other in 1953. The year 1948 marked the return of the order to Scotland. Then in 1953 the motherhouse of the English and thus too of the Irish and ultimately of all the English-speaking provinces of the order, Clare Priory, Suffolk, was acquired and repossessed for the first time since 1538.

There was talk in Dublin at provincial level in 1871 of starting a mission in Glasgow, but nothing came of it[78]. It was not until 1948 that serious thought was given to making a foundation in Scotland. The idea was the brainchild of the coadjutor bishop of Dunkeld, James Donald Scanlan. He had spent many years in Hammersmith and there got to know the friars and formed a close friendship with the community at St Augustine's. Back in his native Scotland, having been appointed coadjutor to Bishop John Toner of Dunkeld, he wrote with the warm approval of the diocesan to the Irish provincial, Michael Connolly, about the possibility of Augustinians coming to work in the diocese. The provincial, to his undying credit, went over to Dundee early that same year, 1948. He discussed the matter both with Bishop Toner and his coadjutor James Scanlan.

The upshot was that Connolly decided to send some friars to Dundee. They were assigned to different parishes, pending the formal handing over to the order of the parish of SS Peter and Paul in the city. Thus Thomas L. McCabe was in Perth by 1 March 1948; Charles R. Hussey was actually stationed in Dundee at SS Peter and Paul itself by April; and John Berchmans ("Berki") Power acted as assistant to Canon Quinn at St Mary's, Dundee. Then at the provincial chapter on July 12 the province formally accepted as a mission SS Peter and Paul, Dundee. Berki Power was appointed rector of the mission. The community consisted of himself, Thomas A. Daly, Tom McCabe and Charlie Hussey. The parish of SS Peter and Paul having been designated by the diocese as a foundation of the order, Rome granted the necessary rescript on 18 January 1950[79].

Dundee, which welcomed the Augustinians back to Scotland in 1948.

Berki Power had suffered a bout of malaria in 1949 and had to return to Ireland. He was advised by his doctor not to go back to Dundee, but he returned for duty shortly after June 18. His health did not improve, and he had to return to Ireland again. Consequently, Tom Daly was appointed vicar-prior on 3 March 1950. As such, he was the first Augustinian prior in Scotland

78. IAPA, vol. 71, doc. 13.
79. Thomas David Tuomey most kindly shared with me his recollections of the beginnings of the order in Dundee. He was himself one of the earliest friars to serve there from 26 November 1948.

since the Reformation. Since Bishop Scanlan wanted an Augustinian full-time in Cupar, Fife, the friars took it in turn to cross the Tay and serve the local Catholic community. This was not an entirely satisfactory arrangement. So Tom McCabe generously agreed in 1950 to reside there. He lived in a small house owned by the bishop. He loved the place and did such marvellous work there as pastor that the Catholic faith was saved in Cupar[80]. Its beautiful church which he built is a lasting memorial to him.

In Dundee itself the parish of SS Peter and Paul thrived, though not without some community difficulties. One proof of the success of the Augustinian administration of the parish is that it was able to create out of SS Peter and Paul two new parishes. The success may also be evaluated perhaps in another way, namely in terms of Augustinian vocations. In this respect Dundee leads the other three pre-1950 foundations, Hoxton, Hythe and Hammersmith but only by a short head[81].

Easily the most momentous contribution to the restoration of the order in England by the Irish province was made in the first place by John Charles Dullea after his election as provincial in 1948. It was his desire, and his alone, that led to the opening of the first school of the Augustinian order in England. He was a man of great faith, and if ever an undertaking required faith this was it. To enter the field of secondary education in England without any first-hand knowledge of the system, without anyone qualified academically to act as headmaster of an English boarding and day grammar school, and without adequate resources in personnel and money, was to court certain disaster.

It might have been said to Fr Dullea what was said by a most respected and cultured friar in a telegram to James Colman O'Driscoll in April 1935 when he was on the point of publishing the first issue of *Good Counsel* : "Stop publication. Are you mad"! [82] There was all the more justification for saying the same to Dullea in 1949, if the word 'school' were substituted for 'publication'. Yet the province, certainly the more forward looking members, it would appear, greeted his initiative with something little short of enthusiasm.

The man chosen by Dullea to further the enterprise was the secretary of the province and one of its most gifted personalities, the aforementioned James Colman O'Driscoll. The choice of him was an inspired gamble. One may confidently wager that there would never have been an Austin Friars school in England only for him. In his diary of the events of the crucial years 1949-50 he recorded that at the end of February 1949, just as he was leaving Dublin to give a series of missions in England, the provincial, John Dullea, said to him: 'Perhaps during your work you may find a suitable opening for an Augustinian college somewhere in England'[83]. It was asking more than anyone could promise.

O'Driscoll's second mission was at Kendal, a parish in the diocese of Lancaster and gateway to Lake Windermere in Cumbria. In the course of conversation on the first night of his arrival, he mentioned to the parish priest, Canon Arthur Gracey, how anxious the order was to revive the English province, and felt that this could best be achieved by starting a grammar school. The canon cocked his ears because there was no Catholic grammar school for boys in the important city of Carlisle. The canon assured O'Driscoll that the Augustinian order would be most welcome to open a school in the diocese and offered to introduce him to a friend, Fr Patrick Begley, parish priest of St Margaret's, Carlisle. They met and from that moment the hunt for a suitable site was on.

It was May before one was found, "Home Acres" on the Brampton Road. After some delay

---

80. During a visit to Cupar in 1970 the parish priest, Fr James Malaney, said to me that the faith would have been lost in Cupar only for the Augustinians.

81. If we exclude aspirants or professed who did not persevere, Dundee has given two to the order (there are three more in formation), Hoxton, Hythe, and Hammersmith one each.

82. So Fr O'Driscoll related to me many years ago.

83. Cf. O'Driscoll's Carlisle diary p. 1. The diary unfortunately ends with 1 January 1951. The chronicle, for such it really is, was not resumed until September 1965. It is preserved in the Anglo-Scottish Provincial Archives with other records of Austin Friars, Carlisle.

an agreement to purchase the building was made with the trustees of the property on July 20. That very same day in 1949 the city corporation placed a compulsory purchase on the property. This had to be confirmed. Matters dragged on and by October the order was thinking of acquiring property in Somerset for a school. A public inquiry was ordered by the Ministry of Education into the rights and wrongs of the Augustinian order *v.* Carlisle corporation[84]. The public inquiry at Carlisle was held on 12-14 April 1950. The result was that the compulsory purchase order on "Home Acres" was upheld by the Ministry of Education.

Contrary to initial and bitter disappointment, this proved to be a blessing in disguise, because a far better and bigger property on the finest site in the whole of Carlisle, one overlooking the city and its surrounds, became available. Before this transpired there was a suggestion in June that the order might buy Grosvenor College, Eden Mount. This property was found to be unsuitable. The infinitely better property was owned by the Poor Sisters of Nazareth. Their mother general wanted to dispose of their imposing property. The bishop of Lancaster, Thomas Edward Flynn,

Austin Friars School, Carlisle. (Photo: Phototronics)

paved the way for the acquisition by the Irish province of the sisters' property. They were all the more willing that the friars should have it, not least because of its beautiful chapel, which naturally they did not want to see defaced. The bishop unhesitatingly granted the order a foundation at St Ann's Hall where the sisters had their convent. His lordship also gave the order the administration of a parish to be constituted at Stanwix of which the school would be initially the centre. O'Driscoll was appointed prior of the priory school on September 12, and John Laurence Cotter, was named parish priest designate of Stanwix[85].

They took possession on Thursday, 21 September 1950, of Nazareth House, soon to be called Austin Friars. The formalities of the sale and purchase between the sisters and the friars were completed later on the 30th. O'Driscoll in his diary wrote opposite the 29th: 'This is a <u>RED LETTER</u> day; but we cannot find red ink'! The occasion was a visit by the prior general, Joseph A. Hickey, who was accompanied by John Dullea, the provincial. The rescript for the foundation was granted by the Holy See on October 3. Eventually the school was formally blessed and opened on 5 July 1951. The occasion was graced by the presence of the bishop, the general, the provincial, the mayor of Carlisle and the vicar-provincial, James Augustine Doyle[86]. Incidentally, on 9

---

84. Before this was held the province was vaguely interested by 20 October 1949 in acquiring one of two properties for a school in Somerset, namely "The Grove", Wrington, or Bindon House, Langford Budville, Wellington. This latter was owned by the Augustinians of the Assumption. In addition there was some interest in buying a Jesuit place, Wardour Castle, Tisbury, Wiltshire. By 22 January 1950 the order was asked if it would open a school at Brighton as the Xaverian Brothers were giving up theirs which was a day school.

85. Before the present parish church was built and dedicated to St Augustine in 1979 a temporary church was erected by Michael Damian Curley who succeeded Fr Cotter as parish priest. He also acquired as a residence the 'mansion' felicitiously nicknamed the 'Taj Mahal'! This has since been demolished and replaced by a new presbytery at no.10 Waverley Road.

86. At the 1948 provincial chapter it was decided to make the houses in England and Scotland into a vicariate of the Irish province under a vicar provincial with two councillors. James A. Doyle was appointed vicar provincial, with James F. Larkin and Richard A. Bell as councillors. The following faculties were granted to the vicar provincial: to arrange 'supplies' for absent friars; to grant leave of absence for a week; and to accept requests for retreats and appoint friars to give them.

Austin Friars School, Carlisle: Pupils relax in the leafy grounds. (Photo: Phototronics)

September, shortly after the blessing of Austin Friars School, the houses in England and that in Scotland were made into a vice-province, of which John Augustine Roche was appointed commissary provincial, a title which was replaced by that of vice-provincial at the special general chapter of 1968 when the new constitutions were devised.

Only a full length study could do justice to the history of Austin Friars school. It is an absorbing story, especially if all is revealed! The school opened on 18 September 1951 with some 80 boys on the rolls, 50 being boarders and day boys in the secondary department, and the rest in the preparatory school. It needs to be recorded that an absolutely crucial role in getting the actual school off to a start was played by a secular priest, Louis Heston. He had been unwell and his bishop, John Carmel Heenan, then at Leeds (later he would crown his career as a bishop as cardinal archbishop of Westminster), asked O'Driscoll, a great friend of his, if he could find a place for Louis on the teaching staff. This was done, and the act of kindness was more than repaid by Heston.

In 1955 the preparatory school was transferred to Ellingham, Northumberland, where the first term began in September 1956. The school was deemed unnecessary by 1962 and was therefore closed. Meanwhile the grammar school at Carlisle, although it did not prosper financially as an independent school (in 1953, for example, the income only covered nine months of the year), it increased its enrolment to 233 in 1961. Ten years later there were 292 students, 167 being boarders and 125 day pupils. The school has won high praise from parents, government inspectors, headmasters of prestigious schools, such as Ampleforth, but its greatest benefit to the church and particularly to the order is the many vocations it has produced.

If the foundation of Austin Friars school, Carlisle, was momentous for the restoration of the English province, the return to Clare Priory, the first Augustinian house ever established in the British Isles, complemented, and in a sense crowned, the establishment of a grammar school of the order in Carlisle just three years earlier. If the Austin Friars school was a leap forward on a road hitherto uncharted by the Irish province with regard to England, the acquisition of Clare Priory marked a return to the roots of the order in England and ultimately in Ireland itself. The last lay owners of Clare, Mrs Stella Mary Augusta de Fonblanque, her sister Iris Olivia Helena Johnston, and Michael Kinchin

Austin Friars School, Carlisle: Chapel. (Photo: Phototronics)

Smith offered to sell - actually it meant selling back - to the order its own property, St Mary's Priory, which had been sequestered by Henry VIII on 29 November 1538. It had been founded in 1248 by the Tuscan Friars Hermits of St Augustine who had expanded beyond the borders of Italy into Gascony which was then an English overseas possession.

On 10 October 1952 the provincial, Michael Connolly, together with the commissary provincial, John A. Roche, and members of the definitory, visited Clare[87]. It was decided to buy the property. The bishop of the diocese of Northampton, Leo Parker, and the local clergy were delighted to hear that the Austin Friars were returning to their original home in England. The sale of the property was completed early the following year, 1953, and a community, with Joseph Curtis as prior, was appointed - the first since 1538. The property needed a good deal of refurbishment before the first public Mass since the Reformation could be fittingly celebrated. This took place on 10 May 1953, in what was originally the medieval friars' refectory. The definitory decided to establish a professorium in the priory, and on September 3 six students, one being the late Joseph Condon from Brisbane, Australia, arrived to begin the study of philosophy.

Clare Priory, Suffolk. The first Augustinian foundation in the English speaking world. Established in 1248 it was suppressed by King Henry VIII. It was acquired again by the Order in 1953 and is now a retreat centre.

The ground floor of the medieval infirmary was re-designed to serve as a public church; it was opened and blessed, followed by Mass on 29 June 1954. The philosophy students, having completed their course, moved out, and in September 1955 Clare became the novitiate for the Anglo-Scottish vice-province. The first postulants were Robert Hickey from Dublin, Garth Marshallsay from Luton, and George Stibbles from Dundee. They received the white habit on October 11, the first aspirants to the order to receive it in England since the Reformation.

Garth and George both came to Clare from Austin Friars, Carlisle, with which Robert also had a connection. The first professions at Clare in over 400 years took place on the site of the medieval church on 12 October 1956 when Robert and George made their first vows as members of the vice-province of England and Scotland[88]. The priory continued to be part of the parish of Sudbury until November 1959 when it was made a parish in its own right, taking in the growing town of Haverhill, now a separate parish. It was entirely appropriate that the first chapter of the vice-province should have been held at Clare Priory, the motherhouse of the order in England and therefore in Ireland, and through Ireland in the English-speaking provinces of the order. The vice-provincial chapter opened on Wednesday, 7 January 1970. Bishop Charles Alexander Grant of

---

87. This and other events concerning the return of the friars to the priory are carefully recorded in the house diary which is preserved in the archives of the province.

88. Garth Marshallsay did not complete the year. He left in May and was later tragically killed in an air disaster. The news was received with very great sadness at Clare and Carlisle; Garth was held in high regard by both communities.

Northampton came on the Friday. He concelebrated Mass with the capitulars and gave the homily. This chapter was in every sense historic, not only because of its setting and attendance, but perhaps most significantly of all in its being the first chapter of the order to be held in England since 1532[89].

With the re-foundation of Clare, preceded by the opening of the school at Carlisle, the stage was set for the formal reconstitution of the pre-Reformation English province. But it would be some years yet before this became a practical proposition. After a lull of some years the expansion of the order in England, and later in Scotland, gathered momentum. First in the line of developments was the taking over of a preparatory school, Bishops Court, Freshfield near Liverpool, in 1967. The headmaster, Henry Gordon Burroughs, some of whose pupils had gained entry into Austin Friars, was anxious that the friars would undertake to buy and staff Bishops Court. The friars thought well of the school and saw it as a replacement for Ellingham from which they had withdrawn five years earlier. Agreement with Mr Burroughs was reached as regard the sale of Bishops Court, a charming property in a select residential area.

Finbarr James Murphy of Austin Friars, Carlisle, arrived at Bishops Court on July 14 to prepare the way for the commencement of the 1967-8 term. In this he was assisted by Michael Alypius Roche also of Austin Friars. James O. Hartnett was appointed prior and Fr Murphy headmaster. The enrolment under new management consisted of 127 boys of whom 70 were boarders and 57 were day boys. The permission of the local ordinary, the archbishop of Liverpool, George Andrew Beck, an Augustinian of the Assumption, had been obtained in advance. He was a good friend of the order, and warmly welcomed the decision of the province to take over the school, as the provincial, Thomas K. O'Mahoney, informed the parents in a letter of May 30. At the request of the provincial, His Grace entrusted the order with a new parish at Woodvale in the proximity of the school, and appointed Robert R. Dunn as parish priest. The church was officially opened and blessed by the archbishop on 18 February 1971 and dedicated to St John Stone, martyr, who had been canonized on 25 October of the previous year. Sadly the school, founded in 1892, had to be closed in 1986, simply because of insufficient numbers of pupils[90]. The parish at Woodvale continued to be served by the friars, and in 1981 their residence was raised to the status of a priory. James Pius Maguire, the then parish priest, was appointed prior.

The remainder of the story leading finally to the re-erection of the Anglo-Scottish province in 1977 can be briefly told. By 1970 the need to expand the apostolate of the friars was keenly felt. Approaches were made to various bishops. All were most willing to have Augustinians working in their dioceses, but none but two felt able to grant a parish. One of the exceptions was Bishop Grant of Northampton. He deeply appreciated the Augustinians' commitment to Clare; Great Yarmount had originally been a Jesuit parish and he felt it should revert to administration by a religious order. A contract was signed on behalf of the diocese and the order in 1972, and St Mary's Priory was canonically erected on August 14. John G. Hyland was appointed prior and parish priest.

The other exception was George Patrick Dwyer, archbishop of Birmingham. An approach was made to him in writing on 24 February 1972, to which he gave an encouraging reply, but no firm commitment. It was something adventitious that led him later to offer the order the choice of either of two parishes, Harborne or Saltley. The Passionist provincial informed him that his order had decided to withdraw from its 1870 foundation at Harborne, whereupon the archbishop invited our vice-provincial to come and have lunch with him on 7 May 1973. It was then that he made the offer of either Harborne or Saltley. As Harborne had been from its foundation a religious order

---

89. It was held at Leicester. His lordship came on day 3 of the chapter and concelebrated Mass with the capitulars and gave the homily. Two outside speakers addressed the chapter members by invitation. They were Mgr Michael Buckley and Fr Michael Richards, both well known public figures. [At this chapter the outgoing Vice-Provincial, Michael Benedict Hackett, was again elected - Ed.]

90. The last to leave was, fittingly enough, the headmaster, James Murphy, who signed out at 5.20 p.m. on 28 January 1987 and locked for good the main door after him.

parish he felt that it would be appropriate if another religious order were to continue the tradition. The vice-provincial and two of his councillors visited Saltley first and then Harborne. They had no doubt that Harborne was the more suitable of the two parishes on offer to the order. The archbishop agreed, and a contract between the diocese and the order was signed, following the erection of St Mary's, Harborne, on October 4 as a priory cum novitiate by the general council of the order. Philip Bernard O'Connor, the new vice-provincial, and his council appointed John Malachy Loughran as prior and parish priest[91].

After the vice-province was raised to the status of a province at the 1977 general chapter, it was thought advantageous if the order had its own house of studies in London where the students could attend Heythrop College, which was linked with London University. Moreover, our two parishes offered a ready-made outlet for the students to gain pastoral experience on home territory. A residence was acquired within our Hammersmith parish at 46 Weltje Road. As it was not large enough, a double house was bought at 17 Dorville Crescent. In 1985 it was constituted priory. Brother Thomas Cyril Counihan was appointed prior, but as this ran counter, unfortunately, to the status of the Augustinian order as a clerical institute according to canon law, the appointment had to be rescinded. The priory ceased to be a student house. It became instead the residence of the provincial, Malachy Loughran, who also assumed the office of prior of the house. Since then it has been designated a guest-house of the order.

A second parish in Scotland was assigned to the care of the order in 1986. It was Our Lady's, Currie, near Edinburgh. Seamus Ahearne was appointed prior and parish priest. The friars serve three more churches in addition to Our Lady's. The churches are St Joseph's, Balerno; St Mary's, Ratho-Saughton; and St Augustine's, Heriot-Watt. Most recently the order was entrusted by the archbishop of Birmingham, Maurice Couve de Murville, with the administration of the parish of the Sacred Heart at Hanley, Stoke-on Trent, Michael Aidan Power becoming the parish priest, assisted by Sean Clement Ahern.

A total of fourteen houses is a far cry from the one foundation which the order had in 1864 at Hoxton. It is a simple fact that none of this build-up of the order in England and Scotland could have been or would have been achieved only for the Irish province. This applies with particular force to the elevation by the general chapter of the order on 8 September 1977 of the Vice-Province of England and Scotland to the status of a province, of which Bernard O'Connor became the first provincial since the Reformation. With that, the desire and efforts of the Irish province down the centuries to restore the order in England and Scotland were finally crowned with success.

The newly reconstituted Anglo-Scottish province in proof of its vitality spread its wings in a remarkable joint-venture with the Australian province in the Far East in 1985. Two English friars of the province, Kevin Lowry and Paul Graham, arrived in Seoul on September 4. Their mission was to work in conjunction with Michael Sullivan and Brian Buckley of the Australian province to lead the way in establishing the order in Korea. Once again it was the restoration by the Irish province of the order in England and Scotland, as well as its foundation of the Australian province, that made this courageous and exciting new venture ultimately possible.

---

91. In 1980 Archbishop Dwyer placed the adjacent parish of Our Lady of Fatima at Quinton under the care of St. Mary's, Harborne. Malachy Loughran thereby acquired a dual role as parish priest. Quinton now has its own resident priest-in-charge, Joseph Benedict Beary, at 23 Upper Meadow Road, assisted by Fionan Columba Heffernan.

THE IRISH AUGUSTINIANS IN NORTH AMERICA, 1794-1992

The Irish Augustinian Mission to the United States of America

Joseph C. Schnaubelt, O.S.A.

THE IRISH AUGUSTINIANS IN NORTH AMERICA, 1794-1992

*The Irish Augustinian Mission to the United States of America**

Joseph C. Schnaubelt, O.S.A.**

I
THE FOUNDING OF OLD SAINT AUGUSTINE'S CHURCH

Twenty years after the American Declaration of Independence in 1776, the Order of Hermits of Saint Augustine was established in the United States. Less than a decade earlier Bishop John Carroll (1790-1815) had been appointed by Pope Pius VI (1775-1799) to organize the Catholic Church in the United States, with Baltimore (the first center of Catholicism in the English colonies) as his episcopal city. Priests were his greatest need, and he appealed in particular to the bishops of Ireland to send missionaries for his widespread diocese, coterminous with the former thirteen colonies[1].

Among the first to heed this apostolic call was the zealous Irish Augustinian, Fr John Rosseter (1751-1812)[2], who landed in Boston in 1794, and quickly took up residence outside Wilmington, Delaware, at the plantation-mission of Coffee Run. Rosseter's positive reports to his Irish brethren crystallized their plan to establish a branch of the Augustinians in the United States. The prior of the Dublin convent, Fr Matthew Thomas Carr (1755-1820)[3], a mature and experienced priest who had been trained in France and had labored for seventeen years in Ireland, volunteered to make the new foundation. He arrived in Philadelphia in the spring of 1796. Together Carr and Rosseter informed Bishop Carroll of the plan to establish the Order of Saint Augustine in North America. The bishop enthusiastically agreed and readily acceded to their desire to make the first settlement in Philadelphia, then the largest city and chief seaport of the newly emerging country. Accordingly, on 12 June 1796, ground was purchased on Fourth Street near Vine, and the cornerstone of Saint Augustine's Church was set in place on 4 September of the same year[4].

Meanwhile in Rome, on 27 August 1796, the Augustinian general and his council had erected a new American province under the title of Our Mother of Good Counsel. Matthew Carr was designated prior of the Philadelphia foundation and commissary general of all Augustinians in the United States. He was also empowered to open other missions and to enroll the laity in the Augustinian archconfraternities[5].

On 26 August 1799, Carr was appointed Bishop Carroll's vicar general for Pennsylvania east of the Susquehanna River and for New York. The care of the congregation of Saint Mary's on

---

*. Father Arthur J. Ennis, O.S.A., is the principal authority on the history of the Augustinians in the United States. He has submitted the first volume of a two volume work on this subject for publication, but it has not yet gone to press. [Edd. note. Since this chapter was submitted, Fr Arthur J. Ennis died at Villanova, 27 March 1994. The first volume of his work, *No Easy Road. The Early Years of the Augustinians in the United States 1796-1874,* was published in 1993].
**. The name of the author's mother is Margaret Mary McIntire Schnaubelt.
1. Thomas F. Roland, O.S.A., *The Order of Saint Augustine in the United States of America, 1796-1946* (Villanova, PA: Villanova College, 1947), p.3.
2. Arthur J. Ennis, O.S.A., 'John Rosseter 1751-1812', in John E. Rotelle, O.S.A., ed., *Noteworthy Augustinians, Province of Saint Thomas of Villanova,* Vol.II of *Men of Heart* (Villanova, PA: Augustinian Press, 1986), pp.1-14.
3. Arthur J. Ennis, O.S.A., 'Matthew Carr 1755-1820', in John E. Rotelle, O.S.A., ed., *Pioneering Augustinians, Province of Saint Thomas of Villanova,* Vol. I of *Men of Heart* (Villanova, PA: Augustinian Press, 1983) pp. 9-25.
4. Francis Edward Tourscher, O.S.A., *Old Saint Augustine's in Philadelphia, with Some Records of the Work of the Austin Friars in the United States* (Philadelphia: The Peter Reilly Company, 1937), pp.1-16; Roland, cit., pp 3-4.
5. Tourscher, cit., p.41; Roland, cit., p.4.

Matthew Thomas Carr, O.S.A.
(1755-1820)
Commissary General of the American
Province (1797-1820)

Fourth Street in Philadelphia also was mostly in his hands. He was greatly assisted at Saint Mary's by his confrère, John Rosseter, who moved in from the country. Later another of their brethren, Fr George Staunton (1768-1815), who arrived from Ireland in July 1800, was added to the staff. But he returned to Europe in 1804[6].

The new Church of Saint Augustine took shape slowly, because funds were scarce in those times. Many prominent leaders in the city, both Catholic and other, were on a list of contributors that included President George Washington, "Father of His Country", and Commodore John Barry, "Father of the American Navy". Some money was raised by a lottery authorized by the Pennsylvania Legislature, but not nearly so much as was needed. Nevertheless, Saint Augustine's was blessed and opened for divine worship on 7 June 1801[7].

Carr and Rosseter took title to this first property in their own names. Later as superior, Carr made acquisitions under his own name alone. But this device to evade the problems of trusteeism was superseded when the Augustinians, on the advice of Bishop Carroll, were registered on 10 November 1804 under the title of the Corporation of Brothers Hermits of Saint Augustine. Among the first members, and one whose arrival in Philadelphia had made the project feasible, was Fr Michael Hurley (1780-1837)[8], the secretary of the new body[9].

Born in Ireland, Michael Hurley was the first aspirant to the priesthood from the American province. He had been sent from Philadelphia to Italy by Matthew Carr in 1797, when seventeen years old, and had recently returned, after his ordination in Rome in 1803. Two years later, Bishop Carroll transferred Hurley at his own request to Saint Peter's in New York, where he became the friend and spiritual advisor of Saint Elizabeth Ann Bayley Seton (1774-1821). With few regrets except for his separation from Elizabeth Seton and her sister Cecilia, Hurley returned to Philadelphia in 1807[10].

In 1811, one year before the death of the pioneer, John Rosseter, and nine years before the death of Matthew Carr, the Augustinians at Saint Augustine's tried another venture. They opened a school on Crown Street, Philadelphia, known as Saint Augustine's Academy. It was closed, however, shortly after 19 June 1815, probably for want of money in the aftermath of the War of 1812 - there was no apparent lack of good will. Carr also made an initial literary effort in 1812 when he edited a manual entitled *The Spiritual Mirror* for the Cincture Society which he had established[11].

On 29 September 1820, Matthew Carr died at Saint Augustine's, the first and only foundation he had been able to make. He was buried in the garden cemetery attached to the church where his tomb can still be seen. At this juncture, only Michael Hurley was left to continue the administration of the province as commissary general, the province, for the moment, consisting solely of himself. There were indeed two other Augustinian priests in the country, Fr Philip Lariscy (1782-1824) and Fr Robert Browne (1770-1839)[12], but they were working independently[13].

---

6.   Tourscher, cit., pp 12, 19, 30; Roland, cit., p.4.
7.   Tourscher, cit., pp 4-15, 20, 26; Roland, cit., p.4.
8.   John J. Gavigan, O.S.A., 'Michael Hurley c. 1780-1837', in Rotelle, cit.(n.3), pp 27-44.
9.   Tourscher, cit., p.29; Roland, cit., p.5.
10. Tourscher, cit., p.43; Roland, cit., p.5.
11. Tourscher, cit., pp 52-60; Roland, cit., p.6.
12. John E. Rotelle, O.S.A., 'Robert Browne c.1770-1839', in Rotelle, cit.(n.2), pp. 15-39.
13. Tourscher, cit., pp 5, 44-45, 61, 173; Roland, cit., p.6.

Hurley's first years in charge of Saint Augustine's were the Times-of the "Hogan Schism", an abortive movement instigated by a renegade priest. The ordinary of Philadelphia, Bishop Henry Conwell (1820-1842), found it necessary to excommunicate the schismatic, because he proposed the founding of an "American Catholic Church". Throughout this stormy controversy, especially in the attempted compromise which recognized the spiritual powers of Bishop Conwell and the temporal concerns of the trustees at Saint Mary's Church, Michael Hurley played a major role[14].

For several years Michael Hurley had to rely on transient priests to assist him at Saint Augustine's. But, finally, in 1828, two of his Irish brethren, Fr William C. O'Donnell (†1832) and Fr Nicholas O'Donnell (1802-1863)[15], came to join the province in the United States. Their arrival marked the beginning of an era of progress. The church was completed and embellished. The new church tower was fitted with the clock and bell that had been removed from the State House; and ground was purchased for a second cemetery. When an outbreak of cholera struck Philadelphia in 1832, Hurley helped bring in the Sisters of Charity to nurse the sick. He even went so far as to convert his own rectory and parish school into a hospital for the term of the deadly epidemic[16].

One of the new arrivals, Nicholas O'Donnell, flourished, and shortly became the first editor of *The Catholic Herald*, published in Philadelphia from January 1833 - without a doubt the outstanding achievement of the Church in Philadelphia in the 1830's. But the health of his companion, William O'Donnell, failed. William then returned to Ireland, where he died in December 1832[17].

Michael Hurley, O.S.A. (1780-1837)
Commissary General of the American Province (1822-1837)

Nicholas O'Donnell's cousin, James O'Donnell (1806-1861)[18], was brought over from Ireland to Philadelphia, where he began his novitiate at Saint Augustine's on New Year's Day 1832, making the first Augustinian profession of vows in the United States on the same day of the following year. He later studied theology under Bishop Francis Patrick Kenrick (1830-1863) as one of the first students of the Philadelphia Seminary. He was ordained to the priesthood on 13 January 1837, the first Augustinian to be admitted to orders in the United States[19].

When Michael Hurley died on 14 May 1837, Nicholas O'Donnell became pastor of Saint Augustine's parish and president of its board of trustees. Coming from his temporary post in Salinas, New York, to attend Michael Hurley's funeral in Philadelphia, James O'Donnell was elected to fill the vacancy on the board[20]. Realizing the need for vocations, Nicholas O'Donnell's first act as commissary general was to dispatch young William Harnett (1820-1875)[21] to Rome to study for the religious priesthood. Harnett, a native of Saint Augustine's Parish, had already been a postulant at the parish for some months. He would become the first native-born American Augustinian. Moreover, Harnett had the great privilege of making his novitiate in Genazzano, the shrine of Our Mother of Good Counsel, where Blessed Stephen Bellesini (1774-1840) was pastor. There the neophyte learned the principles of Augustinian religious life which he in turn would

14. Francis E. Tourscher, O.S.A., *The Hogan Schism and Trustee Troubles in St. Mary's Church Philadelphia, 1820-1829* (Philadelphia: The Peter Reilly Company, 1930), pp 5, 17, 41, 69, 167; Roland, cit., p.7.
15. John P. Pejza, O.S.A., 'Nicholas O'Donnell 1802-1863', in Rotelle, cit. (n.2), pp 41-62.
16. Tourscher, cit.(n.4), pp 81-83; Roland, cit., pp 7-8.
17. Tourscher, cit.(n.4), pp. 62-75; Roland, cit., p.8.
18. Joseph L. Shannon, O.S.A., 'James B. O'Donnell 1806-1861', in Rotelle, cit.(n.3), pp 47-66.
19. Tourscher, cit.(n.4), pp.63-64; Roland, cit., p.8.
20. Tourscher, cit.(n.4), pp 64-66.
21. John P. Pejza, O.S.A., 'William Harnett 1820-1875', in Rotelle, cit.(n.2), pp 75-90.

Old Saint Augustine's Church in Philadelphia before the Burning of 1844.

inculcate as master of novices in his own country[22].

Then, placing James O'Donnell in charge of Saint Augustine's, Nicholas O'Donnell sailed in 1838 for Europe. In Ireland and Rome, he petitioned his brethren to send help to the American mission. The first result of his journey was a response from Fr Thomas Kyle (1797-1869)[23], who arrived in Philadelphia on 9 September of that same year[24]. After his return to the United States, Nicholas O'Donnell wrote to Bishop John Dubois (1764-1842) in New York, requesting a new parish. On 1 July 1839, Bishop Dubois invited the Augustinians to take over Saint Paul's Church, Brooklyn.

Shortly thereafter, both Frs O'Donnell moved to Brooklyn, leaving Thomas Kyle to service Saint Augustine's[25].

The second result of Nicholas O'Donnell's journey was of the utmost importance for the Augustinian mission in the United States. On the other side of the world, just at this time, the Augustinian Daniel O'Connor, Bishop of Madras (1834-1841), India, was sending his Vicar General, Patrick Eugene Moriarty (1805-1875)[26], to Rome to make a report on the diocese to the Holy See. Upon the advice of the prior provincial of Ireland, the prior general appointed Dr Moriarty as commissary general for the American province, where he arrived in Philadelphia in July of 1839. Another Irish Augustinian, Fr John Possidius O'Dwyer (1816-1850)[27], arrived at Philadelphia during the summer of 1840. Dr Moriarty had an unusual gift of eloquence which he manifested on many notable occasions. He stood for the Total Abstinence Movement, and defended the rights of Catholics in general and the Irish immigrants in particular all along the Atlantic seaboard[28].

Like Nicholas O'Donnell, Moriarty realized that new members were needed to ensure the future stability of the American province of Augustinians. Additionally, he perceived that a school or "college" would be an ideal source of vocations for his Order. On 23 March 1843, he wrote to his ex-provincial, Dr Charles Stuart, in Ireland: '. . . the greatest work is yet to be mentioned. I felt deeply the necessity of making an effort to propagate our Order and to secure stability and success, and also that all would be ruin unless we would return to the proper system of religious observance. An opportunity appeared to be offered by Providence. A farm of 200 acres of the best land in Pennsylvania, with a house on it sufficient for a community of 24 persons . . . was offered for sale . . . Here was a chance to employ lay brothers to cultivate the land, whilst the produce would support a religious family retired from missionary trouble and having a Regent of

22. Tourscher, cit.(n.4), p.77; Roland, cit., p.8.
23. Joseph L. Shannon, O.S.A., 'Thomas Kyle 1797-1869', in Rotelle, cit.(n.2), pp 63-72.
24. Tourscher, cit.(n.4), pp 66-67; Roland, cit., pp 8-9.
25. Pejza, cit.(n.15), pp 47-48.
26. Robert J. Welsh, O.S.A., 'Patrick E. Moriarty, 1805-1875, in Rotelle, cit.(n.3), pp 69-85.
27. John E. Rotelle, O.S.A., 'John P. O'Dwyer 1816-1850' in Rotelle, cit.(n.3), pp 87-109.
28. Tourscher, cit.(n.4), p.67; Roland, p.9; Welsh, cit., pp 72-73.

Studies and Master of Novices - Students preparing for the Altar and the Pulpit and in the mean time teaching an Academy of a select number of boys from our Catholic families out of which occasionally we may be supplied with Postulants. In this way a nursery would exist for all future foundations . . . Who could resist the temptation? All was offered by singular chance for $18,000 - and I made the purchase. Where did I get the money? I looked up to heaven'[29].

In 1842, the year before Dr Moriarty's prophetic letter, there were still only five Augustinian priests in the country: Dr Moriarty, commissary general, and Thomas Kyle and John O'Dwyer in Philadelphia, and Nicholas and James O'Donnell in Brooklyn. Some time late in the fall of 1842, or during the early winter of 1843, John O'Dwyer, being in poor health, was sent abroad to recuperate and recruit. With health much improved, he returned in the summer of 1843, bringing with him William Harnett and Fr Francis Ashe (1820-1848), another Irish Augustinian who had completed his studies in Italy[30].

Patrick Eugene Moriarty, O.S.A. (1805-1875)
Commissary General of the American Province (1839-1846; 1850-1858)

II

THE FOUNDING OF VILLANOVA COLLEGE AND ITS EVENTUAL MISSIONS

"Belle Air", an attractive and valuable farm put up for public sale on 14 October 1841, was the private residence of the late John Rudolph for some thirty-five years. Situated in Radnor township, Delaware County (about ten miles west of Philadelphia), Belle Air contained about two hundred acres of high-quality real estate, divided by the Lancaster Turnpike and the Philadelphia/Columbia Railroad. This expansive property included a two-story stone mansion, a two-story kitchen, two barns, a coach house, a farmhouse, a smoke house, a poultry house, a hog house, a double corn crib, and a spring house (there were four large springs on the estate). This premium farmland was divided into fields of convenient size, with an orchard of fine fruit and a woodland of oak and hickory[31].

John Rudolph, the deceased owner of Belle Air, was born in Philadelphia about 1760; served as lieutenant in the Revolutionary War; and was many years in business at Burlington, New Jersey, and in Philadelphia. He was married three times. On 13 October 1806, he made an initial purchase of one hundred acres from Jonathan Miller, of Haverford township, for $10,000. A certain Jesse Horton, carpenter of the neighborhood, was contracted to finish the mansion the former owner had begun. On its completion, Mr Rudolph left Philadelphia for the country and, after a fashion of the day, renamed his new home "Belle Air", in remembrance of his father's native place in Maryland. Three years after her husband's demise on 30 March 1838, the last Mrs Rudolph (Jane Abeel-Lloyd) decided to sell the property[32].

So gracious a country seat did not last long on the market. Its elevated site and beautiful location, its abundance of wood and water, its high state of tillage, and its rich meadow lands, as well as its accessibility from every direction, were advantages more than sufficient to recommend it. It would appear that Fr Thomas Kyle, pastor of Saint Augustine's in Philadelphia, was the first to recognize Belle Air as the appropriate location for a foundation of the Order of Saint Augustine,

29. Provincial Archives, Saint Augustine Friary, Villanova, PA.
30. Tourscher, cit.(n.4), p.76.
31. Thomas C. Middleton, *Historical Sketch of the Augustinian Monastery, College and Mission of St Thomas of Villanova, Delaware County, Pa., during the First Half Century of Their Existence. 1842-1892.* (Villanova, PA: Villanova College, 1893), p.13.
32. Ibid., pp. 9-10.

even though Dr Moriarty claimed that honor for himself in his letter to Dr Stuart - when the potential of the venture was apparent. Hence, on 13 October 1841, the day before the one announced for the public sale, Kyle took it upon himself to purchase this superb tract of land for $18,000 with <u>borrowed</u> money - a seemingly precipitous, but a providential, move, as it turned out[33]. On 5 January 1842, title to Belle Air was granted to the Brothers of the Order of Hermits of Saint Augustine. Shortly after the sale of the farm, the widow Rudolph sold the Augustinian Friars the house furniture and farm utensils for $3,400. In five years' time, the Augustinians would pay off almost all this indebtedness[34].

Although transfer of title to Belle Air was concluded in January 1842, classes at the new "Liberal Arts College" could not begin until September 1843. Nevertheless, the corporate foundation is calculated from 1842. It should be noted moreover that, despite its legitimate title of "college", the institution in its early years served in large measure as a preparatory school[35].

In early spring of 1843, brothers John (Denis) Gallagher (1812-1894)[36] and Jeremiah Ryan were sent from Saint Augustine's to open the house at Belle Air. Ryan, a native of Tipperary, Ireland, and kinsman of the Frs O'Donnell and of the Reverend James Dolan, a diocesan priest of Baltimore, later left the Order. After their return from Europe in the summer of the same year, O'Dwyer and Ashe, together with William Harnett, were directed to form a community with the lay brothers at the new institution. Accordingly, on 28 August, the feast of Saint Augustine, John O'Dwyer first offered Mass in the parlor of the mansion house, then blessed the new monastery, and placed the community under the special patronage of the eminent Augustinian bishop and educator, Thomas of Villanova (1486-1555)[37].

In the early sixteenth century, Thomas of Villanova (in Spanish, "Villanueva") served as prior provincial of the Augustinian provinces of Andalusia and Castile and as Bishop of Valencia. As prior provincial, he sent the first band of Augustinian missionaries to Mexico in 1533 (two years after the apparition of Our Lady of Guadalupe, when the Faith was spreading in the Aztec nation with astonishing rapidity). As Bishop of Valencia - popularly known as the "bishop of charity" - he devoted himself and his income to the care of the poor and the sick and the redemption of captives. He founded colleges for students and, innovatively, for "young women in need". Canonized in 1658, he is one of the glories of the Spanish Church. His charismatic sermons, which influenced Spanish spiritual literature profoundly, are the basis of efforts to have Saint Thomas of Villanova declared "Doctor of the Church". His selection as chief patron of the college was most felicitous, even though it has been suggested that he was initially chosen because he was Thomas Kyle's own patron. The college eventually came to be known simply as Villanova[38].

The three Augustinians (O'Dwyer, Ashe, and Harnett) also formed the nucleus of the first college faculty, which over the first two years included a diocesan priest, the Reverend Florimund Bonduel, and four laymen: E. A. Ansley, John Dalton, Joseph O'Donnell, and a Mr Rogan. Bonduel had been a missionary among the Indians in Michigan for some seven years. Ansley was a convert. Dalton had been associated with the failed Saint Augustine's Academy, and subsequently joined the diocesan priesthood in Virginia. O'Donnell was a graduate of Mt Saint Mary's, and later practiced medicine in Baltimore. Rogan, a very athletic young Irishman, also became a secular priest "out in the West". The first student body of Villanova consisted of thirteen young men, among whom were William J. Turner, Charles F. Kelly, Michael J. Downs, Thomas A. Egan, James Henry Magee, John R. Downing, and three brothers, James P., John S., and Robert P.

33. Shannon, cit.(n.23), pp 64-65.
34. Middleton, cit., p.14.
35. Ibid., p.19.
36. William C. Harkin, O.S.A., 'Lay Brothers John Gallagher, James O'Brien, Owen Maguire, Stanislaus Duffy, Kieran Phelan', in Rotelle, cit.(n.3), pp 115-26.
37. Middleton, cit., pp 15-16.
38. Ibid., pp 16-17; Shannon, cit.(n.23), p.65.

Barr[39].

Tuitions were accepted on 17 September, and classes began the next day. Study carrels were set up in the back of the oratory, over which John Dalton presided as study master. The curriculum included Latin, Greek, English, mathematics, history, and modern languages. At first the former Rudolph mansion housed the entire college. Chapel, classrooms, study hall, dining room, kitchen, and pantry were on the first floor; rooms of the Augustinians and other faculty on the second; and student dormitories in the garrets. Lay brothers were lodged over the kitchen. An increase in the number of students would soon necessitate the demolition of the carriage house and the construction on its site of a new building with a large hall on the first floor which was used as a classroom and study hall during the week and as a chapel on Sundays. Above this hall were additional sleeping quarters for students. Until the erection of the new building in 1844, the students' lavatory was in Rudolph's old wagon shed. On the far side of this shed a long wooden trough was set up to hold basins. The whole arrangement was open in front, and the students had to fetch water from pumps some hundred feet away. Towels, mirrors, and various other items were hung over the trough and against the walls[40].

In the spring of 1844, the first advertisement for Villanova was published in the *Catholic Herald* of Philadelphia:

PROSPECTUS

Saint Thomas of Villanova's College, Pennsylvania - This institution under the direction of clergymen of the order of Saint Augustine, has been established for the purpose of affording the Catholic community a means of giving their children a thorough Catholic education. None but Catholics are received. In accordance with wishes of parents or guardians a classical and scientific, or purely mercantile - education will be given to their children, or the one will be so blended with the other, as to qualify the pupil to embrace any of the learned professions, or to apply himself to business. It is hoped that experience will show that proper attention is paid to the young gentlemen who may be sent to this institution.

The College is situated in the midst of a highly cultivated and salubrious country, close by the Columbia Rail Road, and about eleven miles from Philadelphia. The scholastic year begins in September and terminates in July. No leave of absence is given to any pupil during that time, except at the express request of parents or guardians.

TERMS

For pupils over twelve years $125 per annum, payable half yearly in advance. Under that age $100. Further particulars may be learned on application at Saint Augustine's Church, Philadelphia, or to the Rev. Mr O'Dwyer, president of the College[41].

Everything now pointed to a prosperous future for the plans of the ambitious and active commissary general, Patrick Moriarty, but within half a year the whole project was threatened with collapse. The hatred of the bigoted Nativists, whom Moriarty had dared to confront, focused on him and his works. Bishop Kenrick described the whole terrible event in his diary:

'May the sixth day [1844] - A gathering of Americans, who are known as the *"Native American Party"*, was an occasion for the beginning of strife and a disorderly fight between the Irish and these *Native Americans* in a place called Kensington, not far

39. Middleton, cit., pp 19-21.
40. Ibid., p.21.
41. Ibid., pp 21-22.

from the city.

One American was killed in the fray and one Irishman was wounded. Then some dwellings were looted by the *Americanists*. After night they made a renewed attempt to demolish buildings belonging to the Irish: and set fire to a house which had been the home of some devout women [the Sisters of Charity], proceeding thence to burn the Church [Saint Michael's]: but after the fire was started in the [Sisters'] house the Irish drove them off by force of arm. Two men were killed and many were wounded.

The next day a flag was raised in the city, which bore the legend [untrue indeed] that this [standard of the nation] had been trampled on by the Irish Papists. Then there was a gathering of armed men in Independence Square addressed by two speakers, who, while they pretended to counsel moderation, roused the mad fury of the mob by their words. They proceeded then, about four thousand men in number, to the place of the previous day's fight, threatening death to the Irish. They first demolished the Fire House of an Irish Company of Volunteers. This was the occasion for determined resistance to the action of the mob. A small number, about twenty, among them some non-Catholics, banded together to put down the rule of the mob, to fight for the security of their homes. On the side of the Catholics one man was killed, Joseph Rice. He was betrayed and met his death at the hands of a youth. Twelve, or more, of the *Americanists* [rioters] fell in this fight, and forty were wounded. Later sixty houses, the homes of the Irish were set on fire.

The next day a County official made a search of the homes of the Irish. A [military] guard was stationed there, as renewal of rioting was feared. In the afternoon the priest Laughran gave over the keys of Saint Michael's Church to General Fairlamb, hardly knowing what he did as the mad mob was pressing on. In a short time the church was on fire. The military, as it appears, did not prevent the firing of the church. After night the Church of Saint Augustine was set on fire and burned together with the Library there. The rioters yelled with frenzied applause, when, after a long wait, they saw the Cross falling from its high support.

The mob next moved on to the Cathedral Church of Saint John, designing surely to burn it also: but General Cadwalader, hearing that the Governor of the State [David R. Porter] had arrived in the city, had proclaimed what is called martial law, made the threat that the military would use arms to quiet the mob.

During the days that followed numerous attempts were made to burn the Cathedral Church [Saint John's], also Saint Mary's and Saint Phillip's. It was the design of many to burn every [Catholic] church in the City. Threats were made also against the priests, who, on this account, wore no clerical dress, remained in hiding or went out of the city. Fear and dread paralyzed the [Catholic] community. No one could feel secure. Everyone feared the fire and destruction destined for his own home'[42].

Nothing remained of Saint Augustine's Church but the rear wall of the sanctuary, where among the charred and blackened ruins the symbol of the All-seeing God announced to all who gazed there that THE LORD SEETH[43].

Incidentally, one of the Know-Nothing Nativists who witnessed the burning of Saint Augustine's was Joseph Middleton, a Quaker. Thereafter, discerning the extremes of fanaticism, he turned against the Nativist Movement. Ten years later, on 4 April 1854, he was baptized into the Catholic faith by Fr Michael Domenec, C.M. (1816-1878), subsequently the second Bishop of Pittsburgh. Only fifteen days after this initial baptism, Michael Domenec baptized Lydia Cooke Middleton, Joseph's wife, and six of the Middleton children. The eldest of these was Thomas

42. Tourscher, cit.(n.4), pp 85-88.
43. Roland, cit., p.10.

The Burning of Old Saint Augustine's Church in Philadelphia during the Know-Nothing Riots of 1844.

Cooke Middleton (1842-1923)[44], twelve years old at his baptism. As Fr Middleton, Thomas would figure significantly in Villanova College history[45].

During the Know-Nothing insurrection itself, John O'Dwyer was at the college, Nicholas O'Donnell at Saint Paul's Church (Brooklyn), Thomas Kyle, James O'Donnell, and Francis Ashe at Saint Augustine's (Philadelphia), and Patrick Moriarty down South lecturing and collecting for his church. At the time of the riots, Moriarty was at Charleston, South Carolina. He had left Thomas Kyle in charge of Saint Augustine's. Neither of the two priests who were present in Saint Augustine's rectory the night of the burning, Thomas Kyle and Francis Ashe, have left any record of their experience with the mob beyond the note written in the "Baptismal Record" in Francis Ashe's hand: *"8 May 1844, our elegant church was burned by the Americans"*. An appeal for restraint was made by Bishop Kenrick and printed in the *Catholic Herald*, 16 May 1844. Nevertheless, there was apprehension that the mob would move westward to Villanova and burn the college too[46].

At Villanova deep anxiety prevailed. For weeks after the burning of Saint Augustine's, community and students were kept in a state of continual alarm and panic. On three separate occasions friends in the city warned the college authorities that the college was about to be burned out. But ample precautions were taken for the defense of the property. At night, doors and windows of the lower stories of the monastery were kept heavily barricaded. Lay brothers patrolled the grounds. Younger boys were sent off the premises. Every evening after supper the lads were dispatched in charge of John Dalton to spend the night with the widow Rudolph at her Rosemont mansion on what is now called Lancaster Avenue, about a mile from the college. In the morning, they were marched back to the college for breakfast and class. The weeks from the eighth of May painfully passed until the July commencement brought the first year of Villanova college life to a close[47].

The Augustinians wasted little time weeping over the ruins. Plans to provide the congregation at Saint Augustine's with a temporary chapel were rushed. James O'Donnell went on a collecting tour in the United States and Canada, while Patrick Moriarty and Thomas Kyle embarked for Europe for the same purpose. Kyle sailed to Italy with his nephew, Patrick Augustine

---

44. Joseph C. Schnaubelt, O.S.A., 'Thomas C. Middleton 1842-1923', in Rotelle, cit.(n.2), pp 165-204.

45. Ibid., p.167.

46. Middleton, cit., p.22; Tourscher, cit.(n.4), pp 77, 89.

47. Middleton, cit., pp 22-23.

Stanton (1826-1891)[48], and two brothers, Edward Michael Mullen (1825-1888) and Ambrose Augustine Mullen (1827-1876). These three candidates for the Augustinian priesthood would return to the United States in September 1847[49].

John Possidius O'Dwyer, O.S.A. (1816-1850)
Commissary General of the American Province (1846-1850)

Meanwhile, as long as he had to assist in Philadelphia, Nicholas O'Donnell left the Brooklyn foundation in the care of the local clergy. When it became evident that Moriarty could not return to America as soon as he had planned, the whole burden of administration fell on John O'Dwyer. (John O'Dwyer would be made commissary general in Moriarty's place in 1846.) Consequently, O'Dwyer moved to Saint Augustine's, and Nicholas O'Donnell returned to Brooklyn[50].

Because the Augustinian corporation as owner brought a civil suit against the County and City of Philadelphia for damages caused by a mob which had been aided and abetted by the military, the ruins of Saint Augustine's Church were considered legal evidence and could not be disturbed until a favorable verdict was returned. The litigation tested the value of the incorporation obtained by Carr and Rosseter in 1804. Utimately, the Augustinian corporation was to be awarded $47,433.87[51].

William Harnett was ordained priest by Bishop Kenrick on 21 September 1844. At the beginning of that school year, he and Francis Ashe were still at Villanova, but John O'Dwyer as superior had to reside at Saint Augustine's. Even so, O'Dwyer remained president of the college. In early June, as pastor of Saint Augustine's, he had begun construction of Our Mother of Consolation Chapel alongside the ruined church in Philadelphia. The chapel was opened on Sunday, 27 October 1844. At the same time, as president of Villanova, he had started the new school building on the site of Rudolph's carriage house. The chapel on its lower floor was blessed and dedicated to Saint Thomas of Villanova by Bishop Kenrick on Sunday, 1 September 1844, feast of Our Lady of Consolation[52].

But, with the opening of the second semester in February 1845, O'Dwyer began to feel the stress of the past year's ordeal. He had the responsibility, moreover, of building a new church at Saint Augustine's. To afford some relief, James O'Donnell surrendered his missions on Long Island to Bishop Dubois, and came to Philadelphia. Additionally, Francis Ashe was in delicate health; he died on 13 March 1848, only twenty-eight years old. And William Harnett, just ordained, was convalescent from chronic skin eruptions[53]. These four Augustinians with Nicholas O'Donnell were the only priests of the Order in the country. Therefore, some time in February 1845, John O'Dwyer decided to close the college temporarily; and, on 20 February, he published the following announcement in *The Catholic Herald*: 'In consequence of the losses sustained during the May riots in the destruction of their church and property, the members of the Order of Saint Augustine are compelled to close the college lately opened at Saint Thomas of Villanova near Philadelphia. It is hoped that the justice of their fellow-citizens by awarding a fair compensation for the losses sustained will soon enable the Augustinians to reopen the college'[54]. On the same day, after supper, O'Dwyer assembled the student body and, to their astonishment and regret,

48. Arthur J. Ennis, O.S.A., 'Patrick A. Stanton 1826-1891', in Rotelle, cit.(n.2), pp 93-106.
49. Roland, cit., p.10.
50. Middleton, cit., p.23; Roland, cit., p.10; Tourscher, cit.(n.4), p.76.
51. Roland, cit., p.11.
52. Middleton, cit., pp 23-25; Tourscher, cit.(n.4), p.99.
53. Middleton, cit., p.26.
54. Ibid.

informed them that the college was closed. The very next day the "Villanova boys" were sent home. Villanova had provided them with less than two years of Christian education[55].

The respite afforded the province an opportunity to reorder its monastic and missionary labors. Just at this critical point, Fr George Augustine Meagher (1821-1881) arrived from Italy to assist at Saint Augustine's. Moreover, generous sums for the Augustinian apostolate were collected in Europe, Canada, and the United States. Therefore, during the summer of 1846, the Augustinians resolved to reopen the college, and published the following announcement: 'Saint Thomas of Villanova's College . . . is now reopened . . . each pupil should be provided with three suits for winter and three for summer; three pairs of shoes and one pair of strong boots; a cloak or overcoat; six towels; the same number of napkins and handkerchiefs, and at least a half dozen of the different articles of under dress which require a frequent washing, and a large silver spoon duly marked . . . The terms are $150 a year, with a discount of 10 percent for prepayment[56]'.

Opening exercises for the 1846-1847 term took place on Sunday, 6 September. The Augustinian associates of the president, John O'Dwyer, were Francis Ashe and William Harnett and, a month later, Thomas Kyle, who had just returned from Ireland. E. A. Ansley was re-engaged. His salary was to be one hundred fifty dollars a year, if there were less than forty students, and two hundred, if there were more. John Gibney, a new teacher, was hired at one hundred fifty dollars per annum. Closing exercises for the term were held on Wednesday, 21 July 1847. A canopy over the lawn north of the college building provided protection from the sun. *The Catholic Herald* reported that the train arrived at the college about 10 o'clock. J. D. Bryant read an essay on "Education". Because William Harnett, the "acting-president", was away, James O'Donnell presided. This was Villanova's first public commencement[57].

In early spring of 1848, Villanova College petitioned the Pennsylvania Legislature for a charter, and on Friday, 10 March, of that year, Francis R. Shunk, Governor of the State, signed "An Act to Incorporate the Augustinian College of Villanova, In the County of Delaware and State of Pennsylvania". At the first meeting of the Board of Trustees on 1 May 1848, John O'Dwyer was named the first official president, and Fr Harnett, vice-president. The other five incorporators of the college were James O'Donnell; Edward Mullen; Francis Patrick Kenrick, Archbishop of Philadelphia; William A. Stokes, an attorney; and Daniel Barr, a merchant[58].

There had been talk of having James O'Donnell take over as head of the school, but his experience in parochial work in which he had shown a high degree of zeal and piety proved a barrier, and he was passed over for younger men. Accordingly, he left the Philadelphia area and, by November 1848, was in Lawrence, Massachusetts, where he initiated an Augustinian mission and eventually built Saint Mary's Church[59].

That same spring of 1848 the cornerstone for the new Saint Augustine's was laid on 23 May, and Bishop Kenrick opened the completed edifice for divine service on Christmas day that same year. Since the church was completely free of debt, the bishop consecrated the new Saint Augustine's on 5 November 1848[60]. In April 1848, the administration began the erection of another college building. The plan was to put up only what is now the east wing of Alumni Hall (this was sufficient for the current needs of the college) and let another administration finish the rest of the building. This wing was completed by February 1849 at a cost of $11,958.77. In its second story a large beautiful hall was opened for a library and reading room. Most of the books rescued from Saint Augustine's library during the riots of 1844 in Philadelphia found their way there. These constituted the nucleus of the present collection in Falvey Memorial Library. The hall

55. Ibid., pp 26-27.
56. Ibid., p.28
57. Ibid., pp 28-29.
58. Ibid., pp 29-31.
59. Tourscher, cit.(n.4), pp 76, 134; Shannon, cit.(n.18), pp 56-61.
60. Roland, cit., p.11; Tourscher, cit.(n.4), pp 90-91.

was open to students during free hours and all day on Sundays and holidays. The fee for using the reading room was a dollar a year. At the same time Fr O'Dwyer had a small one-story stone building erected at the railroad for a college station[61].

With the approval of Bishop Kenrick, a manual labor school for orphans over sixteen years of age was opened at Villanova in 1850. Saint John's Orphanage paid twenty-five dollars a year for each orphan and also supplied bed and bedding. But John O'Dwyer did not live long enough to witness more than the initial stages of this program. He was utterly exhausted by his unremitting labors. In the hope he might benefit from a change, he was taken to Mt Hope Hospital near Baltimore. There the chaplain who assisted O'Dwyer and witnessed his pious death was John Nepomucene Neumann, C.SS.R. (1811-1860), later third Bishop of Philadelphia and canonized saint. John Neumann told Patrick A. Stanton that John O'Dwyer in his last illness, out of humble reverence for the Savior, would not receive the Holy Eucharist in bed, but insisted on getting on his knees to receive Christ as Viaticum. O'Dwyer died on Friday, 24 May 1850, at the age of thirty-six. He had seen the college charter granted, stability established, and plans for expansion implemented[62].

William Harnett then succeeded Fr O'Dwyer as president for the second time, having served as "acting-president" for a year (1847-1848) between John O'Dwyer's two terms in the office. A list of college rules which would now be judged extremely confining were drawn up about this time[63]:

COLLEGE REGULATIONS.

Boys to rise at $5\frac{1}{2}$;	Studies to $4\frac{1}{2}$;
Prayer at 6;	Recreation to 5;
Mass at $6\frac{1}{2}$;	Studies from 5-6;
Breakfast at $7\frac{1}{2}$;	Spiritual reading from $6-6\frac{1}{2}$;
Recreation to $8\frac{1}{2}$;	Angelus and supper at $6\frac{1}{2}$;
Studies to 12;	Recreation to 7;
Examen at 12;	Studies from 7-8;
Angelus and Dinner;	Prayer to $8\frac{1}{2}$;
Recreation to 2;	Bed by 9.

SILENCE [in]

Refectory;	Study Hall;
Dormitory;	Wash Room.

PRIVATIONS.

No liquor;	No absence;
No tobacco;	No idleness;
No snuff;	No negligence;
No bad conduct;	No injustice.

Ambrose A. Mullen and Charles Egan were ordained to the priesthood by Bishop Kenrick on 17 December 1850, during Fr Harnett's second one-year term. On the death of John O'Dwyer, Patrick Moriarty returned from Europe, once again with the authority of commissary general. In 1851, he assumed the presidency of Villanova College from William Harnett, and held it until 1855[64].

---

61. Middleton, cit., pp 33, 35.
62. Ibid., pp 35-36.
63. Ibid., p. 36.
64. Ibid., p.37; Welsh, cit., pp 78-79.

On Sunday night, 14 March 1852, another near disaster occurred. While the Villanova community was in chapel at night prayers, the refectory ceiling in the basement caught fire from a lamp. Happily, the monastery was saved from destruction by fire. That same year, the monastery received a stone extension, which made the building eighty-nine feet in length and forty-five feet in width. Refectory, kitchen, and pantry were then moved upstairs. At the same time, a large two-story stone house was constructed some one hundred yards east of the barn to house the laundry and bakery[65].

Meanwhile, the mission begun by James O'Donnell at Saint Mary's in Lawrence, Massachusetts, was extended to several neighboring towns. The first chapel at Andover, for example, which evolved into Saint Augustine's Church, was blessed and opened by Fr O'Donnell on 22 November 1853. Eventually, Archbishop John Joseph Williams of Boston would commit all of the city of Lawrence north of the Merrimack River to the care of the Augustinians. At present, this area includes the churches of Saint Mary Immaculate Conception (1848), Holy Rosary (1884), and Saint Augustine (1935)[66].

Similarly, Saint Denis' Church in Havertown has been under the care of the Augustinians since 1853. This church, like the one at Villanova, began as a mission station attended occasionally from Saint Augustine's and Saint Mary's in the city: the first at the home of Denis Kelly in Haverford Township, the second at the home of John Rudolph in Radnor Township - now Villanova University[67].

In 1854, the few Catholics at Chestnut Hill (northeast of Villanova) began talking about the convenience of having their own mission church and resident pastor. Though only recently converted, Joseph Middleton took up the issue and consulted the bishop about the possibility. Under the proviso that the Catholics in the area would build the church themselves and find a priest in good standing to serve their needs, the bishop, Saint John Neumann, gave his consent. Joseph Middleton then enlisted the help of Dr Moriarty, the superior of the Augustinians in the United States. Dr Moriarty agreed to accept the mission for his Order. Next, Joseph Middleton raised the necessary funds, contributing lavishly from his own means. Thus, it was obvious that he was the leading spirit of the project. Accordingly, the Know-Nothings moved one night against the Middleton homestead, intending to burn the farm buildings. Middleton simply went out to confront them. Apparently, his courage, conviction, and strength of character were sufficient to deter his opponents. Nevertheless, it was necessary for Middleton and other Catholic men (such as Richard Plunkett, the grandfather of Fr Richard M. Plunkett, O.S.A.) to stand guard over the Church of Our Mother of Consolation in Chestnut Hill while it was under construction. The new church was blessed and opened for divine service on 11 November 1855 by Bishop Neumann[68].

It was also in 1854, the year of his baptism, that Thomas Cooke Middleton matriculated at Villanova College, where his maternal cousin and godfather, Joseph Cooke Longstreth (an earlier convert from Quakerism), had attended from 1847 to 1850. Ironically, who would have imagined that ten years after the burning of Old Saint Augustine's, the eldest son of the Middleton-Nativist who abetted the conflagration would be attending a Catholic institution? Moreover, in 1858, the Augustinians would send young Middleton with a fellow Philadelphian, Francis Michael Sheeran (1840-1912) to Italy, as candidates for the Augustinian priesthood, the same year that Dr Moriarty resigned the office of commissary general on 26 April because of failing health, and was succeeded by Fr Patrick A. Stanton[69].

65. Middleton, cit., p.38.
66. Tourscher, cit.(n.4), pp 134-35.
67. Ibid., pp 79-80.
68. Thomas C. Middleton, 'Some Memoirs of Our Lady's Shrine at Chestnut Hill, Pa., with Reminiscences of Still Earlier Days', *Records of the American Catholic Historical Society of Philadelphia,* 12 (1901), pp 38-39, 137-259; Tourscher, cit.(n.4), pp 131-33; Schnaubelt, cit., pp 167-68, 198 n.13.
69. Francis E. Tourscher, O.S.A., 'Fr. Thomas Cooke Middleton, D.D., O.S.A., 1842-1923', *Records of the American Catholic Historical Society of Philadelphia,* 35 (1924), p.21; Schnaubelt, cit., pp 168-69; Welsh, cit., p.80.

Patrick Augustine Stanton, O.S.A.
(1826-1891)
Commissary General of the American
Province (1858-1866)

During the first half of the nineteenth century, the missions of South Jersey were generally attended from Saint Augustine's in Philadelphia. The first Augustinian to care for the Catholics on "Absecon Island", later Atlantic City, was Michael Francis Gallagher (1802-1869), who had charge of the mission from 1855 to 1860. The first resident pastor of Saint Nicholas of Tolentine Church in Atlantic City was John Joseph Fedigan (1842-1908)[70], who was made rector there in 1880[71].

In 1858, Bishop John McCloskey of Albany (1847-1864), later Cardinal Archbishop of New York (1864-1885), entrusted Saint Augustine's in North Troy and Saint Mary's in Waterford to the Augustinians. Saint John's in Schaghticoke (1859) was attended, first from North Troy, then after 1865 from Saint Paul's in Mechanicville, which was founded in 1862, with Fr George Augustine Meagher (1821-1881) as its first resident rector. Saint Patrick's Church in Cambridge and Immaculate Conception Church in Hoosick Falls were also given to the care of the Augustinians in 1862. In February 1880, almost two decades later, Fr Thomas Field (1829-1912) was sent as first permanent rector to Saint Joseph's in Greenwich, which had been attended since 1862 as a mission of Saint Patrick's in Cambridge[72].

Meanwhile, at Villanova College, the faculty for the scholastic year of 1855-1856 included Ambrose Mullen and Lewis Matthew Edge (1825-1870). The latter entered the novitiate at Villanova in 1853, and was ordained by the saintly Bishop Neumann in Philadelphia in the House of the Good Shepherd one year later. There were also two diocesan priests on the faculty, the Reverends John Kelly and Patrick Duffy[73].

In 1855, William Harnett took over as president of the college for the third time, his term lasting two years and unfortunately ending in sadness. The commencement of 1857 should have been a joyous occasion, for it saw the first conferral of the Master of Arts degree on James F. Dooley. This was only two years after the first awarding of Bachelor's degrees to Henry Crabbe Alexander and to the same James F. Dooley. The conferral of these degrees should have signaled the college's coming of age; instead, the commencement marked its second closing. A combination of difficulties made it impossible to continue: too many demands had been made on the time and energy of the Augustinians, and severe economic depression gripped the country[74].

Once again, however, the farm continued to provide for the religious community, and during the eight hard years of the closing it was still possible to educate twenty-seven clerical students at the monastery, mostly for the Augustinian Order. The latter years of the closing were also the time of the Civil War (1861-1865), during which Villanova was used as a hospital[75].

After the conflict, it was feasible to reopen the college. In the summer of 1865, Thomas Middleton and Francis Sheeran (now priests) were recalled to the United States to serve on the Villanova faculty. In Rome, they had had the scholarly Fr Joseph Lanteri (1820-1886) as their regent of studies. Joseph Lanteri, a devotee of Augustinian Order history, was to serve as the last Augustinian prefect of the Biblioteca Angelica, which was confiscated from the Augustinians in the

70. Harry A. Cassel, O.S.A., 'John J. Fedigan 1842-1908', in Rotelle, cit.(n.3), pp 169-85.
71. Tourscher, cit.(n.4), pp 145-46.
72. Ibid., pp 138-44.
73. Middleton, cit.(n.31), p.40
74. Ibid., pp 39-41.
75. Thomas F. Roland, O.S.A., 'The First Half Century at Villanova', *The Tagastan*, 6, No. 2 (1943), p.79; Tourscher, cit.(n.4), pp 117-20.

Italian Risorgimento. Inevitably, the influence Joseph Lanteri exercised over the young Middleton was profound, instilling in him feeling for the past and reverence for books and documents[76].

Ambrose A. Mullen served as president of the reopened college, with the newly arrived Francis Sheeran as vice-president. On the faculty were Thomas C. Middleton, the Reverend Dr P. J. Madden, a diocesan priest, and five clerical students: Michael Mary O'Farrell (1842-1881), Timothy Donovan (1838-1875), Charles Augustine Marsden (1845-1877), John Hugh Devir (1841-1926), and Thomas Cullen, and Mr John K. McGuire, an alumnus of 1857. In addition, Frs Pacifico A. Neno (1833-1891) and Philip Izzo were sent as qualified theologians by the prior general, John Belluomini (1814-1887), to bolster the theological faculty[77].

Thomas Middleton discharged his duties at Villanova for half a century, not only as teacher, but also as custodian of books. His devotion to literature and general antiquarian interests eminently qualified him for the college librarianship, a post he would relinquish only in death. Hand in hand with the librarianship went the appointment to act as archivist of documents and records for the province[78].

Classes resumed in September of 1865. The basic curriculum was somewhat modified and expanded: Greek, Latin, English, French, German, mathematics, natural philosophy, history, poetry, music, and bookkeeping. The next year added drawing under direction of a Mr Reed. From 1867-1869 Robert Brooks was drawing master[79].

In 1866, Middleton, the son of the Nativist who abetted the cruel conflagration, initiated a practice which he would continue irregularly until 1923, the year of his death. This was to record data on life at Villanova in its various and someTimes-strange manifestations, all kept in two ledgers and various other manuscripts. These ledgers, a treasury of otherwise unknown lore and anecdote, are commonly cited as the "Middleton Journal"[80].

In August 1866, the General Curia removed Patrick Stanton from his position as commissary general and reinstated Fr Moriarty. However, Moriarty's reappointment was acceptable to neither the Bishop of Philadelphia nor the Archbishop of Baltimore, both of whom protested to Propaganda Fide. The Curia reacted by revoking Moriarty's nomination and replacing him, on 30 November, with Fr Thomas Galberry (1833-1878)[81]. Patrick Stanton then became president of the college. Under his administration, the first gymnasium was constructed in 1869. Among its facilities were ten-pin alleys, horizontal and inclined ladders, trapezes, swinging and parallel bars, breast bars, a vaulting horse, climbing pole, bouncing board, and punching bag[82].

Early in 1875, Thomas Galberry, who had succeeded Patrick Stanton as president of Villanova College in 1872, was appointed Bishop of Hartford, Connecticut, by Pope Pius IX (1846-1878). Irish-born, Galberry entered the novitiate at Villanova in 1852, and was ordained priest by Bishop Saint John Neumann in 1856. He served as pastor of Saint Denis' Church in Haverford, Pennsylvania, Saint Augustine's in Lansingburg

Thomas Galberry, O.S.A. (1833-1878)
Commissary General of the American Province (1866-1874)
First Prior Provincial of the Province of St. Thomas of Villanova (1874-1876)
Bishop of Hartford, Connecticut (1876-1878)

76. Schnaubelt, cit., pp 169-70.
77. Middleton, cit.(n.31), p.42.
78. Schnaubelt, cit., p.170.
79. Middleton, cit.(n.31), p.42.
80. Schnaubelt, cit., pp 171-72.
81. Welsh, cit. (n.26), p.82; Albert C. Shannon, O.S.A., 'Thomas Galberry 1833-1878', in Rotelle, cit.(n.3), pp 129-39.
82. Middleton, cit.(n.31), pp 43-44.

(Troy), New York, and Saint Mary's in Lawrence, Massachusetts. In 1867, he was appointed commissary general for the American Augustinians. While still president of Villanova, Thomas Galberry was elected first prior provincial on 16 December 1874 after the American Augustinians were authorized by a decree of the prior general dated 25 August of the same year to reorganize into a regular province under the new title of Saint Thomas of Villanova[83].

One of the acts of the Provincial Chapter of 1874 was to transfer Dr Moriarty from Our Mother of Consolation Church in Chestnut Hill to the monastery at Villanova. There he spent his last days suffering, but manifesting interior peace, much to the edification of all, until his death on 10 July 1875. Some seventy priests, three bishops, and a large congregation attended his funeral at Old Saint Augustine's, where he was buried in the Augustinian vault[84].

On the eve of commencement day in 1875, Tuesday, 29 June, the college alumni met in the house parlor with the bishop-elect and formed the Villanova Alumni Association. Galberry's administration at Villanova saw many improvements. In 1872, to meet the needs of the faithful, the gymnasium was dismantled, and the hall arranged as a church. Three altars were erected at its north end, and a choir gallery built at the south. Mass was first offered in the new church on Sunday, 14 July; and on Sunday, 15 September, Archbishop James Frederic Wood (1860-1883) of Philadelphia came to Villanova to bless the edifice. The old chapel of 1844 was reserved as the community oratory, and during Holy Week served as the repository. Ever since 1849, the college administration had wanted to complete the main section of what is now Alumni Hall. Thomas Galberry saw the first stone laid on Tuesday, 1 April 1873; the cross raised atop the copula one hundred feet above the ground on Thursday, 4 September; and the building occupied by teachers and students on Tuesday, 3 February 1874. When Thomas Galberry left Villanova on Tuesday, 7 March, 1876, for his consecration in Hartford, Thomas Middleton was chosen president for the remainder of his term. During Middleton's two year term, the grounds were notably improved and a tree-lined walk to the railroad put in[85].

Elected in 1878, the next president, Irish-born Fr John J. Fedigan added a fourth story to the monastery and introduced steam throughout the building. The former study hall in the east wing of the college building was fitted up for public assemblies. In 1879, Fedigan had it neatly decorated with paintings of Saints Augustine and Monica and "The Charity of Saint Thomas, of Villanova". Then, late 1892, it was adorned with new mural paintings of Saint Augustine, the Prophet David, and Saint Cecilia[86].

Coming from Ireland in 1878, Fr Joseph A. Coleman (1842-1902)[87] replaced Fedigan as president in 1880. On 1 April 1883, his administration began the erection of a church worthy of Saint Thomas of Villanova, patron of the monastery, college, and mission. Edwin F. Durang was architect in charge. The spiritual needs of the college were first serviced by the little oratory in the monastery parlor, next by the church of 1843, then by the chapel of 1844, and still later by the gymnasium church of 1872. The magnificent new Gothic-Revival church, completed in four years, was blessed on 3 July 1887 by Archbishop Patrick John Ryan (1884-1911) of Philadelphia[88].

In 1885, for the convenience of "summer residents" (Bryn Mawr at that time was a summer resort for the residents of Philadelphia), Fr Coleman said the first Mass in the "old school house" north of Montgomery Avenue and west of Penn Street. This practice was continued in the frame chapel built in the spring of 1886. Later, the site of this "old school house chapel" was traded for ground east of Penn Street and north of the Lancaster Turnpike, to which the Chapel of Our Mother of Good Counsel was moved in early 1889 and opened for Mass on Easter Sunday, 12 April

83. Tourscher, cit.(n.4), pp 126-30.
84. Welsh, cit., p.83.
85. Middleton, cit.(n.31), pp 44-46.
86. Ibid., pp 45, 47.
87. Robert J. Welsh, O.S.A., 'Joseph A. Coleman 1842-1902', in Rotelle, cit.(n.2.) pp 117-29.
88. Middleton, cit.(n.31), pp 48-51; Tourscher, cit.(n.4), pp 150-51.

1889[89]. It was also in 1885 that Francis Sheeran, for many years professor and vice-president of the college, received the degree of Bachelorship of Sacred Theology and, in 1886, was elected president of Villanova[90].

In 1890, Christopher A. McEvoy (1840-1914) was elected president of the college, with Richard A. Gleeson (1865-1939) vice-president, who, the year after, was succeeded by Fr Laurence A. Delurey (1864-1922)[91]. In 1892, the second year of Christopher McEvoy's presidency, Villanova College celebrated the Golden Jubilee of its foundation. The fifty years witnessed two closings, and then the gradual stabilization and growth of the college. Each year some seventy students matriculated. The faculty remained rather constant, while the scholastic standards rose, keeping the college apace with secular institutions. Eleven Augustinians served as president of the college, one with two terms and another with three. The celebration of the jubilee reached its climax at the commencement of 1893, over which Archbishop Ryan of Philadelphia presided, assisted by Bishops Keane and O'Farrell. All in all, fifteen hundred forty-eight students had attended Villanova, of whom seventy-five had achieved the Baccalaureate and three, the Masters[92].

To commemorate the event, Thomas Middleton published a slim volume in 1893 entitled *Historical Sketch of the Augustinian Monastery, College and Mission of Saint Thomas of Villanova, Delaware County, Pa., during the First Half Century of Their Existence, 1842-1892.* The slimness of the volume belies its significance, for it provides data available nowhere else, such as the names of all the students educated at Villanova from 1843 to 1893. Middleton's own name appears as an alumnus on page eighty in Appendix IV, the roll of students, and that of his cousin, Joseph Cooke Longstreth, on page seventy-six. But of even greater significance is Middleton's account on pages fifty-three and fifty-four of the Augustinian effort to spread the faith from the motherhouse at Villanova College:

'Since, with the year 1892, closed the fiftieth anniversary of Villanova's foundation, here, as a memorial of the event, are recorded the names of the Fathers in residence and of the officers and teachers, who during that year, were connected with the monastery, the college and the missions of Villanova. They were as follows: Very Rev. Christopher A. McEvoy, O.S.A., prior of the monastery, president of the college and parish rector; Rev. Thomas C. Middleton, D.D., O.S.A., prefect of the ecclesiastical department and professor of moral theology, church history, canon law, and homiletics; Rev. Francis M. Sheeran, S.T.B., O.S.A., subprior of the monastery, cleric-master and professor of liturgy; Rev. Michael J. Locke, S.T.L., O.S.A., professor of dogmatic theology, sacred scriptures, and mental and moral philosophy; Rev. Edward Dailey, O.S.A., rector of Saint Monica's mission at Berwyn; Rev. John H. Devir, O.S.A., rector of Our Lady of Good Counsel mission at Bryn Mawr; Rev. John J. Ryan, B.S., O.S.A., sacristan; Rev. Daniel J. Murphy, A.B., O.S.A.; Rev. Timothy F. Herlihy, O.S.A., professor of Latin, Greek, rhetoric, and mathematics; Rev. Charles J. McFadden, O.S.A., professor of Latin, English grammar, mathematics, reading, and spelling; Rev. Richard A. Gleeson, O.S.A., professor of Latin, Greek, rhetoric and mathematics; Rev. Laurence A. Delurey, B.S., O.S.A., vice-president of the college and professor of elocution and oratory, book-keeping, writing, English, orthography, arithmetic and modern history; Rev. Patrick H. O'Donnell, O.S.A., rector of Saint Denis' mission at Cobb's Creek and professor of physics; Rev. Richard F. Harris, B.A., O.S.A., professor of Latin, Greek, English grammar and arithmetic; Brother Walter A. Coar, O.S.A., professor of United States History and of geography; Mon. Pierre M. Arn, A.M., professor of French and German; Mr Dennis O'Sullivan, professor of higher

89. Tourscher, cit.(n.4), pp 146-48; Middleton, cit.(n.31), pp 51-52.
90. Middleton, cit.(n.31), p .52.
91. Ibid., p.53; Edwin T. Grimes, O.S.A., 'Laurence A. Delurey 1864-1922', in Rotelle, cit.(n.2), pp 131-63.
92. Schnaubelt, cit., pp 180-82.

mathematics; Charles Stockton Gauntt, M.D., professor of chemistry; Samuel K. Murdoch, M.D., professor of elocution and oratory; and Mr George J. Corrie, professor of music; the latter four instructors being non-residents.

The college disciplinarians were: Bro. James E. Vaughn, O.S.A., Bro. James T. Collins, O.S.A., Bro. James F. Green, O.S.A., Bro. Edward P. Flynn, O.S.A., Bro. Walter A. Coar, O.S.A.; and the college physician in charge was George S. Gerhard, M.D., of Ardmore. The religious connected with the monastery and missions of Villanova, Saint Denis at Cobb's Creek, Saint Monica at Berwyn, and Our Lady of Good Counsel at Bryn Mawr, and the college, numbered 45, namely: 16 priests, 10 professed clerics, 5 novice clerics, 4 professed lay brothers, 6 novice lay bothers and 4 postulants.'

Villanova College, circa 1892

III

AFTERMATH OF THE IRISH AUGUSTINIAN MISSION

Villanova's Golden Jubilee in 1892 marked almost a century of missionary effort in the United States by Irish Augustinians, beginning with the founding of Old Saint Augustine's by Matthew Carr in 1796. It also signaled the maturation of the American province, for if the province was still energized by infusions of Irish blood, that blood was becoming more and more native to America. If one surveys Augustinian foundations in the United States from 1796 to 1905, one notes immediately that they all lie along the northeastern seaboard. Only members of the Augustinian Mission Band ventured farther west. It was one of these missioners who made the first contacts in the Mid-West: Fr James F. Green (1867-1936), a native of Chestnut Hill, Pennsylvania. While preaching in Chicago, Illinois, at the parishes of Saint Anne's and Saint Gabriel's, Fr Green became acquainted with Fr Patrick M. Flannigan and Fr Maurice J. Dorney. These dynamic pastors were influential in obtaining permission from Archbishop James Edward Quigley (1903-1915) for the Augustinians to open a school on the south side of the city. To the provincial, Fr Martin John Geraghty (1867-1914), James Green seemed the ideal Augustinian to make the new foundation. Consequently, Fr Green was sent to Chicago, where, on 26 October 1905, he laid the cornerstone for Saint Rita High School at the junction of 63rd and Oakley[93].

By 1940, the Order had six houses in Illinois (three in Chicago and three in Rockford), three in Michigan (two in Detroit and one in Flint) and one in Tulsa, Oklahoma - a total of ten foundations staffed by sixty-six priests and three brothers. Such a large increase was judged adequate for the division of the Province of Saint Thomas of Villanova. Consequently, the Province of Our Mother of Good Counsel was founded on 26 April 1941[94].

Similarly, in the far west, seventeen years after Fr Green was sent to Chicago, Irish-born Fr Thomas Aquinas Healy (1873-1927) was sent to San Diego, California, to investigate the possibility of founding a boarding school. Then, at the behest of Bishop John Cantwell of Monterey-Los Angeles (1917-1947), Fr Alphonse Martel was sent from Villanova College in the east to join Fr Healy in the west, in order to make the actual foundation. (Alphonse Martel, a native of Quebec, Canada, was later incardinated into the Diocese of Lafayette, Louisiana.) Shortly thereafter, on 18 September 1922, Saint Augustine High School was opened on a temporary location opposite Fr Healy's house on Stockton Drive. But by 4 September, the next year, the school opened at a permanent location between 32nd and 33rd Streets on the east and west, and Palm and Nutmeg Streets on the north and south[95].

By 1957, the Augustinian foundations in California included Saint Augustine High School in San Diego, Villanova Preparatory School in Ojai, Saint Patrick's Church in San Diego, Our Mother of Good Counsel Church in Los Angeles, and Saint Thomas Aquinas Church in Ojai. Inasmuch as there were now fifteen Augustinian priests and sixteen seminarians who were natives of the West Coast, all the priests of the Order assigned to California, with one exception, petitioned for the establishment of a California vice province. Accordingly, the prior general, Engelbert Eberhard (1893-1958) issued the rescript which established the Vice Province of Saint Augustine in California as of 1 January 1957. Then, to eliminate the necessity of crossing the continent to attend provincial meetings and to facilitate local decisions, it was proposed on 19 October 1968 that the Vice Province should acquire the status of a Province. The proposal was voted unanimously. The General Chapter of 1968, celebrated at Villanova University, approved the petition submitted by the Vice Province of St Augustine, and the new Province was officially created on 17 March 1969[96].

In his letter of 1843 to Dr Stuart, Patrick Moriarty stressed 'the necessity of making an effort to propagate [the] Order and to secure its stability and sweep'. He 'saw a large province starting up and [its] members, after being well trained, going into the different states to take possession of thousands of acres (which [had] already been offered to [the Augustinians] on condition of erecting churches and schools), stirring up the fires of faith and observing strictly the holy rule of Augustine'. Today, Moriarty's vision has been more than vindicated. Like their Irish forebears, the American Augustinians have gone across the sea to bring the great light of the gospel to those who 'walk in darkness' in Peru and Japan (cf. Isaiah 9:2).

---

93. Karl A. Gersbach, O.S.A., ed., *Province of Our Mother of Good Counsel of the Augustinian Order: Forty Years of Service, 1941-1981* (Olympia Fields, IL: Tolentine Center, 1981), pp 1-3.
94. Ibid., pp 6-9.
95. John R. Sanders, O.S.A., *Before All Else: The History of the Augustinians in the Western United States, 1922-1985* (Villanova, PA: Augustinian Press, 1987), pp 1-17.
96. Ibid., pp 87-88, 129-32.

Augustinian Foundations in the U.S. 1796-1893

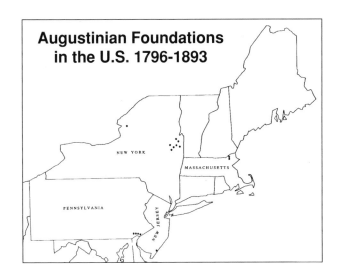

Foundations in Pennsylvania 1796 - 1893

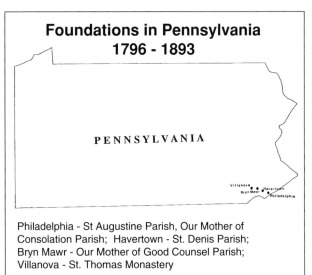

Philadelphia - St Augustine Parish, Our Mother of Consolation Parish; Havertown - St. Denis Parish; Bryn Mawr - Our Mother of Good Counsel Parish; Villanova - St. Thomas Monastery

Foundations in Massachusetts 1848 - 1884

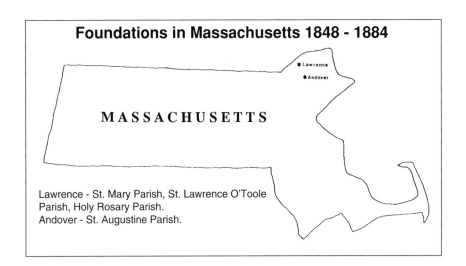

Lawrence - St. Mary Parish, St. Lawrence O'Toole Parish, Holy Rosary Parish.
Andover - St. Augustine Parish.

Foundations in New York 1858 - 1880

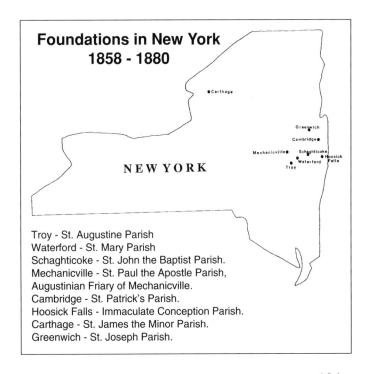

Troy - St. Augustine Parish
Waterford - St. Mary Parish
Schaghticoke - St. John the Baptist Parish.
Mechanicville - St. Paul the Apostle Parish, Augustinian Friary of Mechanicville.
Cambridge - St. Patrick's Parish.
Hoosick Falls - Immaculate Conception Parish.
Carthage - St. James the Minor Parish.
Greenwich - St. Joseph Parish.

Foundation in New Jersey 1855

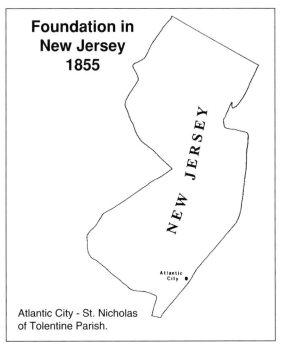

Atlantic City - St. Nicholas of Tolentine Parish.

Irish-Born Augustinians of the Provinces
in the United States
Arranged by Date of Death

Name	Date of Birth	Place of Birth	Date of Death	Place of Death
P. John Rosseter	1751 Feb 23	Wexford, Ireland	1812 Oct. 20	Charles County, MD
P. George Staunton	1768	County Mayo, Ireland	1815	Dublin, Ireland
P. Thomas Matthew Carr	1756	Ireland	1820 Sept. 29	Philadelphia, PA
P. Philip Lariscy	1782	Callan, Kilkenny, Ireland	1824 Apr. 6	Philadelphia, PA
P. William C. O'Donnell	-	Ireland	1832 Dec.	Ireland
P. Robert Browne	1770	Ireland	1839 Apr. 20	Charleston, SC
P. Michael Hurley	1780	Ireland	1837 May 14	Philadelphia, PA
P. Francis Ashe	1820	Cork City, Ireland	1848 Mar. 13	Philadelphia, PA
Fr. Thomas McDonnell	-	Ireland?	1840 May 19	Philadelphia, PA
P. John Possidius O'Dwyer	1816	Callan, Kilkenny, Ireland	1850 May 24	Baltimore, MD
P. William Hogan	-	Ireland?	1852 June 14	Cincinnati, OH
Fr. Philip Shea	-	County Kilkenny, Ireland	1856 Feb. 21	Villanova, PA
P. James O'Donnell	1806	Black Castle, Tipp., Ireland	1861 Apr. 7	Lawrence, MA
P. Nicholas O'Donnell	1802	Cahir, Tipperary, Ireland	1863 July 1	Verplanck, NY
P. Timothy Aloysius Hayes	-	Ireland	1868 Nov. 15	North Troy, NY
Fr. Owen Maguire	-	County Cavan, Ireland	1869 Feb. 14	Villanova, PA
P. Michael Francis Gallagher	1802	Dromore, Ireland	1869 Aug. 25	Lawrence, MA
P. Thomas Kyle	1797	Ireland	1869 Oct. 23	Philadelphia, PA
P. Timothy Alphonse Hayes	1844 May 29	County Cork, Ireland	1869 Nov. 15	North Troy, NY
P. Louis Matthew Edge	1825	County Tipperary, Ireland	1870 Feb. 24	Philadelphia, PA
P. Mark Crane	1832	County Wexford, Ireland	1871 Jan. 19	Philadelphia, PA
P. Peter James Furlong	1849 Mar. 1	County Wexford, Ireland	1872 Sept. 28	Cambridge, NY
Fr. John Kelly	1842 Dec. 13	Ireland	1873 Mar. 12	Templemore, Ireland
P. Timothy Donovan	1838	Skibbereen, Ireland	1875 Jan. 25	Schaghticoke, NY
P. Patrick Eugene Moriarty	1805 July 4	Dublin, Ireland	1875 July 10	Villanova, PA
Fr. Patrick Duffy	-	County Cavan, Ireland	1877 July 11	Villanova, PA
P. Thomas Galberry	1833 May 28	Naas, Kildare, Ireland	1878 Oct. 10	New York, NY
Fr. Nicholas O'Brien	1825	Mullinahone, Tipp., Ireland	1881 July 7	Villanova, PA
P. Michael Mary O'Farrell	1842 Sept. 27	Castlebar, Mayo, Ireland	1881 Aug. 28	Princeton, NY
Fr. Sylvester Hogan	1822	County Kilkenny, Ireland	1882 Jan. 24	Villanova, PA
Fr. Possidius McMahon	1832 Jan. 1	County Monaghan, Ireland	1882 Oct. 6	Villanova, PA
Fr. James O'Brien	1805	County Tipperary, Ireland	1884 Oct. 24	Villanova, PA
Fr. John Joseph Regan	1862 Dec. 23	Clonmel, Ireland	1884 Nov. 24	Lawrence, MA
Fr. Joseph Whittendale	1815 Nov. 6	County Kilkenny, Ireland	1885 Dec. 9	Villanova, PA
P. Michael Joseph Collins	1834 Sept. 23	Dublin, Ireland	1887 Mar. 7	North Troy, NY
P. Francis Joseph Rowan	1852 Nov. 12	Stranorlar, Ireland	1887 Sept. 20	Brooklyn, NY
P. Edward Michael Mullen	1825	Ireland	1888 Aug. 8	Genazzano, Italy
P. Edward A. O'Reilly	1849 Sept. 8	Marlborough, Qu., Ireland	1889 Jan. 2	Villanova, PA

P. Patrick A. Stanton	1826 Jan. 27	Castlebar, Mayo, Ireland	1891 Feb. 28	Philadelphia, PA
Fr. Stanislaus Duffy	1825 Sept. 29	County Cavan, Ireland	1891 Aug. 29	Philadelphia, PA
P. James Joseph Blake	1850 Feb. 28	Clonaslee, Ireland	1892 Jan. 21	North Troy, NY
P. Joseph Augustine Locke	1856 Feb. 9	Callan, Ireland	1892 Apr. 22	North Troy, NY
Fr. Thomas (John) Burns	1831	County Meath, Ireland	1892 Aug. 5	Ardmore, PA
Fr. John (Denis) Gallagher	1812	Tulloughbegley, Do., Ireland	1894 Feb. 8	Villanova, PA
P. Charles Augustine Egan	1821	Ireland	1895 Mar. 4	Boston, MA
Fr. Dominic (James) Byrne	1826 June 2	County Kilkenny, Ireland	1895 Sept. 28	Villanova, PA
Fr. Edward Stack	1826 Nov. 26	County Kilkenny, Ireland	1895 Oct. 14	Villanova, PA
Fr. Joseph Briody	1837	Oldcastle, Meath, Ireland	1898 May 29	Villanova, PA
P. Jeremiah Joseph Ryan	1848	Fedamore, Ireland	1898 Nov. 19	Cambridge, NY
P. Michael Augustine White	1849 Feb. 5	Islandbawn, Clare, Ireland	1900 Apr. 5	Lawrence, MA
P. Bernard A. Dailey	1839 June 9	Enniskillen, Fer., Ireland	1901 Mar. 2	Villanova, PA
P. Patrick Augustine Carr	1847 Aug. 2	Headford, Ireland	1901 Apr. 8	Greenwich, NY
P. Michael Mark Fogarty	1853 Sept. 12	County Tipperary, Ireland	1902 Jan. 21	Diocese of Albany
			NY	
P. Peter Crane	1834	County Wexford, Ireland	1904 Feb. 24	Lawrence, MA
Fr. James (Michael) Fox	1840	County Tipperary, Ireland	1905 Mar. 28	Villanova, PA
P. Maurice Joseph Murphy	1844 Feb. 19	Daugh, Ireland	1905 Dec. 20	Lowell, MA
P. John Joseph Fedigan	1842 Apr. 27	Rathbrau, Meath, Ireland	1908 Apr. 27	Villanova, PA
Fr. Lawrence (William) Kelly	c.1814	County Kilkenny, Ireland	1908 June 7	Lawrence, MA
Fr. Antony Anglin	1868 Aug. 6	County Tipperary, Ireland	1909 Nov. 8	Villanova, PA
P. John Joseph Bowles	1839 June 6	Limerick, Ireland	1911 Sept. 30	Villanova, PA
P. Francis Michael Sheeran	1840 Dec. 6	County Tyrone, Ireland	1912 Jan. 19	Villanova, PA
P. Thomas Augustine Field	1829 Feb. 21	Kilbrin, Cork, Ireland	1912 June 19	Villanova, PA
P. Patrick Hugh O'Donnell	1857 Mar. 7	Arran Island, Ireland	1912 Sept. 24	Philadelphia, PA
P. Christopher A. McEvoy	1840 Dec. 20	Balinakelen, Qu., Ireland	1914 Dec. 14	Villanova, PA
Fr. Kieran (Thomas) Phelan	1827	County Kilkenny, Ireland	1915 June 12	Villanova, PA
Fr. Francis (Denis) Curtin	c. 1844	Emly, Tipperary, Ireland	1916 Dec. 20	Villanova, PA
Fr. Augustine Dougherty	1848 June 8	Lagnahoory, Do., Ireland	1917 Mar. 23	Villanova, PA
P. Daniel Paul Fogarty	1887 Jan. 30	Templemore, Tip., Ireland	1918 Oct. 18	Andover, MA
P. Hugh A.. Gallagher	1853 Aug. 13	Letterkenny, Do., Ireland	1919 May 6	Philadelphia, PA
P. Patrick Joseph Gallagher	1880 Apr. 4	Castlebar, Mayo, Ireland	1919 Apr. 1	Bordeaux, France
P. Patrick Joseph Mayock	1888 Mar. 10	Ballina, Mayo, Ireland	1922 July 30	Ogdensburg, NY
Fr. Possidius (John) Frail	1846 June 24	County Galway, Ireland	1925 June 23	Villanova, PA
P. Daniel James O'Sullivan	1859 Apr. 2	Greenmount, Cork, Ireland	1926 Apr. 8	North Troy, NY
P. William Francis Berry	1897 Feb. 13	Castlebar, Mayo, Ireland	1926 Apr. 17	Philadelphia, PA
P. John Hugh Devir	1841 Dec. 23	Stranorlar, Donegal, Ireland	1926 June 24	Villanova, PA
Fr. Mark Donahoe	1855 Mar. 4	Longford, Ireland	1926 Dec. 28	Villanova, PA
P. Thomas Aquinas Healy	1873 Jan. 1	Athlone, Ros., Ireland	1927 Jan. 27	Rosemont, PA
P. Charles Patrick O'Neill	1871 Mar. 17	Leighlin Bridge, Car., Ireland	1927 Apr. 19	Chicago, Illinois
Fr. Patrick Jarrett	1853	Kilcommon, Mayo, Ireland	1927 Apr. 27	Villanova, PA
P. Patrick Augustine Lynch	1849 Feb. 1	Thomastown, Gal., Ireland	1927 May 6	Philadelphia, PA
P. Michael Joseph Locke	1860 Oct. 8	Callan, Kilkenny, Ireland	1929 Dec. 10	Philadelphia, PA
P. Bernard Edward Daly	1871 Oct. 4	Kells, Meath, Ireland	1931 Jan. 23	Lawrence, MA
P. Francis Joseph McShane	1846 Feb.	Aughnacloy, Ireland	1932 Mar. 28	Philadelphia, PA

Fr. John (William) Gillespie	c. 1866	Killymard, Donegal, Ireland	1934 Aug. 31	Philadelphia, PA
P. John Patrick Whelan	1862 Jan. 27	Dublin, Ireland	1934 Oct. 13	Villanova, PA
P. John McErlain	1868 July	Belfast, Ireland	1935 Sept. 6	Lowell, MA
P. John Augustine Hogan	1862 June 19	County Tipperary, Ireland	1941 July 16	Villanova, PA
P. Robert Fitzgerald	1868 Aug. 20	County Tipperary, Ireland	1943 June 18	Philadelphia, PA
P. Thomas P. Fogarty	1888	Ireland	1950 Oct. 4	Waterford, NY
P. James J. Hasson	1897 May 3	County Donegal, Ireland	1960 Sept. 8	Villanova, PA
P. John Stanislaus O'Leary	1890 Oct. 13	Cork, Ireland	1964 Mar. 2	Villanova, PA
P. Hugh Patrick O'Neil	1893 Sept. 16	Lisburn, Antrim, Ireland	1965 Jan. 4	Lawrence, MA
P. Denis Joseph Kavanagh	1886 Aug. 21	Ballinrobe, Mayo, Ireland	1966 May 2	Bryn Mawr, PA
Fr. James Patrick Lyne	1904 Jan. 4	Kerry, Ireland	1976 Dec. 4	Piura, Peru
Fr. J. Brendan Elliott	1903 Dec. 31	Carrigallen, Leitrim, Ireland	1986 July 7	Villanova, PA
P. John Michael Quinn	1922 Nov. 27	Altaglushin, Tyrone, Ireland	Living	-

(Note: In above lists, P. = Pater, Fr. = Frater)

Augustinian Houses in the United States

1796 August 27: Foundation of American Province under title of Our Mother of Good Counsel.

1874 August 25: Regularization of American Province under changed title of St. Thomas of Villanova.

1941 April 26: Foundation of Chicago Province under title of Our Mother of Good Counsel.

1969 March 17: Foundation of California Province under title of St. Augustine.

Foundation	Canonical Foundation	Title	Location	Province
1796	1796	St. Augustine Parish	Philadelphia, PA	Villanova
1842	1843	St. Thomas Monastery at Villanova University	Villanova, PA	Villanova
1848	1894	St. Mary Parish	Lawrence, MA	Villanova
1853	1935	St. Augustine Parish	Andover, MA	Villanova
1853	1894	St. Denis Parish	Havertown, PA	Villanova
1855	1894	St. Nicholas of Tolentine Parish	Atlantic City, NJ	Villanova
1855	1894	Our Mother of Consolation Parish	Philadelphia, PA	Villanova
1858	1935	St. Augustine Parish	Troy, NY	Villanova
1858	1935	St. Mary Parish	Waterford, NY	Villanova
1859	1935	St. John the Baptist Parish	Schaghticoke, NY	Villanova
1862	1935	St. Paul the Apostle Parish	Mechanicville, NY	Villanova
1862	1935	Augustinian Friary of Mechanicville (Mission Consolidation)	Mechanicville, NY	Villanova
1862	1935	St. Patrick's Parish	Cambridge, NY	Villanova
1862	1935	Immaculate Conception Parish	Hoosick Falls, NY	Villanova
1874	1935	St. James the Minor Parish	Carthage, NY	Villanova
1875	1935	St. Laurence O'Toole Parish (Closed)	Lawrence, MA	Villanova
1880	1935	St. Joseph Parish	Greenwich, NY	Villanova
1884	1916	Holy Rosary Parish	Lawrence, MA	Villanova
1885	1893	Our Mother of Good Counsel Parish	Bryn Mawr, PA	Villanova
1899	1923	Our Lady of Good Counsel Parish	Staten Island, NY	Villanova
1905	1905	St. Nicholas of Tolentine Parish (High School closed)	Bronx, NY	Villanova
1905	1920	St. Rita High School (Moved)	Chicago, IL	Chicago
1907	1907	St. Rita of Cascia Parish	Philadelphia, PA	Villanova

1909	1947	St. Clare of Montefalco Parish	Chicago, IL	Chicago
1920	1920	St. Thomas of Villanova Parish	Rosemont, PA	Villanova
1920	1922	St. Augustine Parish (Closed)	Detroit, MI	Chicago
1920	1920	St. Nicholas of Tolentine Parish	Jamaica, NY	Villanova
1920	1920	St. Rita Parish	Chicago, IL	Chicago
1920	1920	Augustinian College (Moved)	Washington, DC	Villanova
1921	1935	Assumption Parish	Mechanicville, NY	Villanova
1922 OSA	-	St. Vincent de Paul Parish (Ceded)	San Diego, CA	California
1923	1924	Malvern Preparatory School	Malvern, PA	Villanova
1923	1923	St. Augustine High School	San Diego, CA	California
1924 OSA	-	St. Thomas Aquinas Parish	Ojai, CA	California
1924	1924	Augustinian Academy > Mount Augustine Apostolic Centre (Closed)	Staten Island, NY	Villanova
1924	1924	Villanova Preparatory School	Ojai, CA	California
1924	1925	Cascia Hall Preparatory School	Tulsa, OK	Chicago
1925	1925	Our Mother of Good Counsel Novitiate (Closed)	New Hamburg, NY	Villanova
1925 OSA	-	St. Patrick Parish	San Diego, CA	California
1926	1926	Mother of Good Counsel Parish	Los Angeles, CA	California
1926	1926	St. Clare of Montefalco Parish	Grosse Pointe, MI	Chicago
1926	1926	St. Matthew Parish	Flint, MI	Chicago
1933	1933	St. Thomas High School (Ceded)	Rockford, IL	Chicago
1933	1933	St. Mary Parish (Ceded)	Rockford, IL	Chicago
1935	1935	St. Augustine Parish	Lawrence, MA	Villanova
1941	-	St. Monica Novitiate (Closed)	Oconomowoc, WI	Chicago
1947	1947	Our Mother of Good Counsel Monastery at Merrimack College	North Andover, MA	Villanova
1949	-	St. Augustine Seminary (Closed)	Holland, MI	Chicago
1951	-	Carroll High School (Ceded)	Washington, DC	Villanova
1951	-	Mendel High School (Ceded)	Chicago, IL	Chicago
1951	-	Austin Catholic Prep. (Ceded)	Detroit, MI	Chicago
1952 OSA	-	Our Lady of the Angels Parish (Ceded)	Jacksonville, FL	Villanova
1953	-	St. Joseph Friary at Bonner High School	Drexel Hill, PA	Villanova
1953	1956	St. Genevieve Parish	Flourtown, PA	Villanova

1958	1958	St. Nicholas of Tolentine Monastery	Olympia Fields, IL	Chicago
1959	-	St. Joseph Mission House (Closed)	Fort Wayne, IN	Chicago
1961	-	Austin Preparatory School (Ceded)	Reading, MA	Villanova
1961	-	Augustinian Academy (Closed)	St. Louis, MO	Chicago
1961	-	Resurrection of Our Lord Parish	Dania, FL	Villanova
1962	1962	Casa San Lorenzo	Miami, FL	Villanova
1965	-	Santa Ana House (Closed)	Santa Ana, CA	California
1966	-	Casa Adolfo Camarillo (Closed)	Camarillo, CA	California
1966	-	Central Catholic High School (Closed)	Modesto, CA	California
1966 OSA	-	St. Anthony Parish (Ceded)	Baton Rouge, LA	Chicago
1967	-	Augustinian Provincialate (Closed)	Evanston, IL	Chicago
1967 OSA	-	St. Gregory Parish	Cambridge, ONT	Chicago
1969	-	St. Augustine Parish	Casselberry, FL	Villanova
1969	-	San Francisco House (Closed)	San Francisco, CA	California
1969	-	Villa Nueva Community (Closed)	San Ysidro, CA	California
1971	-	St. John Stone Friary	Chicago, IL	Chicago
1972 OSA	-	Immaculate Conception - St. Henry Parish	St. Louis, MO	Chicago
1973	-	Augustinian Midwest Priory (Ceded)	Villanova, PA	Chicago
1973	1985	St. John Stone Friary	Villanova, PA	Villanova
1935 CANADA 1975 CHICAGO	-	Holy Rosary Parish	Kenosha, WI	Chicago
1976	-	Tierra del Sol (Closed)	Boulevard, CA	California
1977 OSA	-	St. Mary Parish (Ceded)	Independence, MO	Chicago
1977 OSA	-	St. Joseph Parish	Pekin, IL	Chicago
1977	1977	Austin Friars Hall (Closed)	Washington, DC	Villanova
1925 CANADA 1979 CHICAGO	-	St. Rita Parish	Racine, WI	Chicago
1980	-	St. Rita Retreat Center	Gold Hill, OR	California
1980 OSA	-	Our Lady of Grace Parish	Castro Valley, CA	California
1981	-	Augustinian Community	North Andover, MA	Villanova
1981	-	Austin House (Prenovitiate)	San Diego, CA	California
1981	1982	Bl. James of Viterbo Friary	Golden Gate, FL	Villanova
1982	1982	St. Augustine Friary (Provincial Offices)	Villanova, PA	Villanova

1983	-	Austin Friary	Olympia Fields, IL	Chicago
1984 OSA	-	Augustinian Friary at Providence High School	New Lenox, IL	Chicago
1985	-	Monica House (Annex to Austin House)	San Diego, CA	California
1986	-	Augustinian National Novitiate	Racine, WI	Chicago
1986	-	Augustinians	Medford, OR	California
1987 OSA	-	St. Peter Parish (Mission Consolidation)	Douglas, MI	Chicago
1988	-	Austin House (Closed)	Scottsdale, AZ	Chicago
1988 OSA	-	Immaculate Heart of Mary Parish	Abbot, TX	Chicago
1988	-	Blessed William of Toulouse Monastery	Chicago, IL	Chicago
1990	-	St. Augustine Friary at Bishop McNamara High School	Kankakee, IL	Chicago
1991 OSA	-	Blessed Sacrament Parish (Mission Consolidation)	Allegan, MI	Chicago

THE IRISH AUGUSTINIANS IN INDIA, 1834-1841

Fr Peter Clancy, P.P., Dublin.

THE IRISH AUGUSTINIANS IN INDIA 1834-1841
Fr Peter Clancy, P.P., Dublin.

BACKGROUND AND PRELIMINARIES

The history of the Irish Augustinian Mission at Madras, in India, 1834-1841, opens up a whole new chapter of development there that had started way back in 1579 when Fr Stephens, S.J., sailed from Lisbon to the East Indies. By 1830 the whole of the South Indian Mission field was bereft of orthodox Catholic clergy, since the Portuguese civil prerogative of nominating to parishes and dioceses had led to much abuse. This was the lamentable *Padroado* custom[1]. The clergy of Portuguese origin had made themselves unacceptable to the majority of faithful Catholics due to their careless corruption. These clergy no longer had any credibility.

"The British Army Brass" had allowed a lack of discipline to develop, and signs of corruption crept down into the ranks. The very luxury of colonial power, the affluence, availability of scores of servants, the native leaders with their addiction to opium and opulence, caused the God-fearing colonists either in the East India merchant class or among the ruling Raj to become victims of greed and corruption.

In 1833 Dr Bramston, as apostolic delegate in London, had received urgent requests to send out English-speaking clerics to India. He wrote to Archbishop Murray of Dublin on 21 December 1833, as follows. 'I have been credibly informed that the District of Madras is very extensive, tho' its precise extent I have not been able to ascertain, and also that there are an immensity of Catholics there, either English or Irish or Natives, understanding the English Language better than any other'[2].

Earlier in the previous year Bramston had nominated an eminent Benedictine to be vicar apostolic at Madras. The nomination was accepted by Rome, and the monk was then appointed formally as vicar apostolic by the Holy See. Bramston stated, 'the proper Briefs were handed to me, he received them from my hands and he wrote to Rome to signify his acceptance of the office . . . afterwards he took fright, and then without my knowledge wrote again to Rome begging to be released from the charge he had accepted . . . [Later] I was informed that he repented of his second letter and would have accepted the office if again offered to him - in the meantime, however, I got another letter from Propaganda dated November 1832 requesting me to propose another person in the place of the one who had prayed to be released . . .'[3]

Bramston then contacted the President of the English Benedictines, as he 'had no secular clergy whom [he] could spare'[4], hoping the abbot would supply a competent number of assistants, but having written to Dr Nicholas Wiseman, his assistant, whom he had sent to Rome, he heard nothing till the end of the summer.

Bramston was ordered to apply to the proper quarter for permission to be given to Pedro D'Alcantara, bishop *in partibus* of Antiphellensis (actually vicar apostolic of Bombay), to go to Madras and exercise there as pastor for the time being. Dr Bramston thought the Benedictines were on their way, and he also surmised that the Capuchins, then supposedly ministering in Madras, would give place, together with their means of support, to the proposed missioners. This was

1. See Thomas F. MacNamara, S.S.J., 'Sketches in Indian Life and Religions. Padroado and Propaganda', in *Irish Ecclesiastical Record,* 38, 1931, pp 181-196, (at p.181), 39, 1932, pp 262-284, (at p.262).
2. Dublin Diocesan Archives, Murray Papers, 31/4.
3. Ibid.
4. Ibid.

really naive. Bramston also thought that the East India Company would assist in sending out the clergymen because of a Bill relating to India passed at the previous session of the English parliament. Here he was again an optimist. Finally, he stated to Archbishop Murray of Dublin, 'From the multiplicity of letters I have received from India . . . it is quite evident to me that the Clerics to be sent to India should be persons possessed of very considerable tact and knowledge and of truly Apostolic Spirit'[5]. Fr Daniel O'Connor was marked out to fulfil this difficult role.

Such was the state of matters at the beginning of 1834. Immediately, according to O'Connor's journal, Archbishop Murray contacted the East India Company with a view to gaining their goodwill, and to explore the possibility of obtaining financial aid to fit out and transport a group of Irish clergy to Madras[6].

It was now that Daniel O'Connor, an Irish Augustinian who had been prominent for some years in English and Irish ecclesiastical affairs, appeared on the India scene. Due to the interest and influence of James Warren Doyle, bishop of Kildare and Leighlin, O'Connor was nominated vicar apostolic for Madras, with the title, 'Bishop of Saldes', an extinct early christian Greek diocese. As vicar apostolic he was linked directly to Rome in theological terms, while, as 'Bishop of Saldes', he was part of the early christian church in Greece. In many ways O'Connor could be seen as a forlorn hope to salvage the Catholic Church at Madras - a Jonah thrown into the belly of the India whale.

Let us return briefly to Fr Daniel O'Connor's earlier years. As a friar and provincial of the Augustinians, he had already been involved in many delicate matters. In the mid 1820s, O'Connor had battled for four years to have the rebuilt Dungarvan church in County Waterford opened against the bishop of Waterford's ruling; eventually he won.

In early 1829 a great crisis arose regarding the religious orders as a result of the Emancipation Act, which aimed to suppress and banish all regulars and to abolish all benefices. This was a critical moment and needed immediate action. O'Connor's day had come. He proceeded to Dublin and, after consultation with the Dominicans at Tallaght, County Dublin, he led post-haste a delegation to London with the Dominican, Dr Leahy, and Mr Edmund Ignatius Rice, founder of the Irish Christian Brothers. This was a do or die effort to save the religious orders from extinction in that ironic twist to the Emancipation Act of 1829.

James Warren Doyle, O.S.A. ("J.K.L."), bishop of Kildare and Leighlin.

This London visit was to be of immense value within the next five years. It was O'Connor's test by fire, in tact, prudence, and the ability to communicate. Further, he was obliged, with speed, to muster arguments. He constructed memorials and petitions which were suited to the formal procedures of the parliament at Westminster.

O'Connor's 1829 visit to London brought him into contact with the heavyweights of the Empire - Peel, Lord Wellington, Sir James Mackintosh, Lord Lansdowne and Lord Clifden. This series of encounters steeled and prepared Daniel O'Connor for the future meetings in 1834 with the East India Company's directors and associated authorities.

Another factor was O'Connor's friendship with James Warren Doyle. Doyle had been trained by the Portuguese Augustinians in Coimbra, at the great medieval university of Portugal. On his return to Ireland and New Ross he taught young Daniel O'Connor theology, and also must have explained much about the Portuguese and their far-flung eastern empire. Doyle was later to be famous as "J.K.L." (James, bishop of Kildare and Leighlin) the mysterious initials under which he anonymously issued so many remarkable pamphlets and letters in the newspapers.

5. Ibid.
6. Irish Augustinian Provincial Archives, Ballyboden, Dublin, Bishop Daniel O'Connor, 'The Madras Mission', p.36.

While Doyle was a student in Coimbra he made several firm friends, one of them, an Augustinian, called Misquita who went as a missioner to East India along the Coromandel Coast. Doyle and Misquita kept contact over many years. This is proved in a letter which J.K.L. sent, on 16 June 1829, to another friend, Fr A. McDermott, O.S.A., living in Coimbra. He quoted a letter from Misquita who was in Calcutta at the time, 'He tells me of the great numbers of our poor Catholic fellow-countrymen who are in that city and its dependancies, destitute almost of the aids of religion'. Doyle continues, 'He presses me not only to request, but to urge our provincial in this country [Ireland] to send to the scene of his own labours two or three steady clergymen, Augustinians. Should you have such persons, I will have an application made at the Colonial Office in London for their transmission; and were they such as I could vouch for, 'tis probable they might be sent to Calcutta free of expense'[7]. This expectation of free travel would very soon prove to be merely wishful thinking. Meanwhile, before the following summer of 1830, J.K.L. was informed about the sad news of Misquita's saintly death on Good Friday[8]. This event fuelled the request Misquita had made to his dear friend, Doyle, in Ireland to send missionary help to India.

Let us fill in the background further. Shortly after O'Connor's ordination as a priest, 1809-1810, J.K.L. and O'Connor were together in New Ross. J.K.L. asked O'Connor's advice about a document he had produced on domestic nomination of bishops. It was a paper produced overnight, of formidable dimensions, which J.K.L. intended to send to the widely-read *Freeman's Journal* for publication. The topic was a lively one at the time and had caused many divisions of opinion. J.K.L. asked Daniel O'Connor to act as literary censor while he read it aloud. When he had finished O'Connor commented briefly, 'Your letter is, no doubt, able; but it seems to me that it will rather tend to provoke further discussion than to allay it'. J.K.L. had a high opinion of his friend's judgement, and so he replied crisply, 'True', then tore the article into fragments[9].

O'Connor's words, as quoted above, in 1812 to his friend, both newly ordained, were typical of his shrewd insight. A few years or so later this gift of forthright candor was to have far-reaching consequences for J.K.L. and eventually for O'Connor himself.

In about 1814/15, Carlow College staff under Dr Staunton nominated Doyle, then at New Ross, for a vacant chair at the College. Fr O'Connor had just been posted to the Augustinian House at Cork. Doyle postponed a decision with a view to seeking permission from his provincial, Fr Sheehan, also in Cork. Dr Staunton commented that it would be no problem as Fr Sheehan was an old friend of his and would agree to release Doyle from New Ross. But Doyle had already written from New Ross, immediately he heard the news, to his old friend, Fr O'Connor, apprising him of moves afoot. He asked O'Connor to convey to the provincial his readiness to accept this position but added his willingness to assume any other lesser position in the Order, if the Augustinian powers-that-be saw fit. O'Connor actedly promptly on his friend's wishes. He proceeded to the provincial's room and stated, but without any further comment, the desire of Doyle to be a professor at Carlow College. 'My dear O'Connor', replied Fr Sheehan, 'it is impossible that we can spare him'. 'Our Order is small, and death has thinned its ranks', he thus began his argument but after some moments O'Connor interjected, respectfully, 'You have little idea, Fr Provincial, of the intellectual power of that man. There is a mine of unwrought and untouched resources within his head. . . his splendid talents are intended for noble purposes. . . Let him to go to Carlow. . .'.[10] O'Connor's insight was to be proved correct. Less than six years later Doyle would be unanimously chosen bishop of Kildare at the exceptionally early age of thirty-three.

Colm Cooke in his article on Irish mission expansion tells that, 'in Ireland, in the years immediately after Emancipation, a number of events took place that gave emphasis to the missions.

7. W.J. Fitzpatrick, *Life, Times-and Correspondence of Dr Doyle,* Dublin 1880, Vol. II, p.28.
8. Idem, Vol. I, pp 20-21.
9. Ibid., pp 41-42.
10. Ibid., p.51.

In 1832 and again in 1834, Bishop John England of Charleston visited Irish seminaries seeking vocations'[11]. The bishop would later be a key ally for O'Connor when he went to Rome, and warned him about Cardinal Mai's niggardliness regarding cash. He would also advise O'Connor of the Pope's high regard towards him. Twenty years previously, at the time of the contentious proposal about an English government veto on the nomination of Catholic bishops in Great Britain and Ireland, Daniel O'Connor and Dr John England, together with James Warren Doyle and Dr Michael Blake, had spearheaded the opposition to it. These men were close knit in their zeal, courage, understanding and drive.

The above few details of persons and circumstances give a brief outline of the background leading to the Indian Mission. In June 1834 Doyle lay dying in "Braganza", his Carlow episcopal home. O'Connor, on his way to London to seek funds for his Mission but as yet not consecrated a bishop, visited him. J.K.L., on the point of death, could hardly lift himself up but to O'Connor he uttered words of blessing, 'Go - do good. God bless you'[12]. O'Connor later pondered on these words. W.J. Fitzpatrick in his well-documented biography of J.K.L. records his comments thus, 'He [Doyle] recommended me to the Holy See through Dr Murray. Being educated in Portugal he was very anxious to promote the mission in the East Indies, and when the opportunity occurred he fixed on me *proprio motu,* and felt gratified that an Irish Augustinian should be the first British-born subject that ever was a R. C. Bishop in British India. I knew nothing of the matter until the [papal] bulls were presented to me'[13].

Most Rev. Daniel O'Connor O.S.A., bishop of Madras, the first Catholic English-speaking bishop appointed to India.

O'CONNOR'S TOUR - LONDON, MAYNOOTH, IRELAND.

The amazing fact of the matter - O'Connor's being appointed to Madras, without any prior knowledge, quite out of the blue, as bishop of Saldes - galvanised him into immediate action. Archbishop Murray of Dublin had already contacted the English authorities in January about the financial help the authorities might give to an Irish Mission to India. As he had no reply by May he suggested to O'Connor, immediately on announcing his appointment as vicar apostolic on 26 April, that he should proceed to London and find out the position regarding funds for outfits; this would be the topic of intense discussion for almost the next year. Money is always a painful nerve with governments!

Following the announcement of 26 April 1834 O'Connor had immediately contacted Bishop Doyle, his trusted friend, who now lay dying, and was very weak. After two weeks studying Doyle's advice, O'Connor agreed to the appointment by mid-May. The papal bulls were handed to him on 7 June, at Cork, and within a week he was on his way to London, calling in at Carlow to get a last blessing from the great J.K.L., who three days later passed to his reward at the same time as O'Connor set sail for the heart of the British Empire. We must remember that England was at its highest point of imperial greatness just then. O'Connor's purpose was to seek funds to outfit his as yet unpicked staff, and also money for fares all the way to India. Every moment was now precious

11. Colm Cooke, 'The modern Irish Missionary Movement', in *Archivium Hibernicum,* Vol. 35 (1980), pp 234-246, at p.235.
12. Fitzpatrick, cit., Vol. II, p.504.
13. Ibid.

as he was to learn, and long delays were to halt him in his work.   English protocol and the letter of the law with all its complexities would dog his steps.

On his arrival in London, O'Connor proceeded to Mr Charles Grant, President of the Board of Control, and Mr Littleton, Secretary of State for Ireland, seeking interviews, and handing to them letters from Archbishop Murray of Dublin.   He now had to delay for a fortnight during which time he contacted Dan Callaghan, M.P. for Cork, and William Roche, M.P. for the City of Limerick. He had meetings with Daniel O'Connell and the Rt Hon. Thomas Spring-Rice, Secretary of State to the Colonies, and also with Rev. Dr Bramston, vicar apostolic at London.   The result of their meetings was the drafting of a memorial in, by our late 20th century standards, most deferential, almost grovelling, terms.

The introduction sets the scene.   'At the audience with which you were pleased to honour me on the subject of the Roman Catholic Mission to Madras, my honorable friend the member for the City of Limerick, William Roche Esq., having suggested the propriety of my setting forth in form of a memorial the grounds of my application to the Right Honorable the Court of Directors of the East India Company and Right Honorable Board of Control for an outfit and passage, etc., for myself and six or seven clergymen who being British subjects might have the superintendance of the Roman Catholick Religion in that District in place of Foreigners who now administer it, I beg leave most respectfully to submit the following view of my case for the kind Consideration of the Right Honorable Court and Board.

First - I beg leave to state that I have been appointed to the Episcopacy and office of Vicar Apostolic of . . . Madras without any previous notification on the subject, that I have accepted the appointment merely in obedience to the Holy See and at a great personal sacrifice, with the sole view of being useful, particularly to that very numerous class, the Roman Catholicks, Natives of Great Britain and Ireland, who are spread along the Coromandel Coast, and who, it appears from unquestionable authority, are most unhappy, discontented and dejected in spirit for want of the Consolations of their Religion.

Secondly - That it would seem from the very nature of the appointment, as if the Holy See intended to meet the views of the East India Company and British Government by preferring a British Subject to a Foreigner and Confiding to his Administration the most ample Spiritual powers; and it is respectfully submitted, that it would be useful to respond to the dispositions of his Holiness [the Pope] in this respect.

Thirdly - That the most feeling appeals have been made to his Holiness to send out such Missionaries - that there are no means of so doing - and that the evils of discontent, blasphemous arraignment of Providence - despair and a horror of entering the Service, which is obtaining at home, by reason of the representations of the deplorable Condition of the Roman Catholicks in that Country for want of the aid of their Religion must unavoidably continue unless the Company and Government provide a remedy for them by granting an outfit, passage, support and protection to said Missionaries.

Fourthly - That it would be a measure of sound policy to send those Missionaries out, must be evident from the precedent afforded by the Government in its Grant to Maynooth College and by the Colonial Department in its grant of an outfit, etc., to the R.C. Missionaries to the West Indies, New South Wales, etc., etc., which was not to be refunded out of their annuities; and that, if it be desirable, upon a principle of State Policy, to have the R.C. Religion administered by British Subjects rather than by Foreigners, it is obvious it cannot be effected unless by a State Provision.

Fifthly - That if ever there existed a Case which may be regarded as an exception to a general rule, it is humbly presumed the present may be considered as such - and that a benignant interpretation to the Act of the last Session, and generous co-operation with the Holy See in sending forth those Missionaries . . . will . . . operate greatly to the benefit of the State, and attract the hearts and excite the gratitude of the Roman Catholic British Subjects, who now so ardently desire this favour - exhibit the Protestant feeling in an amiable light - and directly tend to promote that peace and good will among all. . .

Lastly - That the report of the intended Mission to Madras having already gone forth to that Country, it will no doubt be hailed with joy and be expected with most ardent feelings of desire; that therefore it is much to be feared that a disappointment would only increase those evils, which this Mission was intended to remedy - that it is utterly out of my power to find the means to go out to India, that the Holy See has no means for the purpose and that it will be my duty to send back the Bulls [of appointment] immediately to his Holiness unless the Company furnish the means of an Outfit and Passage, etc., etc., to me and my fellow Missionaries'.

Daniel O'Connor concludes most humbly, 'I earnestly pray to be excused for having trespassed so long on your patience and the attention of the Honorable Court of Directors and the Board of Control, and beg to say, that whatever may be the result of the application, it will be a great favour to inform me, as soon as possible, of it, as I am unable to remain much longer at expense in the City.

I have the honor to remain, with the profoundest respect, your obedient and humble servant, Daniel O'Connor'[14].

Following O'Connor's failure to receive funds he returned from London via Bristol to Cork. He now considered what next could be done to provide for the six priests, at least, which Propaganda Fide desired he should take out with him. His first thought was he should return the papal bulls to Rome and cancel the affair but the matter had become so public and had gone so far that, after having consulted his religious brethren, he decided to accept and go to India alone at his own expense or rather at the expense of his Augustinian Order (since he was a professed religious, he had the strong support of his superior, Fr Charles Stuart O.S.A., Dublin, the provincial). Dr Murray, the archbishop of Dublin, was very pleased and immediately prepared for O'Connor's consecration as bishop on 3 August, 1834.

Meanwhile in Rome Cardinal Weld wrote on 31 July to Archbishop Murray, stating his knowledge of Britain's refusal re funds. 'I have so great an opinion of the good which will result from this Mission that I beg your Grace will open a Subscription for the expenses of the Voyage and put my name down and that of Lord Clifford [his son-in-law] for ten pounds each and think that whatever can be collected towards this good work will have a good effect in showing the willingness of the Catholics at home to assist their brethren in India. You may moreover assure Dr O'Connor, that he may rely upon the money necessary for his outfit being made up in what may be wanting in the Subscription by his Holiness, either from Propaganda or other funds'[15].

In regard to other funds, O'Connor had received information in late August through Bishop John England of Charleston (U.S.A.), then in Rome, that a certain Indian Queen had deposited a large amount of money at the disposal of His Holiness for promoting the Catholic religion. England suggested that a request should be made to the Holy See for a proportion of this bequest from the Indian Begum, as soon as possible. By late August the Irish bishops were conscious that their support would be required. Weld's letter, though doubted by O'Connor himself as being sufficiently official, was passed as such by Archbishop Murray, and so Murray agreed to act as treasurer to the fund. This was a most opportune time as all the bishops, or least archbishops, would meet in Maynooth in September. So, early in that month, O'Connor, as a newly appointed bishop, went to Dublin from Cork to Archbishop Murray. The archbishop mentioned to O'Connor at their meeting the strong desire that the great J.K.L. had expressed that he, O'Connor, should become a bishop.

O'Connor proceeded to Maynooth where the trustees and bishops received him with the utmost cordiality and started to subscribe towards the India Mission, together with the staff of the college. A promise was made that the worthy cause would be recommended to the consideration

14. 'The Madras Mission', cit., pp 37-40.
15. Dublin Diocesan Archives, Murray papers, 31/4.

of the clergy and people of their respective dioceses, and that any students or clergymen who might wish to go to India with him would have their territorial permission. There were nine Irish bishops present, together with Polding, the new vicar apostolic of New South Wales, Australia, and his friend Dr England, bishop of Charleston, U.S.A. It was then and there agreed that a circular should be addressed by O'Connor to the other bishops of Ireland relating the objects of his India Mission, and his intention to visit each diocese throughout all Ireland.

In brief, the circular, dated 22 September 1834, stated that: Bishop O'Connor is willing to sacrifice himself to the Madras Mission, but he needs £1000 to get under way. He tried to get funds from the British, and as that has failed, there is no alternative but to abandon the millions who are within the range of his future jurisdiction to all the horrors of infidelity, ignorance and vice, or to appeal to the humanity, tolerance and charity of our community for the means of sending forth missionaries to avert such calamities from so vast a portion of the human race. He urges them, since they value their faith, to testify to it by generosity. The circular concluded, 'Dr O'Connor will visit each Diocese if possible or send one of his Clergymen to await on the Bishops, the Clergy and the Laity for their Donations, which will be thankfully received. . .'[16]

O'Connor visited all the bishops in Ireland, twenty-seven in number, and, as far as time permitted and in so far as he could meet the clergy, he was tolerably successful in his fund raising. The time had not been right for such visits. It was the winter season when conferences were over and the clergy were occupied in holding confessional stations. O'Connor met few of the clergy, other than those immediately with or near the bishops, and therefore was not as successful as he might have been.

The subscriptions varied greatly. In Cork where he was well-known, and whose Bishop Murphy had consecrated him, almost £250 was subscribed. Dublin was over £150; Ferns, Galway, Limerick and Cloyne, where Augustinian houses existed, gave almost another £250; in contrast Derry, Down and Connor, and Meath gave £19 between them[17]. This was the pattern. Bishop O'Connor was weary with the labour and the large expense of his winter of continual travelling, often to no avail. He writes in his memoir that this state of affairs led him to think he was only collecting for the benefit of stage coaches, steamers and hotels![18] He stated this sombre fact to the Holy See and to his friends at Rome in many letters appealing for their help.

These letters were slow in arriving, and often even slower in being dealt with. A letter from Cardinal Weld is a classic of misinformation or lack of information, and of jumping to conclusions. It is very hard to believe that the cardinal could have been so ignorant of the facts. His letter is dated 21 October 1834, yet O'Connor's friend Dr England could write two months earlier on 21 August saying that he had spoken to the Pope about O'Connor's pressing problem - money. England remarked, too, that Monsignor Mai 'is one of the most difficult men in Rome with whom to treat on money matters, and so much so, that upon every other topick, he and I are the best of friends; but upon some of my own business of this matter, he is unmanageable . . .' England continued with words of advice, 'You have however from your Religious Profession, a nack of winning your way on such occasions, and you are likely to do so on this - but not immediately. Press gently however, and you will do better than any Advocate. . . . the Pope [with whom England had been talking for nearly an hour] . . . expressed his utmost confidence in you, not only from what I said, but from the reports he had had of you, and could not avoid making a remark, . . . respecting the zeal, the ardor and the devotion to the Holy See of the Irish People and their generous contributions notwithstanding their poverty, after the various confiscations for their adherence to their faith. I spoke with Lord Clifford who is deeply interested in Indian Catholick Affairs, and with Cardinal Weld . . . You will succeed'[19]. Compare this letter indicating slow

---

16. 'The Madras Mission', cit., pp 51-52.
17. Ibid., p.53.
18. Ibid., pp 54-55.
19. Ibid., pp 108-109.

progress, with Weld's letter from Rome exactly two months later. A strange pattern emerges regarding the realities of fact as against fiction.

Weld wrote to Archbishop Murray, 'I trust that my letter of the 3rd of August last duly reached your Grace, in time to forward the object of Dr O'Connor, who has, I presume, before this time sailed for Madras. As I have heard nothing further on the subject, I flatter myself that he has been able to undertake the voyage, without having recourse to the source, which . . . was disposed to assist him. Tho' Government at home were backward in helping him, I think . . . he will not find the same backwardness at . . . his destination . . .'[20] Weld then requested Murray to divert all the monies intended for O'Connor, i.e. £20 together with £30 more, to two Sisters from Mecklenburg Street Convent, Dublin, with rental problems, who had been writing very strong letters to the Archbishop's secretary[21]. He obviously thinks a full team of priests has also gone out to India. This is presumed in his letter in which he had first offered help (31 July).

The fact that Bishop O'Connor finally prevailed was in large measure due to his persistent drive and energy in reminding Rome of his predicament, also in canvassing all the clerics, religious as well as secular, and any other persons of influence contactable. Two of these, Lady Wellesley, the Viceroy's wife, and Lord Lismore are worth mentioning, as their influence and letters of recommendation were to be of much value.

O'Connor returned to London in early spring 1835 with a lot less trepidation, since Propaganda Fide had by then given an assurance of £704 from the Begum's bequest being lodged with Dr Bramston in London[22]. O'Connor himself had collected almost £1,000 by sheer hard work and dedication. The exact total is fully detailed in The Madras Mission log book detailing his preparatory travel meetings, letters, staff, fitting out of the ship and the voyage[23]. The sum he gathered single-handed was £942.8s.6p. It was a mighty sum at that particular time in the Irish scene. The methods used were very slow and seemingly archaic, but there were no phones, no postage as we know it today, no motorised transport.

HOPEFUL SIGNS, FITTING OUT AND SETTING SAIL, 1835
Letters etc. - 2nd visit to London - Dockside

The intricate tangle with the Court of Directors in June 1834 steeled O'Connor. At the outset the cruel rebuff by Gordon, as Secretary to the Court of Directors, distinctly stated 'that the Court . . . had no idea that the Roman Catholic Bishops would be appointed, that the East India Company were opposed to the introduction of any other Religion but the Protestant - that Catholics should find the means of sending out their own Ministers. . .'[24] Grant was equally tardy though he made some effort to interpret the proviso of the new Act in a new light. He interpreted the clause, 'Provided that nothing herein contained shall be construed to prevent the Governor General [of Madras] in Council, from granting such sums of Money, as he may deem expedient, to clergymen of other Religious Denominations, for the purposes of Education and the Building and Repairing of churches'[25].

Grant's instructions were to the following effect: 'that by the words building and repairing Churches etc. should be understood not the mere building of walls, etc., but also that they comprehend a provision for the Clergy officiating therein and imparting education and that the Act should be construed in the most liberal spirit'[26]. A change of fortune was to give the bishop a big boost in the next four hectic months. People of influence were to help give him access to the people that really mattered in the Anglo-Indian scenario.

---

20. Dublin Diocesan Archives, Murray Papers, 31/4.
21. Dublin Diocesan Archives, Hamilton Papers.
22. 'The Madras Mission', cit., p.105.
23. Ibid., pp 80-91.
24. Ibid., p.37.
25. Ibid., p.62.
26. Ibid.

A visit to the officials in the Phoenix Park was very much a prestigious exercise. The Lord Lieutenant's wife, Marchioness Wellesley, was very kind, showing her interest immediately the issue became public. Dr O'Connor recorded the visit as having been an event of prime importance; he also wished to give public evidence and recognition to the lady's deep personal faith, conviction, and her witness to the importance of the forthcoming Mission. In using her initiative she asked Dr O'Connor to visit her at the Vice-Regal Lodge, Phoenix Park, which in itself was symbolic of the power and prestige of the British monarchy. A message for O'Connor was communicated to Archbishop Murray and forwarded by his secretary, Dr Hamilton at Marlboro St, to Dr O'Connor at the Augustinian Priory, Chapel Lane, John's St, Dublin. Dated 22 Sept. 1834, it read, 'I am desired by Her Excellency, the Marchioness Wellesley, to say that she would feel gratified if your Lordship would favour her with a visit at the Park on tomorrow, Tuesday, at 12.00 o'clock'[27].

In his memoir, O'Connor refers with gratitude to her gift of £10 and her courteous attention. He formed 'a judgment of [her] superior mind and intelligence, especially her exalted piety and ardent desire to promote the Holy Catholick Religion, to which purpose she seemed anxious to make her exalted Station serve by every means in her power'[28]. He continues in his memoir, 'She spoke of India with peculiar delight, and of the government of the Marquis there'. She then enquired about the progress of religion in the United States of North America, of which country she was a native. Finally, she requested, on her knees in traditional style, the bishop's benediction.

The second important contact Bishop O'Connor made was the friendship and hospitality of Lord Lismore, "Shanbally", Clogheen in South Tipperary. Lord Lismore was most influential, having headed the Liberal poll in the elections of 1832 and getting a thousand more votes than The O'Conor Don. Lismore's brother, Robert William O'Callaghan, had been in all the Napoleonic wars and had been closely noted by Wellington who mentioned him in despatches. O'Callaghan received awards for courage in over ten battles. He was then, in 1815, appointed to be chief-of-staff commanding Flanders and also France. He was, by 1834, filling the office of Commander-in-Chief at Madras, having replaced William Bentinck. Dr O'Connor was to come to know him intimately within the next year.

First of all O'Connor called to "Shanbally" after being invited several Times-by the viscount, who had asked him to stay for a week at his magnificent castle. O'Connor was very busy at the time, making arduous rounds of the country, fund raising. Lord Lismore kept repeating his

Shanbally, Co. Tipperary, where Bishop Daniel O'Connor was a guest of Lord Lismore.

---

27. Ibid., p.69.
28. Ibid., p.70.

invitation, and finally the bishop arrived for a few days at this splendid residence.   There he met the Catholic bishop of Waterford, and many important people who had been gathered by Lord Lismore, among these were Colonel Pretty, former M.P. for Tipperary, and his son Francis Pretty[29].

O'Connor was given the utmost attention and kindness at "Shanbally".   Important contacts were established by letters he received, to be brought to India and also to London; they were vital in those times.   For example, Lord Lismore sent a letter to his brother, Sir Robert, mentioned above.   Lismore's sister and daughter also sent letters to him, and to Lord Lismore's second son who was secretary to Sir Robert.   Colonel Pretty likewise enclosed one for Sir Robert and also for Sir Frederick Adams, governor of Madras.   We quote Pretty's letter, which concluded in very intimate terms and opened the "inner circle" to O'Connor.

'Shanbally, 16th January 1835

My dear William,

This will be handed to you by the Catholick Bishop of Madras, who is just going out from this Country.   He is of the highest Character and his sojourn amongst us here, for a few days, has interested us exceedingly in his favour.   He takes letters from Lismore to you, and I could not let him go without one from me also.   I know you will do whatever lies in your power to assist him, and I shall feel greatly obliged to you.   He will inform you, what I know will give you pleasure, that your old representative M.P. is well etc. - takes his bottle in the Evening after Cock Shooting in the morning, with as much pleasure as ever.

Farewell, my dear William, I am delighted to hear so good accounts of your and young William's health'[30].

Lord Lismore's brother, John, gave O'Connor a letter for Lord Lowther, and Lord Lismore himself passed on letters for Lord Duncannon and Mr Abercromby, Speaker of the House of Commons, Westminister.

A final letter from Lord Lismore, 30 March 1835, to Dr O'Connor, mentions in so many words the close affinity that had been established.   Opening his heart to him, Lord Lismore begins, 'I write with great pain, in consequence of an accident, which has renewed an old hurt, but not withstanding, I have laboured, and as I hope, to do you some service.   You will receive herewith letters [of introduction] . . . and I hope these Gentlemen will receive you kindly.   In my last dispatch there were letters to Lord Clare, Lord William Benti[n]ck, and Mr Prendergast . . .   If you make this road your way to Dublin, pray make this House your Inn, and let me know, should you not travel this way, where I may write to you in London.   I suffer so much pain, that I must conclude.   Believe me, My dear Lord, to be your sincere Friend and hearty well-wisher, tho' at this moment unable to express all I feel, and all I wish for you, who so boldly undertake such arduous duties in a Land so distant from your Friends.   Believe me to be yours, most sincerely, LISMORE'[31].

On his return to London, in late March 1835, O'Connor proceeded to get final details about sailing and the voyage to India into place.   His letter of 2 April 1835 to Archbishop Murray of Dublin gives a general view of progress.

'My dear Lord,

I have been here now a week, and have engaged a Passage for myself and three Clergymen for four hundred pounds.   The Ship is the Duke of Sussex, 1400 Tons, lately belonging to the East India Company, and will sail, as early as possible, in May - she merely touches at Madras, and proceeds thence to China, for which she is now as late as she can be, therefore must necessarily use all possible dispatch in proceeding on her voyage.   I am assured that I shall be in Madras sooner than if I went in the earliest ship sailing this month, as those immense vessels sail faster thro' those

29. Ibid., pp 71-72.
30. Ibid., p.118.
31. Ibid., p.72.

mighty seas - moreover, they afford more room, air, and place for luggage, and are much more respectable, and the price is very little more than a ship half her size. I have been several times with Dr Bramston, enjoyed his hospitable attention, and was introduced by his Lordship at the East India House. His Lordship is anxious your Grace would draw for the £704.3.4 as soon as possible, as he seems to think that it has an unbusinesslike appearance to have it left in the Banker's hands, and I would wish Your Grace to do so, as soon as you could, as I must draw upon that sum, to meet my demands. I intended to return to Cork by Dublin, but as I must be in Cork by the 5th Inst. I shall have to leave London tomorrow for Bristol, to meet the steamer for Cork. I have got an additional clergyman here - from the Diocese of Limerick - one of whom, I have been already speaking to Your Grace - so that now I have four, and may yet be able to make up my number, as the vessel won't sail until May . . . I have had an interview with Lord Lowther, thro' the introduction of Lord Lismore, and he promised to introduce me to Lord Elenborough, President of the Board of Control, [at] the end of the week. On my return to London, I will wait on Your Grace, and in the meantime,

I remain . . . .'[32]

While home in Ireland he gathered over sixty letters and packages for transportation to India from lay people, nuns, priests, and associates in the vast sub-continents. That was an accomplishment in itself. Of special interest were two letters from the Capuchin, Fr Theobald Mathew at Cork, to Quaker religious friends[33].

On his return to London, for the next few days Dr O'Connor was very busy. He presented the letter to Lord Lowther. He also presented letters to the Speaker of the House of Parliament, Mr Abercromby, who introduced him to Sir John Hobhouse, the President of the Board of Control. This was a great break-through. Hobhouse promised to be as useful as he could be, consistent with the duties of his office, and accepted the printed resolutions of the Roman Catholics of Madras which the London Catholic vicar apostolic, Bramston, had given to O'Connor.

Lord Duncannon attended kindly to Lord Lismore's introduction and handed over several letters of introduction to influential people in India. O'Connor also met Spring-Rice, who had been colonial secretary but was now in the "hot seat" as Chancellor of the Exchequer, to thank him for all his previous attention and kindness in giving him letters of introduction. He also waited on Mr Littleton and Mr Grant for similar purposes. He missed no chance in meeting as many people as possible, by trying to pay his respects to Sir Robert Peel and the Duke of Wellington. They were, however, out when he called but as we will see from his final letter, of 7 May, he would meet them just before he sailed for Madras.

Dr O'Connor's comment in his letter to Archbishop Murray above, about the immense vessel the *Duke of Sussex,* which would serve them well on their exciting voyage of 93 days, was full of praise as to its being a comfortable, safe and fast vessel. The fact that he secured passage on board was due in great part to a chance meeting at "Shanbally" when Lord Lismore received him most warmly. While there he had the pleasure to meet a Mrs Capt. Hewson. She was a native of Madras and was present at Colonel Curry's - the agent to the Duke of Devonshire.

Dr O'Connor tells us that 'the meeting which appeared to be purely accidental turned out to be most providential in the useful information and the introductions with which she most kindly, promptly, and under very inconvenient circumstances, furnished him'[34]. One such person was Mr Gutherie of 9 Idol Lane Towers Street, London. This individual was most useful; he made all the arrangements about the ship, the fitting out of the three cabins, the providing of thirty-two chests for books and all the other items being brought out by the ten missionaries. Even more important was his introducing O'Connor to certain merchants and business associates by letter when O'Connor would arrive in Madras. The bishop details a dozen letters from him. He says of Mr

---

32. Dublin Diocesan Archives, Murray Papers, AB3/34/11.
33. 'The Madras Mission', cit. p.77.
34. Ibid., p.74.

Gutherie, regarding his goodness, hospitable attention and counsel in every respect, that all of the Mission staff considered themselves deeply indebted to him[35].

FINAL LETTER BEFORE SAILING, 7 MAY 1835

'My Dear Lord,

I am on the point of proceeding to Gravesend to embark with four Priests, one Deacon, three Catechists and one Servant - and the Ship sails tomorrow morning. Altho' the sea and such an immense voyage may have its terrors, I do assure your Grace it is comparatively to me an occasion of repose from the bustle and fatigue of the past year. It is however a matter of Consolation to reflect that all things have succeeded so well - that nothing has been left undone - that we are so well provided for our voyage and above all that we have before us such encouraging prospects of success. Thanks be to God - the Holy See - Your Grace and the Prelates of Ireland to whom I beg your Grace to convey my most grateful acknowledgment of their goodness and liberality, and that of their respective Clergy.

I received the amount of Your Grace's draft on Wright & Co. for £704.3.4 immediately on my arrival here. The whole amount of our Passage is £630, but as to the Expense of our outfit, travelling and residence here, etc., etc., etc., it is so immense that I shall have very little of the Loan from Propaganda on my arrival at Madras.

I have had interviews with the Speaker; Lord Duncannon - Sir John Hobhouse - the Chancellor of the Exchequer - Lord Lowther - and Mr Gordon, Secretary to the Court of Directors E.I. Company. I visited Mr Charles Grant (now Lord Glenelg) - Mr Littleton, Sir Robert Peel and the Duke of Wellington, and have got letters from Mr Lushington, the late Governor of Madras - and from Lord Duncannon to Sir Frederick Adam the present Governor - and if I had a little more time, would have letters to Lord Hatesburry the present Governor General and to Sir H. Fane, the Commander in Chief of the Indian Forces, but it is likely Sir John Hobhouse will do everything in that way, as he assured me, in the kindest manner, that if bigotry hitherto existed in his department - "the Board of Control" - it would no longer exist, and that he would take care that the Act of the last Parliament concerning Roman Catholics in India should be construed with the utmost liberality, and that he would see his former predecessor in office, Mr Charles Grant, on the Subject: as yet I have not heard the result, but will today. The report of this morning is that Mr Grant, Lord Glenelg, is to be Governor General of India; if so, all is settled - Dr Bramston is well and was concerned to hear of Your Grace's Illness. I cannot have the consolation of hearing from Your Grace, but you may rest assured that if the prayers of so unworthy an individual, as I sincerely believe myself to be, can find any acceptance before God, I shall never cease to remember Your Grace to my latest breath'[36].

VOYAGE AND ARRIVAL

Dr O'Connor was much occupied for several weeks before he embarked for India. His main concern were his staff whom he tried to gather as best he could. They included three Augustinians, Fathers Michael Page and Michael Stephens from Galway, and Fr Patrick E. Moriarty from Dublin, who was to be his mainstay, as the others proved difficult, Page returning to the Cape shortly after arrival, being in danger of death. Fr William Dinan from Limerick, a secular priest and educated in France, was very difficult at first but settled down later. A very promising young teacher, James Olliffe from Cork, who had attained Sizer recognition at Trinity College, Dublin, and whose brother later became Bishop of Calcutta, died on the voyage out. Thomas McAuliffe also part of the team, London-born, fully out-fitted by his family, educated at Cork, was only fifteen years old but very promising. Michael McCarthy, also from Cork, was specially ordained deacon fourteen

---

35. Ibid.
36. Dublin Diocesan Archives, Murray Papers, AB3/34/11.

months before the normal time so that he could be of use on arrival; he was a relative of the bishop of Cloyne, Dr Crotty[37]. The Rev. Fr Page, O.S.A., was to prove very disagreeable to O'Connor on board; this was partly due to bad health, as he was afflicted with scrofula and the doctors told him it would prove fatal. O'Connor comments in his letter of 12 February 1836, 'I was obliged after losing so much by him to let him go on the 16th ult. The ship touches at the Cape and he may stay there, as the climate is good . . .' [38]   Finally, John Walsh, a servant man, was included in the team, and was to walk out on him with seven weeks' wages on 1 December, getting the next boat home, afraid for his health.

O'Connor had been very busy getting books ready; he was to bring out over twenty trunks of books. There were about 5,500, including pamphlets; 2,100 were printed by Coyne's and 3,400 by Battersby. The total number of titles was 130. These had to be sorted, packed and put on board.

Eventually on 8 May 1835 all ten sailed from Gravesend in the afternoon and so started a mighty adventure, taking ninety-three days, going by the Cape of Good Hope. The ship had about three hundred crew and was nearly two hundred feet long; it was in O'Connor's words a majestic ship. When they arrived at the Equator, suddenly on Whit Sunday, 7 June, the thunder and lightning and torrents were terrific. The jibboom was split and became useless. The lightning shot around 'like so much of the purist liquid fire'[39]. The squall returned during the night to be much more violent. This weather continued until 12 June.

Ships rounding the ironically-named Cape of Good Hope, South Africa, en route to Madras in 1835.
The sketch was made on board the ship following that of Bishop Daniel O'Connor, O.S.A.

O'Connor relates that some days later, just as they crossed the Line, the wind came up from the North East and they were brought almost on to a coral bank. Towards the end of the month the East, South-East Trade Wind arose and the ship completed 1,500 miles in six days. Then on 13 July, at 4.30 in the morning, when they were passing the Cape, the ship was wrecked from stem to stern. 'We [had] attempted to go round the Cape too soon',[40] and because of the current and a contrary wind, the ship had gone off course; 'away went the foremast, . . . carrying with it all the

37. For O'Connor's staff cf. 'The Madras Mission', cit., pp 64-69.
38. Dublin Diocesan Archives, Murray Papers, AB3/34/11.
39. 'The Madras Mission', cit., p.126.
40. Ibid., p.127.

rigging of the Bowsprit and main mast down to the Main Top, and having lost the use of our Boom . . . we were in the twinkling of an eye so far a compleat wreck'[41]. They were now 700 miles from the Cape or any land and it was thought better to make their way to Simon's Bay to refit. 'But the Providence of God that had saved us, still favoured us, and we were enabled to stand out to sea . . . whilst we were refitting . . .'[42] Within a week the ship was refitted and during that time 'it was more like a dockyard, with carpenters, sail makers and smiths at work . . .'[43] non-stop.

This is a unique account of a mission voyage, written on board the sailing vessel during the journey. It indicates right throughout a deep sense of dependence on God's providence.

O'Connor continues, 'We have now arrived at Madras, as perfectly fitted up, and painted, as if no such disaster had befallen us. Such the advantage of coming out in one of those fine Ships, so well appointed and furnished with materials and workmen for the purpose'[44]. This account is but a brief summary of O'Connor's diary.

On arrival at Madras Roads - as the beach was called - coming on shore was quite an event as there was no harbour and small row-boats brought the people to the beach. The party were received with the utmost joy by the Catholic population who had long hoped for their arrival. Thousands assembled on the beach having been on the look out, expecting them for some time. There were fifty thousand Catholics in or around the city who had been denied normal spiritual guidance for years. Also in the outer part of the vicariate were scattered about three hundred and fifty thousand more believers, together with about twenty million pagan natives.

SETTLING IN AT MADRAS

When Bishop O'Connor set foot on Indian soil, he states, 'The Vicar Apostolick of Bombay, who awaited my arrival, and indeed the four Capuchin Fathers, received us very graciously . . . and the people were overjoyed. I was installed [in the Cathedral] on Sunday the 30th of August, proceeded at once on the duties assigned to me, and the Vicar of Bombay [Peter of Alcantara] shortly after set out for his own residence where he expected to arrive in December, and I have not as yet [12 February] heard from him.

Nothing could equal the kindness of Government. I had the honor of dining with the Governor, Sir Frederick Adams, and meeting the Commander in Chief [of India], Sir Henry Fane, . . . who arrived the same day, on which we did . . . I was entertained by the Commander in Chief at Madras Presidency, Sir Robert William O'Callaghan, Brother of Lord Lismore, . . . [and many other dignitaries].

I sent in my letters [of introduction] from the ship, by Reverend Mr Moriarty. - The moment he got the letter he left business and the newly arrived Commander in Chief came into town, took me off to his residence in his own Carriage, detained me there for a month - introduced me to all the wealth and respectability of the surrounding Country, made me acquainted with all the particulars of the disputes, and property of the Mission, from the publick Records. Instructed me how I was to address the Government, and procure its approbation and assurance of support - assisted me in getting possession of the funds of the Mission, in opposition to the Advocate General who opposed the recognition of the [Papal] Bulls - also in addressing the Supreme Government on the Clauses in the Charter Act relative to Education etc. and the consequence has been that we got 5,000 Rupees or about 500£ for repairs of this Church. Had the Hospital and Fort Chaplain's salary augmented from 35 Rupees per men. to 150 Rupees per men. and 50 per mensem will be allowed for a British Clergyman at every British Station, and the clause concerning Education and Support for the Clergymen has been referred by the Supreme Government to the Court of Directors'[45]. In this same regard we know that St Leger in Calcutta had also got a small rise in

41. Ibid., pp 127-28.
42. Ibid., p.128.
43. Ibid., p.129.
44. Ibid.
45. Dublin Diocesan Archives, Murray Papers, AB3/34/11.

pay. But the Church of England clergymen were paid ten Times-as much.

The bishop continues, especially praising Mr Henry Chamier, who was of great benefit to him by helping constantly with the many problems which arose. On the bishop's arrival an address of welcome was presented to him and a special address of welcome was also directed to Rome, thanking the Holy See for sending O'Connor to re-establish religion - 'We feel utterly incapable of expressing our sense of gratitude for the deep interest testified towards our spiritual welfare, and for the incalculable boon thus conferred on us by the Holy See; for which act of pious solicitude and kindness, our humble but sincere prayers shall never cease to be offered up . . .'[46] This address was given at a public meeting in the presence of hundreds of Catholic dignitaries.

Bishop O'Connor replied to the Roman Catholic inhabitants of Madras, 'I am deeply sensible to compliments conferred upon me and the Clergymen who have accompanied me hither . . . and charged as I am with the awful care of such an innumerable multitude of Souls, your address is to me peculiarly gratifying and consolatory, in as much as it is the assured test of that spirit of Religion, which you entertain, and of your disposition to uphold it by co-operating with me and my Clergy, in the great and important work, which is given to us to perform in your regard'[47]. The Catholic laity, in their special committee set up to arrange the public address, in their preparatory meeting stated, in their invitation, 'From the incessant engagements of your Lordship since your landing on our shores [20 August], and from the inconvenience naturally attendant while entering a foreign Country . . . we were induced to defer thus publicly intruding on your Lordship at an earlier period' [13 Sept.][48].

The bishop in those twenty days had come to understand the very large problems confronting the Mission. He comments as follows, 'Notwithstanding the good dispositions of the Clergymen connected with . . . the Black Town, and the anxious desire of the Venerable Peter de Alcantara, Vicar Apostolic of Madras, . . . to do the good work, and to restore order and peace, still from age, infirmity and want of the English Language, as well as from a dissatisfaction among the laity arising out of the spiritual privation they endured, much confusion, and misunderstanding arose - a spirit of insubordination crept in - piety decayed and charity grew cold, so that I deeply regret to be obliged to admit that I have found the Roman Catholic Religion in the Mission of Madras reduced to the lowest condition'[49]. This gives some idea of what O'Connor had to tackle and overcome.

In this same document I have quoted from, he lists the churches of Madras, 13 in number, of which only two were working, with practically no funding. He lists the number of Capuchins or Augustinian clergy as thirteen - of which nine were schismatics. The catechists numbered eight.

This was the position as he found it. We have seen from his 12 February 1836 letter the progress he was able to report, regarding the cooperation of the authorities, but the rebellious clergy posed a great difficulty. This was similar to Dr St Leger's problem at Calcutta. O'Connor states, 'I never met Dr St Leger, but am in regular Corrispondence with him, and the Bishop of Pondicherry who is . . . the Vicar of St Thomè or in other words, the Episcopal Governor of the See of Meliapore . . , has given me and Dr St Leger great trouble - he holds two of my churches, and after all my efforts - remonstrance - threats - condescension, etc., - holds out, as he does also against Dr St Leger, but Dr St Leger declared him and the Missionaries of Bengal Schismaticks, the 1st of January last - and still they all hold out, even against the express decree of Propaganda, until the Court of Portugal issues its orders. . . It is likely his Holiness will not only confirm the sentence of Dr St Leger, but deprive the See of Meliapore of all its privileges (if any it had, as the Hierarchical Church of India is now defunct, there being not a single Bishop of the Portuguese appointment under the *juspatronatus* in existence) and declare that my appointment was for the whole presidency of Madras, which would include Meliapore, and that his Holiness will call on me

---

46. Dublin Diocesan Archives, Murray Papers, 31/4-5.
47. Ibid.
48. Ibid.
49. Ibid.

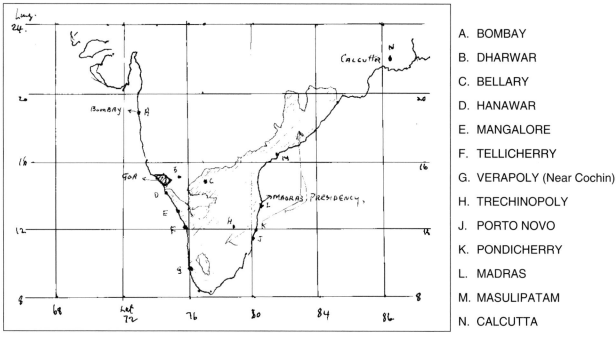

A. BOMBAY

B. DHARWAR

C. BELLARY

D. HANAWAR

E. MANGALORE

F. TELLICHERRY

G. VERAPOLY (Near Cochin)

H. TRECHINOPOLY

J. PORTO NOVO

K. PONDICHERRY

L. MADRAS

M. MASULIPATAM

N. CALCUTTA

Map of India showing Madras Presidency

to exercise such jurisdiction'[50].

O'Connor continues in his letter to Archbishop Murray of Dublin, 'the condition of Religion under the authority of Goa . . . is deplorable - disputes and scandals without end'. He continues, 'I pray your Grace excuse this long incoherant scrawl into which I have been insensibly led, having had so many things to say'[51].

By August 1836, the <u>civil authorities</u> having been given a full account of the situation of dissension, decided through the Governor General of India in Council, to recognise Bishop O'Connor as the only legal representative between the local government and the Court of Rome through which all official business of the Roman Catholic church was to be conducted. This in summary is the result of a memorandum, No. 100, issued from Fort George on 30 November 1836[52].

Moving on to a letter of 9 January 1837 - O'Connor to Murray - the bishop makes in a closely written seven page letter seven repeated calls for extra clergy. It is almost heartrending. He had ambitious plans. In his letter he says, 'There never was such a field for exertion, nor a more favourable opportunity, and I say it with perfect confidence and truth, that if we had about sixteen Irish priests to place at the . . . Military Stations through this Presidency - well prepared to preach and discharge with zeal and example the duties of the Ministry, and about eight Irish students, with a competent professor of Philosophy and Theology - and the same number of East Indian and Native Students, this would be one of the most flourishing Missions in the Church of God. Such is the ardent desire of all, to have the aid and consolations of Religion. The want of them at present is most deplorable'[53]. He continues, 'but what was the use of all this when we had not the clergy to come, or the means of paying for their passage?'[54] He then goes on to suggest that the clergy might be allowed to take free passage on His Majesty's ships or with the troops coming into the country free. He explains he is ready at that moment to receive four Irish students,

---

50. Ibid., AB3/24/11.

51. Ibid.

52. Ibid.

53. Ibid.

54. Ibid.

if they could be sent out to him, and if they would find support *gratis.*

He goes on to outline the problem of bigotry from the fanatics 'who do much mischief and put the cunning Brahmins on their guard to resist Christianity, and keep the people in the thraldom of all that is abominable in Paganism. It is truly afflicting to behold such a multitudinous population, amiable and interesting in their deportment, plunged into the very depths of Idolatry, even to the worshipping of the Devil himself and concilating his friendship by sacrifices of their Cattle, etc., etc., and enjoying the most squalid wretchedness - esteeming themselves as so many degrees of the Diety itself. . . A spirit of Fanaticism has found its way lately into the Civil and Military departments of Government. Our Commander in Chief, Sir Peregrine Maitland . . . has lately issued orders against the profane sports and amusements of Horseracing - Balls, and Plays,'[55] etc. O'Connor mentions he must be very careful in what he writes because whatever is written to Europe returns back at the next opportunity. 'Emissaries are on the watch to know the sentiments expressed by Catholics from this Country, so that we cannot be too cautious in what we say and to whom we write'[56]. Here one senses O'Connor becoming hemmed in and fearful.

There was some good news in the letter, 'The schism[s] of Bengal and Meliapore have received a death blow by the appointment of Dr St Leger and myself as the official organ of Communication between the Roman Catholics and the Government'[57]. Such were the problems facing Bishop O'Connor at the beginning of 1837.

Within six weeks, Rome received a letter from him[58], stating that his left side was completely paralysed and asking immediately for the appointment of a coadjutor who could assume the government of the vicariate in case of his death. He rules out Fr Moriarty, his V.G., as being unsuitable, since he lacked experience and was only thirty-two years old. Thus we enter a new phase with the preparation for the coming of Dr Carew and his team in the following year. Word reached Archbishop Murray of Dublin from Rome by early 1838, as their letter to him was dated 21 Nov. 1837 and dealt with O'Connor's request which he had sent eight months earlier in March 1837.

THE UNSETTLING PERIOD

The strange event of 22 March 1837, when Dr O'Connor reports having had a severe stroke, gives room for speculation. Several factors had obviously built up a tension within him:
1. His almost total lack of staff.
2. The gruelling daily routine - rising at 4.30 a.m. - Mass at 6 a.m. - Confessions for three hours - the vast numbers seeking spiritual assistance etc.
3. The pressing need for educational facilities - the promised bequest of the Begum had not arrived, though he had written to her in October after his arrival.
4. The constant annoyance from the regular clergy, especially from a Capuchin, Fr Louis of Venice, whom he was forced to remove, and who went to ground, O'Connor suspected, at St Thomè, Meliapore.
5. In this context, the Capuchins hatched a calumny against Dr O'Connor and sent a complaint to Rome. He constantly refers to the deep injustice and cunning of these men.
6. O'Connor wrote to Rome to state the real facts of the case on 13 March 1837, just before his stroke. Rome did not reply until mid-October. When he got the reply from Rome exonerating him, he forwarded it to Archbishop Murray of Dublin on 17 March 1838.
7. During this year, 1837/38, he appealed several Times-to Rome where the authorities initially reprimanded him, following the false report of the Capuchins. He also appealed to Bishop Murray, stating his innocence and the deep affliction he felt at being misrepresented[59].

55. Ibid.
56. Ibid.
57. Ibid.
58. Ibid, 31/5-7.
59. Ibid.

These were some of the factors which caused O'Connor to appeal for help and for a coadjutor at his side. Meanwhile, in regard to the matter of church property and the Goan-controlled clergy's *Padroado* claims, great progress took place in April 1838. The document *Multa Praeclare* was published. In a letter to Archbishop Murray on 25 November 1838 Dr O'Connor gives a clear sign of his gratitude for the continued support from Dublin. 'I was favoured with your extremely kind letter of the 10th of March last, on the 6th of July - after having received one equally gratifying from Dr Carew of the 14th of March, on the 9th of May. I have indeed great reason to be grateful . . . for such aid and consolation'[60]. He continues, 'A letter from Fr Moriarty of the 9th of August announces the intended departure of Dr Carew, seven priests and six students per the ship *Lady Flora,* on the 20th of September from Portsmouth, and we expect their arrival early in January next'. We can sense here the bishop's optimism and hope, as he immediately continues to state his new position of authority following the Holy See's brief. 'The Apostolic Brief *(Multa Praeclare)* appointing me Vicar Apostolic of Meliapore came in hand the 27th of August and the Installation took place the 2nd of September. The unhappy Goa clergy at Meliapore, all refuse to obey - but about six or seven from the interior have sent in their submission. I have commenced a Law Suit for the recovery of the property of Meliapore from them, which will be decided next February'. The publication of *Multa Praeclare* resulted in withdrawing all jurisdiction, bequests etc., from the rebels. Now O'Connor showed great determination. 'I receive all their fire and proceed steadily through the ordeal. I have established already three Churches among them, in addition to the one I had there before, and have crowded Congregations, whilst theirs are empty - numbers of their adherents have come over, and I have established schools at all those Churches'[61].

In regard to the last mentioned factor, O'Connor was to institute a law suit, which would be very trying, costly and eventually would be lost. This was also to cause him great anguish as was made evident in the letters between Carew and O'Connor in 1840.

At this stage we should be aware of the historic context of the Indian English-speaking Mission from an overall point of view, in regard to the vast North East Indian, Bengal region. On 18 April 1834, Robert St Leger, S.J., had been appointed Vicar Apostolic of Bengal. He was to arrive there on 8 October, together with his brother Fr John, one lay brother and a French priest, having set out from Plymouth in late May 1834.

The Holy See had for some time been hoping to oust the Goan Augustinian friars from the area. They had been feuding among themselves for several years and refused to recognise Rome's authority. The Roman authorities grasped the opportune moment when Fr Antonio, O.S.A., P.P., appealed to them for the appointment of a Vicar Apostolic. In late 1831, the Metropolitan of Goa who controlled the Vicariates had died, and so all four Vicariates were vacant. In February 1832 Propaganda had notified the lay Portuguese authorities in India to contact Lisbon requesting them to provide bishops. As no reply was received by July - a rather short period considering delays in mail - the Holy Father decided to act while the opportunity was available to terminate Portuguese influence. He established the Madras Vicariate. O'Connor's brief was made public on 10 April 1834. Eight days later, St Leger received notice that he had been chosen as Vicar Apostolic of Bengal.

It seems a strange course of fate that although O'Connor was chosen one week earlier than St Leger to go to India yet, due to the many arduous problems we have mentioned earlier, he did not embark till more than one year later, while St Leger sailed away from Plymouth on 31 May and got to Calcutta on 8 October 1834.

While en route on 12 June 1835, just after the first great storm, referred to in O'Connor's Madras Mission diary above, the former Governor General of India, Lord Bentinck, had come from his sloop of war, *The Curasseau,* to visit the company of the *Duke of Sussex.* Lord Bentinck had

---

60. Ibid.
61. Ibid.

just completed his term of office, and received on board several letters of introduction which were intended to have been handed to him on O'Connor's arrival in India. Undoubtably he would have acquainted Dr O'Connor on the full details of St Leger's progress.

Another benefit for O'Connor were the months of experience which St Leger had gained into an understanding of the complex situation of the *Padroado*. So, as soon as O'Connor got settled, he was in constant touch with St Leger on a very warm and cooperative level. St Leger would undoubtably have given him much sound advice on the best strategies to subdue the rebellious captains and friars who were opposing his authority.

St Leger was never raised to episcopal rank though Vicar Apostolic of a vast area, since Fr Roothan, General of the Jesuit Order, was totally opposed to the appointment, yet Rome recognised St Leger's capabilities and allowed him the privilege of wearing episcopal insignia, a decision which was totally disapproved of by Roothan. St Leger had got many of the Catholic soldiers for his spiritual ministry in the forts at Dumdum, Fort William and also far west to Hazribagh. Nevertheless, St Leger's days were numbered, as he fell foul of the Holy See over the development of La Martiniere, which he had intended to establish as a liberal christian college. This plan was too progressive to be acceptable at Rome in the 1830s. The papal authorities decided that he should return to Europe.

As soon as Rome received O'Connor's request for assistance, moves were set afoot and the archbishop of Dublin contacted. By the beginning of 1838, the eminent Dr Carew was marked out as the most suitable candidate to succeed to O'Connor.

The then Vicar Apostolic in London, Dr Griffiths, wrote to Archbishop Murray on 13 March, 'I was pleased to find from the letter of the 9th March that Dr O'Connor had secured so highly respected a Coadjutor as Dr Carew'[62]. He indicated that several ships would sail in April and May. He also stated that letters from O'Connor made no allusion to his attack of paralysis. However, his vision of Carew sailing in May was rather premature.

Carew was professor of theology, a brilliant priest from Waterford, and he was to be ordained bishop by Dr Murphy of Cork, just as O'Connor had been, since Archbishop Murray was suffering intermittent ill-health. The ordination took place in June at Maynooth College.

During the summer, Carew spent his time preparing for the journey, and some of the time was spent in the Physics Halls of Maynooth, in Stoyte House, helping Callan his special friend, for Dr Nicholas Callan was an outstanding inventor. Carew helped Callan to construct an electro magnetic engine for the college in Madras, and to fit out some other special scientific equipment for Madras. Callan was also instrumental in sending supplies of scientific equipment to St John's College in Calcutta. Later on he would very generously donate his spiritual publications to these two Missions.

"LUNAR" DISINTEGRATION

Carew set sail on 20 September from Portsmouth, according to Moriarty's letter sent to O'Connor on 9 August. He had returned via Rome to Dublin after giving a full report of the developments and great progress of O'Connor's time in Madras. However, Carew states in his letter of 3 February 1839[63] that he did not leave until 10 October 1838, arriving on 30 January after a voyage of 106 days. This meant that from the time O'Connor had initially asked for the help of a coadjutor it had taken almost two years for Carew to arrive at Madras. This was the pace of the tortuous progress, a snail's pace!

On his arrival, Carew sent Archbishop Murray a very detailed account of the wonderful work accomplished by O'Connor. 'Your Grace will be glad to learn that Dr O'Connor is in good health and doing faithfully the work of an Apostle . . . Our arrival has completely renovated his spirits, and thanks to the Divine goodness, Religion is likely to prosper very much in a short time. The

62. Ibid.
63. Ibid.

Schismatics are diminishing in number here and they have lost all respectability . . . They have unfortunately 6 or 7 of the finest Churches in this vicinity in their possession. Dr O'Connor has laboured to mitigate this evil by opening a temporary Church in most of the places where these Churches are situated.

He has fortunately procured some large private dwellings in almost all the above mentioned places, and has thus provided both for public worship, and for schools for the Catholics of these vicinities. Including these temporary Churches, there are altogether 9 Churches in the immediate vicinity of Madras and in Madras itself subject to his jurisdiction. . . There are schools attached to all these Churches and they contain 7 or 8 hundred children. I have attended at the examination of all the schools, and I was astonished to find that education has made such progress here'[64].

He also outlined the many problems O'Connor had to face single-handed - bigotry among the government authorities and Protestants, also the trouble with the schismatics regarding their duties and rights to property. He wrote that within the last few days, 'the schismatic priests have gained at law an advantage which I trust will be only temporary'. The executor of a Mr Del Monte refused to pay them a certain annuity left by Del Monte - this gentleman had been the most generous patron of the Catholic church in Madras. He had built one of the churches with his own funds, and O'Connor had hoped that on his arrival at Madras Del Monte would be one of his most loyal supporters, being very wealthy and a devout Catholic. O'Connor composed a special letter which he intended, on his immediate arrival to India, to present to Del Monte. But this was not to be, as Mr Del Monte had died.

The annuity was for the support of the priests attached to Cochin and to some churches in Meliapore and its vicinity. The executor acted thus on the grounds that the priests in these churches were schismatics and that of course for such persons Del Monte would not have left provision. The Court allowed that, as Bilderbeck the executor swore it would be against his conscience to pay the annuity to such persons, he should not be compelled to do so. But it ordered him to pay the annuity into the Court in order that the Court might appoint respectable Catholics to distribute it to the applicants. The Court added that as Dr O'Connor was an interested party it could not receive his declaration that these priests were schismatics until it had been confirmed by some higher authority. So now Dr O'Connor resolved to write to Rome and request the Holy See to announce clearly that the unhappy men in question were open schismatics, and urgently requested that an authentic document be forwarded to Madras without delay.

This lawsuit was to be a great burden for O'Connor, a worry for the next year and a half, yet from another point of view, great prospects appeared from Carew's quick review of affairs.

As to education and the wider field of evangelisation, Carew within a week of arrival was laying plans for big developments. In regard to the native people, he mentioned, 'They have great emulation, are exceedingly quick in answering the questions proposed to them, and have naturally a gracefulness and energy in their manners and conversation such as in Ireland are rarely found except among children of the highest class in society . . . Perhaps . . . Your Grace would accomplish for us this great benefit. We are making active preparations to open a Lay boarding and Day school in conjunction with our Seminary, I hope we shall have all in full work in two or three months. We want 5 or 6 more hands to help us and as we have not funds I must apply again to the French Society for pecuniary aid. The lawsuit against the Schismatics is very expensive, but if we succeed we shall have sufficient means for every purpose'[65]. Carew continued, 'Dr St Leger's recall will I am assured inflict a deep injury on the Church of Calcutta. I am sorry to hear that neither his successor there nor the new Vicar Apostolic of Ceylon is likely to contribute to the extinction of the Portuguese Schism. The so called Archbishop of Goa is just publishing a pastoral address in which he protests against the separation of Ceylon from the Archdiocese'[66].

64. Ibid.
65. Ibid.
66. Ibid.

Carew's letter has a different tone to all of O'Connor's. It is full of brightness, insights into events, possibilities and people. Within ten days of arriving he has been able to give, in a sixteen page letter, an amazingly clear and detailed account of the situation. He was not aware, however, that within four months or so he would be appointed to Calcutta but would not be able to take up office there for almost two years because of Bishop O'Connor's concern that everything should be left in perfect order. Bishop O'Connor asked Carew to allow him to remain in office. This course of action may seem to show a certain scrupulosity but, in actual fact, O'Connor was by now under deep mental stress and in the next few months, on his journey of visitation as far as Porto Novo to the South of Madras, he contracted the fever. The term that will be used by Dr Manley, will be 'Lunar Fever', it will recur and cause great concern to everybody. Added to this, O'Connor's action in remaining somewhat in control will be misconstrued and so cause him further torture of mind because of his utter sincerity in trying to do God's will. Meanwhile Dr Carew sent forward to Bengal one of his missioners, Fr William Kelly, a very bright and eloquent priest, who had been professor of literature and elocution at Maynooth College[67].

O'Connor's talents served him well as Vicar Apostolic at Madras in resolving a bitter dispute between the rival parties of two newspapers, *The Bengal Catholic Expositor* and *The Catholic Intelligence,* one run by the Cathedral Fathers, the other by the Jesuits. Fr William Kelly resolved the problem by tact and discretion, resulting in their amalgamation as the *Bengal Catholic Herald.*

Dr O'Connor on his return to Madras in May from Porto Novo, due to illness, the heat, and the law suit, comments in a letter of 2 September 1839 that he intends, as bishop of Meliapore, now to go, when the season allows, on his visitation of the north and west which will take him on an extended tour of Bellery, Dharwar, Hanawar right down the west coast to Mangalore, Tellicherry and finally Verapoly, close to Cochin. At this stage, however, according to the close correspondence of a score of letters between Carew and himself[68], also from his doctors, it is evident that he must leave India to seek a cure for the very dangerous state of his health. Dr Carew will show great restraint and kindness during this period. The people of Madras having been informed of the situation will call a meeting to make him a farewell presentation.

The extremely poor state of O'Connor's health required sufficient funds to be made available to support him while waiting and then during his voyage from Bombay to Rome, via Suez. This entailed much effort and negotiations with the Holy See as the funds had run out as a result of the lawsuit being lost. After months of writing Carew managed to obtain sufficient money to ensure O'Connor's every comfort for departure from India[69]. This was forwarded to the Archbishop of Alcantara. The amount which had been requested totalled 3,000 Rupees or approximately £300. A pension for the retiring bishop had also to be negotiated.

To sum up, getting back to Dr O'Connor's frame of mind between the autumn of 1838 and the autumn of 1839, it is evident from his letters and handwriting that a great change must have come over him. He writes to Archbishop Murray just before December 1838 with optimism, looking forward to Carew's arrival. He makes a strange reference to his own health, 'Great labour and care are my best physicians, and I now enjoy better health than when I left Ireland. Indeed I am a subject of surprise to myself and everyone else in this respect and I can only view it in the light of Providence, that it is his will I should only enjoy it by such means and in this Country. Indeed, I know but his will, and I would not, if I had my own, wish to do any other'[70]. He then mentions his longing for Carew's arrival, that he will omit nothing to make him happy, that he will provide every comfort for him and his companions, but he then continues strangely, 'My portion of the vineyard in this quarter is nearly planted, they will only have to water it, and I trust God will give the increase. They will have every comfort on their arrival'. His handwriting showed great distortion

---

67. Cf letters, Irish Augustinian Provincial Archives, Ballyboden, Dublin, O'Connor Papers, MS notebook of letters.
68. Ibid.
69. Ibid.
70. Dublin Diocesan Archives, Murray Papers, 31/5-7

and strain in that paragraph.

Eight months after Carew's arrival O'Connor wrote to Archbishop Murray, 2 September 1839, in a very compact hand, the following statement, which he makes having returned from his visitation of the South through illness:

'My Dear Lord. As you have since the commencement taken such an interest in this Mission, and shewn so much kindness to myself, I feel myself in duty bound to make known to your Grace that I have sent forward by this same post my resignation of these Missions into the hands of the Holy Father, with a view to my retirement altogether from public life and the care of souls, and to my spending the remainder of my days in some religious house, at Rome or elsewhere, on the Continent, for I have no wish to reside in Ireland. This resolution I formed, as soon as I learned the providential appointment of so splendid a Prelate as Dr Carew, and the great and efficient aid he has, and will no doubt have from time to time gathered around him'[71]. He concludes his letter by asking Murray to get Dr Paul Cullen of the Irish College in Rome to help him on his arrival there, as he does not know the Italian language. His final statement is extraordinary, 'I would not presume to make those requests of your Grace if I had not to the utmost of my poor ability, done all in my power to answer to your and our lamented Friend, Dr Doyle's expectations of me'. These words echo the final blessing he received from the great J.K.L., 'Go - do good. God bless you'. O'Connor had indeed gone forth to the Indian vineyard and done all in his power to establish his Mission in the face of normally insurmountable difficulties. Dr Carew realised well his great worth, his endless efforts and now his failing health. He gave him every assistance to ensure his peace of mind and release from India.

CONCLUSION

Concluding this short account of the Augustinian Mission to Madras. The main points to be drawn from it are that it was a pioneering effort into the unknown, fraught with many perils. Great effort was made by Daniel O'Connor. He used every available opportunity to try and get adequate funds and staff for the journey.

There were however many factors militating against O'Connor's progress from the outset, after a year's delay in Ireland, a successful voyage to India and a warm welcome on arrival there. He set himself a punishing programme, to re-evangelise Madras. His many efforts met much opposition, his staff were poor, for the most part; the schismatic priests constantly impeded him by their scheming and treachery; there was the lack of funds to build schools and employ teachers; also the annoyance from bigots in their fanatical methods lead to much suspicion from the Brahmins. Besides, there was the constant problem of ill-health amongst his staff, together with the law suits which cost large sums. All these factors finally resulted in Bishop O'Connor feeling very isolated and becoming morose. As a result he suffered bouts of depression with a persecution complex.

He went on an extended visitation of his vast diocese, he contracted Lunar (or Jungle) Fever, and from then on he was to suffer from bouts of depression. This was a very sad position, and when Dr Carew, his coadjutor, discovered the full extent of the situation he wrote to Dr Paul Cullen, then rector of the Irish College at Rome, explaining the tragic reality[72].

Paul Cullen was a most important figure in the Catholic Church. He held a crucial and influential position between the Vatican authorities and affairs relating to Ireland as well as with the powerful Irish clergy overseas in North America, Canada, Australia, Great Britain and India. There are some dozen letters in the Irish College Rome explaining the predicament. One letter relates how O'Connor twice or trice escaped from the Archbishop of Sardis's House and fled into the nearby woods. On another occasion Carew relates how O'Connor got into a boat seeking to escape his imagined would-be attackers and could not be induced to leave the boat, so that the

---

71. Ibid.
72. Irish College, Rome, Cullen Papers.

people who collected around him were forced to carry him back to the archbishop's house. This state of affairs was resolved when O'Connor departed India in December 1840 and Dr John Fenelly arrived in 1841 with a team of priests from Maynooth, allowing Carew to proceed to Calcutta. Thus the position of the Indian Missions was finally stabilised.

It was the arduous preliminary work of the Irish Augustinian Daniel O'Connor that cleared the way for many years of future progress of the Catholic church in India.

THE IRISH AUGUSTINIANS IN AUSTRALIA, 1838-1992

Australia remembers St Patrick's College, Rome

Thomas A. Hunt, O.S.A.

THE IRISH AUGUSTINIANS IN AUSTRALIA, 1838-1992

Australia remembers St Patrick's College, Rome

Thomas A. Hunt, O.S.A.

Note: in order not to try the patience of the readers by giving extensive footnotes, the sources of this article are from the following: Patrick Francis Moran, *History of the Catholic Church in Australasia,* (Sydney, [1864]); Michael A. Endicott, O.S.A., *The Augustinians in Far North Queensland, 1883-1941,* (Brookvale, N.S.W., 1988); Patrick O'Farrell, *The Irish in Australia,* (New South Wales University Press, 1986); F.X. Martin, O.S.A., 'The Irish Augustinians in Rome, 1656-1956', in *The Irish Augustinians in Rome, 1656-1956,* ed. J.F. Madden, O.S.A. (Rome, 1956), l6-76; Patrick O'Farrell, *The Irish,* No.1017 Bulletin of Foreign Affairs; Frances O'Kane, *A Path is Set,* (Melbourne University Press, 1976).

The editor, Fr F.X. Martin, informed contributors that 'the main purpose of this volume is to show the missionary activity of the Irish Augustinians right down to the present day' and he has graciously commissioned the present writer to contribute the chapter on Australia. The reason being, I presume, is that the writer was the first Vicar General of the Diocese of Cairns when it was raised from being the Vicariate Apostolic of Cooktown in 1942 and later the first Provincial when Australia was severed from the Irish Augustinian Province and became an independent province of the Order in 1952.

Before entering into the history of the missionary contribution of the Irish Augustinians to Australia, it seems to me necessary and essential to understand the type of missionary activity they faced when they came to the new continent. I use the words 'missionary activity' in the sense of Pope Paul VI in *Evangelii Nuntiandi* : 'thus it has been possible to define evangelization in terms of proclaiming Christ to those who do not know him, of preaching, of catechesis, of conferring baptism and the other Sacraments' (No.17).

THE LAST DISCOVERED CONTINENT

Australia was the last continent to be discovered by the white man. It remained a hidden continent until 1770 when the English explorer, Captain James Cook, sailed along the east coast, thus discovering a new continent of 3 million square miles (7,800,000 sq. km). The Great South Land at that time had perhaps 60,000 to 120,000 black Aborigines but had not yet seen a white man. I use the word 'perhaps' designedly because, according to Michael Endicott, O.S.A., and I quote : 'nobody really knows; it is as if the Australia colonial government did not want to know how many Aborigines existed. No census of Aborigines was attempted until well into this century; Aborigines were specifically excluded from the earlier Commonwealth Census laws'. It is interesting to note that as Captain Cook was discovering the east coast and when nearing the far north, his sailing ship struck a reef, on what is now called the Great Barrier Reef, one of the wonders of the world. Thus he was forced to beach his ship at a spot on the mainland now called after him, Cooktown, and it was precisely there that 114 years later the three Irish Augustinians landed to begin the Vicariate Apostolic of Cooktown. Captain Cook, having effected repairs to his sailing ship, returned to England without making a permanent settlement.

A CONVICT COLONY

The politicians decided to make the newly discovered continent into a convict colony. With the American War of Independence being successfully won by the American freedom fighters, the practice of British judges sentencing convicted persons to transportation to the American colonies had therefore to cease. The British Government decided that the new continent of Australia was well suited, in their view, for the transportation of prisoners because, as it was so distant from the rest of the world, escape would be, for all practical purposes, impossible; they could hardly swim home! Australia then became, sad to say, a distant country to get rid of their convicts. In parenthesis, I might add that the Irish Province of the Order was accused in the last century and indeed early this century, of using Australia as a place to send their recalcitrant members! The first archbishop of Melbourne, himself an Augustinian, James Alypius Goold, said so in a report to Rome. Certainly the present writer can well remember, fifty years ago, a certain member of the Irish Province, now deceased, arriving in Australia and declaring he had been sent out as a punishment for having kicked the prior's dog! He should have received sound pastoral advice and counselled to be kind to the prior's dog - or maybe better still, if it serves, kick the prior's dog and enjoy living in the grandest country in the world with a magnificent climate!

THE FIRST FLEET

In 1788, what is now called, THE FIRST FLEET, arrived in Botany Bay, now Sydney, with 1,088 persons who made the first permanent settlement of white people. Of that group 897 were convicted convicts - 717 were men and 180 were women. They were guarded by 191 British marines. Thus began, and continued right up to 1868, a continuous series of arrivals of convicts from Great Britain and Ireland. Up to that year one quarter of all arrivals came from Ireland - about 30,000 men and 9,000 women. The Irish convicts were neither murderers nor thieves and a substantial number were patriots and freedom fighters seeking the independence of their native land. They were almost 100% Catholics. Here was to be the fertile field for an apostolate of Irish missionaries including Augustinians.

To finalise these preliminary observations I quote one of Australia's most noted contemporary historians: 'Australia without its Irish aspects is simply unthinkable. In no other British settlement were the Irish so central to the composition and character of a new nation than they were in the making of Australia: about one third of Australia's present population of 15 millions have some Irish ancestry', (P. O'Farrell in No.1017 Bulletin for Foreign Affairs, Dublin 1985).

THE FIRST AUGUSTINIAN

The Augustinian contribution to pastoral work in Australia had its beginnings paradoxically here in Rome - on the steps of the Church of Santa Maria del Popolo! It began on Holy Saturday 1837 when a young Irish Augustinian, Fr James Alypius Goold, met by accident the Benedictine Vicar General from Sydney, Dom William B. Ullathorne. This was only two years after the arrival of the first bishop in Australia, Bishop John Bede Polding, O.S.B., who was appointed in 1835 as Vicar Apostolic of New Holland, as Australia was called until 1817. Goold had done his novitiate at Grantstown, Co. Wexford, in 1831-1832, having been born in Cork city in 1812. He later studied in Perugia where he was ordained in 1835 and then was appointed assistant master of students at Santa Maria in Posterula, which preceded the present St Patrick's College in the

Santa Maria del Popolo. On the steps of this church in Rome, in 1837, the young Augustinian, James Alypius Goold, met the Benedictine Vicar General from Sydney, Dom William B. Ullathorne, and the Augustinian contribution to pastoral work in Australia was set in train.

Eternal City as the house of studies of the Irish Augustinian Province.

When he heard of the great need for Irish priests to minister to his fellow countrymen and women, on returning to Ireland, he sought permission from his Provincial to go to Australia. In his letter the Provincial, Fr Bernard O'Neill, stated, 'I have known him before he entered college and his conduct was pious and exemplary. During his studies in Italy he had the esteem and regard of his superiors and was distinguished alike for talent and strict observance of Rule'. Goold must have felt great pangs of sorrow when, in the latter part of 1837, he left kith and kin on a sailing ship for the long journey to the Antipodes, landing at Sydney in February 1838. Shortly after arrival, Polding appointed him in charge of Campbelltown where he remained for ten years. The writer remembers in 1955 taking the then Prior General, Fr Englebert Eberhard, on a visit to Campbelltown and amongst other things we saw Goold's neat handwriting in the baptismal and matrimonial registers kept in the presbytery which he bought and converted.

James Alypius Goold, O.S.A., first Bishop, then Archbishop, of Melbourne.

Having been appointed by Pope Pius IX first bishop of Melbourne, Goold was consecrated in St Mary's Cathedral, Sydney, and shortly afterwards left by road for Melbourne, some 600 miles south. He was the first person to make the journey overland in a carriage and four. During the long journey of over four weeks, on Sundays, and whenever a group of settlers gathered, he said Mass, heard confessions and administered the other sacraments.

On 4 October 1848 he was enthroned as first bishop of Melbourne by Fr P.B. Geoghegan, an Irish Franciscan, the first pastor of Melbourne, in the church of St Francis. Geoghegan had arrived in Melbourne in 1839 and celebrated the first Mass there on 19 May 1839. He later was appointed first bishop of Adelaide. It is interesting to note here that Goold in his famous diary stated: 'when I arrived in Melbourne, the diocese had only three clergymen, two churches - one in Melbourne and the other at Geelong - and a commodious little chapel at Portland'. There was also a small presbytery, a hall and a school house, beside the church. Thus began the long and fruitful labours in Victoria of the first bishop and later archbishop of Melbourne. For over 38 years he rode on horseback into the many mining settlements, covering thousands of square miles, preaching to the scattered flocks and administering the sacraments. For the internal organisation and the laying of the foundations of the Catholic Church in the State of Victoria, he was universally regarded, when he died in 1886, as not only the founder of the Catholic Church in that state but one of the great evangelisers of Australia.

In 1874 Victoria was divided into suffragan dioceses with Melbourne becoming an archdiocese. Goold was responsible in having the Irish Augustinian Provincial, Martin Crane, appointed as the first bishop of Sandhurst (Bendigo) and when his sight began to fail Goold suggested the Irish master of novices, Stephen Reville, as his coadjutor. These three Augustinian bishops were responsible for bringing out to Australia other members of the Order - about some of whom, later in this article. I conclude this section on Goold with the well-deserved words of Frances O'Kane: 'He was as meticulous as his records, as solid and perhaps as humourless, but reliable and purposeful, dedicated to his dual vocation as bishop and member of a religious order' (*A Path is Set*, p.156).

OTHER EARLY AUGUSTINIANS

Perhaps the first who should be mentioned is Fr Michael Stephens; he was the second pastor of Port Phillip (Melbourne), the first being the Irish Franciscan, Fr P.B. Geoghegan. Stephens arrived from Ireland early in 1841 - seven years before Melbourne became a diocese. Polding appointed him assistant priest to Geoghegan at Port Phillip (Melbourne) and when, owing to many personal problems, Geoghegan left, Stephens became the second pastor of Melbourne, having been appointed in April 1842. However, the former returned in September that same year when the latter moved to Geelong. He later served at Port Fairy and Portland where he became pastor. According to Frances O'Kane, 'he did not measure up to Goold's high expectations' (p.43). He left the diocese in 1850. O'Kane continues: 'inclined, in his superiors' opinion to be rash and headstrong, though useful subordinately to those who could control him', Stephens had become unsettled in Portland. In December 1849, without seeking the bishop's counsel and much to his chagrin, Stephens announced to the newpapers his imminent departure from his mission. In April 1850 he finally abandoned it! (in the bishop's words of disapproval), without leave or giving notice of his intention to Goold. Portland was left without a priest until May 1850 (see O'Kane, cit. pp 43-45).

Two other early Augustinians in Victoria were the brothers from Cork, Robert and Matthew Downing. The latter was a personal friend of Goold. Robert Downing, however, was a thorn in Goold's side because of his insobriety, against which he had been frequently warned. Goold appointed him pastor of Geelong but because of his drinking problem the bishop brought him to St Francis's church under his own wing, as he usually did with priests with a similar problem. His brother Matthew, on the other hand, was a man of sterling character. He came with a shipload of Irish "convicts" after the so-called Irish Rebellion of 1848. He had been prior of Santa Maria in Posterula, Rome, from 1839 to 1843. Two centuries earlier, due to the British persecution of the Catholic Church in Ireland, the Irish Augustinian Province was informed by the Augustinian Prior General, Paolo Lucchini, in 1656 that Pope Alexander VII had given them the church and priory of San Matteo in Merulana in Rome to train their students for the priesthood. They stayed there until 1798 when they were given a temporary place, at Sant'Eusebio, until they moved in 1819 to Santa Maria in Posterula. After a short stay in San Carlo al Corso from 1888 to 1892 when Santa Maria in Posterula was demolished to make way for a Tiber bridge, the community took possession of a property in the then Villa Ludovisi area of Rome.

The Augustinian bishops who laboured in Australia were all either educated at Rome or were members of the community of Santa Maria in Posterula, namely, Goold (Melbourne); Crane (Sandhurst); Reville (Sandhurst); Hutchinson (Cooktown); Murray (Cooktown); and Heavey (Cooktown/Cairns).

As stated already, Matthew Downing arrived in the Antipodes early in 1849 as chaplain to a shipload of Irish prisoners who were sentenced, after the Rebellion of 1848, to penal servitude in Van Diemen's Land, which in 1835 was called Tasmania. He took up residence in the penal colony at Port Arthur, called "the hell hole" by the convicts. He brought them hope, the Mass and the sacraments. The penal settlement is still preserved as an historical monument and it was a privilege for the present writer to visit there in 1965 and see the little house where Fr Downing lived in the midst of the colony.

When he finished as a convict chaplain after two years, Downing offered his services to his friend from Cork, Bishop Goold, who appointed him the first resident priest at Ballarat, now the centre of a diocese. Later he became the first resident priest at Geelong where he founded St Augustine's orphanage.

While at Geelong he made history because of his attempted but failed effort as the peacemaker before the battle of the Eureka stockade in 1854 - the only armed rebellion or uprising against the government in Australia. Matthew Downing accompanied Bishop Goold on an all night journey to Ballarat in late November 1854 in an eleventh-hour attempt to calm the Irish Catholic diggers on the goldfield who were suffering many injustices. They did not succeed, for on 3 December, led by Peter Lalor, an armed uprising began that ended in the bloody event now known in history as the Eureka Stockade Rebellion. It is interesting to note that when Goold bought a property outside Melbourne in 1852 for a novitiate Matthew Downing was named by the Prior General as novice master but nothing came of it . . . it came 100 years later!

Perhaps two other early Augustinians should be mentioned, James B. Hayes and Charles O'Hea. They arrived in 1853. Hayes, who was later known as Dean Hayes, was immediately stationed at St Francis with Goold, and O'Hea became the first pastor at Pentridge. Some fourteen years later when Goold, according to his diary, arrived in Santa Maria in Posterula in Rome in late 1867, he was visited by the minutante in charge of Australian affairs at Propaganda Fide and during the visit he proposed Dean James Hayes as the first bishop of Armidale, in the ecclesiastical province of Sydney. He was duly appointed but when the Papal Bull arrived he refused for reasons unknown. Shortly afterwards he returned to Ireland where he died a few years later.

DIOCESE OF SANDHURST (BENDIGO)

Archbishop Goold returned to Rome in 1870 to take part in the first Vatican Council together with five other Augustinian bishops from different parts of the world. On 10 May 1870 he was invested with the pallium as the first archbishop of Melbourne. On 8 June 1870 he called a special meeting of all the Australian bishops at the Council which took place at Santa Maria in Posterula, under his chairmanship, at which they petitioned the Holy See to erect two new dioceses in Victoria, Sandhurst (Bendigo) and Ballarat. Nothing happened, so Goold returned to Rome in 1873-1874 to speed up the creation of the two dioceses. During that visit he assisted at the consistory when Cardinal Tommaso Martinelli, O.S.A., received the red hat.

Martin Crane, O.S.A.,
first Bishop of Sandhurst.

In 1874 Fr Martin Crane, O.S.A., was named the first bishop of Sandhurst. He had been prior of Posterula in 1850 and twice Provincial in Ireland. He presided over the diocese from 1874 to 1901, new parishes were established, the number of clergy increased and convents of school Sisters opened in many parishes. He was an experienced church builder in Ireland having built the magnificent John's Lane Church in Dublin which was designed by the famous English architect, Pugin. The Sacred Heart Cathedral in Bendigo was built early on in his episcopate in the same style as John's Lane in Dublin. It was completed by Bishop Bernard Stewart, and the bodies of the first three bishops were interred in a vault underneath.

When Crane's sight began to fail, Fr Stephen Reville, master of novices in Ireland, was appointed coadjutor and on the death of Crane in 1901 he took over the reins of government. He was a very gentle and kindly man beloved by priests, religious and laity. He had rather strict ideas of clerical behaviour as is evidenced by this fact: Bishop Heavey told the writer that when he arrived in Australia in 1914 he called to Bendigo to see Bishop Reville. During the visit Reville noticed that Bishop Heavey was a snuff taker, and clearly told him 'snuff taking is unbecoming for a bishop in this country!' Bishop Heavey in reminiscent mood told the present writer, 'From that day I gave up taking snuff, which was a terrible sacrifice'. When Reville died in 1916 the Augustinians had already made foundations in the diocese: at Echuca 1875, Rochester in 1889 and at Kyabram in 1901.

THE VICARIATE APOSTOLIC OF COOKTOWN

The reason why the Irish Augustinians went to North Queensland is explained by a meeting of Irish tin-miners which took place in Herberton in the Far North of Australia in the early

Stephen Reville, O.S.A.,
Bishop of Sandhurst,
in succession to Martin Crane.

part of the year 1884. A very serious situation had developed between them and the Pro-Vicar, Monsignor Fortini, an Italian, who had been sent there by Propaganda Fide in 1882. Fortini wanted to sell the property on which the church was built, but the Irish miners had the title deeds and quite rightly refused to hand them over because history has proved Fortini lacked prudence or, quite plainly, common sense. He promptly placed the church under an interdict which meant Mass could not be celebrated there, nor weddings or funerals take place! It is the only time in Australian history that a church was placed under an interdict! The present writer was parish priest in Herberton from 1936 to 1939 and lived in the old presbytery where the 1884 meeting took place. He found in an old bookcase the draft of the letter, with many corrections, which the Irish miners wrote to Pope Leo XIII. They made bitter complaints against the Pro-Vicar Fortini; amongst the complaints was the fact that he had gone into the houses of Protestants in Herberton and held the Irish Catholic miners up to ridicule, as well as trying to sell the church property. They asked the Pope to send them Irish missionaries who would care for them spiritually. The writer knew personally two sons of those who signed the letter to Pope Leo XIII - one was Alderman Willie Collins, mayor of Cairns for many years, and the other was Alderman Dick McManus, chairman of the Cairns Harbour Board.

Pope Leo was a great friend of the Augustinians, three of whom he created cardinals. Thus the Prior General, Pacifico Neno, was informed of the request from the Irish miners in North Queensland, and he in turn asked Prior Patrick Glynn, then prior of Santa Maria in Posterula, to inform the Irish Province and suggest they send one priest to North Queensland. Fr John Hutchinson was Provincial and, together with his Council, it was agreed to send three missionaries to the Vicariate of Cooktown. It is a vast area of some 137,000 square miles. To make a European comparison : Italy is 121,000 sq. miles and Ireland 32,000 sq. miles.

These missionaries were agreed on to begin the work of evangelisation; the Provincial himself volunteered and together with Fr James Dominic Murray and Fr William O'Brien they set sail for their far-distant mission. They arrived at Cooktown on the eve of Pentecost Sunday 1884 when a great crowd awaited them on the Cooktown wharf. The present writer got a first-hand account of the scene from a man in Cairns who, as a boy of twelve, was amongst the crowd. His name was Paddy O'Neill who served their three Masses the following morning in the old church at Cooktown. Paddy said: 'I was standing on the wharf as the ship came in, the three priests were very handsome and wore high Roman collars and rather long black coats. The people cheered and clapped as they stepped off'. It is worthy of note that 60 years later, in 1944, Paddy O'Neill, then 72, served the present writer's Mass in St Monica's Cathedral, Cairns, when the 60th anniversary of their arrival was being commemorated. Thus began 64 years of Augustinian service under Augustinian bishops in the vast Vicariate Apostolic of Cooktown, situated in the far tropical north of the continent.

John Hutchinson, O.S.A.,
Vicar Apostolic of Cooktown.
One of the three pioneer priests to
arrive in North Queensland in 1884.

The territory had no roads, no trains, and travel was on horseback or by launch. The climate, being tropical and very humid for the greater part of the year, must have put severe strains on the three missionaries used to a temperate European climate. Having to make long journeys on horseback certainly added to their hardships. Before going to Australia John Hutchinson lived in Limerick city and James Dominic Murray lived in Hoxton, London, so the life style had certainly brought about major changes for them. After arrival, Murray went to Herberton, O'Brien to Cairns and Hutchinson himself stayed in Cooktown. Two notable historical facts perhaps could be

mentioned here. The first regarding Murray's arrival in Herberton. The writer, having lived in Herberton from 1936 to 1939, found the minute book in the old presbytery of the meetings of the lay committee of trustees. They were informed by Hutchinson that an Irish missionary, by name Fr James Dominic Murray, would be arriving there to take charge. The committee decided to send a delegation of men on horseback to "the four mile" to accompany him in to the presbytery. When he had settled down he wrote to the Prior General in Rome and stated 'this must be the loneliest place on earth, coming from London, I hear no sound after sun-down except the howling of the dingoes in the

Innisfail, June 1984. Fr Hunt with the two daughters of Paddy O'Neill, who, 100 years earlier, in 1884, met the steamer that brought the first three Augustinians to Cooktown, North Queensland.

bush!' Then he added that 'because of their differences with Fortini, having placed the church under an interdict, they regard me just as their chaplain!'

The second interesting historical fact concerns Hutchinson himself in Cooktown. Shortly after arrival he got a message from some miners in a mining camp over 50 miles from Cooktown asking for Mass and the sacraments. He rode out alone on horseback. The present writer found a letter, in the Augustinian General Archives in Rome, which Hutchinson wrote to the Prior General stating that the local sergeant of police had called on him shortly after making the above-mentioned journey and said 'you must never again ride out there without getting a policeman to accompany you because last week two Chinamen were speared to death by the blacks on that track!'

James Dominic Murray, O.S.A., Vicar Apostolic of Cooktown, in succession to John Hutchinson.
With Hutchinson, he had been one of the three Augustinian pioneers to come to North Queensland in 1884.

With the arrival of four more Augustinians from Ireland in 1885 and Hutchinson being consecrated bishop, the Vicariate was well on the way to making solid progress. However, Hutchinson died rather suddenly in 1897 and was succeeded by Fr James Dominic Murray. At that time Murray had left the Vicariate claiming health reasons, and was prior and pastor of Echuca, Victoria. He was aged 51 and had been a Christian Brother in Ireland for eleven years before joining the Augustinians. When Bishop Murray took over the Vicariate in 1898 the population in Cooktown was going down and the place carried a heavy debt. When James Hutchinson, the brother of the late bishop, demanded the return of a large sum of money he loaned for the building of the Cooktown convent, Murray had to take off on a great collection campaign to meet the debts. The writer met several people over fifty years ago in Cairns who knew Murray personally and described him as a very energetic bishop and outgoing personality. When he left for Rome, Ireland and America on the campaign to meet the Vicariate's debts he found success. In Rome Propaganda Fide gave him written authority to collect in dioceses where the local bishop gave consent. In England and Ireland he found a ready response especially in the churches of the Augustinian Order. In the United States he found the former Prior General, Sebastiano Martinelli, O.S.A., the Apostolic Delegate, who gave him great assistance. The Hutchinson family were eventually repaid and other debts taken care of. Murray once admitted, 'I am a notoriously bad beggar. I have not asked anyone personally for a donation, nor have I written to anyone. I simply state our needs and take what I get' (Endicott, *The Augustinians in Far North Queensland*, p.91).

He made many friends amongst the Protestant community and was a truly ecumenical figure long before the word was thought of. He frequently travelled the length and breadth of the vast Vicariate from the time of his taking over in 1898 until his death in 1914. With the decline of the goldmining at Cooktown and district and the consequent reduction of the population he changed the episcopal seat from Cooktown to Cairns. However in his will he asked to be buried in Cooktown beside John Hutchinson.

1984. On the occasion of the centenary of the arrival of the Augustinians in Cooktown.
Bishop Torpie, Cairns, Fr J. Newman, Adm., and Fr T.A. Hunt, O.S.A., at Bishop's House, Cairns,
formerly St Monica's Priory built by Fr J. Phelan, O.S.A., in 1930.

It was a great privilege for the writer, in 1984, to have been invited by that much beloved bishop of Cairns, John Torpie, now retired in Brisbane, for the centenary celebrations of the arrival of the Augustinians, and to be able to visit Cooktown and pray at the graves of Hutchinson and Murray. It was a further privilege in 1988 to have been invited back once again by the Sisters of Mercy and by the beloved friend, Bishop John Bathersby, now archbishop of Brisbane, for the centenary celebrations of the arrival of the first five Sisters of Mercy from Dungarvan, Ireland, who came to Cooktown in June 1888. Together with the two bishops, the Augustinian Provincial, Fr Kevin Burman, and some 60 Sisters of Mercy we held a liturgical ceremony in the Cooktown cemetery to pray for the pioneer Sisters and the two bishops. The writer personally knew two of that missionary band of five Sisters, Sr M. de Sales and that wonderful and dedicated Mother Evangelist Morrissey who died in Herberton in 1950 and at whose Requiem Mass and burial he presided.

BISHOP HEAVEY
It is not easy for the writer, having been closely associated with Bishop Heavey for the last 12 years of his life, to give an objective assessment of the man, especially when the writer lived in the same house with him and finally gave him the last sacraments and prepared him for death in June 1948. Fr John Heavey was prior of New Ross when he was appointed successor to Bishop Murray. He was consecrated bishop in 1914 and that same year arrived in Cairns. He presided over the Vicariate for 34 years and when it was raised to a diocese in 1941 he thus became the first

bishop of Cairns. He can be justly described as an ascetic, a gentle and reserved person, especially in the presence of lay people. It can be rightly said of him he ruled more by personal example than by precept or command. He was always seen in public, no matter how hot or humid the tropical climate was, in a black suit with a purple stock. Frequently he would be seen walking on the esplanade at Cairns reading his breviary! This will explain the following incident. Some ten years after John Heavey's death the present writer, walking in one of the main streets in Brisbane, where he was stationed, was stopped by a stranger. The man said: 'I have often seen you in Cairns many years ago with Bishop Heavey and, though I don't belong to your Church, whenever I saw that Bishop walking on the esplanade I thought of God'!

John Alphonsus Heavey, O.S.A., first Bishop of Cairns.

Certainly, he could be described as a "godly" person: he appeared to the public as rather a distant, severe personality, but those of us who lived with him found an ideal community man, friendly, and always good-humoured. His conversations at meals were always on an elevated level, about the books he was reading, Dickens, Shakespeare and so on. Until he was appointed bishop he had mostly been engaged in secondary education at New Ross and Dungarvan. All his life he read extensively English, French and Italian literature. He once told the writer that when he went to Rome in 1930, to make the *ad limina* visit, Pope Pius XI complimented him on his Italian. 'The reason, I think', the bishop added, 'that the Pope thought I spoke the language well is that I am used to the style of Manzoni's *Promessi Sposi,* and Pope Pius being a Milanese would have appreciated that'!

Like his two predecessors he travelled widely visiting the parishes, and every two or three years made the arduous trip by truck into the Gulf of Carpentaria over rough bush tracks. He was gentle and understanding with the priests, he had a deep reverence and respect for the nuns and a keen appreciation for the Marist Brothers. If he were to be found in a *Who's Who* his recreations would be listed as 'walking, and playing bridge with the nuns'!

Theologically he might be described kindly as tending towards Jansenism! When on 12 June 1948 the writer had anointed him about 11 p.m. and said 'I shall now bring you holy Viaticum', the bishop said 'but I am not fasting'. My reply was 'you don't have to be fasting'!. He then said 'I'll leave it on your conscience'! He died an hour later. At 2 a.m., assisted by Fr James Hooper, now at Dungarvan in Ireland, and by the good Mother M. Oliver, ex-Mother General of the Sisters of Mercy who looked after him in his last illness, we carried his body down to the ground floor chapel of the Bishop's House so that the people coming to the 6.30 a.m. Mass in the nearby St Monica's Cathedral could come and pay their respects. Afterwards, about 2.30 a.m., the writer remarked to his companion in the dining room, partaking of light refreshments, 'we have now come to the end of an era'; for it was certain that shortly a bishop would be appointed from the secular clergy. Thus ended the Augustinian government and pastoral care, after 64 years, of the vast territory in tropical North Queensland. During that period, the evangelising zeal and dedicated labours of the Augustinian bishops and priests combined with the Sisters of Mercy, the Sisters of the Good Samaritan and the Marist Brothers. As a combined apostolic team they studded the territory with churches, schools, convents and presbyteries. They created a Catholic laity well grounded in the Faith, built on solid Christian family life.

It fell to the present writer as Vicar Capitular in March 1949 to formally hand over the diocese to Bishop Thomas Cahill at his solemn enthronement as the first bishop from the secular clergy. For several years the Order kept up the supply of priests until the bishop was able to carry

on with his own newly ordained priests from Banyo seminary.   The Augustinians have retained
two parishes in the diocese, at Innisfail and Mareeba, which they first founded in 1894 and 1911
respectively.   Bishop Cahill was translated to Canberra as archbishop where he died in 1978.   He
was succeeded at Cairns by two close friends of the Augustinians, Bishop John Torpie, now retired
in Brisbane, and Bishop John Bathersby just recently appointed archbishop of Brisbane.   At the
time of writing (1992) a successor at Cairns is awaited.   [Edd note: Since this chapter was
submitted, Bishop B. Foley has been appointed bishop of Cairns. Further, the Augustinians, in a
quest for renewal as a Province by means of a planned redeployment of human resources, handed
over in November 1993, to Bishop Foley and his diocesan clergy, the parish of Innisfail.]

Finally, it should be pointed out in this centenary booklet that, without exception, the bishops
and priests of the Augustinian Order mentioned so far were all past students of either Santa Maria
in Posterula or of the present St Patrick's College, Rome.

BRISBANE, SYDNEY, MELBOURNE.

In 1952 a new era opened up for the Order in Australia when the Australian Province was
established as separate from Ireland.   The present writer, who until then was Vicar General of the
Diocese of Cairns, was elected the first Provincial.   Formidable tasks lay ahead.   That great and
true friend of the Order, Archbishop Sir James Duhig, handed us the magnificent parish of
Coorparoo that had been pioneered by Dean Jeremiah O'Leary.   It became for many years the
Provincial headquarters of the Order in Australia.   But there was a snag!   The archbishop asked
that a college for boys be built and staffed by Augustinians on a nearby hill.   The Villanova
Province in the U.S.A. must be thanked for coming to our aid with a fairly large loan free of
interest.   "I dips me lid" to the memory of that big-hearted American Provincial, the late Fr Joe
Doherty.   The Irish Province also came to help.   Thus Villanova College was built and opened in

Foundation Stone, Villanova College, Brisbane. Fr Hunt revisits the College which he built in 1952-53

1953, staffed by Augustinians and a dedicated lay staff. Blessed by the Lord over the years, today it now has a student body of approximately 1,000 boys with a teaching staff of over 60. No wonder the writer felt constrained at the invitation of the archbishop, the truly great Sir James, to go into his residence every evening between 8.30 and 9 p.m. (including Christmas night and New Year's) to take him for a drive along the Brisbane River and then, on returning, have a cup of milo with him and chat until 10 p.m. That was done for twelve years until James Duhig died at the age of 94 in 1965. Even archbishops can be lonely men in their old age!

Cardinal Gilroy at the opening of St Augustine's College, Sydney, 1955.
Speaker: T.A. Hunt, O.S.A., Provincial

In 1953 the Augustinians moved to Sydney. In long negotiations with another close friend, Cardinal Sir Norman Gilroy, we were given the parish of Manly Vale in 1953, but again with the obligation of building and staffing a boys' college at Brookvale, within the parish. When grave difficulties were foreseen during the negotiations the cardinal said to the writer: 'I think, Father, your problem boils down to this, can the Augustinians afford <u>NOT</u> to be in Sydney?' The college was opened and blessed by the cardinal in 1955, and has never looked back. Today it has a student body of some 800 boys.

Under the provincialship of Fr John Barry we returned to Melbourne in 1976, taking over the parish of South Yarra. It was strange that during the long reign of Archbishop Goold the Augustinian Order never secured a permanent foundation there. It is interesting to recall that when the present writer accompanied, in 1955, the then Prior General, Fr Eberhard, to meet Archbishop Mannix, His Grace, with a subtle sense of humour, said to the Prior General, 'Fr Hunt is always telling me that Augustinians began the Church in Melbourne and I am always telling him, why don't you come back and finish it!' Well we have gone back, but not to "finish it"!

Archbishop Daniel Mannix at his home, "Raheen", Melbourne, in 1955, with Frs E. Eberhard, O.S.A. (Prior General), N.P. Duffner, O.S.A. (Provincial, Ireland), T.A. Hunt, O.S.A. (Provincial, Australia), and T. Tevington, O.S.A.

KOREA

A new chapter of Augustinian history in Australia was opened when the Province under Fr Kevin Burman, Provincial, sent its first missionaries in 1985 to Korea. They went at the invitation of the bishop of Inchon and already have a house of formation in Seoul, as well as a parish in Inchon. The three Australian missionaries are the brothers John and Michael Sullivan, and Brian Buckley. All three are past pupils of Villanova College, Brisbane, and also of St Patrick's College, Rome.

AUGUSTINIANS AND THE ABORIGINAL AUSTRALIANS

I feel that some of the readers will be asking or thinking of what we have done, or rather not done, for the Australian aboriginal people. When the First Fleet landed in Sydney in 1788 with the first white settlers, Australia already had on its soil, maybe for 40,000 years, an ancient people, called Aborigines by the white settlers. At that time and for a century later they were a nomadic, tribal people coming, as their folklore states, from "the dreamtime". Sad to say they never built any permanent dwellings, like the Aztecs in Mexico, for example; they were mainly hunters wandering, on what they still call "walk-about", in search of food, mostly fish and birds. In the early days of the white, penal settlement they someTimes-attacked the white invaders with bows and arrows as well as spears. The colonial soldiers and police did not hesitate to shoot them. Perhaps it is not unfair to say that the colonial government and the powers that be as well as the early settlers regarded them as non-people! When Pope Paul VI came to Australia in 1970, in a public address, he reminded all Australians that when the white explorers came to the continent two hundred years before 'they found that this land was already inhabited by a very ancient people'. A delegation of them came from Darwin in the Far North of the continent to Sydney in order to meet the Pope. To this writer's knowledge it was the first time they ever had the privilege of being presented as a formal group of people to a world leader such as Pope Paul VI.

It should be stated that when the first Augustinians arrived in Australia, from Archbishop Goold in 1838 to Bishop Hutchinson in 1884, they considered themselves as missionaries to the Catholic convicts, miners, explorers and white settlers, who were scattered over a vast continent with no roads or public transport. In the reports to the Congregation of Propaganda Fide in Rome the six Augustinian bishops from 1848 to 1948 made little reference to the aboriginal people. Some other bishops had contrary ideas about evangelising the Aborigines. Michael Endicott, O.S.A., in *The Augustinians in Far North Queensland, 1883-1941*, p.175, quotes a report of the English Archbishop Vaughan, O.S.B., second archbishop of Sydney, to the Congregation of Propaganda Fide at Rome in 1878. He states: 'The Australian savages are extremely uncivilised, and those in the north are the worst of the lot. They live in rudimentary shelters and have no fixed abode, living from hand to mouth as they move from place to place. There have been some previous attempts to civilise them, but all have failed including the project of Bishop Salvado, O.S.B. . . . All in all, I believe there is no hope'.

It must be said, however, that after the first Plenary Council in Sydney in 1885, when Cardinal Moran with the other bishops suggested that the Spanish Augustinians, who had successful missions in the Philippines, be invited to come to North Queensland to open missions to the Aborigines, Bishop Hutchinson followed up the proposal. It was suggested to the two Spanish Augustinians, when they came to Cooktown, that six Augustinians, three priests and three brothers, from the Philippines and from Spain, should begin evangelising the Aborigines in the Far North. Problems arose about financing the mission and John Hutchinson rightly stated that he personally could not be responsible but it should be for the whole Catholic Australian Church as had been decided on at the Plenary Council in Sydney. Finally, Fr Villar, O.S.A., the senior of the two who had come to Australia to discuss the proposal, stated in a letter to his superiors in the Philippines: 'I cannot see how we could succeed, because the authorities intend the complete extermination of the black people. In the south they have been the victims of a cruel war of extermination, and have been almost annihilated. In the north there remain 50,000 of them, but they too will be decimated before very long.' (Endicott, cit., p.184). If, but IF, Fr Villar's report is true, then let us Australians hang our heads in shame!

It was left to the Protestant churches almost up to the end of the last century to evangelise this ancient people. It was only towards the end of the latter part of the last century that the Catholic Church made any serious and organized attempt at evangelising the Aborigines, and this was done mainly by the Missionaries of the Sacred Heart in the Northern Territory, and in a smaller way by the Spanish Benedictines in New Norcia in West Australia and the Pallottines in Broome. Tribute must be paid to Bishop McGuire who opened the Palm Island mission in 1930. Lastly, but not least, tribute must be paid to Fr Roderick Cameron, O.S.A., who, for many years, is carrying out an extensive apostolate to this ancient people all over North Queensland.

THE IRISH AUGUSTINIANS IN NIGERIA 1939-1992

Raymond Hickey, O.S.A.

THE IRISH AUGUSTINIANS IN NIGERIA, 1939-1992
Raymond Hickey, O.S.A.

The decision taken at the Provincial Chapter in 1936 to apply to Rome for a mission territory in Africa should be seen in the context of a wave of missionary enthusiasm then sweeping through the Irish Church. It gained momentum after the establishment of the Maynooth Mission to China in 1918 and, inevitably, was experienced in the mendicant orders. An Augustinian Foreign Mission Association was established in 1935 and the *Good Counsel* quarterly, founded in the same year, was 'designed primarily to help the missionary activity of the Augustinian Order' (*editorial of the first issue, April 1935*). The proposed mission had the enthusiastic backing of the newly-elected Provincial, Fr Thomas Cooney, but there were also those who had their reservations and counselled caution. The Province already had a growing commitment to the Vicariate of Cooktown in North Queensland and it was feared that another mission might be beyond the resources of the Province.

The delay in receiving an answer to the application for a mission territory in east or west Africa caused some perplexity to the Provincial and his Council. A year passed and it was decided that Frs Luke Maddock and John Berchmans Power should take up an assignment under Bishop Chichester, S.J., in the Vicariate of Salisbury (now Harare, capital of Zimbabwe). Fr Maddock had spent many years in the tropics in North Queensland while Fr Power was a young priest with a great love for travel and the missions. On 10 October 1937 they left London by sea for Cape Town and from there made the long rail journey to Salisbury. It was the start of a lifelong fascination with Africa for Fr Power and he would be drawn back there time after time throughout the course of his life.

The Augustinian application for a mission territory coincided with a petition from Msgr Josef Kirsten, C.S.Sp., of Benue Prefecture in Nigeria, to Rome that the eastern section of his prefecture be constituted a separate jurisdiction. The Apostolic Delegate to British East and West Africa, Archbishop Riberi, visited Nigeria in April 1937 and discussed the matter with the prefects apostolic of Jos and Benue. They agreed that the proposed mission territory would comprise the province of Adamawa in Nigeria and the adjoining League of Nations mandated territory of Northern Cameroons (formerly part of the German colony of Kamerun). The territory would come under the Prefecture of Jos until it developed sufficiently to be constituted a prefecture *sui juris*. The Congregation of Propaganda Fide in Rome offered it to a newly-established Swiss missionary body, the Bethlehem Foreign Mission Society, but they considered it to be too remote and difficult for their inexperienced missionaries to take on. The offer from the Irish Augustinian Province was still on the table and in February 1938 it was offered to them.

The picture of the mission territory outlined in the letter from Rome to the Irish Provincial contained no reference to the remoteness of the region or the special difficulties it presented. In optimistic tone it noted that Adamawa had 'the best climate in all Nigeria, [was] elevated, well-watered and agricultural' and had a 'more than 60% pagan population'. This was indeed true and these positive features would become more and more appreciated and important as the mission grew. They were secondary considerations however for Fr Cooney and his Council, whose application for a mission territory had been made in a spirit of faith and without preconditions. The offer was accordingly accepted and by the end of April the Prefect of the Congregation of Propaganda Fide, Cardinal Fumassoni Biondi, informed the Provincial that the first missionaries should proceed imnmediately to Jos.

Shortly afterwards Frs D.B. Redmond, P.A. Dalton and T.G. Broder were appointed to

Nigeria and Frs Maddock and Power were recalled from Rhodesia. It came as a shock to Fr Power who was under the impression that the Augustinian involvement in Salisbury Vicariate was a permanent commitment. Subsequent events would show that the assignment to Northern Nigeria was, despite initial appearances to the contrary, more promising and important for Church and Order than anything Rhodesia had to offer.

Frs Redmond, Dalton and Broder set out from Liverpool on 12 October 1938 and arrived in Jos on 2 November. Fr Redmond, who had worked in North Queensland and was the oldest of the three, was the Superior. Fr Maddock, who was his senior, failed a medical test before leaving Rhodesia and never saw Nigeria. Fr Power got a passage from Cape Town to Nigeria and joined the other three priests in Jos in February 1939. The Adamawa mission territory had been incorporated into the Prefecture of Jos and the Augustinians came under the jurisdiction of its Prefect Apostolic, Msgr William Lumley, S.M.A. As there was no mission station in Adamawa Province and the Augustinians had no missionary experience in West Africa they were posted to various mission stations in and around Jos. They would spend the next year learning the rudiments of mission life and methodology and studying the Hausa language. Although they did not realize it at the time it was a valuable apprenticeship for the task which lay ahead.

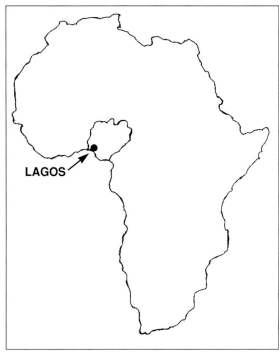
Map of Africa, showing Nigeria.

THE PROVINCE OF ADAMAWA

In sending missionaries to Nigeria the Irish Augustinian Province was following in the footsteps of Portuguese Augustinians who had laboured in West Africa from the early 16th to the mid-18th century. Their work had been made possible by the great exploratory journeys of Prince Henry the Navigator and Vasco da Gama which opened a sea route to India. Three dioceses were established to cover the western coast of Africa, with sees in Cape Verde, Sao Tomé and Sao Salvador (in modern Angola). That of Sao Tomé included the kingdoms of Warri and Benin, west of the Niger delta and now part of Nigeria.

The best known of the four Augustinian bishops of Sao Tomé is Gasper Cao. To remain in such a remote and inhospitable place for twenty years (1554-74) was in itself a considerable achievement. During these years he established a seminary on the island and sent Augustinian missionaries to Warri. The link between Sao Tomé and Warri was maintained for the following 160 years and it is on record that an Augustinian, Fr Francisco a Matre Dei, baptized the heir to its throne. Even today part of old Warri is known to the local population as "Santomé". We know too that missionaries from Warri preached the Gospel in Benin but with less success than in Warri. When left without priests in the eighteenth century the Catholics of Warri reverted to a syncretism with the traditional African religion in which, even today, some elements of Catholic ritual are clearly discernable.

The territory confided to the Irish Augustinian Province in 1938 was far removed from the coastal region in which Warri and Benin are situated. Adamawa was one of the twelve provinces which formed the Northern Region of Nigeria. It lay in the eastern border area and included for administrative purposes most of the mandated territory of British Northern Cameroons. This was a throwback to the First World War in which a combined British and French operation had defeated the Germans in Kamerun. The larger portion of the colony was placed under French administration and today (with the British Southern Cameroons) forms the Republic of Cameroon. The smaller Northern Cameroons voted in a United Nations supervised plebiscite in 1961 to unite with Nigeria and became the thirteenth province of the Northern Region.

Historically Adamawa and most of Northern Cameroons belonged to the Fulani-controlled emirates of Adamawa and Muri. The first of these had Yola as its capital and was the largest of the associated states which formed the Caliphate of Sokoto. It was also the least homogeneous of these states as about three quarters of the population were non-Fulani who had never been fully subjugated. The ethnic composition was similar in neighbouring Muri Emirate and the British united the two emirates in a single civil province in 1926. All the emirates of the Northern Region of Nigeria continued to administer their own affairs under colonial rule in a system of Indirect Rule devised by the territory's first High Commissioner, Sir Frederick Lugard.

The indigenous population of Adamawa was thereby ruled by a dual administration from 1901 to 1960 when Nigeria gained her independence. The system of local government by which the emirs appointed district heads was maintained, although the latter were supervised by British divisional officers. The emirs were likewise answerable to a British Resident in each province. All the emirate officials were Muslims and in Adamawa the great majority of these belonged to the ruling Fulani tribe. They formed an 'ascendancy' similar in many ways to the Protestant Ascendancy in Ireland of the eighteenth century. The ruling elite in Adamawa were Muslim and the Fulani were a people set apart who seldom mixed with the settled tribes. The latter were cultivators and followed their traditional religion. The Fulani were mainly pastoralists and their nomadic lifestyle also marked them off from the other ethnic groups.

This cleavage helped to limit the normal process by which subject people tend to adopt the religion of the ruling class in the hope of bettering their condition in society. Although the Fulani language (Fulfulde) was widely accepted and used as the lingua franca of the one hundred ethnic groups of Adamawa, Islam was resisted and individual cases of conversion were usually referred to as 'becoming a Fulani'. This attitude changed in the years after independence (1 October 1960) as the power of the emirates declined and education opened the eyes of the younger generation to a bigger and brighter world. Membership of a world religion, while retaining one's ethnic identity, became possible and highly desirable and the changed attitude benefitted Christianity much more than Islam.

This is borne out by the official census returns of 1952 and 1963. They show that whereas the Muslim population of Gongola State (which substantively corresponded with the old Adamawa) increased from 28.6% to only 32%, the Christian population grew fourfold - from 4.0% in 1952 to 16.7% in 1963. The disparity in the rates of growth has continued and in 1989 I estimated from available data that the population of Gongola State (and of Yola Diocese) was 45% Christian, 35% Muslim and 20% Traditional. The last-named is concentrated in the older generation and has no future as a formal organised religious body. The figures are based on an estimated population of $5\frac{1}{2}$ million people.

ARRIVAL IN YOLA

Time passed slowly for the young Augustinian missionaries doing their apprenticeship in mission stations in and around Jos. Their goal was Adamawa and they were impatient to get there. Relations with Msgr Lumley became strained and morale must have been weakened when, in May 1939, Fr Redmond abruptly returned to Ireland. The next in seniority was Fr Dalton, then just 30 years of age and four years a priest. A graduate of University College, Cork, and the Gregorian University in Rome, he had been a teacher in the Augustinian schools in New Ross and Dungarvan before volunteering for the Adamawa mission. He was appointed Superior in Nigeria at the provincial chapter held in July 1939 and would spend the remaining 30 years of his life as the anchorman of the mission.

The clouds of war which had been hanging over Europe for over a year grew more ominous during the summer of 1939. When German troops invaded Poland on 1 September fears gave way to the reality of war. The implications of the conflict for a mission which had not yet got off the

159

ground were apparent to Fr Dalton and he wrote to Msgr Lumley : 'In view of the recent grave happenings I felt it my duty to ask if you have any information about our future prospects. They will no doubt be affected by the restrictions but what I'd like to know now is whether we shall be allowed into Adamawa at all. It is very near the former German territory and may be forbidden to us.'

The Prefect Apostolic was able to allay Fr Dalton's fears and assured him that the authorities would welcome their good influence on the people of Adamawa. Msgr Lumley had visited Yola in February 1939 and explained the purpose of the Augustinian mission to the Resident (senior administrative officer of the province). This paved the way for a reconnaisance expedition to Adamawa in May by two of his most experienced missionaries. They trekked the mountainous country south of Yola and the riverain plains to the west, and selected sites for three mission stations in the villages of Demsa, Boi and Sugu.

Msgr Lumley decided to apply for only two stations, in Boi and Sugu. Demsa would not have been granted as it was close to Numan where the Danish Lutherans had a long-established mission. It was also unlikely that permission would be granted for a mission in Yola. A Christian mission in the seat of a large Fulani emirate would not be seen as conforming with the treaties signed between the British and the emirates which guaranteed to respect and safeguard their Muslim culture and religion. None of the expatriate Protestant missions then operating in Adamawa had a station in Yola.

The outbreak of war brought many matters to a head and the application for a mission in Sugu was approved in early September. The site in Boi however was not granted, probably because of the emir's opposition. Msgr Lumley had the foresight to purchase a supply of building materials in Jos and arrange for their transport to Adamawa. This proved to be of immense value in view of the shortages which the war would soon cause. He had also been assured that good roofing timber was available near Sugu. It seems that the outbreak of war was a spur to all concerned to get moving and establish the mission in Adamawa as soon as possible.

The same sense of urgency was apparent in the unexpected visit of the Apostolic Delegate to Jos in November. Archbishop Riberi was surprised to learn that the Augustinians were not already in Adamawa and there was a candid exchange of views between him and the parties concerned on this point. Msgr Lumley wished to appoint an experienced S.M.A. missionary to be in charge in Adamawa and supervise the building of the mission in Sugu. This was unacceptable to the Augustinians who wanted to plan and develop their mission from the start. The disagreement was settled amicably by the Delegate and it was decided that the Augustinians would move to Adamawa in January 1940. While remaining under the jurisdiction of Msgr Lumley they were free to work on their own initiative and administer their own accounts.

Archbishop Riberi, Apostolic Delegate to British East and West Africa.

Accordingly, on Friday 19 January 1940, Frs Dalton, Broder and Power packed their belongings into the truck they had purchased and set out for Yola. It was the dry season and the dirt track was open to traffic. They took three days to do the journey of 325 miles and arrived in Yola in the evening of Sunday, 21 January. They put up in the only Catholic church in all Adamawa Province, a grass-matting structure erected ten years earlier by the handful of Catholics - mainly from the south of the country - who had settled in Jimeta, the commercial area of Yola. In his diary Fr Dalton described the church as follows : 'This church was an oblong structure of about 30'x15', the sides were merely a number of stakes. These held the roof of grass and were in turn surrounded by native mat. Into this we put our bed, kitchen and Mass box - and there we lived until we got use of a government rest house, the first headquarters of the Augustinian Foreign Mission in Nigeria.'

THE MISSION IN SUGU

The outbreak of the Second World War was a matter of grave concern for the newly-elected Irish Provincial, Fr J.B. O'Donoghue. He took action on two vitally important points, finance and personnel, before the means of communication with Nigeria were severely restricted. A lodgment of £1,000 was immediately made to the Augustinian account in Jos and three young priests were appointed to the mission. In the event only two of these travelled, Frs H.A. Garman and P. O'Shea, and they arrived in Lagos on Christmas Eve 1939.

The situation of the Spiritan (C.S.Sp.) mission in Benue Prefecture was at this time in dire straits. The missionaries there belonged to the German Province and since the outbreak of the war were classified as enemy nationals by the British administration. They were able to carry on their work subject to some restrictions for some months but in 1940 they would all be interned and deported to Jamaica. Being aware of this possibility, the Apostolic Delegate requested that the two Augustinian missionaries en route from England in December 1939 assist in staffing the Benue Prefecture for some time. Fr Dalton agreed to this and Frs Garman and O'Shea were accordingly instructed to proceed to Onitsha where they would receive their appointments.

Other counsels prevailed in Onitsha and more experienced missionaries were sent to take over from the Germans in Benue Prefecture. The two Augustinians thus served their missionary apprenticeship among the Igbo of Onitsha-Owerri Vicariate rather than in Makurdi. In March 1940 Fr Dalton wrote to the Delegate in Mombasa and requested permission to recall Fr Garman to Yola. It was his last communication with Archbishop Riberi and there was no reply. When Italy entered the war on the side of Germany the Delegate was forced to leave British-ruled Mombasa and return to Rome. He had been a good friend of the Augustinian mission in Nigeria and when he was appointed Nuncio to Ireland in 1959 Msgr Dalton took the pains to write and congratulate him.

Meanwhile in Yola the need for a pied-à-terre in the provincial headquarters had become clear. The only organised Catholic community in Adamawa was there (in Jimeta). There was no road to Sugu and the position of the missionaries there could be untenable during the long rainy season. The nearest Catholic mission was in Jos and it would remain the indispensable supply point and fall-back position for the Augustinians in Adamawa for many years. Despite the difficulties involved in siting a Christian mission so close to emirate headquarters Fr Dalton pressed the case for it forcefully with the Resident. The latter was sympathetic and accepted that the Catholic community in Jimeta had a right to the services of the priests. He suggested that the mission apply for 'a church for local Catholic adherents, rest house and store for Rev. Fathers'. Thus worded it won the approval of the colonial and emirate authorities and a site on a rocky eminence outside the town was granted. It was known to the local population as the Hill of Snakes.

A week after their arrival in Yola the three missionaries set out for Sugu. There was a motorable track to Jada, some 60 miles from Yola and 25 from Sugu. Fr Power returned to Yola and Frs Dalton and Broder proceded on horseback to Sugu. They arrived in the evening of 30 January and, in keeping with the African tradition of hospitality, were given round houses for accommodation by the Fulani District Head. There was no building of any sort on the approved site and the enormity of the task confronting them was immediately apparent. Building materials would have to be brought from Yola, trees felled for timber, stone and sand brought to the site and stone masons and carpenters sought. They soon found out that the Hausa they learned in Jos was of little use to them in Sugu or anywhere outside Yola and that they would have to learn Fulfulde.

Meanwhile back in Yola Fr Power decided to tackle the problem of communication head on. He would load the truck with building materials and clear a trail to Sugu. He did so and some days later arrived at the mission site to the utter amazement of Frs Dalton and Broder. Work commenced on a mud-block room built on stone foundations. It was completed in August at the height of the rainy season, in time for a delayed St Augustine's Day reunion of the Adamawa missionaries. Fr Garman had just arrived from Onitsha and was critical of the mud-walled building. The missionaries spent some days together and Fr Dalton recorded in his diary : 'Our little house came in for a lot of criticism from Fr Garman's experienced mind, a lot of the gilt was worn away but it was in a good cause'. Such was the beginning of St Augustine's, Sugu, the first station of the Adamawa mission.

THE SECOND WORLD WAR

By the summer of 1940 the Second World War had erupted into open conflict in Europe and when the Germans established a puppet government at Vichy in France there were fears that there would be conflict on the Nigeria-Cameroon border. The war, known in Nigeria as "Hitler's War", did not spread to Nigeria but it did cause severe shortages and curtailed the anticipated expansion of the Adamawa mission. One other mission station however was opened before the effect of the shortages began to bite. This was in the Chamba village of Mapeo in the mountains south of Yola and close to the border with Cameroon. The site was chosen by Fr Power and was approved in November 1940. By then work had commenced on building the Fathers' rest house in Yola and Frs Dalton and Power moved in there on Christmas Eve.

Thus it was that within a year of their arrival in Yola a framework had been established which would endure for the next five years. Three mission stations had been, or were in process of being, established, the first elementary school had been opened by Fr Broder in Sugu, and all five priests appointed to Nigeria were on the spot in Adamawa. Fr Dalton as Superior of the mission resided in Yola, where Fr Power was in charge of the parish. The latter would leave Yola to open the station in Mapeo with Fr O'Shea in February 1941. The building programme had been confided to Fr Garman and despite the shortages caused by the war he built the mission residences which are still in use in Sugu and Yola and the small church which would serve as the first cathedral of Yola Diocese.

At the same time the work of the Augustinian Foreign Mission Association in Ireland was expanding rapidly. The missionaries in Adamawa were financially dependent on their support and, apart from an annual grant from Rome, there was no other source of income. As the number of missionaries in the field increased greater demands were made on the Association. It was established in all churches of the Irish Province and local promotors, co-ordinated by a Mission Director in Dublin, brought in the funds. A monthly news-sheet, *Mission News,* was established by Fr J.L. Cotter in May 1949 and this brought a new fillip to the Association at a time of rapid expansion on the mission field.

The Province was also supportive in the number of priests appointed to Nigeria. Despite the perils of war they were able to get a passage on the occasional convoys which set out from the U.K. to West Africa. In this way Frs M. Cullen, J.O. Hartnett and P.A. Harney got to Yola in 1942 and Frs T. Cotter, A.J. Hanly, S. Anderson and J.C. Fitzsimons in 1943. The ship carrying the last two named was bombed by the Germans off the Spanish coast and sunk. The passengers took to the life-boats and were picked up by other ships. After a week in Casablanca the two priests were able to continue their journey to Nigeria.

No other missionaries arrived until after the war ended in 1945. Conditions then improved and it became possible to make a wider reconnaisance of the Adamawa mission territory with a view to further expansion. The longest of the exploratory journeys was that undertaken by Frs Broder and Cullen to the Mambilla Plateau in March 1945. Travelling by horse and on foot from Sugu they trekked a distance of over 700 miles through rugged mountainous countryside. They marked a site for a mission on the plateau but it was considered to be too isolated from Yola, and Mambilla did not get a resident priest until 1975. Other journeys of note were made by Fr T. Cotter who went overland from Shendam (south of Jos) to Lau on the River Benue in December 1945 and visited distant Tiv fishing villages on the same river.

By then Fr Cotter had opened the next mission station at Jauro Yinu and was operating from there. It was the first venture into Muri Emirate and the village was only six miles from the emirate headquarters in Jalingo. The sparse population was mainly Jukun, a former ruling tribe who had been displaced by the Fulani. Although it was not a good centre for evangelization Jauro Yinu served as a base to open outstations in southern Adamawa. It was also close to the densely-populated Mumuye region, a tribe which in later years would yield a rich harvest for the Gospel message.

Always an ardent advocate of missionary expansion Fr Cotter was intimately involved in the opening of the next mission station at Bare in February 1948. Situated on the River Gongola, ten miles north of the town of Numan and outside the Muslim emirates, the mission in Bare was hampered by the surrounding swampy terrain. Nevertheless it opened up a new area to the Gospel and would spawn other more accessible mission stations. This was also true of the mission in Kaya (Gulak) opened by Frs M. Cullen and J. Seary in 1948. It provided an opening to the large Marghi tribe and was the springboard from which the missions were established in Bazza (1950), Mucella (1957), Mubi (1960) and Shuwa (1966).

Frs Tadhg Cotter and Basil Hannon outside the grass hut in Bare
in which they lived for some months after their arrival.

THE PREFECTURE OF YOLA

In October 1948 the Augustinian mission to Adamawa was ten years old. The anniversary was marked by the first visitation by a Provincial to Nigeria. Fr C.J. Dullea spent six weeks in Adamawa in December 1948-January 1949 and visited all six mission stations. He also met Msgr Lumley, Prefect Apostolic of Jos, who was the ecclesiastical superior of the Adamawa mission. His Vicar Forane or local representative for the territory was by then Fr Hugh Garman - while Fr Dalton held the position of Augustinian Religious Superior. The time was approaching for the appointment of a Prefect Apostolic for Adamawa and the normal process of consultation had started. Frs Garman and Dalton held senior positions and would certainly have been considered for the office. The two men had widely different backgrounds and personalities and did not always see eye to eye but both had the calibre for leadership. There would be scope and fulfilment for both of them on the Adamawa mission.

Fr Dullea's visitation also led to the coming of the first missionary sisters to Adamawa. On his return to Dublin the Provincial contacted the Mother General of the Franciscan Missionaries of

Divine Motherhood (F.M.D.M.) and appealed for their help in Nigeria. They were needed both for health care and the education of women and girls. The response was positive and the Mother General visited Yola to finalize arrangements in March 1950. A small convent residence was built beside the mission school and the first three sisters arrived in Yola on 8 July 1950. One was employed in the Government hospital while another took charge of the mission school.

The Prefecture of Yola was formally constituted on 14 July 1950 and on 27 October Fr Dalton was appointed Prefect Apostolic. He was in Ireland at the time and his first act was to appoint Fr A.J. Hanly Pro-Prefect (substitute superior). Fr J.A. O'Connor was appointed Augustinian Religious Superior in place of Fr Dalton and so the two offices were kept distinct. Fr Garman returned to his native England in November and did not return to Nigeria until 1960.

Msgr Dalton returned to Nigeria in March 1951 and was installed as Prefect Apostolic in Yola on the feast of St Patrick. It was an opportune time to take stock of the situation and plan for the future. The Prefecture had seven mission stations, sixteen priests and three F.M.D.M. sisters (although it would lose the services of Frs M. Cullen and J. Seary later that year). The next phase in the development of the Adamawa

A short halt on a trek by jeep: Frs Corny Madden, Charlie O'Reilly, and Malachy Cullen, with native helpers.

mission would last for eleven years, until the Prefecture became the Diocese of Yola in July 1962. They were years of profound social and political change in Nigeria as the country progressed towards independence and successive steps towards a fully representative government were taken.

The F.M.D.M. sisters opened their second convent in Sugu in January 1954. As in Yola they took care of the mission school and became involved in health care. They managed a health centre in collaboration with the Adamawa local government authority and opened a domestic science centre for adult women at a time when women had a very lowly status in society. Having seen this in action the North Regional Director of Women's Education was so impressed that she claimed that 'Sugu Housecraft Centre was the most practical of all Government and Voluntary Agency institutions in Northern Nigeria'.

Four beaming beauties from F.M.D.M. school.
Helen Edward (front left) is a teacher leader of Catholic women in Maiduguri. Mary Vandu (front right) - her father gave the land for O.S.A. mission site at Bazza.

The need for a much greater involvement of the Church in education became apparent as independence approached. The lack of trained teachers was a crippling obstacle to the development of a Catholic school system in Adamawa. The effectiveness of the mission school as a means of evangelization had been demonstrated in the south of the country and, given sufficient time, could be expected to bear comparable fruit in the north. The time factor was all-important as the first full (i.e. seven year course) Catholic primary school outside Yola was not opened until 1955. Fr W. Power, brother of the pioneer-missionary J.B. Power, was by then Catholic Education Supervisor for the Prefecture and was successful in getting government approval and grant-in-aid for this and many other schools in the years leading up to independence.

The school in question was in Bazza and it led to the opening of a Catholic Teachers College there in January 1958. The first Principal of St Augustine's T.C., Bazza, was Fr A.B. Kennedy, a priest who had been involved in education since his arrival in Nigeria in 1946 and who imported a printing press to Yola for mission needs. It was used to print his short catechism in Hausa, *Karamin Katekism,* which has had a number of revised editions and is still in use. The college in Bazza provided the regulation three year course and its first graduates were ready for appointment in the schools of the Prefecture in January 1961. Thereafter, until it was taken over by the government in 1973, the college provided a steady flow of teachers to staff the mission schools of Yola and Maiduguri dioceses and played a major role in the evangelization of north-east Nigeria.

Aidan B. Kennedy, O.S.A.,
with his printing press.

Villanova Secondary School was the second post-primary school in the Prefecture of Yola. It was opened by Fr J.A. O'Connor in temporary accommodation in Bazza in February 1960 and occupied its permanent site in Numan in November. It too was a boarding institution and it played a significant role in creating a well-educated Catholic elite, many of whom would hold prominent academic and government posts in later years. Fr P.O. O'Keeffe was appointed Principal in 1961 and, aided by a highly-qualified team of Augustinian priests and lay teachers, brought the school to the level of excellence over the next ten years. As in the case of Bazza T.C. it was taken over by the government in a unilateral decree in 1973 and soon lost the Catholic character.

Two other post-primary institutions were opened in the Prefecture in January 1962. The sisters in Sugu opened Madonna W.T.C., a teachers' college for girls and Fr A.B. Kennedy opened St Michael's Advanced Teachers College in Yola. The latter was converted into a day secondary school in 1965 and was in time taken over by the State. Although Fr D. Kelleher stayed on as Principal of St Michael's until 1976 the era of the mission school had effectively ended with the government take-over of schools.

THE PREFECTURE OF MAIDUGURI

Shortly after Msgr Dalton's installation as Prefect Apostolic of Yola the Apostolic Delegate, Archbishop David Matthew, requested the Irish Augustinian Province to assume responsibility for

The early days!
A youthful Fr Bresnan prepares the football for his young athletes.
Fr Malachy Cullen receives a lesson in the use of the bow and arrow.

165

the neighbouring province of Borno. Like Adamawa it formed part of the Prefecture of Jos and Msgr Lumley had let it be known that he was anxious to get Borno off his hands. Msgr Dalton was consulted and was not at all enthusiastic about the proposal. Unlike Adamawa, Borno had a predominantly Muslim population and prospects for establishing the Church there were bleak. The Provincial headquarters, Maiduguri, was the capital of the long-established Kanuri state and seat of the Sheikh (or *Shehu*) of Borno.

The proposal about Borno was discussed at the Irish Provincial Chapter in July 1951 and received a qualified approval. A brisk correspondence ensued between the newly-elected Provincial, Fr Michael Connolly, the Apostolic Delegate and Msgr Dalton. Many of the missionaries in Adamawa had reservations about taking on Borno and felt that the resources of the Irish Province should be concentrated in Adamawa. Msgr Dalton suggested that one mission station, situated in Maiduguri, would be able to care for the scattered pockets of immigrant Catholics in Borno Province.

The Apostolic Delegate pressed the matter forcefully and a reluctant Msgr Dalton bowed to the inevitable. He wrote to the Resident of Borno Province in October 1952 to inform him of the impending change in jurisdiction and of his intention to post two priests to the province in the near future. He went there in person two months later and marked an extension to a plot on which a small church had been built in 1945. As in Yola in 1940 a mission in Maiduguri was a delicate matter and the application needed tact and patience to succeed. There were an estimated 400 Catholics in Maiduguri, the great majority being Igbos from the south of the country, and they could not be denied a religious ministry. Approval was accordingly granted for a church and Fathers' residence but an application to the Native Authority for a school was rejected on the grounds that 'such a school would be a menace to the religion of the people'.

Monsignor P.A. Dalton, O.S.A., when Prefect Apostolic of Yola, Nigeria, in 1951.

In this way the wheels were set in motion whereby a separate Prefecture of Maiduguri was established on 29 June 1953. The first priest to be appointed to Maiduguri was Fr A.J. Hanly. He arrived there from Yola on 1 April 1953 and got accommodation in a government rest house. A small mission house was built that year and was followed by a new church in 1956. Permission was given for a school to serve the Catholic population and it opened in early 1954. In general it was an easier task to establish the mission in Maiduguri than in Yola but it was specified that the Fathers there could operate only 'amongst the non-Muslim stranger community'. The Kanuri had been Muslim for centuries and there was no realistic hope of their conversion to Christianity. They had a tradition of tolerance and hospitality to strangers and this no doubt eased the way for the establishment of St Patrick's mission at Maiduguri.

An unconvinced Msgr Dalton was appointed Apostolic Administrator of Maiduguri Prefecture on 26 February 1954. 'Since I have had this inflicted on me, I should like to know what plans if any are being made about staff for the two Prefectures in the coming year', he wrote to the Provincial some weeks later. A separate prefecture meant that he would receive an annual grant from Rome, so progress had to be made. The second visitation by an Irish Provincial took place in January 1956 when Fr N.P. Duffner visited Maiduguri and all the

Frs N.P. Duffner and Columba Heffernan - with Sr Francis - visit the hospital at Sugu, for maternity cases and abandoned lepers, run by the Franciscan Missionaries of Divine Motherhood.

stations of Yola Prefecture. He confirmed the Irish Province's commitment to Maiduguri Prefecture. More priests were appointed there and stations were opened in Nguru (1956), Potiskum (1959) and Pulka (1962). In this way the scattered Catholic communities of the prefecture were adequately served.

Msgr Dalton's fears concerning the difficulty of evangelization in Borno Province were borne out although his belief that 'Priests, unless they be Francis Xaviers, will be just idle for years' was an over-pessimistic assessment of the situation. It was only in Pulka that a local church took secure root among a hill people who had preserved their traditional religion (although strictly speaking Pulka was outside the prefecture). It was due in large measure to the patient spade work of its pioneer missionary, Fr T.A. Walsh who, in the absence of a mission school, directed all his efforts to winning the hearts and minds of the adult population. It was a new departure in mission strategy in the region.

Fr Hanly remained in Maiduguri as Msgr Dalton's Vicar Delegate for the Prefecture until he had a near-fatal accident and was invalided home to Ireland in 1960. He was succeeded by Fr M.T. Flynn who had only just opened the mission in Potiskum. In the same year Fr J. Curtis was elected Provincial. He was in office for six years and the big number of priests he appointed to Nigeria brought about a new impetus to all aspects of the mission apostolate. The growth of the commitment of the Irish Province to Nigeria can be seen in the number of Augustinians working there at ten-year intervals :

1940 - 5	1960 - 34
1950 - 17	1970 - 61

In all, to date (1992), 116 Irish Augustinians have served in Nigeria. There have also been three English Augustinians, two Spaniards, a Scot and an Australian.

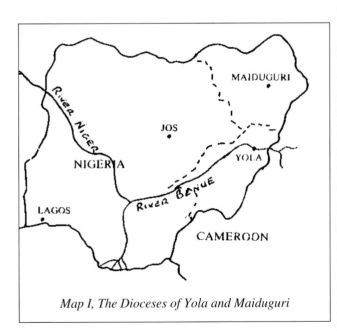
Map I, The Dioceses of Yola and Maiduguri

TWO AUGUSTINIAN BISHOPS

After the normal process of consultation Fr Timothy Cotter was appointed Prefect Apostolic of Maiduguri on 5 July 1962. The prefecture could now develop under its own momentum and in its own right. Msgr Cotter had never served in Borno and after his installation in Maiduguri on 28 October he undertook a number of familiarisation tours of the prefecture. He had just three mission stations (four if Pulka is included), five priests and six churches. The only indigenous Catholics were a group of schoolboys who had been baptized in Potiskum that Easter. All the others were immigrant Catholics from other parts of Nigeria. Borno presented as bleak a picture to him as it had to Msgr Dalton in 1952.

Msgr Dalton had been Administrator of Maiduguri Prefecture for eight years (1954-62) and was fully aware of the difficulties faced by Msgr Cotter. In a generous act of solidarity he agreed to cede the northern districts of Yola Prefecture which could be conveniently administered from Maiduguri to his episcopal brother Ordinary. This part of the old Northern Cameroons (by then known as Sardauna Province) had mission stations in Pulka and Kaya and was mainly non-Muslim. It would constitute an invaluable base for building up an indigenous community and a source of badly-needed teachers and catechists. It is not for nothing that the Diocese of Maiduguri has always been looked upon as the daughter and sister jurisdiction of Yola.

The agreement to transfer this territory to Maiduguri Prefecture was finalised when the

Apostolic Delegate, Archbishop Pignedoli, visited Maiduguri in May 1963. The Delegate also assisted in getting the agreement of the Immaculate Heart Sisters (a Nigerian congregation) to establish a community in Maiduguri. Plans were made for mission stations in Biu, Gashua and Shuwa and for a day secondary school in Maiduguri. All of these, apart from the last-named, would come to fruition during the next three years. Fr D. Coleman was placed in charge of an extensive building programme, beginning in Gashua and moving on to Shuwa in 1965. A Catechetical Training Centre was opened by Fr N.C. O'Reilly in Kaya in 1964, a Trade School by Fr P.I. Farrell in Shuwa in 1965, and a convent with a community of Immaculate Heart Sisters in Shuwa in 1966.

The pace of development in Maiduguri Prefecture would not have passed unnoticed by the Apostolic Delegate. The Second Vatican Council, which was taking place during these years, favoured the rapid development of mission territories into fully-constituted dioceses. This helps to explain the reasoning behind the establishment of the Diocese of Maiduguri on 7 June 1966 and the appointment of Msgr Cotter as its bishop-elect. He was ordained bishop in the Augustinian church in his native Limerick on 8 September 1966. In view of the tragic developments in Nigeria which affected his diocese later that month - to which we shall return - his episcopal motto *Dum Spiro Spero* was indeed apt.

Monsignor Dalton in the 1950s with some of his intrepid helpers.
Front row: Fr Bill Power, Sr Philippa, Mother Bernard, Mgr Dalton, Sr Paul, Frs Malachy Cullen and Andy Hanly.
Back row: Frs Fionan Heffernan, Philip Martin, Jed Roche, John O'Connor, Jack Seary, Tadhg Cotter, Aidan Kennedy

In treating of the growth of the Church in Borno our narrative has now moved ahead of events in Yola. As noted earlier there was rapid expansion there in the field of education prior to and after the granting of independence in 1960. The number of missionaries increased steadily in Yola Prefecture but most of them were drawn into the new post-primary schools. As a result less emphasis was placed on direct and primary evangelization. New stations were opened in Yakoko (1955), Numan (1958), Mubi (1960) and Zing (1961) but vast areas of southern Adamawa were still untouched. Another area which saw little development lay north of Yola on the road to Mubi. Sadly, the first death of a missionary in the field took place when Fr J.V. Butler died in Yola on 11 June 1959. He was aged 28 years.

The Prefecture of Yola was formally constituted a diocese on 2 July 1962. Msgr Dalton was appointed bishop-elect and arranged that his ordination would take place in Ireland. Before leaving Yola he sent a moving personal letter to his fellow-missionaries in which he said :

'It happens through an accident of time and circumstance that I am the one appointed bishop. I was one of the first to come here, the longest, the oldest but one etc. An accident such as this scarcely makes one worthy of such an exalted position as Bishop of a diocese, of which truth I can never be but painfully conscious.

There is another feature about our work here and that is its continuous and phenomenal success. I used to think that it was God's way of preparing young and inexperienced missioners; to prepare them for the Cross, the seal of perfection, by handing out a little of the crown first.'

In keeping with this line of thought Msgr Dalton chose *Triumphans in Cruce* as his episcopal motto. It would epitomise the next seven years of achievement in spite of adversity for him. He was ordained bishop in the Augustinian church of SS John and Augustine, John's Lane, Dublin, on 28 September 1962. The principal celebrant was the Apostolic Delegate, Archbishop Pignedoli. President Eamon de Valera was there as was the Taoiseach (Prime Minister), Seán Lemass. It was time for "a little of the crown" that Msgr Dalton referred to in his letter. The new bishop did not enjoy good health and he seemed to foresee the Cross that would be his for much of the remainder of his life.

THE NIGERIAN CIVIL WAR

The crown was also present for Bishop Dalton and his missionaries in the Silver Jubilee celebration of the Adamawa mission. It took place in Yola on 24 January 1965 and was attended by the Provincial, Fr J. Curtis (who was conducting his second visitation), Fr R. Shuhler (Assistant General, O.S.A.) and the founding father of the mission, Fr T. Cooney. A parish hall, which now serves as a busy Pastoral Centre, was built to mark the occasion. The Silver Jubilee coincided with the opening of St Peter's Minor Seminary, a sure sign of progress and a turning point in the history of the diocese. It was opened by Fr M.O. Flynn in renovated school buildings in Bare but moved to Jauro Yinu in 1967. The site there was unsuitable for a number of reasons and it was only when the seminary transferred to a new site in Yola in 1973 that its future was assured.

The Diocese of Yola was not affected to the same extent as Maiduguri by the trauma of the Civil War (1967-1970). The majority of the Catholic population were indigenes of the diocese and the parishes were not built on the Igbo diaspora. The opposite was the case in Maiduguri Diocese and hundreds of Igbo Catholics lost their lives there during the pogrom of September 1966. Bishop Cotter was still in Ireland and his newly-appointed Vicar General, Fr J. Crean, was in charge in the diocese. The Igbos who survived the slaughter were evacuated from the Northern Region, and the parishes of Nguru, Gashua and Biu were no longer viable. The Igbo Sisters in Maiduguri and Shuwa were evacuated to the Eastern Region and the convent in Maiduguri was rented to a Protestant mission.

At this bleak moment for Maiduguri Diocese Bishop Dalton of Yola once again showed extraordinary generosity and solidarity with his brother Augustinian bishop. In order to make the new diocese a viable unit he agreed to transfer to it a much larger part of his diocese than in 1963. It included mission stations in Mubi, Bazza and Mucella, out-stations such as Michika, Kala'a and Gombi, and St Augustine's Teachers College, Bazza. Mubi was the largest town in his diocese after Yola, St Augustine's T.C. the most important Catholic institution. Their addition to Maiduguri Diocese would more than make up for the closed parishes of Borno Province.

The change in diocesan boundaries took effect in September 1968 and brought about a revitalisation of Maiduguri Diocese. A community of four Augustinian Sisters of the Mercy of Jesus from Park House, Liverpool, (Sisters Carmel, Agnes, Kevin and Concepta) reopened the convent in Shuwa in 1970 and in the following year opened a very successful Health Centre. The first Irish de la Salle brothers came to St Augustine's T.C., Bazza, that year and in 1972 the last Augustinian Principal, Fr S.L. O'Donnell, handed over responsibility to Bro. Michael Fergus, F.S.C. New mission stations were opened in Madagali (1968), Buma (1970) and Kala'a (1972), thereby opening up new areas to the Gospel message.

As the work progressed in both Yola and Maiduguri dioceses attempts were made to recruit more personnel. A proposal to hand over most of southern Adamawa to the American Spiritan (C.S.Sp.) Province was made to the Apostolic Delegate in 1965. Bishop Dalton was in favour of incorporating the area in question in a new jurisdiction to be based in Wukari (in Makurdi Diocese) but his suggestion was not acted upon. Seventeen years later English Spiritans undertook to work the area and the Wukari region was soon added to Yola Diocese. By then the time for primary evangelization of the indigenous population had passed and a golden opportunity had been lost.

From an Augustinian point of view the proposal that the region west of the River Gongola in

Yola Diocese should be handed over to Spanish Augustinians is more interesting. Two of their number, Frs L. De Sande and J.M. Vazquez, had been working in the diocese since 1957 and 1963 respectively and the proposal was seen as an extension of their work. Three other Spaniards volunteered for the mission in 1967 and the two priests in the field were accordingly posted to the two stations in the proposed Spanish region, Bare and Lafiya. Nothing more was done however and Fr De Sande left the diocese abruptly in early 1969.

It was the start of a very difficult year for the Diocese of Yola. The changes brought about by the Second Vatican Council had an unsettling effect on many missionaries world wide and Yola was not an exception to a general trend. Over the next few years three priests in the diocese would resign in order to get married. At the annual general meeting of missionaries in Yola in January 1969 there was a frank exchange of views and Bishop Dalton came in for stinging criticism. He returned to Ireland shortly afterwards charged with getting ten more priests for his diocese. He attended the Provincial Chapter in June and was preparing to return to Nigeria when he received word that Fr Garman had been killed by a mentally-deranged man in Yakoko. The lives of the two men had been interwoven for many years and word of his colleague's violent death came as a great shock for the bishop. He returned to his diocese not knowing that he himself was seriously ill. In September he was back in Ireland and there he died, *triumphans in cruce,* on 29 November.

Shortly after word of Bishop Dalton's death was received in Nigeria Fr J.D. Gough - who had been Vicar General - was appointed Vicar Capitular of Yola Diocese. The cup of bitter adversity for the diocese that year had not yet been drained and the year ended with another grievous loss. On 12 December a young English missionary, Fr C.P. Bowlby, scarcely two months in the country and only 28 years old, was thrown from the truck he was driving and died shortly afterwards. The only ray of light to brighten an otherwise bleak year was the arrival of the first Sisters of Mercy (from Dungarvan) in Yola on 30 October. In the following year they opened another convent in Bare.

ESTABLISHING THE ORDER

The office of Augustinian Religious Superior in Nigeria was concerned from the beginning with the organisation of the Adamawa mission and the religious observance of the missionaries. Fr Dalton held the post, which was separate from that of ecclesiastical superior, until his appointment as Prefect Apostolic in 1950. He was succeeded by Fr J.A. O'Connor and then Fr T. Cotter. The latter was responsible for building the mission residence in Mubi, which would also serve as a residence for the R.S. (by then known as Provincial Vicar) in 1961. Fr S. Coffey was appointed to the office in 1963 and it was during his tenure (1963-69) that the first steps were taken towards establishing a Nigerian Augustinian Province.

The position of Mubi as an Augustinian house was clarified at the 1963 Provincial Chapter and Bishop Dalton agreed that it should be an Augustinian canonically formed house and parish. Fr M.T. Flynn, who had been pastor in Mubi since 1963, was appointed its first Prior in 1965. There were also plans for a minor seminary at Kala'a, within the Augustinian parish. It would cater for vocations to the Diocese of Yola, the Prefecture of Maiduguri and the Order. A residence for the Provincial Vicar and adequate accommodation for visitors and newly-arrived missionaries were included in the plans. Unfortunately they came to naught because of the ethnic disturbances of 1966 and the resulting instability of the country. Bishop Dalton went ahead with the transfer of his minor seminary from Bare to Jauro Yinu in 1967 and it became an interdiocesan institution with Maiduguri Diocese when it was moved to Yola in 1973.

Plans for another Augustinian foundation in a totally different area did come to fruition before the Biafran civil war put further development on hold. The acceptance of a parish in the small town of Iwaro-Oka in Ondo Diocese in 1966 was significant as it was the first Augustinian commitment outside the jurisdictions of Yola and Maiduguri. It gave the Order a presence among the Yoruba, the second-largest ethnic group in the country (after the Hausa). The appointment of

Fr J.G. Cunnane as Superior and Parish Priest and Fr G.J. Bresnan as Rector of St Patrick's Secondary School was confirmed at the 1966 Provincial Chapter. Both had served for many years in Adamawa and the transfer to Iwaro-Oka meant a change to a completely different cultural milieu. Fr Cunnane therefore spent some months studying the Yoruba language in Ibadan before joining Fr Bresnan in Iwaro-Oka. Bishop Field of Ondo was keen that the Augustinians take care of the Marian shrine of Oke Maria nearby but local community rivalries made this impractical.

Although Iwaro-Oka was a rural parish and did not have great potential for growth it had a strong Catholic tradition and the large number of vocations to the priesthood and religious life from the area testifies to this. It would provide the first Nigerian vocations to the Order and its first professed members. Joseph Mary Omerigbe was accepted as a postulant in 1968 and having completed his novitiate in Orlagh (Dublin), made simple profession of vows on 16 September 1969. He went on to study theology in Rome and Louvain but was not passed for solemn profession. The next to join the Order was Samuel Oluwole, an electrician by trade and a candidate for the brotherhood. He completed his novitiate in Mubi and made his profession of simple vows there in 1972. Because of family responsibilities he sought a dispensation shortly afterwards and left the Order.

The disturbances of 1966 and their aftermath were the occasion for the establishment of a third Augustinian community. It followed an earlier (1963) request from the Ordinaries of the Kaduna Ecclesiastical Province that the Order staff and manage a major seminary in Zaria. The proposal was discussed at the Provincial Chapter in 1963 and was accepted. Shortly afterwards, however, the project was abandoned as it did not have approval from Rome. A decision in favour of a single national seminary was overtaken by the turmoil which followed the military coup d'état in January 1966. A widespread transfer of population took place in the weeks following the September pogrom of Igbos in the north and the few northern seminarians in Enugu and Ibadan returned to their homes. Their continuing formation and education became a matter of grave urgency and the Augustinians were again asked to open and staff a major seminary in the north.

This was the background to the assignment given to Frs M.T. Flynn and G.B. O'Brien at the end of 1966 to open St Augustine's Major Seminary. Temporary accommodation was found in the minor seminary for Makurdi Diocese at Keffi and St Augustine's Seminary opened there on 1 March 1967. There were just 13 students on the roll, among them the future bishop of Makurdi, Athanasius Usuh, and a future Governor of Benue State. Frs Flynn and O'Brien had scarcely any teaching aids or text books but they improvised as best they could and completed the first academic year in December. Meanwhile the political situation deteriorated rapidly and when the Eastern Region (Biafra) seceded from the Federation in May it was clear that there would be no quick solution to the country's troubles. Paradoxically, they guaranteed the permanence of St Augustine's Seminary.

ST AUGUSTINE'S MAJOR SEMINARY

The involvement of the Irish Province in Nigeria took on a new dimension during the six years spent by Fr S. Coffey as Provincial Vicar. He was the first Augustinian religious superior to function above and apart from the missionary structure in Yola and Maiduguri and thereby break the accepted mould. The establishment of the parish in Iwaro-Oka and the acceptance of responsibility for a major seminary served to broaden the horizons of the Order in Nigeria and to making it national rather than regional in scope. The Priory in Mubi constituted a secure base for the Order in the original mission territory assigned to it and close to the missionaries in the field. It would continue to serve as headquarters until 1978.

When Fr Coffey returned to Ireland because of ill-health in 1969 a great deal had been accomplished and the office of Provincial Vicar had assumed a new importance. Fr P.L. Lyons, the Prior of Mubi, acted as superior until the Provincial Chapter of 1969 when Fr P.F. Sheehan was appointed Regional Vicar of the Nigerian Vicariate. He held the position until his appointment as

Bishop-elect of Yola in 1970. Fr Lyons then became substantive Regional Vicar and remained so until 1977. His years in office coincided with a period of national reconstruction after the horrors of civil war. The economy of the country was buoyant as its oil resources were exploited and there was rapid development in all fields.

It was also a period of rapid Nigerianisation of Church structures and saw the appointment of many Nigerian bishops. It became increasingly difficult to get visas for new missionaries in the years after the civil war. Numbers in the field began to drop and many missionaries believed that it was too late in the day to establish the Order in the country. They felt that all the resources on hand should be directed to the primary task of evangelization and building up a strong local church. Promoting vocations and seminary formation assumed enormous importance in this scenario as there was not yet a single Nigerian priest in either Yola or Maiduguri Diocese. Alternative systems of ministry were debated and a centre for the formation of permanent married deacons was opened in Bazza in 1972.

The pivotal importance of St Augustine's Major Seminary and, to a lesser extent, St Peter's Minor Seminary in Yola, was obvious in view of the urgency of the situation. The episcopal Ordinaries of the Kaduna Province had decided in 1967 that a permanent site for the major seminary would be sought in Jos. While the site was being acquired and developed the seminary would move from Keffi to a newly-built centre for the formation of married deacons in Sabon Gwong, Jos. As in Bazza the project had encountered difficulties and the staff house was vacant. The seminary would function in the classrooms of an adjoining mission school. Facilities were rudimentary and there was no piped water supply but it would house the seminary for two years from January 1968.

The future of St Augustine's Seminary was now assured and a comprehensive syllabus for a full seminary course was drawn up. The staff was augmented when Fr M.C. Fitzgerald arrived from Ireland in January 1968. He was joined by Fr J.A. Downey at the end of that year and by Frs T.D. Mason and M. Nolan in 1970. All were highly qualified in theology or philosophy and their appointments show the importance attached to the seminary by the Irish Province. In January 1970 the permanent site in Laranto was occupied and over the next few years a spacious assembly hall and diamond-shaped library were added to the original functional buildings.

Relations between the Irish Province and the Ordinaries of the North were formalised in a contract signed between them in February 1971. The Order thereby accepted the direction and ordinary administration of the seminary for a period of ten years. The Rector and all staff members would be presented by the Irish Provincial for appointment but he would not be required to supply more than eight staff members. The contract stipulated that 'Every effort shall be made, with due consultation between the Hierarchy and the Order, to work towards the provision of a Nigerian staff . . . and to have this achieved as soon as is prudently possible and circumstances allow' - more an aspiration than a practical proposition at that time. The contract was renewed in 1982 and again in 1987, on each occasion for a five year period.

As the number of seminarians grew (from 31 in 1969 to 186 in 1975) so did the number of staff members. The first Nigerian priest came in 1974, the first non-Augustinian expatriate in 1975. The first Rector, Fr M.T. Flynn, returned to Ireland because of persistent ill-health in 1973 and was succeeded by Fr M.C. Fitzgerald in January 1974. His $4^1/_2$ years in office were a time of rapid growth when many of the seminary's notable buildings were constructed. Both he and Fr G.B. O'Brien resigned from the staff in 1978 and Fr J.A. Downey was appointed Rector. By then the seminary was beginning to reap the harvest of its endeavours and past pupils began to return as staff members. The aim of having a Nigerian staff was being gradually realized and in January 1984 Fr Downey handed over to the first Nigerian Rector, Fr C. Gotan.

GROWTH IN YOLA DIOCESE

Our narrative now returns to the cradle of the Augustinian Order in Nigeria, the Diocese of

Yola. The term "Adamawa Mission" became an anachronism after the break-up of the Northern Region into states in 1967. The old Adamawa Province then became part of North-East State which had Maiduguri as its capital. Adamawa (with the addition of Wukari Division, Benue Province) was reconstituted a separate political unit in 1976 and renamed Gongola State. At a much later date (1991) this State would be divided into Adamawa State and Taraba State, thus bringing back the old name of Adamawa to common usage.

Fr Patrick Sheehan was only 38 years of age when he was ordained second bishop of Yola on 6 January 1971. The ordination took place in Yola and was attended by the Augustinian Prior General, Fr A. Trapé, the Irish Ambassador in Lagos and, to the delight of all present, the bishop's mother and sisters from Ireland. So began a new chapter in the history of Yola Diocese. Fr P.O. O'Keeffe was appointed Vicar General and Fr J.K. Moylan Chancellor. A general meeting of all missionaries in the diocese was held shortly after the Bishop's episcopal ordination and a policy of extensive evangelization to cover the whole diocese was adopted.

By the end of March Fr R.P. Hughes had opened a new station in temporary quarters in Bali, a small town on the main road south from Yola and ninety miles from the nearest mission in Jalingo. It was an important breakthrough into the sparsely-populated area of southern Adamawa. There were small Catholic communities in the larger towns but very few of them were indigenes of the region. The largest Catholic community was in Gembu, administrative headquarters of the Mambilla Plateau and a gruelling 150 miles from Bali. There were also many outstations among the Tiv farmers in the fertile lowlands of the Benue Valley and their number would increase greatly in the years to come.

The mission in Bali led to the opening of other stations in Gembu (1975) and Garba Chede (1976). A drop in the number of missionaries prevented further expansion and soon caused the temporary closure of Garba Chede. In 1979 an agreement was made with the English Spiritan Province whereby they would take over Bali parish. The first Spiritan priest arrived in January 1980 but shortly afterwards the mission house in Bali was destroyed by fire. Fr Hughes returned to rebuild the house and it was handed over to the Spiritans in November. It was seen at first as an extension of their work in Makurdi Diocese but in November 1982 all of Wukari Division (with parishes in Wukari and Takum) was transferred from Makurdi to Yola Diocese. This brought the diocesan boundary into line with the civil boundary of Gongola State.

The evangelization of Adamawa was a wholly Augustinian enterprise from 1940 to 1980. The coming of the English Spiritan missionaries brought a new fillip to the work and another tradition meant new ideas and methods. The process of diversification continued when a community of De la Salle brothers took over the management of St Peter's Seminary in Yola in 1984. The last Augustinian Rector, Fr D.V. Loughran, built on the earlier work of Fr M. Sexton (who was Rector from 1971 to 1979) and was successful in having the seminary recognised as a centre for the State school certificate examination. St Peter's Seminary has fulfilled its purpose admirably and has been a fertile seedbed of vocations for Yola and Maiduguri dioceses and the Nigerian Augustinian Vice Province.

The first priest to be ordained for the Diocese of Yola was Fr Aloysius Jella, on 16 December 1973. The first for Maiduguri was Fr Thomas Kambasaya, on 14 December 1975. He and almost all the priests of the two dioceses who followed since then were past pupils of St Peter's Seminary and St Augustine's Major Seminary, Jos. The link between the diocesan priests of Yola and Maiduguri dioceses and the Order is therefore very close and many of them have received hospitality and accommodation in Augustinian houses in Ireland. Their number has increased greatly in recent years and when the Golden Jubilee of the Adamawa Mission was celebrated in Yola in 1990 there were 21 diocesan priests in the diocese, as against 12 Augustinians and 11 Spiritans.

As the number of diocesan priests increased and the diversification of missionary personnel noted above took place (bearing in mind the contribution made by communities of five congregations of Sisters to the apostolate), the number of Augustinians working in Yola Diocese began to decrease. As the post-primary schools were taken over by the State in the early seventies there was less demand and fewer outlets for them in education. At the same time a future Nigerian Province of the Order was taking shape and there was the need for personnel in formed houses of the Order. The process of disengagement in the two dioceses was gradual and the transfer of responsibility to the diocesan clergy orderly. The sharp decline in the number of ordinations in the Irish Province in the eighties accentuated the process and it shows that the era of the expatriate missionary is nearing its end. Thankfully, vocations to the priesthood in Yola Diocese are numerous and as the number of diocesan priests increases the specific role and contribution of religious communities can be seen in their true light.

THE NIGERIAN VICE PROVINCE

When the parish of Mubi was transferred to the Diocese of Maiduguri in 1968 the Augustinian Order was left without a canonically formed house in the Diocese of Yola. This anomaly was raised with Bishop Sheehan shortly after his episcopal ordination in 1971 and again at the Provincial Chapter in 1973. At first Ganye was favoured as a location for a formed house but eventually, on 28 October 1974, a formal request was made for a parish and house in Jalingo. Bishop Sheehan readily consented to this and in 1975 the parish priest of Jalingo, Fr T.D. Hegarty, was appointed Prior. He would continue to serve in this capacity until he left Jalingo in 1980.

As the boundaries of an Augustinian parish were never delineated its area of pastoral responsibility remained an unwritten arrangement over these years. The future of the Priory in Jalingo came up for discussion after Yola became the capital of Gongola State in 1976. Bishop Sheehan offered the Order the option of a parish in Yola town or in Bekaji estate. It was felt that the Order should have a house in the State capital and the parish in Bekaji was accepted in May 1980. The Order agreed at the same time to relinquish the priory in Jalingo.

It will be recalled that the Irish Chapter of 1973 was held at a time when it was almost impossible to get visas for new missionaries and the whole feasibilty of establishing the Order in Nigeria was being questioned. Fr Martin Nolan was beginning his eight-year tenure as Provincial while Fr P.L. Lyons was confirmed in office as Regional Vicar for the Nigerian Vicariate. Despite the problems posed by the visa question the Chapter came out strongly in favour of working towards the establishment of a Nigerian Province and of taking immediate steps towards this end.

Some months later Fr V.B. Hickey was entrusted with the task of establishing a house of formation in Jos. It was a full-time appointment, unconnected with the Major Seminary. A site had been applied for in 1972 and was approved shortly after the Chapter. Fr Hickey arrived in Jos in October 1974 and work commenced on the first buildings in 1975. The design of small circular chalets around two large community houses was based on the style of the traditional African compound in Northern Nigeria. The design posed special problems for the contractor and delayed the work with the result that Fr Hickey and the students did not occupy the monastery until late 1976.

By then the difficulty in getting visas for new missionaries had been overcome and prospects for a future Nigerian Province of the Order were much brighter than in 1973. At the Irish Chapter in 1977 Fr T.D. Brosnan was appointed Regional Vicar and the offer of a house and parish in Benin City was accepted. The outgoing Regional Vicar, Fr P.L. Lyons, was appointed superior of the new venture. It was an important milestone in the growth of the Order and, as Portuguese Augustinians had preached the gospel in Benin 300 years earlier, was of symbolic value. The city had not lost its historic importance and in 1977 it was the capital of Bendel State.

Fr Brosnan would remain at the helm of the Order in Nigeria for the next twelve years. When he assumed office in April 1977 there were 52 professed Augustinians in the Vicariate, but not a single Nigerian among them. In these circumstances the decision of the 1977 General Chapter to make Nigeria a Vice Province of the Order was deemed by many in the field to be premature. It should be remembered however that only a General Chapter has the authority to make such a decision and had the opportunity not been grasped in 1977 it would not have arisen again until 1983. By then there would have been many Nigerian professed members of the Irish Province. This anomaly was avoided by the decision taken at the 1977 General Chapter. Many in Nigeria felt that there had not been adequate consultation of the brethren before taking such a decision and it remained a controversial subject for some time.

Fr Brosnan transferred the headquarters of the Vice Province from Mubi to Jos in early 1978. It was a more central location for the various communities and the move underlined the growing importance of the monastery. An extension to the compound, approved in June 1978, gave ample room for future development. Later that year quarters for the Vice Provincial, with an office and six guest rooms, were built. The monastery was gradually becoming the hub of the Vice Province and in January 1980 it was the venue for the first specifically Augustinian retreat for all the brethren. This has become an important annual event in the Vice Province and is as much a celebration of Augustinian fraternity as a retreat.

AUGUSTINIAN HOUSES IN YOLA AND MAIDUGURI

The first Ordinary Chapter of the Nigerian Province was held in the monastery in Jos in June 1981. It was the first Augustinian Chapter to be held on the African continent. The Assistant General of the Order, Fr T.A. Hunt, presided over the historic gathering and Bishops Cotter and Sheehan attended as honoured guests. Fr Declan Brosnan had been elected Vice Provincial before the Chapter - and would be re-elected before the next Chapter in 1985. He also served as President of A.F.A., the Augustinian Federation of Africa, a consultative co-ordinating body formed at a meeting of Augustinian superiors in Africa at Hippo in 1979.

Fr P.O. O'Keeffe, formerly Vicar General of Yola Diocese, was appointed Prior of the Monastery community at the 1981 Viceprovincial Chapter. At the same time Fr V.B. Hickey was appointed to establish the "New Priory Foundation, Yola". It was another challenging task, made all the more difficult by the fact that the Catholics in Bekaji estate formed part of Yola Cathedral parish and did not have a sense of separate identity. There were no buildings on the site and no demand for the new parish. The site was in the farthest corner of the estate and was inconvenient for the people. A community would have to be won and then held.

A start was made when a parish hall was built in 1982. Frs Hickey and J. Daman moved into staff quarters in 1983 and the parish slowly took off. The Priory was completed in 1985 and by 1989 there was a community of three priests with five Masses on a Sunday. They are chaplains to St Peter's Minor Seminary and have looked after the Nigeria Army barracks community for long periods. As noted earlier the house in Jalingo reverted to the diocese in 1980 and as the town is now a State capital, it is one of the busiest parishes in Yola Diocese.

The building of a new cathedral in Yola was a sign of the growth of the Church in the diocese. It took $3\frac{1}{2}$ years to complete and was first used for the ordination of five priests on 4 October 1986. One of these, Fr S. Tagisa of Mapeo, was the first Augustinian priest from Yola Diocese. The new St Thérèse's Cathedral was dedicated by Bishop Sheehan a year later, on 3 October 1987. His fellow Irish bishops in the North, from Maiduguri and Makurdi, were present as was the Irish Provincial, Fr T. Cooney, and former Diocesan Administrator, Fr J.D. Gough. It was Bishop Cotter's last visit to Yola before he died.

The Augustinian foundation in Maiduguri Diocese followed the pattern set in Yola. Following a consultation of the brethren Fr Brosnan and his Council decided in 1986 to accept Bishop Cotter's offer of a parish in the State capital in exchange for the house and parish in Mubi. It was a difficult decision to make and somewhat controversial as Mubi had been an Augustinian house since 1961. Both it and St Augustine's, Maiduguri, were considered "plum" parishes of the diocese and Bishop Cotter and his Council felt that they could not give both to the Order as permanent foundations.

The transfer from Mubi to Maiduguri took place shortly after Easter, 1987. Fr T. Sexton was the Prior and Parish Priest at the time. The parish in Maiduguri had been opened in 1980 and served the University and a large urban population coming from all over Nigeria. The parish house was too small for a community of three priests and a new Priory was built during 1988. As the parish community grew the need for an extension to the church built in 1980 became urgent. This was carried out in 1991 under the Nigerian community appointed to St Augustine's at the 1989 Chapter.

It will be recalled that there is also a community of Augustinian Sisters of the Mercy of Jesus at Shuwa in Maiduguri Diocese. Their house of formation opened there with a single postulant in 1984. Their number grew steadily and on 4 May 1988 the first three Nigerian Sisters made profession of vows. It was an occasion that Bishop Cotter had looked forward to dearly but did not live to see. He had returned to Ireland for medical treatment in December 1987. A malignant tumour was found on his chest and he died peacefully in John's Lane Priory on 15 March 1988. Before he died he wrote his last Easter message to the people of Maiduguri Diocese. 'Easter is a time of good news and I am happy to let you know that I hope to return to Maiduguri very soon', he wrote. 'I shall then have the pleasure of meeting you face to face and together we shall praise God for his care and blessings'. But it was not to be and his Easter was spent with the Risen Lord in the communion of saints.

A few days after receiving word of Bishop Cotter's death the diocesan consultors in Maiduguri elected Fr S.L. O'Donnell Administrator of the Diocese. He had been Vicar General under Bishop Cotter and parish priest in Nguru-Gashua parish. It was a time when relations between the Christian and Muslim communities in Nigeria were strained and the position of the mainly immigrant Catholic population of Borno State was delicate. The situation has not changed since then and the appointment of a bishop in such a strongly Muslim area is a sensitive issue. This may help to explain the long delay in appointing a successor to Bishop Cotter. More than two years elapsed before Fr O'Donnell was appointed Apostolic Administrator of the diocese on 14 May 1990. Maiduguri is on the frontier of the sub-Saharan Church and the core of the diocese still lies in the territory given up by Bishop Dalton in 1963 and 1968. It has a Catholic population of about 60,000, less than half that of Yola Diocese. The number of vocations there is not as great as in Yola Diocese and the diocese will need the services of Augustinian missionaries for many years to come.

[Edd note: Since this chapter was submitted a successor to Bishop Cotter has been appointed - Fr Senan Louis O'Donnell, O.S.A., was ordained Bishop of Maiduguri in November 1993]

Bishop Senan Louis O'Donnell, O.S.A., with his brothers, Ben and Columba, both also Augustinians, after the Bishop's Ordination in Maiduguri, Nigeria, November 1993.

GROWTH OF THE VICE PROVINCE

As the number of expatriate Augustinians began to decline after 1980 the first Nigerian members of the Vice Province made solemn profession of vows and were ordained priests. Frs Joseph Ekwu and Bart. Chidili were ordained in December 1980, Fr J. Daman in 1982 and Fr C. Mbanusi in 1983. As the number of students grew the need for more accommodation in the Monastery became acute. A separate novitiate was built in 1984 and a library in 1987. Fr M. O'Sullivan was appointed Prior at the 1985 Chapter and was re-appointed in 1989. The importance of the Monastery in the life of the Vice Province continued to grow and by 1988 there was a community of 48 priests, students and novices. By then an internal school of philosophy had been opened there while professed students continued to

176

attend St Augustine's Major Seminary for theology.

The monastery was also the centre for Augustinian Publications, established in 1979 to meet the needs of the growing literate Catholic population. Bro. Cyril Counihan was appointed General Editor and the first five booklets were published in 1980. The venture built on the earlier work of Frs Malachy Cullen and Aidan Kennedy and by 1991 over a million copies of 27 different titles had been published. The booklets are in Hausa as well as English and prices are kept as low as possible. Most are the work of Fr M. Cullen while the first by a Nigerian Augustinian was published in 1988.

The apostolate of higher education is closely related to that of the written word and Augustinians have been active in this field too. Fr T.D. Mason of the Monastery community served in the University of Jos as lecturer, Associate Professor of Religious Studies and Dean of the Faculty of Arts from 1974 to 1987. In the Diocese of Maiduguri Fr P.D. Daly was a lecturer and Head of the Department of English in Maiduguri University from 1975 to his death in May 1980. And in Yola Fr M. Sexton, ex-Rector of St Peter's Seminary, was Head of the Religious Department in the Federal College of Education from 1981 to 1985. In all three cases academic involvement was wedded to important chaplaincy work among the Catholic student body.

The eighties were a decade which saw the Nigerian Vice Province take shape and grow. Strictly speaking this is outside the scope of this essay - which deals with the activities of the Irish Province - but salient events and dates must be mentioned. As the activities of the Vice Province grew some missionaries in the field grew uneasy lest the establishment of the Order take precedence over the evangelization of Yola and Maiduguri dioceses - the primary purpose for which the mission had been established. The matter was raised at the Irish Provincial Chapters in 1985 and 1989 and the commitment of the Province to the two dioceses was reaffirmed. The work of evangelization and the establishment of the Order would proceed hand in hand and both had the backing of the Province.

As the number of solemnly-professed Nigerian Augustinians increased it became possible for the Vice Province to undertake further expansion. A house and parish in Lagos had been mooted since 1967 and it became a reality in 1987 when Fr M. Crean was appointed Superior and Parish Priest of what soon became the busiest parish in the Vice Province. It had been an out-station and had a house and temporary church building but a community of three priests was able to give a good service and the Mass congregations grew rapidly. A year later Fr V. Aherne opened another important parish in the former North Regional capital of Kaduna. A house was rented beside the temporary church building in Malali and it served the community until a large Priory was built on a new site in 1990.

Meanwhile the older parishes in Iwaro-Oka and Benin City had been consolidated and built up. Fr J.B. Grace succeeded Fr Cunnane as Prior in Iwaro-Oka in 1973 and was responsible for building a two-story Priory. In all he spent ten years in the parish before being appointed to Benin City in 1978. The Augustinians there had been engaged in supply work for Bishop Ekpu for their first three years and the Priory was not built on their own site until 1981. A temporary church, built in 1978, served the needs of St Augustine's parish for nine years. Work on a new church commenced in 1985 and took two years to complete. Fr P.L. Lyons returned to Ireland because of ill-health in 1988 and was

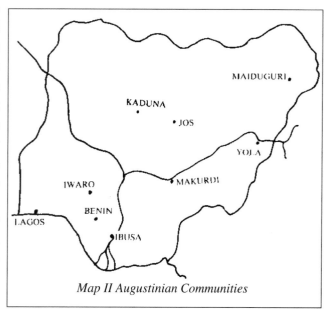

Map II Augustinian Communities

succeeded as Parish Priest by Fr M. Sexton. St Augustine's had by then grown into a thriving parish, second only to Lagos among the eight parishes of the Vice Province.

THE GOLDEN JUBILEE

In the elections prior to the 1989 Viceprovincial Chapter Fr V.B. Hickey was elected to succeed Fr Brosnan as Vice Provincial. By then there were 24 affiliated members of the Vice Province, eleven of whom were priests. The increasing number of Nigerian brethren was reflected in the new Council, which had two Nigerian members, and in the appointment of the first Nigerian Priors. The Chapter also considered the following far-reaching proposals for further expansion :

(a) the acceptance of a parish in Ibusa in the Diocese of Issele-Uku (in the Igbo area of Bendel State).

(b) the closing of the internal school of philosophy in the Monastery in order to assist in staffing the Philosophy Campus of St Augustine's Major Seminary in Makurdi.

(c) the establishment of a community in Ishiara in the Diocese of Embu (Kenya) where there were two convents of Augustinian Sisters.

The first two proposals were approved by the Viceprovincial Council and were implemented in the months following the Chapter. The last did not have the support of the Chapter members and no action was taken. In 1990, however, following further consultation and a change in circumstances in Ishiara, it was agreed that the Vice Province would accept responsibility for the Ishiara project. The Irish province would co-operate with it in the all-important fields of finance and personnel. A programme for the implementation of the project was drawn up and in September 1990 Fr T. Sexton went to Kenya to get the project off the ground. He took over the parish of Ishiara on behalf of the Order the following Easter.

In addition to the three proposals put before the 1989 Chapter the Vice Province accepted a parish in the suburbs of Jos later that year. Bishop Ganaka confided the out-station of Rantya to the Order in November and Fr T. Lyng was appointed pastor of the new parish. As in Kaduna a house was rented close to the existing temporary church structure and plans were made for a permanent church. This was built during 1991 and was in use by Christmas. By then Fr R. Hughes, who had spent some years in Ireland, was back in the country and was the full-time parish priest in Rantya. It was in Jos that the first Augustinian missionaries began their apostolate in Nigeria in 1938. St Monica's Parish, in building on their work and that of the Major Seminary and Monastery, has forged a new link between the Order and its origins in Nigeria.

The Golden Jubilee of the arrival of the first missionaries in Yola in 1940 was celebrated both as the Jubilee of the Catholic Church in Yola Diocese and the Augustinian Order in Nigeria. A Jubilee Year was proclaimed by Bishop Sheehan on Sunday 21 January 1990, fifty years to the day that Frs Dalton, Power and Broder arrived in Yola. The year, which had "The Christian Family" as its theme, was marked by numerous ceremonies. At an Augustinian celebration in May the old cathedral was used for a Mass of remembrance. In his homily Bishop Sheehan said : 'Yola is the seed bed from where all other Augustinian commitments began. This, somewhat smaller then, was the first church, the first symbol of the faith, brought by the Augustinians to Yola. It is a church that has been prayed in for 50 years; and these very walls and stones have heard the prayers of many people over these years.'

The position of Parish Priest of St Thérèse's, Yola, had been held by an Augustinian ever since the arrival of the first missionaries in 1940. The Jubilee Year was a very busy time for the incumbent, Fr Colin Fives. Later that year he handed over the office to a Nigerian priest of the diocese. Similarly, in 1988, a Nigerian had replaced Fr A.K. O'Leary as Vicar General. Both appointments were proof of the growing strength and maturity of the diocesan clergy. The whole purpose of a missionary assignment was being achieved.

The closing ceremony of the Jubilee Year took place on the feast of St Thérèse (celebrated on Sunday, 30 September), patroness of Yola Cathedral. It was attended by Fr Brian O'Sullivan,

Augustinian Assistant General, and a number of former missionaries from Ireland. Among them was Fr Dan Kelleher who spent some months helping out in the Cathedral parish. Fr F.R. O'Shaughnessy, Director of the home Augustinian Mission Association for the previous 24 years, was also present. In this capacity he represented the thousands of Irish people who supported the "Adamawa Mission" over the past fifty years and contributed, by their prayers and contributions, to its flowering and success.

LAUS DEO SEMPER
* * * * * * * * * * * * *

ADDENDUM

SOURCES

I began to collect information on the establishment of local Catholic communities in Borno State shortly after my posting to Maiduguri in 1960. This proved to be invaluable in view of the disruption and massive transfer of population which preceded the outbreak of the Nigerian Civil War in 1967. By then I had detailed accounts of the origins of Catholic communities in Maiduguri, Nguru, Potiskum and other towns - long before a priest was posted to Borno. Many of the informants were either killed during the pogrom in 1966 or did not return to the province when the civil war ended in 1970.

On a visit to Jos about 1968 Bishop Reddington kindly gave me the files dealing with Borno when it formed part of Jos Prefecture and was served from St Thérèse's Parish at Jos. Fr Frank Hughes, S.M.A., shared with me his recollections of pastoral visits to Maiduguri between 1942-52 and gave me a valuable photo of the first church built there in 1945. This was all very useful when I was asked to write, in 1973, a history of the mission to Borno. Bishop Cotter gave me full access to the archives in Maiduguri and lent me his diaries. I also drew from the mission diaries of the Augustinians of early days in Kaya (Fr Malachy Cullen), Mubi (Fr John Seary), Mucella (Fr M. Tom Flynn), Maiduguri (Fr A. Justin Hanly) and other stations. These led to the publication of my *Heralds of Christ to Borno*, marking the Silver Jubilee of the Prefecture of Maiduguri in 1978.

I also had access to the Irish Augustinian archives at Ballyboden for the work and found the Acts of Provincial Chapters, correspondence between Nigeria, the Irish Province, the Apostolic Delegates in Mombasa and Lagos and the Congregation of Propaganda Fide in Rome, and *Good Counsel* and *Mission News* periodicals, to be valuable sources for checking facts, figures and dates. The same was true when I was working during 1988-89 on the history of Yola diocese. Bishop Sheehan put the archives in Yola at my disposal for this work as well as mission house books and registers. These had been expertly catalogued by Fr Aidan B. Kennedy, O.S.A. His notes and analyses, especially in the field of education, eased my task.

The first volume of Bishop Dalton's diary, dealing with the years 1938-42, is a frank account of a difficult period and has the freshness of a narrative written on the spot by a deeply-involved protagonist. The same is true of many of the mission diaries, kept regularly in all stations until about 1975. Those from Yola Diocese are now in the Augustinian archives at Jos. I found Fr Hugh Garman's diaries of his years in Yakoko especially helpful. They give not only an account of the growth of the Catholic Church among the Mumuye but an analysis of underlying trends and missionary methods. Baptism and Mass registers were also useful in establishing dates of arrival or transfer of missionaries. I found an old Augustinian Mass register in Sugu, and Fr Colin Fives gave me a similar register which covered the fifty years of Augustinian stewardship of St Thérèse's Cathedral Parish, Yola.

Background information on Adamawa and Borno Provinces is available in numerous Government publications and in the published work of such well-known figures as A.H.M. Kirk-

Greene (*Adamawa: Past and Present*), E.P.T. Crampton (*Christianity in Northern Nigeria*), J.B. Grimley (*Church Growth in Central Nigeria*) and D.J.M. Muffett (*Let Truth be Told*) - all of whom served in Adamawa in the pre-independence period.   There are also many useful articles in *The Annals of Borno,* published annually by the University of Maiduguri.

The first Nigerian *Catholic Directories* were published in 1965 and 1966 but then, because of the civil war, had a gap until 1973.   The most reliable source for recent Catholic Church statistics and information is the annual *Catholic Diary and Directory,* published by the National Missionary Seminary.

An edited version of my work on the history of the Adamawa Mission was published as *A History of the Diocese of Yola* by the diocese of Yola on the occasion of the Silver Jubilee of the Catholic Church there in 1990.   As in the earlier work on Borno it contains a bibliography.   At much the same time I was asked to compile booklets to mark the Silver Jubilee of St Peter's Minor Seminary, Yola, and the Golden Jubilee of the Augustinian Order in Nigeria.   This resulted in the publication of my *The Augustinians in Nigeria* in 1990.   It contains a list of the 123 Augustinian missionaries (all but seven of whom were Irish) who served in Nigeria between 1938 and 1990.   It also refers to the work of the early Portuguese Augustinians who brought the Gospel message from Sao Tomé to Warri and Benin.   The research for this period was undertaken by Fr J. Kenny, O.P., an American Dominican, and published in *The Catholic Church in Tropical Africa, 1445-1850* (Ibadan University Press, 1983).

St Augustine's Major Seminary, Jos, celebrated its Silver Jubilee in 1992.   A special issue of the seminary periodical *Jos Studies* has marked the occasion.   An article I was asked to write on the birth and growth of the seminary covers this area of the Augustinian involvement and commitment to the Catholic Church in Nigeria.   The information for my article was readily available in the archives in Jos Monastery and from the Major Seminary (thanks to the secretary, Sister Máire Blair, S.S.L.).   The article completes the picture of the Augustinian presence in Nigeria : Yola, Maiduguri, the Major Seminary at Jos, the establishment of the Order.

Other Augustinians have published articles on our missionary endeavours in Nigeria.   As early as June 1944 F.X. Martin, then a student of philosophy at Orlagh, Dublin, published an article, 'The African Venture', in *The Tagastan,* of Washington D.C., U.S.A., vol.7, no.3, pp 142-152.   This was superseded in 1956 when Michael Benedict Hackett provided a detailed survey,'Irish Augustinian Mission in Nigeria', in *Augustiniana* of Louvain, 6(1956), pp 791-814.   I edited a selection of Bishop Timothy Cotter's pastoral letters and messages, published under the title *Hearts as well as Souls,* Augustinian Monastery, Jos, Nigeria, 1990.   The involvement of the Irish Augustinian Province in Nigeria has therefore to date been well documented, but for future research scholars there is a wealth of information available in the archives at Jos, Yola, Maiduguri, Ballyboden, and at the Congregation of Propaganda Fide, Piazza di Spagna, Rome.

As an additional bonus the Ballyboden Augustinian Archives include the rich systematic collection of the papers of Fr Tom Cooney, O.S.A., (†29 Feb. 1992) - founder of the Augustinian Mission in Nigeria - whose papers were carefully examined by Fr Peter Haughey, O.S.A., in 1992 and deposited in the Ballyboden Augustinian Provincial Archives.   They are available for consultation by all qualified historians.

LIST OF AUGUSTINIAN MISSIONARIES WHO SERVED IN NIGERIA, 1938-1994.

(The list of 123 missionaries has been arranged in chronological order according to the year of their first arrival in Nigeria. Whenever a period of over two years was spent outside the country it has been indicated. Where two entries are given for 'origin' the first indicates the place of birth, the second where most of the formative years were spent. All but seven of these missionaries were Irish: there were also three English, two Spaniards, a Scot and an Australian. The information given here has come mainly from the catalogues issued by the Irish Province from time to time and from the List of Arrivals and Departures compiled by Fr A.B. Kennedy.)

Name	Origin	Birth	Arrival & Departure		Death
1. Redmond, Denis Brendan	Tipperary	1-2-1899	1938	1939	29-10-1974
2. Dalton, Patrick Anthony	Tipperary	29-3-1909	1938	1969	29-11-1969
3. Power, John Berchmans	Limerick	8-6-1908	1938	1941	27-7-1987
			(Returned later)		
4. Broder, Thomas Gabriel	London	18-7-1912	1938	1949	
5. O'Shea, Michael Philip	Offaly	22-5-1915	1939	1942	8-12-1983
6. Garman, Hugh Augustine	Kent(U.K.)	24-12-1911	1939	1950	
			1960	-	8-6-1969
7. Cullen, Kevin Malachy	Wexford	25-11-1914	1942	1951	
			1967	-	
8. Hartnett, James Otteran	Waterford	8-3-1917	1942	1946	6-6-1977
9. Harney, Patrick Alphonsus	Cork		1942	1947	1988
10. Cotter, Timothy Kieran	Limerick	16-6-1916	1943	1987	15-3-1988
11. Hanly, Andrew Justin	Tipperary	1-8-1914	1943	1960	
			1962	1983	10-1-1991
12. Anderson, Sean Kevin	Limerick	21-8-1915	1943	1944	28-2-1989
13. Fitzsimons, Joseph Cyprian	Galway	5-7-1916	1943	1946	
14. Roche, Edward Gerard	Cork	25-4-1917	1945	1970	26-3-1990
15. Hannon, Donal Basil	Kerry	4-12-1919	1945	1963	
16. O'Connor, John Augustine	Limerick	24-9-1918	1946	1993	
17. Kennedy, Brendan Aidan	Limerick/ Dublin	27-1-1919	1946	1966	
			1977	1988	14-7-1990
18. Martin, James Philip	Limerick	24-5-1919	1946	1987	20-6-1992
19. Flynn, Michael Thomas	Waterford	26-6-1919	1946	1973	11-12-1974

20. O'Mahoney, Pearse Aloysius	Antrim/				
	Galway	6-4-1919	1946	1970	
			1981	-	
21. Seary, John Leslie	Cairns	10-8-1914	1947	1951	
	(Australia)		1965	1991	4-5-1992
22. Power, William Clement	Limerick	22-12-1916	1948	1966	
23. Heffernan, Fionan Columba	Kerry	1-8-1919	1948	1968	
24. Callaghan, Patrick James	Meath	6-4-1923	1948	1969	
25. Coleman, Denis	Cork	2-2-1924	1949	1960	
			1964	1991	
26. Madden, Patrick Cornelius	Cork	11-3-1924	1949	1968	
27. Crean, John Joseph	Limerick	29-11-1925	1951	1971	
28. Gough, John Declan	Waterford	11-8-1926	1951	1974	
29. Cunnane, James Gerard	Mayo	17-10-1914	1952	1975	
30. Lyons, Patrick Lawrence	Galway	19-9-1925	1952	1988	
31. O'Donovan, Timothy Alypius	Cork	28-6-1925	1952	1958	
32. King, Desmond John	Carlow/				
	Dublin	3-12-1920	1954	1957	12-4-1971
33. Bresnan, Gerard John	Cork	8-7-1925	1954	1969	
34. Moylan, John Kevin	Limerick	6-8-1929	1954	1981	
35. Sheehan, Patrick Francis	Roscommon/				
	Wexford	28-5-1932	1956	-	
36. Butler, John Vincent	Waterford		1956	-	11-6-1959
37. Flanagan, Patrick Sylvester	Limerick	31-3-1923	1956	1957	21-12-1985
38. Walsh, Timothy Augustine	Limerick	10-2-1931	1957	1977	
			1981	1989	
39. Dowling, Sean Colman	Cork	1-6-1932	1957	1967	
40. De Sande, Luis	Spain		1957	1969	
41. O'Reilly, Noel Charles	Dublin	28-12-1932	1958	-	
42. Sheehan, Jeremiah Sylvester	Cork	10-10-1932	1958	1982	
43. Brennan, Richard	Dublin/				
	Waterford	11-4-1931	1958	1973	
44. Sheehy, Kevin Hilary	Kerry	30-1-1934	1959	-	4-2-1990
45. Moore, John Philip	Antrim	14-5-1933	1959	1972	
46. Donnelly, John Michael	Dublin	9-1-1932	1960	1990	
47. Flynn, Michael Oliver	Waterford	7-1-1932	1960	-	
48. O'Leary, Aidan Kevin	Wexford	24-10-1932	1960	1970	
			1977	1988	
49. Bolger, Patrick Fintan	Limerick	8-5-1934	1960	1973	
50. Hickey, Raymond Francis	Dublin	21-4-1936	1960	-	

51. Ryan, James Albert	Limerick	2-1-1913	1961 1978	
52. O'Keeffe, Patrick Otteran	Waterford	16-3-1923	1961 1991	12-3-1992
53. Brosnan, Thomas Declan	Kerry	27-10-1936	1961 1964	
			1971 1989	
54. Sexton, Michael Fachtna	Cork	6-8-1932	1962 -	
55. O'Donnell, Senan Louis	Clare/			
	Wexford	24-2-1927	1962 -	
56. Loughran, Vincent Damian	Dublin/			
	Drogheda	18-8-1936	1962 -	30-11-1984
57. Farrell, Patrick Ignatius	Dublin	28-11-1935	1962 -	
58. Slattery, Sean Joseph	Clare/Meath	6-7-1932	1962 1969	4-4-1991
59. Mansfield, Michael Columba	Waterford	31-12-1936	1963 1964	
60. Kiely, James Oliver	Waterford	15-11-1936	1963 1970	
61. Coffey, Sean Thomas	Cork	11-3-1906	1963 1969	
62. Vazquez Bracho, Jose Maria	Spain	9-3-1933	1963 1973	
63. O'Brien, Gerard Benignus	Wexford	3-4-1938	1964 1978	
64. O'Sullivan, Michael Aidan	Tipperary/			
	Kerry	22-6-1936	1964 1993	
65. Baldwin, William Peter	Waterford	28-9-1935	1964 1968	
66. Fortune, Gerard Finbarr	Dublin	3-10-1931	1964 1966	
67. Hickey, Bartholomew Vincent	Cork	7-10-1935	1965 -	
68. Hughes, Richard Patrick	Louth	4-4-1938	1965 1985	
			1991 -	
69. Stibbles, George Gabriel	Angus			
	(Scotland)	11-4-1930	1965 1966	
70. Moore, Oliver Killian	Cork	19-11-1937	1965 1973	
71. O'Regan, Michael Leonard	Cork	1-6-1935	1965 1971	
72. Humphreys, Seamus Martin	Dublin	6-9-1938	1966 1969	
			1974 1979	
73. Mernagh, Michael Paul	Kilkenny	7-10-1937	1966 1974	
74. Kelleher, Daniel Dominic	Cork/			
	Waterford	2-2-1938	1966 1980	
75. Brennan, Patrick Ailbe	Galway/			
	Dublin	8-8-1937	1966 1970	
76. King, Martin Jude	Galway	10-9-1936	1967 1977	
77. Crean, Martin Oliver	Limerick	12-5-1941	1968 -	
78. Fitzgerald, Michael Christopher				
	Limerick	15-12-1937	1968 1978	
79. Grace, John Bernard	Cork/			
	Waterford	25-1-1938	1968 1982	

80.	Downey, James Augustine	Cork	8-1-1939	1968	1985
81.	Mason, Thomas Denis	Waterford	11-1-1932	1969	-
82.	O'Farrell, Patrick Joseph	Offaly	27-1-1916	1969	1981
83.	Sinnott, Philip Benedict	Wexford	16-9-1943	1969	1985
84.	Hegarty, Timothy Dominic	Waterford/ Cork	1-6-1943	1969	-
85.	O'Connell, John Colman	Cork	4-6-1943	1969	-	24-5-1983
86.	Bowlby, Christopher Paul	Durham (England)	1941	1969	-	12-12-1969
87.	Flatley, John Gerard	Dublin	10-2-1935	1969 1990	1984 -
88.	Nolan, Thomas Martin	Sligo/Dublin	9-3-1933	1969	1972
89.	Hooper, James Augustine	London/ Cork	29-12-1912	1970	1977
90.	Fitzpatrick, Richard Carthage	Waterford	19-9-1936	1970	-
91.	McCarthy, Patrick Vincent	Waterford	18-10-1942	1970	1976
92.	Cooney, Patrick Matthew	Tipperary	6-4-1943	1970	1980
93.	O'Brien, Paul Maurice	Dublin	29-4-1942	1970	1993
94.	Loughran, Sean Malachy	Dublin/ Drogheda	2/8/1933	1971	1973
95.	O'Halloran, Michael Giles	Cork	27/9/1945	1971 1978	1974 1982
96.	Aherne, Francis Vincent	Cork	2/3/1947	1971	-
97.	McManus, Thomas Kevin	Dublin	3/11/1940	1971	1977
98.	Haughey, Francis Peter	Dublin	1/10/1924	1973 1979	1977 1980
99.	Spring, Francis Finbarr	Kerry	21/8/1938	1974	1975
100.	Fives, Colin Richard	Waterford	8/12/1947	1974	-
101.	Lyng, John Kieran	Kilkenny	23-12-1946	1974	-
102.	Daly, Patrick Dominic	Limerick	6-12-1921	1975	-	11-5-1980
103.	Twohig, Padraig	Cork	12-3-1951	1977	1983
104.	O'Brien, Nicholas Bernard	Kilkenny	1-4-1931	1977	-
105.	Boyle, John Michael	Dublin	23-9-1945	1977	1988
106.	O'Connor, John Joseph	Kerry	25-12-1951	1977	1991
107.	McNamara, Henry	Cork	13-11-1951	1978	1981
108.	Brennan, Declan	Dublin	2-2-1956	1979	-
109.	Counihan, Thomas Cyril	Kerry	7-7-1930	1979	1981
110.	Sexton, Thomas Kieran	Cork	12-5-1939	1979	1989
111.	Foley, Desmond Thomas	Kilkenny	9-5-1945	1979	1987
112.	Fitzgerald, David Martin	Tipperary	22-4-1941	1980	-

113. Walsh, Michael	Limerick	17-12-1955	1980	1982
			1986	1991
114. Whelton, Denis Fintan	Cork	29-11-1926	1980	1985
115. Corcoran, Michael Gervase	Wexford	8-7-1944	1981	1981
116. Kelly, Declan	Dublin	4-6-1952	1982	1984
117. Egan, Anthony	Offaly	24-2-1953	1982	-
118. Sexton, Francis Nicholas	Cork	8-3-1936	1982	-
119. McDonnell, Brendan Finbarr	Cork	25-9-1943	1983	-
120. Campbell, Michael Gregory	Antrim	2-10-1941	1985	1989
121. Furlong, Shem	Wexford	4-5-1960	1985	1987
122. Crowley, Tadhg	Dublin/			
	Kildare	8-7-1959	1985	-
123. Roche, Michael Alypius	Tipperary	1-2-1933	1986	1988

EXPATRIATE AUGUSTINIANS IN NIGERIA AT 5-YEAR INTERVALS.

1940	- 5		1970	- 58
1945	- 10		1975	- 52
1950	- 17		1980	- 53
1955	- 23		1985	- 45
1960	- 35		1990	- 32 (+1 in Kenya)
1965	- 54			

In each case the figure as on 31 December is given. The highest number attained was in 1971 when there were 60 on the Mission.

THE IRISH AUGUSTINIANS IN ECUADOR, 1977-1992

Paul G. O'Connor, O.S.A.

THE IRISH AUGUSTINIANS IN ECUADOR 1977-1992
Paul G. O'Connor, O.S.A.

When the Irish Provincial Chapter accepted the invitation of the Ecuadorian Province to take over the mission in Chone in 1977 Fr Declan Deasy had already been working there for two years. His letter in the *Mission News* with a map of South America and a little point marked Quito made it all seem so far away, so distant from the well known names from Australia and Nigeria. For many that distance may have remained; for most, it will have gained a little corner in the mission memory of the Province; for a few, Chone means every-day life.

Of the four appointed that year, only three arrived, as Fr Declan Gough could not persuade his doctor to let him tackle a new mission-field. Declan Deasy went back to Ecuador immediately and Frs Tom Tuomey and Paul O'Connor followed on in autumn 1977.

QUITO

The Augustinian Province of San Miguel de Quito had been founded in 1573. Looking up at the dark outline of the statue of Saint Augustine which crowns the dome of our church there, one could be forgiven for wondering why Ecuador should need missionaries more than four hundred years later. The beautiful cloister with its palm trees, flowering shrubs and square stone fountain, speaks of a teeming Augustinian presence in the past centuries; the three friars who greeted us, wrapped in heavy black cloaks against the cold and old age, reflected an even colder reality. In the huge dining room they gave us a warm welcome. Once, before the War of Independence, there had been more than three hundred Augustinians in the province, now there were twenty four.

Map of South America, showing Ecuador.

In the monuments of the old colonial city important moments in the history of the country's christianity are prolonged: the church of Santo Domingo, with its treasured Virgen del Rosario given them by Charles V of Spain, brings to mind the first Dominican Chaplain, Fray Vicente de Valverde, who arrived on the coast of Esmeraldas with the Pizarro expedition which, with a force of only a hundred and sixty seven men, conquered the Inca king Atahualpa in 1533. It was the beginning of a colonialism and christianizing that was as vigorous as it was disquieting; a time of incredible sacrifice for the sake of the faith and of unbelievable misunderstanding of what that faith involves.

Only a block away is the most ornate church in Ecuador, La Iglesia de la Compañia, the Jesuit church begun in 1605. One looks uncomfortably at the gilded interior: its walls, roof and altar shine in coverings of pure gold leaf. It is said that it took seven tons of gold to gild those interiors. In front of the tomb of the Quitaña saint, Mariana de Jesús, who died in 1645, dark little hands are raised in a devotion and in an interior faith that owes nothing to its garish surroundings, while outside the doorway a crumpled little Indian woman enveloped in a thick poncho tries to interest us in votive candles. How is one to know the depths of folk memory that hide in the guarded looks of those seemingly expressionless dark eyes? The Incas had overrun Ecuador for only a hundred years; the Spaniards for another four hundred; but what is that when compared with the thousands of years that have formed the Indian culture?

It is this Indian population of the high Andean plateau which has suffered most by being despoiled of their lands and culture. Several areas have preserved their dress, customs and Quichua language, but it is only recently, urged on by a new spirit of indigenous American identity, that they have made others aware of how deeply held are their traditions and devotion to the land. In their culture, the Goddess Earth, who gives them everything that they have, is to be revered. Without their lands they are exiles in their own country.

It would be a very undiplomatic government (or church) that would remember the fifth centenary of 1492 as an unqualified moment of celebration.

A further monument that remembers a period that must have been of importance in church history is that of Mariscal Sucre in the Plaza Santo Domingo; this Mariscal of Simon Bolivar's army is pointing to the Pichincha mountain where he had won his decisive battle against the fleeing Spaniards on 24 May, 1822. One wonders how true it is that multitudes of serf-monks escaped from their monasteries to follow the Liberator in these battles for Independence. Did the new found liberty of Gran Colombia leave the Church with it first shortage of vocations?

A third monument, this time not among the huddle of churches, but rather symbolically on the edges of the new Quito, records a much later event. It is the statue of Eloy Alfaro (1842-1912), the hero of the Liberal Revolution of the turn of the century, an upheaval which had dire consequences for the Church, especially in the area of Manabí where it had come to head-on collision with the bishop of Portoviejo, Bishop Schumacher, an arch Conservative whose thinking was in line with the most rigid European thinking of the period. The Liberal victor carried no flag for organized religion and those who came after him showed scant respect for church lands and property.

DIFFERENT WORLDS

It is hardly surprising that all but one of the main cities of Ecuador are situated high up along the Andean Ridge and that these should have become the focus of secular and religious development during the centuries. From Ibarra in the north to Cuenca in the south stoutly built cathedrals have resisted earthquakes or have been rebuilt after them. From these towns have come the majority of Ecuadorian vocations to priesthood and religious life. The lowlands of the coast to the west and the Amazonian selva to the east are still in varying degrees mission territory. Nor is it surprising that, when we need a rest from the humidity of Chone, we should head for the thin air of Quito, the second highest capital city of South America (9,300 feet). The city is built in a valley from which the mountains rise up in a steep wall that dwarfs the high-rise American type buildings of the

Painting of Quito, the capital city, by Ecuador's most famous artist, Guayasamin.

190

newer section.   Away to the south across rich arable land the snow-capped volcanic cone of Cotopaxi rises up to nearly twenty thousand feet.   The climate is beautifully temperate all the year round; some like to say that Quito passes through the four seasons each day, from the fresh blue light of the morning air to the summer warmth of mid-day and afternoon and on to the bone-chilling cold of night-time.   For us it is a pleasant change to see the cattle graze on short grasses or watch the clouds move in darkening patterns on the colourful patchwork quilt of fields that stretch up the mountainside.   All so civilized, really.

If it were not for the mid-day bus ride from the Catholic University where we had been doing an intensive course in Spanish, I would have said that nothing in Quito could quite prepare us for Chone.   The pushing clammy closeness to humanity and the suffocating heat of those airless buses introduced us to a crowded lack of privacy that makes one's psyche scream for individual space, but which does not seem to bother Ecuadorians a whit.   Later I found this crowded unprotectedness accentuated in the out-stations, by one's being the focus of every curious eye even in delicate ablutionary moments.

CHONE

The Ecuador Provincial, Fr Aurelio Zarate, his secretary, Fr Guillermo Castro, Tom Tuomey and I travelled down to Chone a few days before Christmas, a journey of nearly three hundred kilometres that takes one from the temperate altitudes of Quito to the tropical heat of Chone, not five metres above sea-level.   We could have wished the road down the Cordillera a little wider or, at least, that the buckled crash barriers on the turns be more reinforced to protect us from the chasms.   The aerial view of tree-tops and electricity pylons below us accentuated the depth of the valleys and did little to comfort us.   Miles of twists and turns in the road offered short straight sections of risky odds to tanker and bus drivers who played Andean roulette, overtaking one

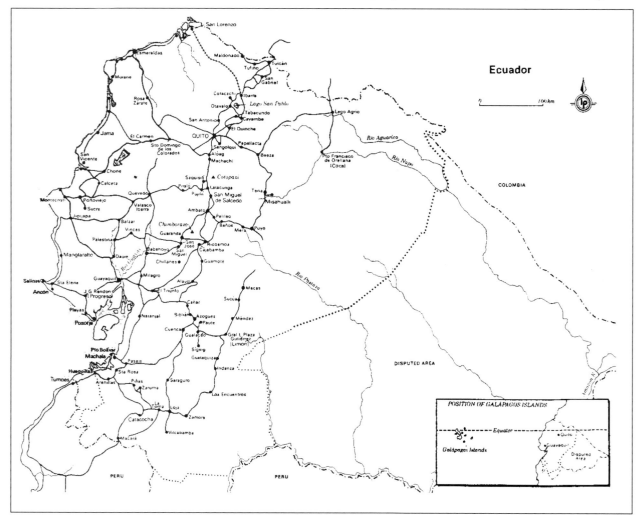

another with blaring horns and fatalistic unconcern.

The vegetation changed gradually as we left the short grasses and poplar trees of the sierra for the wild giant plant abundance of the tropical coast, where bony shrunken-uddered cows struggled in wildernesses of grass that reached high over their heads. The heat of the Nissan Patrol car became oppressive. Jumpers and shirts were discarded and moist Tshirts clung to our bodies, cooled a little by the breeze of the car's motion.

We were not impressed by the two towns we passed through. Santo Domingo de los Colorados, home of the Colorado tribe renowned for its skill in natural medicine, seemed to be a haphazardly built town of unplastered block houses, uncared-for food and fruit stalls, but with an unending list of signs advertising the services of lawyers, obstetricians and odontologists. Thirty kilometres further on we were in El Carmen, a smaller town recently taken as a mission by the Comboniani, the Verona Fathers. These priests would be our nearest neighbours on the north-east. Chone is still a hundred and twenty kilometres away, but some of our new territory is not more than twelve kilometres from the El Carmen mission.

Since Santo Domingo the road had levelled and narrowed. It seemed to fight its way through palm trees, banana plantations and tall grasses that want to invade it. Another seventy kilometres winding uncertainly through huge clay hills, dotted with palm trees and cane houses built on stilts, brought us to Flavio Alfaro, a village of five thousand people which had neither electricity, running water, parish house nor church. It was the first of our new parishes to be met on the way to Chone and was being attended to by Fr Oswaldo Alban, O.S.A., who lived in a dilapidated cane hut and was struggling to build the church.

The Ecuadorian Fathers pointed out the little chapels along the way and we were soon confused by strange new names, Zapallo, Sesme, Pavón, Ricaurte, Garrapata and El Bejuco. They were all communities that we would soon try to serve and we did not, as yet, realize that they were the lucky ones who had all year round asphalt road. No one mentioned Convento, Eloy Alfaro or Boyacá, three large parishes that could be attended only for a few months of the year when the bulldozers had ploughed open the dirt tracks which had disappeared during the winter rains.

On the outskirts of Chone the tarmac petered out, as if the county council did not wish to share its resources with the town. Dust whirled up behind the jeep and seeped in through the back door. Half way down the main Calle Bolivar we could see the tower of the church rising above the trees of a little park, two prongs of armed concrete rising to a clock-tower and at one side a façade of plaster relieved by geometric designs and a statue of St Cayetano. At the left of the church was the monastery - a long building with a colonade at ground level and a row of dormitory windows shuttered against the heat. At the beautifully carved door on which the old stylised coat of arms of the Order is held up by bouncy wooden angels, Declan Deasy met us.

* * * * * * * * * * * * * * * * * * *

Fifteen years later, Chone is much changed and it is difficult to remember just what it was like in 1977 when, as Christmas approached, we began to settle in to our new domain. Certainly there was not a square foot of tarmac in the town; no one could ever forget that, because the winter rains turned the streets into quagmires and the brethren were equipped with rubber boots for trips to the post office, the hospital or other pastoral concerns. The raised sidewalks on the main street were boarded and broken; even the bank was a wood and cane structure that had one teller's window with five rusting vertical bars. Saloons did not have bat-wing doors but there were horses hitched to the hard guayacan wood posts that held up the portals of the two storey cane houses.

It was a town that was changing rapidly even then. The cane houses which often had remnants of beauty in their intricately worked wooden windows and doors, were being torn down to make room for permanent multi-storied premises that owe much of their design to models from the United States. The new banks have marble floors and a row of computers. Looking back now it was a time of relative prosperity; there was a good price for cocoa and coffee; the cattle industry was thriving. The country was about to revert to democratic government and had already enjoyed some years of petroleum prosperity. The Ecuador sucre was one of the more stable currencies of South America and valued at twenty-five to the American dollar. (Today - 1992 - the sucre fluctuates around 1350 to the dollar and no longer boasts of any degree of stability).

AUGUSTINIAN PRESENCE IN CHONE

It is practically impossible to imagine what Chone must have been when, on 17 October 1937, the Ecuadorian Augustinians, Frs José Tejada and Cirilo Pozo, took over the immense parish. There was no road to Quito nor were there permanent roads within the mission itself. The journey from Flavio Alfaro to Chone, which today takes forty-five minutes by car, was then a two-day journey by horse. The two priests came by boat from the large sea port of Guayaquil to Bahia de Caráquez, a town fifty kilometres distant on the mouth of the Chone river.

Nor was the politico-religious situation very clear either. The Augustinians had been invited to Chone by the Jesuit Vicar General of Portoviejo, Mons. Felix Heredia, since the bishop who had been appointed in 1908 was never recognized by the Liberal Government and would not be allowed into the diocese. It had to await the signing of the *Modus Vivendi* between Church and State in 1937 for Portoviejo to have its fourth bishop, Mons. Nicanor Gavilanes, who took possession of the diocese in June of 1938. On 2 February 1947, Mons. Gavilanes handed over 'definitive, *pleno iure et in perpetuum*' the 1500 square miles of impenetrable hill country to the Augustinians. They were to provide at least three priests to attend the area, some parts of which did not even have formal owners and could be bought from the government at nominal rates. Huge claims were staked out in those years by enterpreneuring families and no amount of land reform has been able to wrest these disproportionate holdings from their grasp.

In the last days of 1977, when the Ecuadorian Augustinian Province, in informal agreement, handed over the administration of the mission to the Irish Province, the then bishop of Portoviejo, Mons. Luis Carvajal, seemed happy to endorse the new beginnings in the hope that further priests would arrive later, even though the initial group barely fulfilled the conditions of the 1947 agreement. Part of our informal agreement was that the territory should revert to the Ecuadorian Province should the Irish decide to retire from it.

In the last four years however, with the arrival of the present bishop, Mons. José Mario Ruiz Navas, the question of parts of the diocese being '*iure et in perpetuum*' in the hands of religious groups has arisen. One can have a certain sympathy for a newly appointed bishop who finds huge blocks of his diocese only very indirectly under his authority, especially for a bishop whose motto is "Que sean uno" (That they may be one). The first steps in building a new relationship with the diocese have been taken recently when the Ecuadorian Augustinian Chapter decided that, since the Irish Province is the one involved in the pastoral work of Chone, it should also be the one involved in moves to further integration at diocesan level. Here it should be noted that the new bishop has made every positive move possible to build the

Diocesis de Portoviejo para Manabi

diocese into one "community of communities". For three years now there have been week-long meetings for planning and evaluation for the diocese that have allowed us to get to know all the priests and a goodly number of sisters and pastoral agents. Fr Chris Fitzgerald, as a member of the animation team and representative for religious on the bishop's Council, had the daunting task of guiding this year's meeting (1992). We are invited to the diocesan retreat and encouraged to assist at renewal courses that are held for the diocese.

We hope that this new direct relationship with the diocese will result in a more realistic involvement on the part of the Irish Province. It is now seven years since a fresh new face has appeared on the Augustinian mission team here to revive our drooping spirits.

WALKING THE LAND

Ecuador is a country which falls into three broad geographical regions: the Coastal Plain; the Andean Highlands which have an average height of ten thousand feet and a large number of ice-capped volcanic peaks, the most famous of which are Cotopaxi and Chimborazo; and finally on the east, the Selva of the upper Amazonian tributaries. This last is the region where petroleum has been found and is also the domain of tribes which resist the intrusion of white men with their religion and their concept of progress.

Chone is situated mid way down the coastal plain, about fifty kilometres from the sea, in the Province of Manabí, which is coextensive with the diocese of Portoviejo. The diocese has a territory of approximately 20,000 sq. kms and a population that approaches 1,400,000 who are attended by some ninety priests and probably over two hundred sisters. The Chone/Flavio area covers some 3,500 sq. kms; has a population of 240,000 people who are attended at present by six priests and eight full-time missionary sisters. A further ten sisters work in school, hospital and social apostolates. The people with whom we work are not indigenous Indians, but rather the mestizos - people of mixed blood - settlers and homesteaders who do not have the community traditions and folk memory found in the Andean Highlands.

At Times-one wonders why the area is called the coastal plain, because the major part of our mission is a series of hills that can rise to three hundred metres and river valleys that have cut their way through soft stoneless soils, urged on by torrential wet season rains that swell to dangerous flood levels whenever the now famous Niño Current warms the Pacific Ocean coasts of Ecuador and Peru. The soil formation is intriguingly important and would seem to have been caused by wind-blown loess, volcanic dusts that have covered parts of South America to depths of even two thousand feet. Because of the nature of this soft earth there are very few quarries and most of the hills that make the terrain so difficult to travel have not a stone in them. Even the best made roads, therefore, are merely thin strips of tarmac perched along hillsides that have no permanent base and which can move and shift in winter rains, causing landslides and five metre deep cuts in the permanent roads.

The same soil structure plays havoc with all clay dry-season roads. The first four days of heavy rain in the beginnings of January turn all the country roads into clinging mud and wash away the summer "bridges". From then on until July there is no means of communication with the majority of outstations. This is one of the most important considerations in the deployment of personnel and it is even conceivable that extra missionaries could work here on a semester basis from August to December once they are familiar with the language and have got to know the territory.   Not that one cannot be busy all the year round; there are more than sufficient people living in the towns of Chone, Flavio Alfaro and the accessible parts of San Antonio, Santa Rita and Ricaurte, to keep us occupied.

Volcanic soil is rich and fertile and the lands around Chone are no exception; it is one of the more fertile regions of Manabí, with crops of cocoa, coffee, maize, rice and banana; recently, citrus fruits are being developed for the internal market.   The cattle trade is also well developed, but one doubts if it should be continued in its present form, because large tracts of land must be cleared of trees to fodder cattle and already much of the southern part of the mission is becoming dry and dusty.   Cattle farming gives quick cash results and is not labour extensive, so it is easy to understand how people involved in it turn a blind eye to the ecological damage they are causing. One wonders if cattle could not be stall-fed from maize crops as is done in the basin of the Po at Padua in Italy.

It is not surprising that Chone is a market town with large 'pistas', open cemented areas where grains are dried and improved before being resold for export from Guayaquil, the largest port town of Ecuador.   There is no refinement of produce; no factories that might give employment to young people - just an endless buying and selling of every possible kind, from sweet and cigarette sellers at every corner, to children who sell soft drinks and home-made meat loaves, from country peasants with three chickens to sell, to commercial people who sit next to their weighing scales accepting cocoa, coffee, maize and rice by the pound, the hundredweight or the truck load. Everyone is willing to be a potential middleman, unproductive and inflationary.

In the years that we have been in Chone a new product has risen high on the export charts - prawn farming.   Though it is only in the parish of San Antonio that Chone has prawn beds, many of the rich farmers of our area have invested their money in this new and prosperous industry that has a large export to the United States and is projecting itself towards Europe.   In San Antonio some developers were not too scrupulous as to the ownership of the land which they converted into prawn beds; recently, however, the people who live along the river have become more careful about the title to their own pieces of land.   The companies that have grown have shown unusual acumen in trade and have risen to quality levels that are so necessary in this highly competitive market.   There is, however, a dark cloud.   The building of artificial beds along the river-mouths and coastland has been destroying the natural growth of 'manglares' (mangrove trees, which are the habitat of prawn larvae).   People who are concerned for the ecology, and for the future possibilities for simple fishing folk, see this growth of the prawn industry as just another get richer quicker scheme for the already rich and as short-sighted economic insanity.   There is no doubt, however, that there is quite a deal of employment generated by the industry and we, Irish, should be the first to understand how a struggling country can grasp at any hope that will boost exports.

RICH AND POOR

The unequal distribution of wealth, whether it be based on land ownership, prawn farming, commercial middlemanship, transport facilities or medical clinics, seems to be accepted with a kind of fatalism.   Each family unit is so involved in the mere process of survival, or in the avid scramble to make money and clamber up the ladder, that there is very little social conciousness or civic pride; nor is there much genuine organization to demand justice or respect for the individual.

It is difficult to gain precise statistics on the distribution of land wealth; the Basque Fathers in the next county to us state that on their mission eight per cent of the population owns eighty per cent of the land; in Chone the proportion is not so drastic.   In Flavio Alfaro 3,100 families have farms of above 100 hectares and some ten per cent of those have between 500 and 1,200 hectares - which really does not leave too much to be shared between the rest of the forty thousand parishioners. Unfortunately the rich people are not conscious of any social obligation to help in building schools or medical centres and will help in summer road building only in so much as it is to their own personal benefit.

The poor suffer deprivation on every level with a stoic acceptance. Most of them will never receive the minimum wage (which today is a little over a pound sterling per day). Medical services are so inadequate that they have to buy medicines at prohibitive prices and they often turn to 'curanderos', empirical quacks, simply because of the prices doctors charge. Civil registers cannot find their births registered, so they become non-persons without access to justice or even schooling for their children. And school teachers, who seem to be protected by laws and by a very agressive union, can blatantly play with the future of children in poor out-of-the-way schools. Some have been known to arrive for class only from Tuesday to Thursday, while others pay a substitute a fraction of a salary and then continue with a job as taxi-driver or housewife without let or hindrance.

Party politics is so plainly divisive that people have become apathetic and disillusioned. There are seventeen parties, each of which demands open affiliation on the basis of which, if victorious, they will share out the spoils of war down to the tiniest job in a local registry office or typist's desk in the municipal building. It is hardly to be wondered that the people consider their vote as one would the few bob he puts on the Grand National - if he backs the winning party there may be something in it for him.

It would be too cynical to say that nobody in power is concerned about these situations: it is simply that a good man's efforts will get caught up in interminable bureaucratic tangles, hidden interests, and an incredibly porous legal system. There will be no funds available: since the country has lived on the providence of God through successive booms - the war-time rubber boom, the banana boom and now the petrol boom - it has never really developed a proper taxation system nor got adequate returns from those who can live in luxury. Consequently it has never been able to offer systems of equal opportunity in health or education. If one adds to this the fact that "friendly" countries have allowed more than a century of incessant borrowing, with repayments calculated on the present-day value of the dollar, a gloomy picture of crisis and confusion reveals itself. (Shortly after our coming here the country paid off the final instalment of its debt to Britain incurred during the war of independence in the eighteen twenties!)

POPULAR RELIGION

In the midst of this confusion of agricultural riches, privileges, down-trodden poor, torrential rains, chickens and muddied sows, maniac drivers and Sunday markets, one begins to realize after a time that there is a deep innate, confused and ill-informed sense of religion here that antedates the arrival of the Spanish caravels on the shores of Esmeraldas in the sixteenth century. Diggings around the Basque mission of Bahía de Caráquez, home of the Cara civilization of 3000 B.C., continue to turn out religious figurines, fish-bone priestly breast-plates and reliques that hint at a religious past. The importance given to the dead, the fixation with hours and dates of death, the attention to tombs and, above all, the celebration of All Souls' Day, are all so exceptional that one cannot believe they are the product of a mere four hundred years of Christianity.

On the one hand there is an obsession with an immortality that has little to do with the Christian other life, but which concentrates, rather, on the procreation of as many children as possible or the building of some memorial that will prolong one's presence here long after the ornate coffin has been fitted away in its massed concrete tomb. On the other hand, there is a vivid realization, not untouched by fatalism, that we are in the hands of God: everything comes from Him; the rains, the floods, the good harvests and the death of a new-born child. 'Dios sabe lo que hace' (God understands what he is doing). People are not beyond twisting his arm a bit, however. They plea bargain. 'If You don't let the fowl pest kill my chickens, I'll give one to the Lord of Good Hope'. Or more generously they come to offer the price of an animal to the priest. 'The

196

cow was sick and I promised that if it recovered I'd give it to the church'.

It may be because of the isolated homestead nature of living in the campo or even because the Church has had more than a century of individualistic spirituality, but fundamental communitarian aspect of sacramental life has very little meaning for our people. Traditionally Baptism and Confirmation are sought after at all cost, more in the sense of fully paid-up membership than with a sense of commitment to a community. This is not to deny that there is a longing for community; quite the reverse. All over our mission there are little villages growing up, calling themselves 'comunas' and choosing very communitary names like "The Alliance", "La Unión" - yet hidden behind this growth one often finds that there is someone who wants to be 'casique', strong man upon whom all decisions depend and to whom others defer. Being Church President or even catechist is often seen as part of the pecking order. The result, of course, is a static non-participation and disunity.

It is the hope of the New Image of the Parish (NIP) that small dynamic communities with real Christian commitment will eventually grow and replace this power-seeking imitation.

Confession and Communion celebrated in these villages are moments of festive celebration, but they are exclusively for children and very often of a one-off nature. Since the celebration of Marriage is very infrequent there is a built-in time limit to children's continued participation. Naturally the Eucharist has lost its communitary aspect and, in line with devotion to the dead, Masses are sought mainly and individualistically for dead relations.

When called out to attend a person who is seriously ill one should be ready for requests for marriage, because country people believe that they may not be present at a partner's death bed if they have not been married. I have celebrated a marriage that lasted only fifteen minutes; the bride was in a coma, but her Legion of Mary friends assured me that she had always wanted to be married. Another story, which may be apocryphal, tells how Davy Crean married off a mother to her son in the confusion of the moment.

In every house in the countryside, far from the churches of the town, there will be a family altar, where, amid decorations of coloured paper, candles are lit before the 'santitos', pictures or statues of saints who are considered particularly powerful in the face of distinct dangers - St Roc against animal diseases and St Paul because of his proven powers against deadly snakes. Many families have a tradition of holding a Velorio (or vigil) for their preferred saint. This is a celebration that includes prayers said by a 'rezador', a prayer man who knows interminable litanies and complicated prayers. There will be a meal for the guests and, if the owner of the saint is sufficiently broad-minded, a dance which begins at twelve (with the permission of the saint) and goes on until morning. People are not expected to last till dawn without some alcoholic refreshments.

Had we had some realization of what celebration and formal activities mean to our people we might have had a smoother entry to our pastoral work and, even today, were we more creative and dramatic, we might come closer to them. The Inca culture, (and presumably the Ecuadorian Shyris which preceded it), had not developed a written language. It is said of Atahualpa that when he heard of the 'word of the Bible' he took the book and held it to his ear and announced that he did not hear it speak. Even today our people are not really a people of the written word, but not a movement of the eye nor a change of expression on the face will escape their notice. Abstract concepts of celebration do not move them; a celebration must be seen, acted out or danced and enjoyed; above all, something must be eaten. Endless verses in simple rhythms and of doubtful theological content can fill a night of the Christmas Child Novena. A tiny sliver of celebration cake and a minuscule glass of rompope will be accepted with a gravity that we would reserve for the sacred. There are fiestas for Saints' Days, Baptisms, First Communions, Weddings. They go on all night and an invitation is treated with seriousness. The taking down of the Crib in the church or in a community demands 'Priostes', persons selected for that year who are responsible for providing home-made sweets and biscuits to be taken with poor-grade wine shared out in thimblefuls. Even death is celebrated solemnly with the community gathering at the home of the deceased for nine nights, praying, chatting or sitting for long moments of contemplative silence; later in the night, with meticulous attention paid to social importance, the guests will be invited in turn to the family table for a meal of chicken and rice.

OUR IGNORANCE

Coming new to the mission all this slipped by us or was even treated with suspicion. That first Christmas, as the endless repetitive rhythms of the local carols, chigualos, came wafting faintly through the dark from some happy family gathered round its crib, I lay on my bed listening to this strange threatening sound with as much trepidation as if it were the beat of unfriendly pagan tribal war-drums. Today it is the heart-warming sound of simple religious enjoyment.

We could see only the dire ignorance of doctrine, the lack of reverence in church ceremonies and the grim determination to have private and exclusive celebrations of sacraments. When we realized that schools never taught children their catechism, we were amazed and could only remember the day when we, little theologians, with a red arm-band on our new grey suits, had confounded Bishops and Bishops' secretaries with our definitions of sacrifice, lists of marriage impediments and the distinction between fasting and abstaining.

We did not know that, in their very recent history, between 1895 and 1937, our people had gone through a period of civil and religious trauma, when the Church and, in particular the bishop of Manabí, had sided with the Conservatives in the Liberal Revolution; had sided with them and lost. Nor did we know that the bitternesses and antipathies generated against the Church had been particularly strong in Manabí, the home province of the Liberal hero, Eloy Alfaro. This antipathy shares much of the ambivalence we associate with the alienation of Fenian supporters in Ireland.

Portoviejo had been made a diocese by Pope Pius IX in 1870, but the first bishop never really lived there and he resigned in 1881. The second bishop, Peter Schumacher, a vigorous man who brooked no opposition to his running of the local church, is the one to whom it fell to establish the diocese of Portoviejo and Esmeraldas. He even managed to bring sixty priests to Manabí and a number of sisters from Europe, among whom was the sister who later founded the Franciscan Congregation of sisters who now work with us in Chone, having come back exactly a hundred years after the foundress's first coming. Bishop Schumacher became bishop in 1885.

Ten years later the civil strife broke out between the Conservatives and Liberals. Though the bishops of the Sierra were far more circumspect, Bishop Schumacher was vehemently and openly opposed to the Liberals; so much so that the Conservative forces are still spoken of as "The Bishop's Army". The bishop had to abandon the diocese and take refuge in Samaniego, Colombia. Manabí, under the leadership of Eloy Alfaro (who was born not fifteen miles from Portoviejo in the town of Montecristi), became a leading force in the Liberal victory.

In the beginnings of this century the new Ecuadorian state declared itself a lay state: its declared separation of church and state was little more than an open persecution of the church. It ignored the concordat with Rome and invoked an ancient law of the Spanish Patronato in order to have a determining voice in the appointment of bishops - thus the new bishop of Portoviejo, Juan María Riera, appointed in 1908, was never recognized by the Government and was not allowed to take up residence in Manabí. Religious communities were expelled and no foreign religious could enter the country; religious schools were subjected to the state and the teaching of religion in state schools was totally forbidden.

Manibí had to wait until 1937 and the signing of a *Modus Vivendi* between Church and state for the appointment of its fourth bishop, Mons. Carlos Nicanor Gavilanes, who took possession of the diocese on 5 June 1938 and served until 1965.

We have no way of knowing how many of today's attitudes to the Church in Manabí stem from those war-torn years, but there are probably traces of that antipathy still extant in the reluctance of men to attend church and the ambivalence about church marriage. The prohibition on teaching religion in state schools continues unquestioned today as a hallmark of liberty.

The *Modus Vivendi* accepts that children may not be baptised until they have been inscribed in the civil register. One is tempted to believe that civil authorities are taking advantage of the deep-seated desire of the people for baptism as a lever to have them comply with the law of civil registration, as no amount of pleading on the part of the Church has managed to abrogate the law. Not even Pope John Paul's visit and request for a change have been heard.

Occasionally one meets Liberals today who have problems as to how they should address a priest. "Señor Cura" has become pejorative and they are not keen on a "Father" relationship, so they have opted for the title "Doctor". . . so why bother spending years researching a thesis?!

Another relic of those Times-may be the manner in which certain of the more well to do (and those who can be manipulated by them) feel they can impose upon the clergy, violently rejectng them or impeding their transfer when they so prefer. Shortly before our arrival in Chone, a priest from Pichincha, about 90 kilometres from us, had had a year's sabbatical in the U.S. and had returned with some new ideas about getting rid of the statues in the parish church. He was bundled unceremoniously, vestments and all, into a car and dumped outside the bishop's house in Portoviejo - they did not accept him back and the bishop did not insist. His replacement, Fr Luis Leon, told me that he himself had had to discharge his revolver over the heads of an unruly mob of parishioners the first day he arrived - in order to establish a new relationship with his people.

BLIND BEGINNINGS

With the adrenalin of mission fervour (or fever) running freely and in blissful unawareness of their inheritance, the Irish group took over the administration of Canton Chone on 28 December 1977. Until that time it had been run by Fr Federico Ibañez, Fr Declan Deasy and a Fr Oswaldo Alban who had a cane residence in Flavio Alfaro. A brother, Hermano Miguel, was to stay with us to see us through the initial period, but Father Ibañez, who had become a legend in Chone and whose departure would not have been very acceptable to the populace, slipped his mooring quietly and left during the somnolent quiet of siesta time without creating a ripple of protest. He had spent twelve years in Chone and his burly gruff kindness had won him friends in the most remote corners of the mission. They were his loved people and it did not matter at what hour they came for baptism, he attended them with water that was slightly green and not quite a symbol of purification. If four different families wished a Mass for their dead in the morning, he said the four Masses. Each afternoon at two thirty, when we were collapsing in the 90 degree heat, he could be seen bouncing along the corridor on his way to do the radio programme, a canvas bag on his shoulder and his battered straw hat protecting him from the searing sun. His old Willis jeep, "The King of the Mountain", part of his image, he preferred to the new Nissan Patrol which he had damaged slightly in a head-on confrontation with an obstinate cow. Shortly before our arrival he had finished the building of the new Chone church, more with a spirit of high-powered enthusiasm than with any concessions to the reforms of Vatican II, and, as yet, his parting gift to Chone, an enormously complicated clock worked by motor and emergency weights and pendulum, had not been installed. It never did work properly; the rains got into the motor, and the people, whenever they wished to demonstrate their non acceptance of the new gringos, complained that we could not even keep a clock going.

Looking back now on the first year of the mission, it was all rather dreadful. We had really no idea where we were going. School teachers from a planned curricular life, we were unprepared for pastoral work with adults. If there were planning, it was about some things that Declan Deasy had decided should be changed; after all, he had had two years of Ecuador already.

So the changes came; they were sudden, confrontational and they achieved their objective. We may not have examined the new medicine with sufficient care however, as the side effects were rather upsetting.

There would no longer be a succession of Masses each morning in the Chone church, but rather a concelebrated Mass each evening. Baptisms would have a fixed time on Saturday afternoons and would be preceded by an explanatory talk. Premarriage talks would be held each month. No deviation from this pattern would be countenanced as the slightest weakness would be like a crack in a Dutch dam. Those who had booked Masses as far forward as the following October could reclaim their deposit.

People were vociferous in their dislike of these changes and we undoubtedly allowed ourselves to fall into a siege mentality that was neurotic. Each night we gathered together with enormous sympathy for ourselves to recount the day's happenings. On the first Saturday that I refused to baptize again after evening Mass, a group of about twenty people crowded into the sacristy shouting their vehement disapproval. The Ecuadorian brother, Hermano Miguel, blanched as he heard them threaten to drive my likes out of the town 'a balazos'. One man insisted that he was Military Governor of Manabí and ordered me to have my papers ready to be checked on Monday morning. Not knowing what a governor was, I was equally abrupt with him - calling his bluff, if you like. He did not come back. Only later did I find out that 'a balazos' meant 'with bullets flying'. Today, if the same threats were made, I would take them more seriously.

Meanwhile the town-folk were not inactive; one enterprising gentleman collected signatures to have us removed. The Marianita Sisters, who could not quite fathom us either, defended us with a blind fidelity. Someone went to the bishop with the sad tale of Chone's undeserved fate at the hands of these newcomers. And finally word reached the Cardinal in Quito, Mons. Pablo Muñoz, a friend of many Augustinians who had had him as Rector in the Gregorian. Then we had a rather irate Father General, Fr T.V. Tack, enquire what we were doing to upset the people of the mission. It is probably a measure of our extraordinary foolhardiness that we prepared an apologia for the Primate and the benjamin was sent off to seek audience. The Cardinal could not have been more kind and gentle: he even recounted how his people had threatened to burn down the church when he raised the age of Confirmation to ten. He promised to read our report the following day on the plane to Rome, as he was due to fly out for the *ad limina*. Somewhere in the Chone archives there is a relieved letter from the Father General enquiring how we had managed to turn the Cardinal, who had called to say how he approved of our outlook. Our report, after all, had been a rather coloured and optimistic one.

REACHING OUT

Whatever one might feel about our kingdom of the blind, there was one area where Declan Deasy had twenty twenty vision. Always an ardent explorer, whether in the vast realms of the night sky over Carlisle or on the cliffs of Skellig, his understanding of the geography of the mission was unrivalled and he was anxious that attention be given to the more remote and semi-abandoned parts. Very quickly we heard of Convento, El Mate, Barraganete and San Pedro Latacoso. We even had our own remote Mongoya. And Declan wanted us to know these places. We never really got a chance to put on our water wings - just a sudden push at the deep end of the pool. A hardened missionary of four months, with mosquito net, wellingtons, army boots and an umbrella to protect me against the sun on the long canoe journey, I headed out for Barraganete, the first village on a ten-day trip up the river Daule. Never since have I been on such a long trip and only grim determination kept me paddling towards the shallow end. In those few days I came to know a new side of the Ecuadorian character, the gentle generosity of the simple river people. I also learned to detest horses and was introduced to the national pastime of waiting: waiting for buses, canoes and congregations.

Later on in the year, when the mud had dried up, Tom Tuomey became the patron saint of Convento, a thriving village and parish some seventy kilometres from Chone. He had had to await the opening of the summer road by county council bulldozers. They had smiled in the Head House, Santa Monica's at Rome, when Tom had announced his determination to spend a while in the third world of Latin America, yet they should have known the stout heart that pounded away to

Two seasoned missionaries: Tom Tuomey and James Ryan.

keep that rotund figure bouncing merrily along through life. Tom's little two-room establishment at the rear of the church in Convento was, in later times, a lesson to newcomers in the art of simple living, but they had never seen it when Sisters Olga and Ana Isabel, two Marianita sisters who shared his work in Convento and Eloy, had had it brightly papered and shining. Some have even giggled on seeing that his second and quite ample room had no other furnishing than a hole in the middle of the floor!

In Flavio too there had been problems. Declan was determined that the sacristan's term of office terminate with the handing over of the parish; the sacristan was quite opposed to such plans for his future and proceeded to put a second lock on the church door. This lock-out détente lasted until March 1978 when week-end attention was resumed. A Church Committee was elected to build the priest's house and to finish the building of the church. By a narrow margin the people had elected as President a stout red-faced farmer called José Ricarte Cedeño. The Spirit was certainly hovering over the community that day, for Don Ricarte assumed the building of the house and church as his vocation in life. He died before he could see the church façade finished, but his name deserves to appear in any note on the history of Flavio. Since someone had sold the Irish Province the idea that Chone would be self-sufficient economically, we were precluded from appealing for funds and the building of the house took more than a year. On 5 July 1979 the priest took up permanent residence. We had begun to decentralise.

And then Fr Joe Beary came on the scene. His time in Mexico had made him suspect that Latin American cooking had little in common with the Latin cuisine of Rome, and he had found that his talent for language was more suited to recounting incredibly funny stories than to the construction of Spanish adverbs. Manfully he survived for months on cups of coffee and nicotine nourishment, his head buried in *Spanish Made Easy*. Once, when Tom Tuomey was *hors de combat* because of a burst blood-vessel that had temporarily damaged his memory, Joe baptised a hundred and fifty babies at the Convento Fiesta, following word by word the baptismal ritual that must have been for him a mystery of faith and understanding. Shortly after that, Joe decided to get out while he was still winning. Years later, in Liverpool, I heard him brighten the evening for a group of friars with hilarious reminiscences of those few months, new grist for the old mill of his Kerry *seanachaíocht*.

A senior citizen at Flavio: Don Euclides Cedeño, c.75 years.

Fr Chris Fitzgerald arrived in November of 1979, the first inflow of experience and creativity from the Nigerian mission. His arrival coincided with our own dawning realization that the lodestone of Chone was drawing us towards catechesis and that the formation of catechists must be a primary objective. We were no longer lost, since we at least knew where we wanted to go. Now we had only to find out how to get there.

201

ON COURSE

It seems so simple now to say that the better one knows the reality around him the clearer the way forward will be, but the years of trying to work with purpose, while gaining that understanding bit by bit, can be frustrating and hindsight could very easily snigger at one's efforts.   And then there is the serious question as to whether one has a healthy understanding of what evangelization really means - or what it means in our specific context.

We could identify the real need to attend to the innumerable villages spread across the canton and the lack of Christian formation was brought home to us every day.   We were not too quick in recognizing the positive elements in popular religious practice: the tenacity with which a traditional people held on to celebrations of village fiestas that centred on baptism and a procession; the velorios, rezadores and prayers for the dead.   We did identify some obstacles - the difficult terrain that hindered movement and communication;   the shortness of the dry working season in the campo;   the lack of accommodation in remoter parishes;   and the shortage of personnel at all levels - priests, sisters, catechists and other pastoral agents.

We had arrived in South America in exciting times: nine years before, the bishops of CELAM (The Conference of Bishops of Latin America) had nailed their colours to the mast in Medellín and now, even as we were trying to settle in, the preparation was going on in the dioceses for the meetings of Puebla that would result in the analysis of "Evangelization in the Present and Future of Latin America" (The Documents of Puebla).   Community, participation of all in evangelization, and Comunidades Eclesiales de Base (Basic Ecclesial Communities) came into focus as objectives and means of evangelization.   A preferential option for the poor and for youth crystalised the metanoia of the American Hierarchy and threw down a challenge to the Church at large.

Two attractive young parishioners.

The year after Puebla, in 1980, Chone was chosen by our bishop, Mons. Luis Alfredo Carvajal, as the centre for monthly meetings of clergy, sisters and lay pastoral agents of the north of the diocese.   Here Ecuador's own new pastoral options were to be clarified and made effective at a local level.   The diocese has four zones and these meetings gave us our first opportunity to meet with the clergy of our section, to hear them analyse the reality and search for a way forward.   Each year there was to be a day's get-together of all four zones . . . and so the seeds were set for a far greater integration with the coming of the new bishop years later.

It would be probably true to say, however, that we were more involved in Chone's particular problems than in the fate of the Church at diocesan level.   Two Marianita sisters, Ecuadorians both, were working full time with us; they had built a house in Convento.   In Barraganete a simple cane structure had been built to lighten the burden of those who visited the river mission - the two sisters, Olga and Ana Isabel, spent some time there in fruitful isolation. Moves were made for this latter to become a parish but this never came to fruition.

In March 1980, a lay volunteer from Ireland, Brigid Lyons, came to help us.   She had the advantage that this was her second tour in Ecuador: neither the language nor driving a heavy jeep presented a problem.   More important, however, was the flexibility that she showed in working with us along the pastoral lines that were beginning to emerge.   She taught catechism and helped to form catechists;   she worked with women's groups and, in general, acted as a catalyst among the small group of lay people who were beginning to support our pastoral efforts.

Declan Deasy had given the initial thrust to organized catechetical preparation.   It fell to

Chris Fitzgerald to keep the momentum going. Several priests of the diocese helped us in this work, more notably Fr Francisco Pazmiño of the Redemptorists in Manta and the Italian Salesian, Fr Luis Ricchiardi, who worked in Rocafuerte. The formation of catechists is not an easy task, however essential it may be. Those involved are mainly young girls and married women, who consider it an honour to be the village catechists, but whose lives are surrounded by so many restrictions in a jealous macho world that they find it exceedingly difficult to continue faithful to any formation courses which may involve travelling away from home. Long distances are involved; husbands may refuse permission arbitrarily, and catechists have to find someone to accompany them. Obviously the villages that are furthest away and in need of highly responsible catechists are still the ones that suffer most. It is cruel to ask such people to make giant sacrifices for one-day courses for which they may have to set out on foot at four in the morning. The centre for catechetics in Flavio was built to respond to this need; so far it has not reached anything of its potential and will probably have to wait until there is sufficient personnel and until the distant communities become more acutely aware of the need for trained catechists.

CATEQUESIS FAMILIAR

Occasionally, when we went to visit the villages on the River Daule, we stayed overnight with Irish priests of the St James' Society in El Empalme. There we discovered a system of catechesis to which they had become completely converted - Family Catechesis, an approach which seemed to attack our problems at its roots. It originated in Chile.

The adoption of this system was yet a long way from us when in the final months of 1980, Frs Ted McCarthy and David Crean came to swell the ranks.

A recent article in *Intercom* lamented the decline of religious formation in the Irish home and wondered about the attitude of parents who see such formation as part of the teacher's work at school. Twenty-five years of catechetical renewal in Ireland has been insisting on greater participation on the part of parents, but one wonders if the Church has been sufficiently radical in its demands. The decision of the Chilean Bishops may question our real commitment to the ideal. In the whole of Chile it has been ordained that a child may not be accepted for first Communion if its parents have not participated fully in the two years' preparation course. This move devolves to parents the obligation that they accepted, maybe lightheartedly, at the child's baptism, but which has been gradually usurped by other agencies until it has come to the point where parents feel no longer capable of fulfilling that promise. Catechesis of the Family is designed to help parents deepen their own faith commitment and their understanding while they themselves prepare their children for Penance and Eucharist.

It takes a long time for radical ideas to become acceptable to a community and the seeds of Family Catechesis went through long periods of drought before they began to blossom in Chone. There was a course given by Br. Enrique García, the Chilean animator of this new model, and tentative pilot schemes were undertaken.

In the Year of the Floods, when the rains began in September 1982 and did not subside until August of 1983, a dream of Declan Deasy's had come true. The Irish Presentation Sisters had accepted the invitation to work in Chone. If it were Declan's dream, it must have been a nightmare to the sisters. They had nowhere to live, as the warm Pacific Current, the Niño, which caused these rains, had never let up and the building of the sisters' house in Flavio had run seriously behind time. Sisters Colette, Mary, Martina and Josephine survived as best they could, in a wing of a local clinic, in a house that had been built in Santa Rita for the Marianita Missionaries and, finally, in Flavio. Their coming, however, had an importance for the development of Catequesis Familiar because they took it under their wing. The onus of preparing people to animate and guide this system fell very much on them and they have borne the brunt of introducing it to the main centres of population. Now the other congregations of sisters and many lay people are involved in the process. The system deserves some explanation.

Its aim is that children absorb their christian faith in the atmosphere of the home and from their parents, who are, at the same time, deepening their own commitment through weekly meetings for prayer, biblical reflection and study. These reunions, facilitated preferably by a couple of parents, give the people an opportunity to talk together about an organized series of faith themes, to find their way through the Bible and to shake off infantile ideas of religion and their shyness about praying together. Parents, in their turn, help their children to absorb a simpler version of the theme as presented in the pupil's book. Once a week the children come together under the guidance of animators whose function is not directly catechetical but rather to celebrate the gift of God's goodness seen in the theme and to reinforce the learning that they have received at home. Four or five times a year both parents and children come together for a celebration of broad themes reflected on during the year.

The system demands organization and preparation of facilitators for parents' reunions and younger animators for children's meetings. Parents, too, have to be sincerely responsible in their role of passing on to the children what they themselves have received.

The introduction of this model of catechesis has not always been greeted with cries of joy; doubts have been expressed about the parents' ability to transmit the content of faith; some have wondered if the books even have a comprehensive picture of the faith. Others balk at the tremendous organization needed for preparation of personnel, and there is an uphill struggle to interest parents who are not very keen to be involved one night a week for two school years. The men, true to their liberal macho image, shy off completely. Religion in the home is strictly the domain of women, and some fathers are not even sure that they want their boys to prepare for Communion at all. The girls? Well, the mother can look after their upbringing.

PERIOD OF EXPANSION

The description of family catechesis above has telescoped the chronology of development of the mission and focussed too much on one aspect. In fact the years from 1980 to 1985 were years of growth and expansion on every level. Ted McCarthy and David Crean, who arrived at the end of 1980 were quickly followed by Fr Vincent Kelly in 1981 and Frs James Ryan, Paul Flynn and John Grace in 1982. A convent for Marianita Sisters working fulltime on the mission was guided into existence by Dave Crean and opened in April 1982. A young lay man, Pat Ryan, came to accompany us in 1981, and early in 1982 a volunteer nurse, Vera Lynch, with a nutritionist, Susan Nagle, responding to an invitation from Chris Fitzgerald, Superior of the Mission, came on a two year tour hoping to establish a service in the health and health education field. The Irish Presentation Sisters, after a sojourn at language school in Cochabamba, Bolivia, an O.S.A. Dutch centre, were established in their house in Flavio by early 1983. Later, at the end of 1983, three more nurses, all midwives, came to continue the health mission. They were Liza O'Connor, Margaret Clark and Ann Millar. Finally in the last months of 1985, Frs Chris Traynor, Kevin McManus and Ned McGrath drained the Irish Province's resources of man-power for Ecuador.

With the advent of so many priests, each parish could have its own parish priest; the growth in the number of sisters working full time on the pastoral mission guaranteed that little villages would get catechetical attention. And the sisters were willing to go anywhere and, seemingly, to tackle anything. Russian four-wheel-drive Nivas had a brief and not unremarkable climb to infamy. The Province had realized that we were not really economically solvent and we had also discovered the German Catholic Church Aid Programme, ADVENIAT. Once priests were appointed to individual parishes, reconstruction and building of churches and houses began . . . with all the attendant strains. It once took Ted McCarthy more than twelve hours to traverse twenty-six kilometres accompanying a Scania truck loaded with roof girders. In a very wet year he had done that same trip to Convento in eight minutes by helicopter; the journey home, however, without the aid of the army, took him 32 hours.

Houses or churches, or both, have been built in Pavón, Santa Rita, Convento, San Antonio,

Eloy Alfaro, Chibunga and Boyacá (see map).   In Puerto Arturo, the poorest part of suburban Chone, a community centre has been built: in Flavio, a Catechetics Centre that has yet to come into full use.   In the parish of Santa Rita a multipurpose centre is under construction and the main house in Chone itself has been completely rebuilt.

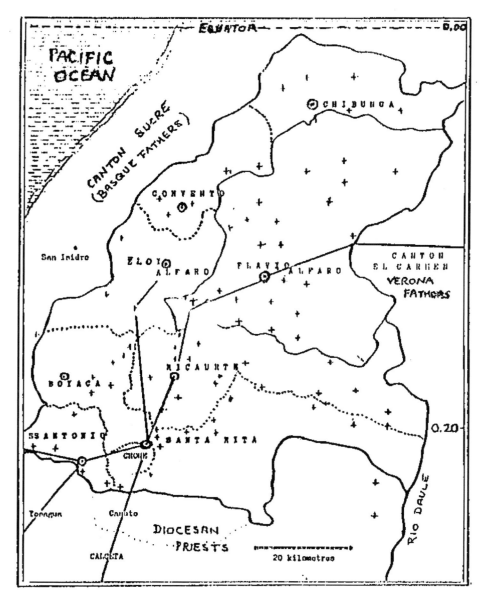

The house that was originally built for the Marianitas in Santa Rita is now occupied by the Franciscan Sisters who arrived to us in 1988, a hundred years after their mother foundress had arrived to work with Bishop Schumacher. These sisters work, for the main part, in Santa Rita in various pastorales - youth, women's groups, catechesis and NIP.   One of the Franciscans, Sr Maritza, has practically been parish priest of Convento - with great success.

Not to be outdone by the friars in this spate of building, the village communities all over the mission responded to this new attention by building their chapels too.   First Communions and the visits of the sisters spurred on their efforts and a large number of hitherto unknown communities have begun to stake their claim on a visit from the priests at least for the day of their annual fiesta. (And now in 1992, when our numbers have gone down to half, these communities still ask for the same attention).

ORGANIZED COMMUNITIES

Such growth cannot be without its problems.   With such talent how could we organize the concert?   The emphasis on our objective had begun to shift, probably because of the South

205

American's insistence on small communities. The community as the source, framework and end result of catechesis and evangelization, was forcing its importance upon us and we needed to work as a team. We could see vaguely what our objective must be, but the vision was partial and we each seemed to have focussed on different parts. We needed an organized structure to coordinate disparate efforts and talents into a Pastoral Team - a difficult marriage.

The Basque Liberation Team from the parish next to us came to help, but they may have been a bit too anxious to have us united by their own vision and their own liberation goal. We toyed with the idea of working in groups of parishes and this could probably have worked had we not each been too taken up with our own little patch. Finally the Augustinians from the Mission in Chulacanas, Peru, came to sell us their wares - the Better World Programme for the New Image of the Parish - and we bought the basic design of their potter's wheel. So far, the artefacts are coming off a bit wobbly with little of the Chulacanas coordination or perfection; the wheel is going a bit slowly and unevenly and some have not managed to get their hands to the clay yet. We like the few results, however, and are steadying our arms to the job. But more of that later, as there is one interlude that seems to deserve further mention: the time spent by the nurses of APSO on the mission.

THE APSO NURSES

We were neither ready nor sufficiently organized for their coming. Other missions which have clinics or hospitals and their own doctors can easily absorb nursing volunteers and are probably incredibly happy to have nurses of the calibre of our Irish nurses. Though our volunteers were hampered by the inferior position that nurses have in the Ecuadorian medical scene and by the fact that they had to find a niche for themselves in a rather experimental way, they did do wonders. In bringing triple vaccines to remote rural areas they suffered frustrations and annoyances as they waited for the vaccines to come from Portoviejo, or as they tried to keep them frozen on long canoe journeys to the safety of kerosene-burning fridges in the villages. They sought openings to give health and nutrition lectures in colleges; they gave instruction in preventive medicine to the poor, to whom they had the gift of going out in real friendship. In a way, they were witnesses to a level of cooperation that can exist between missionaries, lay and religious, in the activities of the Church, even though they had to contend with the layers of cottonwool with which religious communities have surrounded themselves through the centuries.

Had their interest been in catechesis their time might have been more satisfying for them, but they had come as nurses and midwives and we were not capable of availing, to any great extent, of their rich talent. Their dedication to the sick and the poor has probably opened us up at least to an awareness of the suffering that is a back-drop to everyday living for thousands of people, though we have not, as yet, been capable of coming up with an organized answer to that suffering. (Some individual efforts have been made in the social field, as, for example, the school, "Escuela San Agustín", which Chris Fitzgerald and a group of Chone people have managed to get permanently established, and the school meals that have been set up in conjunction with the diocese for thousands of children).

THE NEW IMAGE OF THE PARISH (NIP)

A cohesive plan that would unite our various efforts, had evaded us for years. We may not have been really aware, then, of the importance of the introductory seminar which Chris Fitzgerald asked the Chulacanas Augustinians to give us on the Better World programme of the New Image of the Parish, or NIP as it is commonly called in this age of initials. In January 1988 Fathers Aquilino and Guillermo came to Chone to initiate us.

Their basic thesis struck chords in our memory, bringing back Fr Johnny Bresnan's efforts to have us distinguish between objectives, goals and targets as he introduced us to the Berger Method in Ireland a long time ago. They forced us to consider our reality and to clarify our concept of the ideal parish. And to put the skids under us they made us spell out what would happen if we continued in our present pastorale. When they had us properly on the run they began to offer us criteria and planning for reconstruction that were so profoundly Christian that they caused us much soul-searching.

Every Christian is called to take his or her part in the mission of Christ, to sanctify one's own life and to open up the way for others to do the same, but always in community. The Parish Team's job, therefore, is simply to open up to EVERYBODY the possibility of responding freely to this calling and to animate every baptised person towards participation . . . in season or out of season. You just keep on inviting everybody.

This involves the setting up of a "Telecom" with human cables; zoning the parish, establishing coordinating teams in the zones with a network of messengers who would each have ten families with whom they would be in constant and friendly contact. Once this is set up there is the hope of two way communication, so essential for participation. With this done, evangelization has, at least in theory, ceased to be the P.P.'s personal headache. The whole community is invited to share the problem. The central parish coordination team becomes a listening post that encourages. It encourages the people to paint their own picture of what the ideal parish might be; it encourages a sincere and candid description of the present reality 'warts and all'; it encourages analysis of this reality with a view to identifying the fundamental problems that are strewn like boulders in the way from the real to the ideal. Once a parish feels that it has a pretty clear idea of what its number one problem is, then by common accord, all activities in the parish are directed towards overcoming that fundamental problem. One becomes very conscious that we are all pilgrims on a road from the reality to the ideal, and the NIP programme has a gradual step by step development of that journey.

The poor parish priest comes tumbling from his wobbly pedestal from where he had previously, 'ad modum recipientis', identified the fundamental problems himself. Now he has to listen to the people identify the problem and may even find that he himself is an integral part of it. The Spirit of God is moving in everyone in his parish, so he can no longer afford to write off the exploiter, the manipulator or those sowing corruption in the community; if he is to be a true pastoral agent he must try to smoothen paths so that all can freely choose God's will. He will have to start from the poor and see the reality from ground-level, but a preferential option for the poor is not an exclusive option for the poor. Nor can the P.P. come with a new broom to sweep away the past: that past is the fruit of goodwill of previous generations and cannot be put down like an ailing nag. More often than not, the customs of the past hold, hidden within them, the core and kernel of the communities' spiritual identity; the natural process of growth will assimilate the values and discard useless trappings.

There is a lot of dying involved in this new birth, a lot of letting go and a whole world of community spirituality to be learned both by the clergy and the laity. It is a slow process that demands a discipline to which we are not accustomed and a growth in awareness of what God's alliance with mankind really involves.

So far we are only scratching the surface of this new path; we have problems in keeping the zonal coordination functioning and the network of messengers can get their lines crossed. Yet there has already developed a sense of participation and the anonymity of the large parish is giving way to zonal community identity.

Fortunately for us this type of pastoral planning has recently been adopted by the Diocese: we will not have structures that are discordant; the back-up of the diocesan animation group and the aids they provide for Christian Assemblies, etc., will renew our flagging fervour. In fact, at diocesan meetings we feel very much more integrated now that we are all in the same boat together.

CONCLUSION

TODAY

It has become the lot of Kevin McManus, as Superior, to coordinate the efforts of the group now, and the awareness of how few we are is like a back-drop to every decision. That there are over 4,500 children baptised each year is an indication of the tremendous numbers of Catholics there are on the mission. Each parish has its outstations, with fiestas and celebrations that are a constant call. Three parishes now have no priest and Ted McCarthy tries to give them some attention despite heavy demands in his own area.

The radio programme each day is important, but we are amateurs. Jokingly a Basque priest told us of a parishioner who said that the priests in Chone have a programme in English but if you listen closely you can understand a bit of it.

The Presentation Sisters have established a second mission in Quito and are working from both Chone and Flavio Alfaro centres. They visit homes a great deal, have women's groups for a variety of interests, (even a little marmalade industry), and are encouraging small prayer groups in different barrios. They keep on with the Family Catechesis.

The Lord is watching over us on difficult terrain and we have not had any serious accident: Declan Deasy does have a hill named after him, since his brakes went and he kept toppling over until he got to

Ecuador - Mighty men in the front line!
The Irish Augustinian friars at San Antonio parish house, Chone,
on St Patrick's Day, 1992.
From left: John Grace, Paul Flynn, Chris Fitzgerald, Ted McCarthy,
Paul O'Connor. In front: Kevin McManus.

the bottom of the hill. And James Ryan's driver decided once to drive over a high river bank, depositing them both in the river, when returning from a sick call. John Grace did have a serious viral complaint but it has not slowed down his efforts in building elegant churches and a beautiful house in San Antonio.

We have lost two of our younger priests: Chris Traynor who was here only for a short time and Vincent Kelly who had laboured hard for ten years with us.

We have become reduced in numbers of priests since those halcyon days of 1985 and on 1 December, 1991, Ned McGrath died of a massive cardiac arrest. Ned was a challenge to everybody and single-minded in his concern for the poor. Though he had suffered for years from heart trouble, he worked at a merciless pace all day and long into the night. Even in moments of relaxation Ned's mind was turning over new ideas for organizing church committees, a catechetics course or even a second-hand sale.

He had been working late on Saturday night and arrived a bit up-tight from a fiesta that had not gone too well. Ned had so many irons in the fire that no one was surprised when he did not turn up for meals on Sunday; it was after Morning Prayer on Monday that the community found he had died in his bed.

That day we began to feel something of the consolation hidden behind the Ecuadorian respect for the dead. Everybody helped. The sisters took charge of everything in the house and the church. The bishop and priests, who had come for the zonal meeting, stayed and accompanied us in the funeral. Two of them went to Ned's newly-built church in Boyacá to tell the people and to celebrate a funeral service with them.   Several people in the town offered a tomb, because we did not have our own.

The youth and the poor crowded into the church for the funeral.   It was being shared, as another funeral had been scheduled for the same time.   All day people had come to pay their respects, and, as the two coffins, so contrasting in the simplicity of Ned's, were carried down the main street to the Chone cemetery, Fr Luis Tomás from Quito lead the rosary.

The evening was fading when the people had finally put their wreaths and flowers into the tomb and the heavy flags were put in place, but the prayers and hymns did not cease.   As we were withdrawing from the grave-yard, the youth of the Puerto Arturo barrio continued with Monseñor Proaño's hymn, Ned's favourite, "Solidaridad".

Edmond Martin McGrath, O.S.A. Died at Chone in Ecuador, 1 Dec. 1991, aged 56 years.

To feel as it were part of you
the suffering of your brother;
To make your own the anguish of the poor
is solidaridad, solidaridad, solidaridad.

To give one's life for love
is friendship's greatest sign.
It's living and dying with Jesus Christ . . .
It's solidaridad, solidaridad, solidaridad.

[Edd note: Since this chapter was submitted, two Irish Augustinians, Fr Philip Kelly and Brother Michael Danaher, joined their confrères in Ecuador in 1993.]

THE IRISH AUGUSTINIANS IN KENYA, 1991-1992

Declan T. Brosnan, O.S.A.

THE IRISH AUGUSTINIANS IN KENYA, 1991-1992

Declan T. Brosnan, O.S.A.

BACKGROUND

Kenya, known to the ancient Greeks as Azania and to the Persians as Zanji, is also known today, as THE PRIDE OF AFRICA. It is an independent republic on the East Coast of the Continent. The country, once a British colony, became independent in 1963. It remains, however, a member of the Commonwealth. It is bounded on the north by Sudan and Ethiopia, on the east by the Somali Republic and the Indian Ocean, on the south by Tanzania and on the west by Uganda. Lake Victoria forms the most westerly border. The sea coast is a low-lying strip and the northern part, making up about three-fifths of the country, is an area of dry plains and scanty pastures abounding in wild animals. The equator runs across the middle of the country. The northern part being dry and hot, the shores of Lake Victoria having a tropical climate and the coast is hot and rather damp.

Kenya is perhaps the best known African country for its wildlife and has game parks, where frequent tourists can watch animals roaming freely, ranging in size from the lion and the rhinoceros, to the tiny antelope, called the dik-dik, which when fully grown stand only about 30 centimetres high. Tourism is one of the nation's fastest growing industries. However, being a fertile agricultural country it is more than self sufficient in food, producing abundant quantities of corn, coffee, tea, sugar, cotton and cashew nuts, and also raising cattle, pigs, poultry and sheep. It has many exports but mainly fresh milk and canned butter.

In some circles Kenya is known as THE CRADLE OF OUR ORIGINS. Many believe that here lie the origins of the human race and where HOMO SAPIENS first emerged[1]. Certainly there is archaeological evidence of a pre 2,000 B.C. stone age that had definite contact with the civilizations of Egypt and Mesopotamia.

The country covers an area of 582,646 square kilometres and has an estimated population of 18,000,000. Most of the inhabitants are African, but there are small numbers of Europeans, Asians and Arabs. The most common language is Swahili, derived from the Arabic word for "shore", but English which is taught in the schools, and other indigenous languages, such as Kikuyu and Masai, are also spoken.

Kenya has had contact with the Arab world from time immemorial. The Portuguese came at the end of the 15th century. The British annexed it as part of their East African Protectorate in 1895 and gave some of the best farming land to white settlers[2]. This decision was to have decisive effect on the history of the country in this century. During World War I most of the farmers joined in the campaign against Tanganyika, then a German colony. In 1920 the protectorate was made a British colony and became officially known as Kenya. In World War II, Kenya was the centre of operations against Italy, in Ethiopia and Somaliland. After the war the number of white settlers increased, taking much of the land from the Kikuyu people, who rebelled in 1952, leading to what is known today as the Mau Mau War. It ended in 1969 leading to Independence four years later.

ARRIVAL OF THE FIRST AUGUSTINIANS

As mentioned above, the Portuguese came to East Africa at the end of the 15th century.

---

1. R.E.F. Leaky, 'New Hominid Remains and Early Artefacts from Northern Kenya', in *Nature*, 226, (1970), pp 223-224.
2. Cf. 'Correspondence Relating to the Resignation of Sir C. Eliot', in *Africa*, 4, 1904.

Having rounded the Cape of Good Hope in 1497, Vasco da Gama, in March of the following year, planted the Portuguese flag at Mozambique. One of the main attractions was the route to India and the demand in Europe for the spices, jewels and silks of those regions. To consolidate their presence in Mombassa the Portuguese built in 1593 a massive fortress calling it Fort Jesus, still standing today, and for the next almost two hundred years this became a Portuguese stronghold, the centre of their colonial rule in East Africa and their gateway to the Indian Sub-Continent.

While the fortress was being built the newly appointed Viceroy, Francisco da Gama, realised that the garrison needed spiritual guidance. He approached the Primate of India, Archbishop

Fort Jesus, Mombassa. (Photo: Frank Ltd., Mombassa)

Alexius de Meneses, O.S.A., to send Augustinians to Mombassa[3]. It is interesting to note that the Augustinians were selected, 'because their Order specialised in the particularly difficult and little rewarding mission work among the Moslem, and had already a house in Muscat and Ormuz in the Persian Gulf'[4].

The exact population of Mombassa at the time is not known, but it is true that like all along the East Coast of Africa, due to many years of contact with the Arab world, the majority were Muslim. However, the inhabitants of the interior followed their local Traditional Religion. In 1597 the first Augustinian Prior was appointed there. He was Father Peter of Nazareth and it was he who chose the site and supervised the building of their monastery, near the fortress, dedicating it to St Anthony of Padua, who was himself born in Portugal. The monastery was to be the centre of much Augustinian history and welcome haven, for many a weary missionary, going to and coming from India, the site of much heroic missionary endeavour and even martyrdom, until when the last Prior, elected on 2 December 1729, Father Anthony da Silva Teles, perished in a hurricane in the middle of the Indian Ocean, with 556 others, on 18 May 1730.

While it is true that the Augustinians were initially invited as chaplains to the garrison, it was not long until they widened their apostolate. Barely three years after their arrival they baptised 1,200 people including a Bantu chief. Soon they moved up and down the coast not only taking care of the foreign merchants but continuing to baptise large numbers of the indigenous. They had

---

3. For this section I am much indebted to the excellent booklet by Raymond Hickey, O.S.A., *Augustinian Martyrs of Africa,* Augustinian Publications, Jos, Nigeria, 1987. Cf. also Arnulf Hartmann, O.S.A., 'The Augustinians in the Land of the Swahili' in *Analecta Augustiniana,* 25 (1962) pp 326-329. Also Carlos Alonso, O.S.A., *Los Agustinos en la Costa Suahili, (1598-1698),* Valladolid 1988. This latter has an extensive bibliography on the period.
4. Charles R. Boxer, Carlos de Azevedo, *A Fortaleza de Jesus e os Portuguese em Mombaca,* Lisboa 1960, p.29.

many converts and built churches at Ampaza and Zanzibar.

OUR UNSUNG MARTYRS

From the arrival of the Portuguese, there was continual tension between themselves and the local Muslims, who saw their hitherto autonomy now challenged. The Augustinians, being part of the colony, inherited this animosity. A further difficulty for the missionaries was that often they were identified with, and embarrassed by, the lifestyle and cruelty of their colonial brothers towards the local people. Added to this, was the displeasure they incurred, by the conversion to their faith of many locals including some Muslims. The situation was bound to ignite.

The central figure in much of what followed was Yusuf al-Hassan. He was the son of the Sultan of Mombassa who was slain in 1607. Yusuf, brought up as a Muslim, was sent by the Augustinians to Goa, where he was educated and baptised, being given the name Dom Jeronimo Chingulia. Dom, meaning that he had been made a Knight of Christ and Jeronimo being the Portuguese for Jerome. Later, he joined the Portuguese navy and married a girl from Portugal. Returning to Mombassa in 1626 he was immediately acclaimed Sultan. However his conversion to Christianity was resented by the local Muslims. He was never accepted by the Governor, Peter Leitao de Gamboa, who openly showed his dislike for him, even though Jerome, after his appointment as Sultan, wrote to the Pope professing his obedience as a Catholic. When he reverted to the faith of his youth we are not certain but he did use his military training and his knowledge of the customs of the Portuguese to their full advantage.

He selected the Feast of the Assumption of Our Lady, 15 August, 1631 for his planned assault on the garrison at Mombassa knowing full well that the Portuguese would be slack. He entered the Fort in lay attire, with his followers, as if to attend the Church functions. The captain

Fort Jesus, Mombassa. (Photo: Panthra Ltd., Nairobi)

and garrison were slain before they could offer any resistance. Others were asked to renounce their faith and affirm Islam. Those who refused to do so were killed immediately. Among those who died was one Andrew, a member of the Cincture Confraternity, an ancient world-wide Augustinian devotional society.

In the days that followed an estimated 300 Christians were killed. According to the evidence available they were given the option of renouncing their faith. While the massacres continued many Christians took refuge in the Augustinian monastery. On 21 August the monastery was surrounded. The Prior, Father Anthony of the Nativity, ordered the doors to be opened. Exhorting the Christians to give their lives for Christ he walked out with a crucifix in his hands. They were attacked with arrows and javelins. In all 152 were killed. Among them were four Augustinians that we know of: the Prior, Father Anthony, a native of Lisbon who had made his profession in 1611, also Father Anthony of the Passion Ferriera who had entered the Order in India in 1599 and was a well known preacher, Father Dominic of the Nativity de Cosa and Brother Diogo of the Mother of God. Sultan Yusuf had attained his objective. The Portuguese were defeated and the Christians annihilated. In the years that followed at least three more Augustinians were martyred and the Portuguese garrison was finally routed in the year 1729, the year of the appointment of the last Prior, Father Anthony da Silva Teles, who as we saw died tragically the following year. Thus ended a brave effort by our Portuguese confrères to re-establish our Augustinian Family in the continent where it all began.

THE PROCESS OF CANONIZATION

The Church in Mombassa, at the time of the massacre, was under the Archbishop of Goa. There, in 1631, an enquiry was set up into the Mombassa events. Witnesses were heard. The evidence was overwhelming. Many had freely and willingly died for the faith. About 400 did not die, choosing instead the option of going as slaves to Mecca. After two years of sittings, documents were prepared for the process leading to canonization. In all there were 150 people among whom were the 4 Augustinians and many Africans. The documents were sent to Rome, keeping the originals in Goa. We know they arrived in 1634. We have a copy in the Curia Archives. We also know that the process was favourably received in the Congregation of Rites. But for some strange reason the process seems to have finished there. G.S.P. Freeman-Grenville, who has done an in-depth scientific study of the case writes, 'Whereas both Pope Urban VIII, by report, and Cardinal Pamfili, Cardinal Prefect of the Sacred Congregation of Rites, and later Pope as Innocent X, in a minute in his own hand, appear to have been favourable, the documents cease abruptly'[5]. Why, we do not know. Historians so far have failed to find the missing link.

However the martyrs have not been forgotten. They were very much remembered, when in 1989, Kenya celebrated the centenary of the rebirth of the Catholic Church in their country[6]. Some popular devotion after all these years still exists. The hierarchy, clergy and many faithful are anxious to get the process moving again in order to promote the cause.

It no longer now depends on Goa and on 28 November the present Archbishop-Patriarch of Goa wrote to the Archbishop of Mombassa, John Njenga, stating that the original documents were no longer in their archives, but that they 'were extremely happy to see that the process of the Mombassa Martyrs is going ahead leading to beatification and canonization'. On 17 June, 1991, His Eminence Cardinal Maurice Michael Otunga, Archbishop of Nairobi, received Father Lucian Borg, O.S.A., President of the African Federation of Augustinians, at his residence in Nairobi and expressed his great hope that the case of the Martyrs would go ahead.

Whatever was the obstacle after 1634, there is a renewed interest today[7]. Fernando Rojo, O.S.A., has done an excellent job in having the original document restored and encased in a beautiful leather covering. Freeman-Grenville's book has made the whole story available in English. The evidence and testimonies are unquestionable. For martyrs, miracles are not necessary. The Church in Kenya waits for the final push to have these unsung heroes raised as witnesses to Christ as we approach the second millenium.

A NEW BEGINNING

The people of Kenya had to wait until 2 November, 1889, for the Gospel message to return

5. G.S.P. Freeman-Grenville, *The Mombasa Rising Against the Portuguese 1631. From Sworn Evidence*. Oxford University Press 1980, p.viii.

6. *Pastoral Letter of the Kenya Catholic Bishops, Centenary of Evangelization, 1889-1989*. Cf also Baur John, *La Chiesa Cattolica in Kenya*, Sermis, Bologna 1990, pp 11-14.

7. Information received from Fernando Rojo, O.S.A., Chief Archivist and Postulator of Augustinian Causes for Canonization, Augustinian Curia, Rome.

when a new era of evangelization began with the arrival of the Holy Ghost Fathers from France. Later they were to be followed by others from Ireland: Kiltegan, Mill Hill, Capuchins, Consolatas, Dominicans and many more. This time the soil was more fertile. There was less political trouble. It was possible to offer the people schools, hospitals and social development. Their work was blessed.

The Gospel seed took deep roots within the Kenyan culture and at the time of the Centenary the Bishops would write in their Pastoral, 'The fruits of a century of evangelization appear today: 5,000,000 Catholics distributed in 18 dioceses, 5 national major seminaries, many minor seminaries and catechists' training centres as well as a good number of novitiates and formation houses for men and women religious. All this is but a sign of the vitality of our church. Vocations to the priesthood and to religious life are flourishing now among the sons and daughters of this country and local religious congregations, both of men and women, are growing together alongside the international ones which count an increasing number of Kenyans among their members'. And they also wrote, 'The blood of these "Mombasa Martyrs" was indeed a fruitful seed of Christian faith in our land'[8]. Our Augustinian confrères had not died in vain. 'Unless the grain of wheat falls to the ground and dies, it remains just a single grain of wheat. But if it dies, it produces a rich harvest'[9].

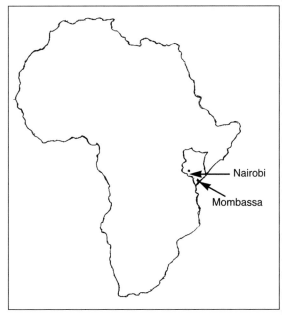

Map of Africa, showing Kenya.

THE AUGUSTINIANS RETURN

A. *Invitations.*

When, precisely, the first concrete invitation came to the Order to return to Kenya, is difficult to ascertain. The Augustinian Contemplative Sisters from Mira Porte, in the Archdiocese of Venice went to Ishiara, Kenya, to open a convent there in 1977. The then Patriarch Archbishop of Venice, Cardinal Albino Luciani, later Pope John Paul I, whose diocesan priests were working in Ishiara, was in those days a frequent guest in St Monica's Augustinian College, Rome. Was it he who first mentioned the possibility of having male Augustinians there? During the Nigerian Vice Provincial Chapter, held at Jos in June 1981, the President, Tom Hunt, then Assistant General for the Fourth Assistancy, made various references to the needs of Ishiara. In 1983, in his report on the State of the Order, Ted Tack out-going Prior General, wrote, 'plans are being made by the Province of the Philippines to open a new mission field in Kenya, where there is already a community of our Nuns'[10]. Well, the Philippine Province did not go there and during subsequent years hopes were expressed that some other Province might be in a position to fulfill the need.

The parish priest of Ishiara was Don Mario Meggiolaro from the Archdiocese of Venice. Over the years he had expressed the desire of having male Augustinians where the Contemplatives were already, and had made various requests. He came to Dublin during Easter Week, March 1989. He had heard that the Vice Province of Nigeria was contemplating a foreign Mission. While there he had meetings with the out going Vice Provincial of Nigeria, Declan Brosnan, the newly elected Vice Provincial, Vincent Hickey, and Tom Sexton, Prior and Parish Priest of St

8. *Kenya Catholic Bishops' Letter,* op. cit.
9. Jn 12:24.
10. *Acta Ordinis,* Vol. XXVIII, 1983, p.10.

Augustine's, Maiduguri, Nigeria. Don Mario explained the role we could play in the parish. It could be divided. There was plenty of pastoral work there for the Venice priests and the Augustinians. Moreover they could help the Sisters in their formation programmes. Also the educational needs were great. Vocations abound.

B. Clarifications and encouragement.

In May, Tom Sexton went to visit Ishiara and see for himself, and with a view to presenting the appeal to the Vice Provincial Chapter later that year in Jos. Ishiara is in the diocese of Embu,

Tom Sexton, O.S.A., sits in the ruins of what was the church of St Anthony in the old Augustinian convent at Fort Jesus. The Portuguese Captain of the Fort lived in the house situated behind the trees in the background - Captain's House. It was a great source of scandal to the friars. The building on the right is a museum.

so the bishop, Right Reverend John Njue, sent a letter to Declan, with Tom, on his return to Nigeria. In it His Lordship wrote, 'I hope that we can get a positive answer because your presence at Ishiara is really very necessary . . . I earnestly ask you to recommend this venture to the new administration'. Tom presented his report to the Vice Provincial Chapter, on 6 June[11]. Benedict Hackett, President of the Chapter and Assistant General, also put the case for Ishiara[12]. However the mind of the Chapter was that due to other commitments it could not accede to the request. Later at the General Chapter, in September, the request from Ishiara was again presented. The proposal was passed stating, 'That the Prior General and his council consider the request for help for the Ishiara (Kenya) Convent of Augustinian Contemplative Nuns'[13].

On the 27 October Bishop John Njue visited the Augustinian Curia, in Rome, and spoke with length to the Prior General, Miguel Angel Orcasitas. He explained the necessity of having male religious in the diocese and the many educational and vocational prospects. He would be most happy if the Augustinians came. On 27 October the Prior General wrote to Vincent Hickey urging him to reconsider the Chapter request. In his reply on 22 November Vincent stated, 'I would be happy if it were possible to give a favourable reply here and now to your request. There are, however, some complications which make this a very difficult question'.

There were real, well grounded, fears in the Vice Province, already in its infancy, that it would not be able to fulfil the pastoral demands in Ishiara. Our presence was still needed in the Dioceses of Yola and Maiduguri. We would be needed for many years to come in the Major Seminaries at Jos and Makurdi. Many things had to be clarified: how many personnel would be needed, necessary qualifications and commitments to the local schools, the relationship with the diocesan clergy from Venice and the Embu diocesan clergy, the role of the contemplative nuns and our role in their formation, and of course the immediate and long-term financial demands. And since the Vice Province of Nigeria depended on Ireland, as its Mother Province, on whom would the contract with the Diocese of Embu depend? The Mother Province, with its many commitments at home, Australia, England and Scotland, Equador and elsewhere, was not in a position to branch out into new fields. However the Irish Provincial, John Byrne, was most anxious to help and so over the next few months many letters were exchanged between Jos, Rome, Dublin and Embu. Also in Nigeria Vincent Hickey continued to keep the brethren aware of developments.

---

11. *Acts of the Chapter,* Jos, 1989, p.4.
12. Ibid., p.25.
13. *The Augustinians Towards 2,000,* n.34.

C. Irish-Nigerian cooperation.

On 31 January 1990, the Prior General wrote a personal letter to each member of the Vice Province in Nigeria. In it he referred to the proposal of the General Chapter on New Frontiers and specifically with regard to Ishiara. He also recalled our presence in Kenya in the 16th Century and the Mombassa martyrs. He emphasised the role we could play in helping the Contemplative and Misioneras Sisters in their formation apostolates, quoting the present Holy Father and our role as an Augustinian Family[14]. He added, 'I am now formally asking the Vice Province of the Order in Nigeria to accept the invitation from Bishop Njue'.

Then on 9 February John Byrne wrote to Vincent Hickey stating that:

1 The basic decision should rest with the Vice Province.

2 If the Vice Province could not meet the commitments in the immediate future, then they could spell out the exact help and support needed at the moment (personnel, finance, etc.).

3 The Irish Province would not be in a position to undertake a long term commitment especially with regard to personnel but could offer some short term help, depending on the nature of the job.

4. The basic contract should be between the Vice Province of Nigeria and the Bishop of Embu. However a subsidiary contract, or agreement, could be made between the Mother Province and Vice Province, with regard to specific help.

On 28 March the Prior General met the Patriarch of Venice, Cardinal Marco Ce. They discussed Ishiara. His Eminence would be happy if the Order were to go to Ishiara. He could foresee no problem. Also in a phone call to the Curia on 26 January, Bishop Njue said, 'I do not expect the Augustinians, in coming to Ishiara, to take on a big financial work'. He said he wanted all his parishes to be self sufficient financially.

With these and other correspondence the invitation and commitment was becoming clearer. And so when Vincent Hickey met with his Council, in Yola, on 3 May, 1990, it was decided to accept Bishop John Njue's invitation to go to Ishiara. In his letter to the Prior General on 9 May, a few days later, Vincent wrote, 'It is a happy coincidence that the decision to open a mission to Kenya, from the Vice Province of Nigeria, falls on the year that we are celebrating the Golden Jubilee of the arrival of the first Irish Augustinians in Nigeria'. Thus the Order was to return to the land which had been nurtured by the blood of their Portuguese and African brothers more than 350 years earlier.

OUR PRESENCE THERE

A. Ishiara.

Ishiara is in the Diocese of Embu which was part of the Diocese of Meru until 1986. The diocese is in the middle of the country at the foothills of the majestic Mount Kenya. The parish itself is territorially quite small, certainly in Nigerian standards. Until our arrival the parish had been under the care of priests from the Archdiocese of Venice. There are 14 outstations with 12 Churches. The farthest away is 19 kilometres. They are accessible the whole year round. The climate is described as mild and pleasant. There are long rains from March to July and a shorter period from October to December. In comparison to the rich farming areas in other parts of the country the land is mostly savannah highlands and thus not so fertile. Hence many of the men migrate, seeking work in the cities. This puts a definite strain on the stability of family life.

In the parish there are Augustinian Contemplative Nuns who came from Mira Porta, Venice, in 1977. Already they have 3 indigenous solemnly professed, 10 simply professed and many applicants. There are also Augustinian Missionary Sisters (Misioneras) who came from Spain in 1985. They run a Craft and Technical Centre and also St Monica's Girls Secondary School. At the moment they have 3 Sisters in the community. There are also 2 Felician Franciscan Sisters

---

14. *Augustinum Hipponensem,* p.39; *The Augustinians Towards 2,000,* p.40.

who came from Poland in 1991. They help in the running of the local St Augustine's Teacher Training College. With these establishments and the presence also of 12 Catholic primary schools the educational needs of the people are adequately catered for.

B. Arrivals.

Tom Sexton arrived on 21 September 1990. After a warm reception by the parishioners and various communities in Ishiara, Tom went to Nairobi, 120 kilometres away, to do an intensive course in the local language Kikuyu. After his return to Ishiara he took over the parish. David Crean came to help him for 6 months last year (1991) and John Joe O'Connor came to stay on 25 November also last year. It is hoped that they will be joined by an indigenous brother from the Vice Province of Nigeria later this year (1992).

From all accounts our brothers have settled in very well though no doubt finding it a different culture from that of Nigeria. Already they are involved in youth organizations, training of catechists, visiting the many schools, organising different liturgies and helping the Sisters in their different apostolates.

Tom, writing in the *Irish Newsletter* stated, 'We will need a community with the ability to live together creatively, not as nodding robots, but as men of faith who are able and willing to highlight in themselves and in others the wonders of grace working in our lives. We will need men who are able to discern and creatively nurture the Spirit and his demands in our midst'[15].

C. Visitors.

Though isolated from other Augustinian confrères they have not been left as orphans. Lucian Borg, of the Province of Malta and stationed at Hippo, visited Ishiara, as President of the African Federation of Augustinians from 16-21 June 1991. Lucian was high in praise of what he saw and full of hope. In his report he wrote, 'Another important element I found in Ishiara is the extraordinary possibility we have to live the Augustinian Charisms in their threefold expressions: our Community, the Contemplative Nuns and the Augustinian Missionary Sisters of active life. Ishiara could be an unique example: in an area of less than a kilometre in diameter, we have the various forms that compose our Augustinian Family. I am sure that the Brothers in Ishiara will not underestimate this topological and sociological situation'. During Lucian's meeting with Cardinal Otunga, His Eminence mentioned his love for the Augustinians, having had the privilege of studying at the feet of Father Casamassa, the renowned Augustinian professor of Patristics at Propaganda College, Rome. Vincent Hickey, the Vice Provincial from Nigeria, visited from 2-14 September of the same year (1991). Vincent in his report highlighted the warm reception given to him by all and the happiness expressed everywhere with the arrival of the Augustinians. In his report he also wrote, 'There are positive signs which indicate a strong possibility of establishing the Order'. While there he met Bishop Njue and together they discussed the proposed contract between the Diocese of Embu and the Order in Nigeria.

The Prior General, Miguel Angel Orcasitas, visited from 26-30 December 1991. In a letter to Tom and John Joe on 7 January 1992, the Prior General wrote, 'I am very happy with the work you are doing and the community life you are leading . . . I am convinced that the Order can render a great service to the local Church and the whole Church of Kenya through your being there. It is a good thing to offer the human and spiritual witness of Augustine to his brothers in Africa. At the same time you have an excellent opportunity to restore the Order in Kenya. The heritage that comes from their faith and their martyrdom is part of our own historical and spiritual patrimony, which now, thanks to your work, we can regain and lend continuity to our past. So the presence of the Vice Province fills us with hope. We in the General Council feel a special gratitude for the generosity shown by the Vice Province when it accepted this mission and also to the Province of Ireland for its cooperation'.

---

15. *Provincial Newsletter*, Easter 1991, p.15.

D. The future.

Finally, after much negotiation, discussion, dialogue and discernment the Order has returned to Kenya. It was a brave decision on the part of the Vice Province in Nigeria, still very much in its infancy, to accept the challenge. No doubt it will prove a blessing and a further step in their development. It was also a further example of the long Missionary dimension and selfless sacrifice on the part of the Irish Province in offering to help in the project.

In the days of our Portuguese confrères the political and cultural climate was very difficult.

Fr Tom Sexton, at the main entrance to Fort Jesus, Mombassa.

Also the missionary approach was quite different. For them it was not easy to lay solid foundations in the indigenous soil. Inculturation and assimilation were not understood as today. However they made heroic sacrifices, leaving their own homes with very little hope of ever returning. Then, much more than today, they faced a totally unknown situation, with much less preparation, for the often traumatic encounter with a totally new culture. But they were men of Faith and proved it by their heroic stand. We pray that our return will re-awaken in our Augustinian Family the great debt we owe to these unsung heroes and that they will be an example to us, to the people of Kenya, and to future Augustinians wherever they may be.

I leave the final word to Fr Tom Sexton, 'The bishop hopes that Ishiara will become a spiritual centre for the diocese. Perhaps in time it can become a sort of retreat centre, maybe a little Kenya "Taizé", a place where young people can gather to find their spiritual bearings. The long term hope is that native vocations will manifest themselves and firmly root the Augustinian presence once more in the land of Kenya, the land of their martyred predecessors. The signs are full of hope, the hopes are full of promise - "Speak, Yahweh, your servants are listening!"[16]'

We hope and pray that the Bishop's and Tom's dream come true. Our return to Kenya is only at the beginning. As St Peter wrote, "Do not ignore the fact, beloved, that with the Lord one day is like a thousand years and a thousand years like one day"[17]. There is a long road ahead but as a Chinese proverb says, "Even a journey of one thousand miles has to begin with a single step". *Laudetur Jesus Christus.*

16. Ibid., p.16.
17. 2 Pt 3:8.

A MEMORY OF ST PATRICK'S COLLEGE FIFTY YEARS AGO

<u>June 4th 1944!!</u>   <u>And Now!!</u>

Thomas David Tuomey, O.S.A.

This coming June, fifty years ago, recalls a very memorable occasion in my life.   The mighty Germans had been passing through Rome for some years previously, to take up their positions in North Africa. Yes, it all fell, due to the unique leadership of General Montgomery, and finally the Germans had to retire from there and move first of all to Sicily, and finally to the Italian mainland well south of Rome. Many thousands of troops on all sides were actually slain there. It was only later that we discovered the long and bitter acrimony among the Allied generals, who would finally destroy the sacred heritage of Christian monasticism which had lasted through centuries!

Yes, the monastery of Monte Cassino was bombed by American planes. Jimmy Doolittle was the initial bomber and he was the man who dropped the bombs on Rome, 19 July 1943. Still the ravages of war carried on, and thousands of lives were again lost. The aim of the Allies was to get to Rome and thus force the Germans to leave this ancient city of one time Roman paganism and which later became the site for Peter and Paul. Those of us who were there in Rome realised that the breakthrough in the Via Casalina would eventually be accomplished. Actually we did not understand when the city would be completely relieved of German troops, so that once again ordinary people would walk through the streets of their glorious city.

Curfew was imposed firmly from 6 p.m. to 6 a.m. the following day. The Wehrmacht was absolutely in control and all of us had to accept the power of the German fatherland, Germany over all!! Strange things actually took place in our regard on the third of June that year. First of all a German officer from the Luftwaffe came in for afternoon tea. He had become quite friendly with some of the priests. He was a Bavarian and occasionally assisted at Mass in the College. His English was quite perfect, while at the same time he was armed to the teeth, and I imagine ready to shoot, at any given moment. In the course of conversation he did reveal to us that the Allies were quite close to Rome, while at the same time the Germans were still retreating. He did assure us, too, that they would not fight to retain the city, as word had arrived from Hitler that Rome should be spared. Such information came as a tremendous source of joy to all of us in St Patrick's at the time.

While this Luftwaffe officer was with us, the door bell rang and one of the group went to open the door. Another German Wehrmacht officer wished to have a word with the priests. So I had to leave the table for my conversation with this particular warrior of Hitler. He gave me his history including the fact that he had been an organist in a Catholic church in Berlin, and had actually fought on most of the fronts where Hitler's men had been fighting. He also mentioned that a Polish gentleman told him to come to the Irish Augustinian Fathers and they would definitely assist him.

I listened with care and then showed him the various documents in Irish, English, German and Italian. In these documents it was stated quite clearly that the College was Irish and was not to be the source of harbouring any of the belligerent countries presently at war. Each of these documents was signed by the Irish Minister to the Holy See. The officer realized quite clearly what they stated and asked me could he stay till the following Monday, as then the Allies would be in Rome. He stated that he had sufficient food to keep him for the days. He was quite fluent in

English and I still listened to him, but finally I had to explain that it would not be possible for him to remain. He stood up rather depressed and in real German fashion gave me the Hitler salute, and departed. It was really quite amazing that two of Hitler's men should have been in the house at the same time. What a contrast!!

The extraordinary thing was that if the Luftwaffe officer had imagined the Wehrmacht man was in the house there could have been violence in the College! The Luftwaffe officer was young, ardent, really full of life, and it would have surely tested his German ardour to find another German who would have then and there given himself entirely to the Allies. It was not to be, and how glad we all were that they did not meet in an Irish College. What would we have done?

One could actually see that very afternoon that the Germans were about to abandon Rome. Trucks, lorries, cars and motor cycles were heading to the highways leading North of the city and so by early Sunday afternoon, General Mark Clark entered eternal Rome. What a reception was given by the Romans to their new liberators! One could almost say that every man, woman and child filled the main thoroughfares in the city. Liberation had finally come and so once again the Romans could walk around their beloved streets. In the following days it was mostly Americans who were seen in the city, and it seemed that the British Eighth Army continued to battle against the Germans north of the city. These battles were quite ferocious and, again, so many died.

For many days the Germans kept retreating towards the North. It was during all this fighting that I happened to be with a group of Allied soldiers and in the course of the conversation I happened to mention that the "unfortunate Huns" had taken much of the wine from the country villa. I did not realize that there was a reporter present from the then *Union Jack;* he put my words into the paper that very next day. It was seen by the German Ambassador to the Vatican, Doctor Weizsächer, who protested quite strongly to the then Irish Minister to the Holy See, Dr Kiernan. Now it was at this point the Germans made a terrific onslaught on the Allies and drove them back towards Rome. It was then that I got rather nervous and kept my ears quite close to the radio. Yes, I thought if the Germans came to near Rome, I might have to leave St Patrick's and perhaps go into hiding for some time. However, this did not happen and so we continued to enjoy the charmed liberation of the Allied armies.

What a joy it was to see Romans sitting out once again and so happily enjoying the glorious glamours of their city! Pope Pius XII appeared on the balcony of St Peter's and what a really tremendous reception he received from the assembled thousands! He thanked the people for their steadfastness during the previous occupation of Rome and once again he prayed that this scourge of the second world war would speedily come to an end. Yes, Pius was a Roman and not very far from St Peter's was he born. He was a man who was *Pio, Dotto e Prudente* and it was this fundamental attitude that he used so much during the Second World War, which started so shortly after his election on the 2nd of March, 1939. It might be well to recall that on that particular day he was 63 and with what particular love, kindness and firmness he guided the destinies of the Church for the next nineteen years! It has been often said that he should have spoken more firmly against the awful Nazi holocaust of the 6,000,000 Jews and the countless people destroyed by Hitler's regime and why didn't he do so? Prudence, discretion and Christian leadership were on his side, and his thoughts were made known to all the leaders of the nations at the time. Yes, he spoke of the awful ravages in so many parts of Europe and begged the leaders to abandon all, and live in ordinary human comradeship. We now realize he was not listened to, and vicious struggles continued in many European countries. We still recall the unspeakable tragedies of Cardinal Stepinac of Zagreb (Yugoslavia), and Cardinal Mindszenty of Hungary! Bitterness was not yet overcome, and we still have to wait for the moments when final peace may reign once again in Europe of today. Pius too must have really wondered what might ultimately happen in the continent of Europe, but his strong and vital faith in Divine Providence must have surely enabled him to foresee that the cause of final human rights would win what we now all hope may be the dawning of a new era in the texture of Christian rights at the end of the twentieth century.

Fr Thomas David Tuomey, born at Tralee, Co. Kerry, 1 Dec. 1915; secondary school at Good Counsel College, New Ross; joined the Augustinians as a novice in 1933; studied philosophy and theology at the Jesuit Gregorian University, Rome, 1934-45, where he was awarded a doctorate in theology (1941); ordained priest on 16 July 1939, and was master of students at St Patrick's Irish Augustinian College, Rome, 1942-44; became prior of St Patrick's on the death of Dr Alphonsus Maurice McGrath, 7 Jan. 1944.

Fr Tuomey was transferred to the Augustinian temporary house of students in the old priory at John's Lane, Dublin, as professor of theology, 1945-8; moved in November 1948 to the Augustinian parish house at Dundee, Scotland, then in 1950 to parochial work at Carlisle, England; master of students in the temporary house of students at Raheny, Co. Dublin, 1954-56; appointed master of novices and prior at Clare, Suffolk, in 1956-65, in the English Augustinian Vice-Province.

Clare is the root from which have come the Augustinian houses in Ireland, and thus the Irish Augustinian foundations in the United States (1794), Australia (1838), Nigeria (1939), and Ecuador (1977). Clare Priory thus merits special mention in the world-wide view of Augustinian history.

The Augustinian property at Clare was confiscated by Henry VIII during the English Reformation, but eventually in the 1950s the then owners, Stella de Fonblanque, who was a convert to Roman Catholicism, and her sister, offered to sell Clare back to its original owners. So, in 1953, it returned to the Augustinian friars.

Fr Tuomey is renowned among his Augustinian brethren for his photographic memory of events over decades past. He recalls the most precise details, which in many cases have been checked and found to be accurate. Hence the value of his memories of what took place at Rome on 4 June 1944, on the eve of the arrival of the Allied and American forces in the city.

SIGLA

A.G.A.	Augustinian General Archives, Rome.
Anal. Aug.	*Analecta Augustiniana.*
Annals National Church	*Annals of the Irish National Church of St Patrick, Rome,* Dublin 1889.
A.P.F.	Archives of Propaganda Fide.
Archiv.Hib.	*Archivium Hibernicum.*
Arch.Hist.Nac.,Madrid.	Archivo Histórico Nacional, Madrid.
Archiv.Segret.Vat.	Archivio Secreto Vaticano.
Battersby, *Hist.Aug.Ire.*	Battersby, W.J., *History . . . of the Hermits of St Augustine in Ireland,* Dublin 1856.
Bibl. Comm., Siena.	Biblioteca Communale degli Intronati, Siena.
Henze, *Miscell.Ehrle.*	Henze, C., C.SS.R., in *Miscellanea Francesco Ehrle,* Rome 1924.
I.A.P.A.	Irish Augustinian Provincial Archives, Dublin.
N.H.I.	*New History of Ireland.*
Pastor, *Hist.popes*	Pastor, Ludwig von, *History of the Popes,* London 1940.
P.N.L.	*[Irish] Provincial News Letter.*
Prop.Arch.	Propaganda Fide Archives, Rome.

INDEX

Cameron, Roderick, O.S.A., 153.

Campbell, Michael Gregory, O.S.A., 185.

Cantillon, Henrietta, 68.

Canton, Patrick, O.S.A., 68.

Cantwell, Bishop John, 103.

Cao, Bishop Gasper, O.S.A., 158.

Cappellari, Dom Mauro, see Gregory XVI, Pope.

Capuchins, 115, 128, 129, 131, 217.

Cara civilization, 196.

Carew, Rev. Dr Joseph, 131, 132, 133-7.

Carlyle, T., 7 n.2.

Carmel, Sr, (Augustinian Sister of the Mercy of Jesus), 169.

Carocci, Fr, S.J., 18.

Carr, Patrick Augustine, O.S.A., 106.

Carr, Thomas Matthew, O.S.A., 66, 85-6, 94, 102, 105.

Carroll, Bishop John, 85-6.

Carroll, William, O.S.A., 65, 66.

Carton, Sydney, 21.

Carvajal, Bishop Luis Alfredo, 193, 202.

Casamassa, Fr, O.S.A., 220.

Casement, Roger, 38.

Casey, Patrick, O.S.A., 53.

Cassel, Harry A., O.S.A., 98 n.70.

Castro, Fidel, 20.

Castro, Guillermo, O.S.A., 191.

Catequesis Familiar, (Family Catechesis), 203-204.

Catherine of Braganza, 63.

Ce, Cardinal Marco, 219.

Cedeño, Don Euclides, 201.

Cedeño, José Ricarte, 201.

CELAM (Conference of Bishops of Latin America), 202.

Celestines (Benedictines), 21, 23.

Challoner, Bishop Richard, 49 n.150, 68.

Chamba people, 162.

Chamier, Henry, 129.

Charles II, King, 13, 62, 63, 64.

Charles V of Spain, 189.

Charlie, Bonnie Prince, 15.

Chichester, S.J., Bishop, 157.

Chidili, Bart., O.S.A., 176.

Chigi, Fabio, see Alexander VII, Pope.

Chigi family, 10.

Chingulia, Dom Jeronimo, see Yusuf al-Hassan.

Cincture Society, 86.

Clancy, Fr Peter, P.P., 49 n.151, 115.

Clare, Lord, 124.

Clark, Margaret, 204.

Clark, General Mark, 224.

Clement XII, Pope, 16, 48.

Clifden, Lord, 116.

Clifford, Lord, 120, 121.

Coar, Walter A., O.S.A., 101, 102.

Coffey, Sean Thomas, O.S.A., see Coffey, Thomas J., O.S.A.

Coffey, Thomas J. (Sean), O.S.A., 42, 47, 55, 170, 171, 183.

Coghlan, Tadhg, O.S.A., 63 n.25.

Coleman, Denis, O.S.A., 168, 182.

Coleman, Joseph A., O.S.A., 100.

Colette, Sr, (Presentation Sister), 203.

Colgan, Thady, O.S.A., 13 n.39.

Colledge, Edmund, O.S.A., 43.

Collins, James T., O.S.A., 102.

Collins, Michael Joseph, O.S.A., 105.

Collins, Alderman William, 146.

Collis, Maurice, 64 n.29.

Colorado people, 192.

Comboniani, see Verona Fathers.

Comunidades Eclesiales de Base (Basic Ecclesial Communities), 202.

Comyn, Francis, O.S.A., 66.

Concepta, Sr, (Augustinian Sister of the Mercy of Jesus), 169.

Condon, John A., O.S.A., 74.

Condon, Joseph, O.S.A., 79.

Conference of Bishops of Latin America, see CELAM.

Congregation of Lecceto, 12-13.

Congregation of Perugia, 12-13, 16, 17-18.

Connolly, Fr, O.P., 20.

Connolly, Michael, O.S.A., 54, 75, 79, 166.

Consolata Fathers, 217.

Conventual Franciscans, 27.

"Convitto Nazionale", 35.

Conway, D., 60 n.8.

Conway, Vincent, O.S.A., 45.

Killykelly, Peter, O.S.A., see Kilkehy.

Kiltegan Fathers, 217.

King, Desmond John, O.S.A., 182.

King, Martin Jude, O.S.A., 183.

Kirby, Archbishop T., 29.

Kirk-Greene, A.H.M., 179-80.

Kirsten, Mgr Josef, C.S.Sp., 157.

Kirwan, James, 69.

Kirwan, Marcus, O.S.A., 14.

"Know-Nothing Nativists", see "Native American Party".

Kyle, Thomas, O.S.A., 88, 89-90, 93, 95, 105.

Lalor, Peter, 144.

Landucci, Ambrogio, O.S.A., 13.

Lansdowne, Lord, 116.

Lanteri, Joseph, O.S.A., 14 n.41, 98-9.

Laoghaire, King, 38.

Lariscy, Philip, O.S.A., 86, 105.

Larkin, James F., O.S.A., 77 n.86.

Laughran, Fr, 92.

Lavery, Robert Banks, 73, 74 n.75.

Lawlor, Brian, O.S.A., 74.

Leahy, Rev. Dr, O.P., 116.

Leahy, M., O.S.A., 47.

Leaky, R.E.F., 213 n.1.

Legion of Mary, 197.

Leitao de Gamboa, Peter, 215.

Leith, W.F., 67 nn 49-50.

Lelli, Giovanni Antonio, 11.

Lemass, Seán, 169.

Lenthal, William, 7 n.2.

Leo XIII, Pope, 28-9, 30, 31, 44, 48, 146.

Leon, Fr Luis, 199.

Leoni, Felice, O.S.A., 68.

Leonori, Aristide, 35.

Limerick Volunteers, 37.

Lindsay, Mary, 60.

Lismore, Lord, 122, 123-4, 125.

Little, Archbishop Francis, 24 n.97.

Littleton, Mr, 119, 125, 126.

Locke, Joseph Augustine, O.S.A., 106.

Locke, Michael Joseph, O.S.A., 101, 106.

Logue, Cardinal, 31.

Lomas, S.C., 7 n.2.

Longstreth, Joseph Cooke, 97, 101.

Lopez Bardón, T., O.S.A., 7 n.1.

Loughran, John (Sean) Malachy, O.S.A., 81, 184.

Loughran, Vincent Damian, O.S.A., 173, 183.

Louis of Venice, Fr, 131.

Lowry, Kevin, O.S.A., 81.

Lowther, Lord, 124, 125, 126.

Lucchini, Paolo, O.S.A., 7, 9, 144.

Lucci, Breeda O'Donoghue, 43.

Luciani, Cardinal Albino (later Pope John Paul I), 217.

Lugard, Sir Frederick, 159.

Luijk, Benignus van, O.S.A., 8 n.5.

Lumley, Mgr William, S.M.A., 158, 159-60, 163, 166.

Lushington, Mr, 126.

Lutherans (Danish), 160.

Lynch, John, O.S.A., 69.

Lynch, Patrick Augustine, O.S.A., 106.

Lynch, Philip, O.S.A., 54.

Lynch, Vera, 204.

Lyne, James Patrick, O.S.A., 107.

Lyng, John Kieran, O.S.A., 184.

Lyng, T., O.S.A., 178.

Lyons, Brigid, 202.

Lyons, Patrick, O.S.A., 54.

Lyons, Patrick Lawrence, O.S.A., 171-2, 174, 177, 182.

Macauley, Geraldine, see Brady, Duchess Geraldine.

Macauley, William, 40.

McAuliffe, Thomas, 126.

McBride, Maude Gonne, 34, 37 n.140.

McCabe, Thomas L., O.S.A., 75-6.

MacCann, Nicholas, O.S.A., 18 n.64.

MacCarthy, James, O.S.A., 7-8, 9-10, 12-13, 49, 53, 62-4.

McCarthy, Michael, 126.

McCarthy, Patrick Vincent, O.S.A., 184.

McCarthy, Ted, O.S.A., 203, 204, 208.

McCloskey, Bishop John, (later Cardinal), 98.

McDermott, A., O.S.A., 117.

McDonagh, Bernard, 43.

MacDonagh, Gabriel, O.S.A., 47, 55.

240

241

Reed, Mr, 99.

Regan, John Joseph, O.S.A., 105.

Reid, Edward Dominic, O.S.A., 73, 74.

Reville, Bishop Stephen, O.S.A., 143, 144, 145.

Riberi, Archbishop, 157, 160, 161.

Ricchiardi, Fr Luis, S.D.B., 203.

Rice, Edmund Ignatius, 22, 116.

Rice, John, O.S.A., 22-3, 54.

Rice, Joseph, 92.

Richards, Fr Michael, 80 n.89.

Riera, Bishop Juan María, 198.

Robinson, Senator Mary, 52.

Robinson, Nick, 52.

Roche, Edward Gerard, O.S.A., 168, 181.

Roche, John Augustine, O.S.A., 78, 79.

Roche, Michael Alypius, O.S.A., 74 n.76, 80, 185.

Roche, Stanislaus, O.S.A., 16 n.52, 23 n.91, 25 n.99, 26 n.100, 53 n.152.

Roche, William, M.P., 119.

Rodriquez, Thomas, O.S.A., 73.

Rojo, Fernando, O.S.A., 216.

Rogan, Mr (later Fr), 90.

Roland, Thomas F., O.S.A., 85 nn 1,4-5, 86 nn 6-7,9-11,13, 87 nn 14,16-17,19, 88 nn 22,24,28, 92 n.43, 94 nn 49-51, 95 n.60, 98 n.75.

Roothan, John, S.J., 133.

Roquevodi (Rochford?), Mathias de Spirito Santo, O.S.A., 60.

Roquevodi (Rochford?), Robert, 60.

Rosa, painter, 40.

Rosseter, John Baptist, O.S.A., 20, 49, 66, 85-6, 94, 105.

Rotelle, John E., O.S.A., 11 n.22, 86 n.12, 88 n.27.

Roth, F., O.S.A., 59 n.2, 60 n.8.

Rowan, Francis Joseph, O.S.A., 105.

Royal Irish Constabulary, 30.

Rudolph, Jane, 89, 90, 93.

Rudolph, John, 89, 91, 94, 97.

Rushe (?) (Rustea), Peter, O.S.A., 65.

Ruskin, John, 26.

Ryan, D., 37 n.141.

Ryan, James Albert, O.S.A., 183, 201, 204, 208.

Ryan, Jeremiah, O.S.A., 90.

Ryan, Jeremiah Joseph, O.S.A., 106.

Ryan, John J., O.S.A., 101.

Ryan, Maurice M., O.S.A., 73.

Ryan, Michael Clement, O.S.A., 68.

Ryan, Pat, 204.

Ryan, Patrick, O.S.A., 55.

Ryan, Archbishop Patrick John, 29, 30, 100, 101.

St Anne, 11.

St Anthony of Padua, 214.

St Augustine, 100, 220.

St Brigid, 30, 39, 40.

St Cayetano, 192.

St Cecilia, 100.

St James' Society, priests of, 203.

St Joachim, 11.

St John Stone, see Stone, John.

St John the Baptist, 22 n.85.

St Laurence, 22 n.85.

St Leger, Fr John, 132.

St Leger, Robert, S.J., 128, 129, 131, 132-3, 134.

St Luke, 22 n.85.

St Margaret, 67.

St Mark, 22 n.85.

St Matthew, 11, 22 n.85.

St Monica, 72, 100.

St Nicholas of Tolentine, O.S.A., 11, 70.

St Oliver Plunkett, see Plunkett, Oliver.

St Patrick, 29, 30, 32 n.132, 33, 38, 39.

St Patrick's Roman Legion, 30.

St Paul, 11, 22 n.85, 197, 223.

St Peter, 22 n.85, 221, 223.

St Roc, 197.

St Simplicianus, 22 n.85.

St Thomas of Villanova, O.S.A., 90, 94, 100.

Salerno, Nicola, O.S.A., 69.

Salvado, Bishop, O.S.B., 152.

Sanders, John R., O.S.A., 103 nn 95-6.

Sanders, Thomas, O.S.A., 60.

Scanlan, Bishop James Donald, 75, 76.

Schnaubelt, Joseph C., O.S.A., 19, 85, 93 nn 44-5, 97 n.68-9, 99 nn 76,78,80, 101 n.92.